THESAURUS
of ALTERNATIVES
to Worn-Out Words and Phrases

ROBERT HARTWELL FISKE

WRITER'S DIGEST BOOKS
Cincinnati, Ohio

Thesaurus of Alternatives to Worn-Out Words and Phrases. Copyright ©
1994 by Robert Hartwell Fiske. Printed and bound in the United States of
America. All rights reserved. No part of this book may be reproduced in any
form or by any electronic or mechanical means including information storage
and retrieval systems without permission in writing from the publishers, except
by a reviewer, who may quote brief passages in a review. Published by Writer's
Digest Books, an imprint of F&W Publications, Inc., 1507 Dana Avenue, Cincinnati, Ohio 45207. 1-800-289-0963. First edition.

This hardcover edition of *Thesaurus of Alternatives to Worn-Out Words and
Phrases* features a "self-jacket" that eliminates the need for a separate dust
jacket. It provides sturdy protection for your book while it saves paper, trees
and energy.

98 97 96 95 94   5 4 3 2 1

Library of Congress Cataloging-in-Publication Data

Fiske, Robert Hartwell.
   Thesaurus of alternatives to worn-out words and phrases / by Robert Hartwell
Fiske. — 1st ed.
      p.   cm.
   ISBN 0-89879-601-6
   1. English language — Synonyms and antonyms.   2. English language —
Usage.   3. Vocabulary.   I. Title.
PE1591.F57   1994
423'.1 — dc20   94-18618
                                                                      CIP

Edited by Jack Heffron
Designed by Brian Roeth

To Brad and to Bruce —
and, of course, to Rebecca

About the Author

Robert Hartwell Fiske is the author of Webster's New World *Guide to Concise Writing* (New York: Simon & Schuster, 1990). A former editor at a well-known publishing house, he now owns Vocabula Communications Company, a writing and editing service in Andover, Massachusetts.

Opening Comments

Whereas a *witticism* is a clever remark or phrase — indeed, the height of expression — a *"dimwitticism"* is the converse; it is a commonplace remark or phrase. Dimwitticisms are worn-out words and phrases; they are expressions that dull our reason and dim our insight.

Thesaurus of Alternatives to Worn-Out Words and Phrases is a compilation of thousands of dimwitticisms (clichés, colloquialisms, idioms and the like) that people speak and write excessively.

Many of the entries in this book are followed by synonyms that may be used in place of the dimwitticism; others are followed by commentary; and still others by both. But even the mere inclusion of an entry — that is, one unaccompanied by synonyms or commentary — damns it as a dimwitticism.

Dimwitticisms cannot always be avoided, nor should we always seek to avoid them. A dimwitticism that expresses a thought or feeling more aptly than any other mix of words is better used than not. But these instances are rarer than people seem to realize, for we depend far too much on dimwitticisms to express ourselves.

It is the least effective speakers and writers who use the most dimwitticisms. A person's ability to express himself well — interestingly and persuasively — is inversely proportional to the number of dimwitticisms he uses. Writing or speech that is free of dimwitticisms is more likely to be memorable than mediocre. A person who expresses himself with genuineness instead of in jargon, with feeling instead of in formulas, is capable as few have been, as few are, and as few will be; this is a person to heed.

Thesaurus of Alternatives to Worn-Out Words and Phrases will aid us in our quest for more purposeful speech and writing. The goal is to promote understanding and rouse people to action. The goal is to express ourselves as never before — in writing that demands to be read aloud, in speech that calls to be captured in print.

Robert Hartwell Fiske

Editor's Preface
HOW TO USE THIS BOOK

When we speak and when we write, we're all susceptible to using clichés, reaching for the easy word or phrase rather than seeking the most accurate, most vigorous one. In *Thesaurus of Alternatives to Worn-Out Words and Phrases*, you can find out if, indeed, the phrase you've chosen is fresh or if, through misuse and overuse, it has lost its power. Author Robert Hartwell Fiske offers fresh alternatives for many of the worn-out words and phrases listed in this book; for others, he tells you why the word or phrase no longer works, advice that should ease your hunt for a substitute.

This thesaurus, however, is more than simply a reference book. The lively, pointed commentary makes for enjoyable browsing. And as you browse, you'll notice a theme developing. The language we use, of course, reflects who we are, and we all want to appear at our best, especially on the page, where there's no denying what we say or how we say it. But, more importantly, the quality of our words also suggests the quality of our thoughts and feelings. When we strive for more meaningful, more thoughtful words, we begin to see ourselves and the world around us more clearly.

A lofty goal. And one the author takes seriously. The tone of the commentary in this book is sometimes pointed. In the tradition of Ambrose Bierce and H.L. Mencken, Mr. Fiske spares no feelings when writing about lazy language. At times, as you read, you may feel like one of the "dimwits" referred to in the commentary. But the author's method is pedagogical, not misanthropic. In short, there's a point to his pointedness. We all use "dimwitticisms." The sting of recognition will help us remember to avoid the words or phrases we now use without thinking. As I edited this book, I felt that sting more than a few times. Mr. Fiske is one tough teacher. But I also remember his lessons well. And I frequently laughed out loud. He is an insightful teacher and often downright funny.

THE ENTRIES
In this book you will find several types of entries, which are explained below.

Explanatory Entries
The author has given names to the types of worn-out words and phrases that you will find in this book. *Thunderous applause*, for

example, is called an "inescapable pair." We use these words together reflexively, without thinking. And the phrase loses whatever real thunder it once possessed. You will find an entry for "inescapable pair," as well as for "moribund metaphor," "suspect superlative" and many other types of formulaic expressions. The author frequently refers you to these explanatory entries, which appear in larger types for easier reference. In these larger, explanatory entries, you learn why this type of word or phrase should be avoided and how to avoid it.

Regular Entries

The regular entries in this book vary in type and format. Some entries simply cite the offending word or phrase. Through its mere presence in the book, the entry instructs us that the word or phrase is worn out and will not reflect well on us if used in our writing. For example, you will find an entry that reads:

it (just) goes to show (you)

This tired expression should be avoided, because it has become a sort of syntactic tic. No explanation and certainly no synonyms are needed. The message: Cut it.

Other entries include the word or phrase as well as a crossreference to the appropriate explanatory entry. For example:

at the breaking point   A moribund metaphor (SEE).

Many listings also offer synonyms and commentary, even a sample sentence in which the offending phrase appears. For example:

at this time   A dimwitted redundancy (SEE). This phrase and several others like it, including *at the present time, at this juncture in life, at this moment in our national life, at this point in time, at this stage in the history of my life, at this time in our history*, mean no more than *at present, now, today,* or *yet* and ought not to be used for them. ■ We don't see any significant breakthroughs *at this juncture.* USE *now.* ■ *At this point in the current time*, the conditions for an agreement have not been met. USE *at present.* The conditions for an agreement have not *yet* been met. SEE ALSO *at that time.*

I hope you find this book useful and fun. And I hope it helps you recognize and cut all those suspect superlatives and torpid terms and inescapable pairs that keep our writing from being *crystal clear*. Oops. I mean *crystalline* or *lucid* or *unambiguous* or . . .

Jack Heffron
Editor
Writer's Digest Books

A

a bad penny   A moribund metaphor (SEE). *bastard; blackguard; cad; charlatan; cheater; fake; fraud; impostor; knave; mountebank; phony; pretender; quack; rascal; rogue; scoundrel; swindler; undesirable; villain.*

a bad penny always turns up
A popular prescription (SEE).

abandon all hope, ye who enter here   An infantile phrase (SEE).

a barking dog never bites   A popular prescription (SEE).

a barrage of   A moribund metaphor (SEE). If our language seems languid, it's partly because our metaphors are moribund.

This, *a barrage of*, is one of a certain kind of moribund metaphor that is especially irksome to come upon; *a bastion of, a chorus of, a deluge of, a firestorm of, a flood of, a mountain of, an army of, an avalanche of, an explosion of, an ocean of, an orgy of, a rising tide of, a sea of, a small army of, a spate of, a storm of, a torrent of, a world of* are all shabby, unimaginative expressions.

These are the least evocative, the least metaphorical, of metaphors.

a bastion of   A moribund metaphor (SEE). SEE ALSO *a barrage of.*

(like) a bat out of hell   An insipid simile (SEE moribund metaphors). *abruptly; apace; at once; briskly; directly; expeditiously; fast; forthwith; hastily; hurriedly; immediately; instantaneously; instantly; posthaste; promptly; quickly; rapidly; rashly; right away; speedily; straightaway; suddenly; swiftly; wingedly.*

a beacon (ray) of hope   A moribund metaphor (SEE).

(catch) a bear by the tail   A moribund metaphor (SEE).

a beautiful person   A suspect superlative (SEE). SEE ALSO *an amazing person; the rich and famous.*

a beehive of activity   A moribund metaphor (SEE).

a bee in (her) bonnet   A moribund metaphor (SEE). *caprice; crotchet; fancy; fixation; humor; impulse; maggot; notion; obsession; urge; vagary; whim.*

a bevy of beauties   An infantile phrase (SEE).

(like) a big weight has been lifted from (my) shoulders   An insipid simile (SEE moribund metaphors). 1. *allay; alleviate; assuage; lighten; mitigate; relieve; soothe.* 2. *deliver; disburden; disencumber; disentangle; emancipate; extricate; free; liberate; manumit; release; relieve; save; set free; unburden; unchain; unencumber; unfetter; unshackle.*

a bird in the hand (is worth two in the bush)   A popular prescription (SEE).

a bitter (tough) pill to swallow   A moribund metaphor (SEE).

abject poverty   An inescapable pair (SEE).

a blessing in disguise   A moribund metaphor (SEE).

a bolt from (out of) the blue   A moribund metaphor (SEE). *bombshell; shock; surprise; thunderbolt; thunderclap.*

abortive attempt (effort)   An inescapable pair (SEE).

above and beyond   *apart from; aside from; besides; beyond; further; furthermore; likewise; more than.* SEE ALSO *over and above.*

above and beyond the call of duty

above par   A moribund metaphor (SEE). *excellent; exceptional; first-class; first-rate; outstanding; remarkable; superior; superlative.*

(like) a bowl of cherries   An insipid simile (SEE moribund metaphors).

agreeable; ambrosial; beguiling; celestial; charming; delectable; delicious; delightful; divine; enchanting; engaging; enjoyable; fun; glorious; gratifying; heavenly; inviting; joyful; joyous; luscious; pleasant; pleasing; pleasurable.

a (welcome) breath of fresh air   A moribund metaphor (SEE). *animating; arousing; bracing; enlivening; exciting; exhilarating; inspiring; inspiriting; invigorating; provoking; refreshing; rousing; stimulating; vivifying.*
■ A toy industry analyst called the news *a breath of fresh air*. REPLACE WITH *refreshing*.

a breed apart (unto itself)   *aberrant; abnormal; anomalistic; anomalous; atypical; bizarre; curious; deviant; different; distinct; distinctive; eccentric; exceptional; extraordinary; fantastic; foreign; grotesque; idiosyncratic; independent; individual; individualistic; irregular; novel; odd; offbeat; original; peculiar; puzzling; quaint; queer; rare; remarkable; separate; singular; uncommon; unconventional; unexampled; unique; unnatural; unorthodox; unparalleled; unprecedented; unusual; weird.*

(it's) a breeze   A moribund metaphor (SEE). *apparent; basic; clear; clear-cut; conspicuous; distinct; easily done; easy; effortless; elementary; evident; explicit; facile; limpid; lucid; manifest; obvious; patent; pellucid; plain; simple; simplicity itself; simplistic; straightforward; translucent; transparent; unambiguous; uncomplex; uncomplicated; understandable; unequivocal; unmistakable.*

absence makes the heart grow fonder   A popular prescription (SEE).

absence of   A torpid term (SEE). SEE ALSO *lack of; less than (enthusiastic).*

absolutely   An overworked word (SEE). *altogether; categorically; completely; entirely; fully; perfectly; positively; quite; thoroughly; totally; unconditionally; unreservedly; utterly; wholly.* SEE ALSO *definitely; most assuredly; most (very) definitely.*

absolutely, positively   An infantile phrase (SEE). ■ A programmer must *absolutely, positively* keep a finger on the format's pulse. DELETE *absolutely, positively.*

absurd   An overworked word (SEE). *comical; extravagant; farcical; foolhardy; foolish; idiotic; illogical; imbecilic; impractical; inane; incongruous; irrational; laughable; ludicrous; moronic; nonsensical; preposterous; ridiculous; senseless; silly; unreasonable.* SEE ALSO *insane.*

(like) a bull in a china shop   An insipid simile (SEE moribund metaphors). *awkward; blundering; bumbling; bungling; clumsy; gauche; gawky; inapt; inept; lubberly; maladroit; uncouth; ungainly; unhandy; unskillful; unwieldy.*

(like) a bump on a log   An insipid simile (SEE moribund metaphors). *dead; dormant; dull; inactive; inanimate; indolent; inert; inoperative; languid; latent; lethargic; lifeless; listless; motionless; phlegmatic; quiescent; quiet; sluggish; stagnant; static; stationary; still; torpid.*

a call to arms   A moribund metaphor (SEE).

(open up) a can of worms   A moribund metaphor (SEE). *complication; difficulty; dilemma; mess; muddle; ordeal; pickle; plight; predicament; problem; quandary; trial; trouble.*

a case of much ado about nothing

(it's) a catch-22

(like) a cat on a hot tin roof   An insipid simile (SEE moribund metaphors). *agitated; anxious; eager; edgy; excitable; excited; fidgety; frantic; jittery; jumpy; ill at ease; nervous; on edge; restive; restless; skittish; uncomfortable; uneasy.*

accent (accentuate) the positive

accidents will happen   A popular prescription (SEE).

according to Hoyle   An infantile phrase (SEE). *accurately; by the rules; conventionally; correctly; customarily; properly; regularly; rightly; traditionally.*

ace in the hole   A moribund metaphor (SEE).

a certain something

(that's) a chance (I'm) willing to take

a chicken in every pot   A moribund metaphor (SEE).

(like) a chicken with its head cut off   An insipid simile (SEE moribund metaphors). *agitated; crazed; crazy; demented; deranged; distraught; frantic; frenetic; frenzied; insane; mad; raging; wild.*

Achilles' heel (tendon) A moribund metaphor (SEE). *defect; deficiency; disadvantage; failing; fault; flaw; foible; fragility; frailness; frailty; handicap; limitation; shortcoming; susceptibility; susceptibleness; vulnerability; vulnerableness; weakness.*

a chip off the old block A moribund metaphor (SEE).

a chorus of A moribund metaphor (SEE). SEE ALSO *a barrage of.*

acid test A moribund metaphor (SEE). *assay; crucible; ordeal; proof; test; trial.*

(breathe; heave) a collective sigh of relief ■ Today, there were more cheers than jeers and an almost *collective sigh of relief.*

a comedy of errors

a creature of habit

across the board A moribund metaphor (SEE). *all; all over; everywhere; throughout; universally.*

a crying shame

action-packed adventure

action plan *action; course; direction; intention; method; move; plan; policy; procedure; route; scheme; strategy.* ■ The UN is expected to produce a global *action plan* aimed at reducing demand and improving treatment, rehabilitation and interdiction. REPLACE WITH *strategy.*

actions speak louder than words A popular prescription (SEE).

active An overworked word (SEE). ■ Please believe me when I tell you that the only thing that stands between you and a better, more responsive government is your *active participation* in the process. DELETE *active.* ■ Nor did the president demonstrate *active interest* in the issue. DELETE *active.* SEE ALSO *actively.*

actively An overworked word (SEE). The popular use of *actively* suggests that any verb not affixed to it is feckless.

We cannot simply *consider* an idea lest we be accused of not thinking; we cannot simply *engage* in a pursuit lest we be accused of not trying; we cannot simply *participate* in a conversation lest we be accused of not speaking. ■ Legislation encourages employers to *actively resolve* the results of past discrimination by developing affirmative action plans. DELETE *actively.* ■ Another possibility is *actively being considered* by the administration: the use of force. DELETE *actively.* ■ I have no intention of mailing a second letter to anyone who does not *actively show* an interest in becoming part of my collectors club. DELETE *actively.*

Here is an example of just how absurd our fixation on *actively* has become: ■ Among the new features of WSF2 R3.3 that he is *actively looking forward to* is the statistical information that can be provided through SMF records. DELETE *actively.* SEE ALSO *active.*

act your age A popular prescription (SEE).

a cut above (the rest) *abler; better; exceptional; greater; higher; more able* *(accomplished; adept; capable; competent; qualified; skilled; talented); outstanding; standout; superior; superlative.*

acutely aware   An inescapable pair (SEE).

adamantly oppose   An inescapable pair (SEE).

a dark day   A moribund metaphor (SEE).

a date with destiny

a day at the beach   A moribund metaphor (SEE).
1. *easily done; easy; effortless; elementary; facile; simple; simplicity itself; simplistic; straightforward; uncomplex; uncomplicated.*
2. *agreeable; beguiling; charming; delightful; enchanting; engaging; enjoyable; fun; glorious; gratifying; inviting; joyful; joyous; pleasant; pleasing; pleasurable.*

add fuel to the fire   A moribund metaphor (SEE). *activate; agitate; animate; arouse; awaken; encourage; enkindle; enliven; exacerbate; excite; feed; foment; ignite; impassion; incite; inflame; intensify; invigorate; make worse; nourish; prod; provoke; rejuvenate; revitalize; revive; rouse; shake up; stimulate; stir up; vitalize; worsen.*

add insult to injury

a deal is a deal   A quack equation (SEE).

a deluge of   A moribund metaphor (SEE). SEE ALSO *a barrage of.*

adequate enough   A dimwitted redundancy (SEE). *adequate; enough.* ■ Another 46 to 48 percent of the priests in his study practiced celibacy *adequately* well *enough* to be called celibate. USE *adequately* or *enough.* SEE ALSO *sufficient enough.*

a diamond in the rough   A moribund metaphor (SEE).

a dime a dozen   A moribund metaphor (SEE). *average; basic; common; commonplace; customary; everyday; normal; omnipresent; ordinary; prevalent; quotidian; regular; standard; typical; ubiquitous; unexceptional; universal; unremarkable; usual; widespread.* ■ Sikhs in Kenya are *a dime a dozen.* REPLACE WITH *ubiquitous.*

ad infinitum   A foreignism (SEE). *ceaselessly; endlessly; forever; forevermore; to infinity; without limit.*

(score) a direct hit   A moribund metaphor (SEE).

a dirty word   A moribund metaphor (SEE). *abhorrent; abominable; a curse; an abomination; anathema; antipathetic; detestable; execrable; hateful; loathsome; monstrous; offensive; repugnant.* ■ Some in the academic community may disagree, but to working families corporate takeovers are still *a dirty word.* REPLACE WITH *anathema.*

ad nauseam   A foreignism (SEE).

a dog-eat-dog world   A moribund metaphor (SEE).

(lead) a dog's life   A moribund metaphor (SEE).

a done deal   *absolute; completed; concluded; conclusive; consummated; definitive; final; finished.* ■ There seems to be a misconception that this is *a done deal.*

adoring fans

(it's) a dream come true

a drop in the bucket (ocean) A moribund metaphor (See). *frivolous; immaterial; inconsiderable; insignificant; meager; meaningless; next to nothing; paltry; petty; scant; scanty; scarcely anything; slight; trifling; trivial; unimportant; unsubstantial; worthless.* ■ Relative to need, it's *a drop in the bucket.* Replace with *next to nothing.*

a drowning man will clutch at a straw   A popular prescription (See).

(like) a Dutch uncle   An insipid simile (See moribund metaphors).

advance planning   A dimwitted redundancy (See). *planning.* ■ This project will require a lot of *advance planning.* Delete *advance.*

advance warning   A dimwitted redundancy (See). *warning.* ■ Although the bank's seventeen thousand employees have known for more than a month that the ax was about to fall, the *advance warning* did little to blunt the effect. Delete *advance.* See also *forewarn; warn in advance.*

advice and consent

advice is cheap   A quack equation (See).

a dying breed   A moribund metaphor (See).

a fairy tale come true   A moribund metaphor (See).

(lull into) a false sense of security   ■ But concerns are growing that savings bank customers are being *lulled into a false sense of security* by believing, incorrectly, that the state has guaranteed the safety and protection of their life's savings.

a fate worse than death

a feather in (his) cap   A moribund metaphor (See). *acclaim; acclamation; accolade; approbation; approval; commendation; compliment; endorsement; honor; praise; sanction; tribute.*

a few choice words

(has) a few screws loose   A moribund metaphor (See). *batty; cracked; crazy; daft; demented; deranged; fey; goofy; insane; lunatic; mad; maniacal; neurotic; nuts; nutty; psychotic; raving; squirrelly; touched; unbalanced; unhinged; unsound; wacky; zany.*

a fifth wheel   A moribund metaphor (See). *extraneous; immaterial; incidental; inconsequential; insignificant; irrelevant; nonessential; superfluous; unimportant; unnecessary.* ■ With his mother doing the cooking and other household chores, I would feel *like a fifth wheel.* Replace with *superfluous.*

a 50-50 proposition

a fine (pretty) kettle of fish A moribund metaphor (See). *complication; difficulty; dilemma; mess; muddle; ordeal; pickle; plight; predicament; problem; quandary; trial; trouble.*

a firestorm of   A moribund metaphor (SEE). SEE ALSO *a barrage of.*

(like) a fish out of water   An insipid simile (SEE moribund metaphors).

a flood of   A moribund metaphor (SEE). ■ The evidence indicates NAFTA will lead to *a flood of* auto exports from the United States to Mexico. SEE ALSO *a barrage of.*

a fly on the wall   A moribund metaphor (SEE).

(bid) a fond farewell   An infantile phrase (SEE).

a fool and his money are soon parted   A popular prescription (SEE).

a fool for love

a fool's paradise   A moribund metaphor (SEE).

a force to be reckoned with   *adversary; antagonist; competitor; contender; contestant; opponent; rival.* ■ The combination of Walsh, the broadcast of Celtics games this season, and hot Fox network programming will make WFXT *a force to be reckoned with.* REPLACE WITH *a contender.*

a for instance   ■ I'll give you *a for instance.* REPLACE WITH *an example.*

afraid (frightened; scared) of (his) own shadow   A moribund metaphor (SEE). *afraid; alarmed; apprehensive; cowardly; craven; diffident; faint-hearted; fearful; frightened; pusillanimous; recreant; scared; terror-stricken; timid; timorous; tremulous.*

a friend in need (is a friend indeed)   A popular prescription (SEE).

after all is said and done   A dimwitted redundancy (SEE). *all in all; all told; altogether; eventually; finally; in all; in the end; on the whole; overall; ultimately.* ■ *After all is said and done,* it truly was an exceptional decade. USE *On the whole.* SEE ALSO *when all is said and done.*

(a man) after my own heart

after the fact   *afterward; later.* ■ We don't have a choice, *after the fact.* REPLACE WITH *afterward.*

(then) a funny thing happened

a funny thing happened to me on the way to   An infantile phrase (SEE).

again and again   A dimwitted redundancy (SEE). *frequently; habitually; often; recurrently; regularly; repeatedly.* ■ I called her and left messages *again and again,* but she never got back to me. USE *repeatedly.* SEE ALSO *over and over (again); time and (time) again.*

against the tide   A moribund metaphor (SEE).

age before beauty   A popular prescription (SEE).

age-old problem

a glimmer of hope   A moribund metaphor (SEE).

a gold mine of (information)   A moribund metaphor (SEE). SEE ALSO *a barrage of.*

a good catch   A moribund metaphor (SEE).

a good man is hard to find   A plebeian sentiment (SEE).

a good read   This is a hideous expression that only the very badly read—those, that is, who read merely to be amused—could possibly verbalize. The people who use this phrase are the people who read only *bestselling authors* (SEE). ■ This bookstore caters to those looking for *a good read in paperback*. REPLACE WITH *a readable paperback*. ■ While Foley's piece on football stadiums was *a good read*, it is entirely off the mark in terms of the proposed megaplex. REPLACE WITH *entertaining*. SEE ALSO *(take) a look see; a must read; an entertaining read*.

(and) a good time was had by all   An infantile phrase (SEE).

agree to disagree   An infantile phrase (SEE).

a guilty conscience needs no accuser   A popular prescription (SEE).

a hard (tough) act to follow   A moribund metaphor (SEE).

a hard (tough) nut to crack   A moribund metaphor (SEE). *conundrum; difficulty; dilemma; enigma; mystery; nut; plight; poser; predicament; problem; puzzle; quandary; question; riddle*.

ahead of the game   A moribund metaphor (SEE). *advantageous; auspicious; blessed; charmed; enchanted; favored; felicitous; flourishing; fortuitous; fortunate; golden; happy; in luck; lucky;* *propitious; prosperous; successful; thriving*.

(stay) ahead of the pack   A moribund metaphor (SEE).

(has) a (good) head on (his) shoulders   A moribund metaphor (SEE). *able; adroit; apt; astute; bright; brilliant; capable; clever; competent; discerning; effective; effectual; efficient; enlightened; insightful; intelligent; judicious; keen; knowledgeable; learned; logical; luminous; perceptive; perspicacious; quick; rational; reasonable; sagacious; sage; sapient; sensible; sharp; shrewd; smart; sound; understanding; wise*.

a heartbeat away   A moribund metaphor (SEE).

(like) a herd of elephants   An insipid simile (SEE moribund metaphors).

a hop, skip, and a jump   A moribund metaphor (SEE).

a house divided against itself cannot stand   A popular prescription (SEE).

a house of cards   A moribund metaphor (SEE).

aid and abet   An inescapable pair (SEE). *abet; aid; assist; help; support*.

airtight alibi   An inescapable pair (SEE).

a (man) is known by the company (he) keeps   A popular prescription (SEE).

a jack of all trades (and master of none)

a Johnny come lately   A moribund metaphor (SEE).

a joy to behold

(it's) a jungle (out there)   A moribund metaphor (SEE).

a kick in the pants   A moribund metaphor (SEE).
1. *encouragement; fillip; goad; impetus; impulse; incentive; incitation; incitement; inducement; jolt; motivation; motive; prod; provocation; push; shove; spur; stimulus; thrust; urge.*
2. *admonishment; castigation; censure; chastisement; disapprobation; disapproval; rebuke; remonstrance; reprimand; reproof; scolding; upbraiding.*

a kick in the teeth   A moribund metaphor (SEE). *abuse; affront; contempt; contumely; derision; disdain; impertinence; indignity; insult; offense; outrage; rebuff; rebuke; rejection; scorn; slight; slur; sneer; snub.*

(like) a kid in a candy shop (store)   An insipid simile (SEE moribund metaphors).

à la   A foreignism (SEE). *according to; in the manner of; like.* ■ I don't want to put myself in a bad position and get beat *à la* this man. REPLACE WITH *like.*

a labor of love   A moribund metaphor (SEE).

alas   An archaism (SEE). *regretably; sadly; sorrowfully; unfortunately; unhappily.*

alas and alack   An infantile phrase (SEE). *regretably; sadly; sorrowfully; unfortunately; unhappily.*

a late bloomer   A moribund metaphor (SEE).

(she's) a laugh a minute

albatross around (my) neck   A moribund metaphor (SEE). *affliction; burden; charge; cross; difficulty; encumbrance; hardship; hindrance; impediment; load; obstacle; obstruction; onus; oppression; ordeal; problem; trial; trouble; weight.*

albeit   An archaism (SEE). *although; even if; even though; though.* Like other archaisms, *albeit* strikes some people as more exquisite sounding—and therefore, apparently, more intellectual sounding—than any of its synonyms. But this is perceived by only the deaf and the dimwitted. ■ *Albeit* somewhat dated, a study performed eight years ago is attracting attention once again. USE *Although.*

a legend in (his) own mind   An infantile phrase (SEE).

a legend in (his) own time

(has) a leg up on   A moribund metaphor (SEE).

a leopard cannot change his spots   A popular prescription (SEE).

a light went on in my head   A moribund metaphor (SEE).

a little bird told me   An infantile phrase (SEE).

a little (honesty) goes a long way   A popular prescription (SEE).

a little knowledge is a dangerous

thing   A plebeian sentiment (SEE).

a little known fact

alive and kicking   A moribund metaphor (SEE). *alive; blooming; doing well; fit; energetic; flourishing; growing; hale; hardy; healthful; healthy; hearty; lively; prospering; robust; sound; strong; surviving; thriving; vigorous; vital; well; well-off.* One of the consequences of endlessly saying and hearing and writing and reading formulaic phrases is that, eventually, people *do* become weary of them.

But instead of expressing themselves differently — more eloquently or more inventively, perhaps — people will simply substitute one word in these selfsame formulas for another.

Thus, along with *alive and kicking*, there is, for instance, *alive and well* (SEE) and even *alive and thriving*; along with *a thing of the past*, there is *a phenomenon of the past*; along with *business as usual*, there is *politics as usual* (SEE) and the deadly *life as usual*; along with *mover and shaker*, there is *mover and shaper*; along with *needs and wants*, there is the needless *needs and desires*; along with *remedy the situation*, there is *rectify the situation*; and along with *nothing could be further from the truth*, there is, incomprehensibly, *nothing could be further from the actual facts.* People propagate these monstrosities. Equally unspeakable is that, in doing so, they think they *are* being clever and inventive. Among dimwitted people, this is what it means to be thoughtful, this is what it means to be creative.

Is it any wonder that speech is so often soporific, writing so often wearisome?

alive and well   An infantile phrase (SEE). *alive; blooming; doing well; energetic; fit; flourishing; growing; hale; hardy; healthful; healthy; hearty; lively; prospering; robust; sound; strong; surviving; thriving; vigorous; vital; well; well-off.* ■ Scholarship and readership are *alive and well* and will outlast the publishing binge of the commercial houses. REPLACE WITH *flourishing.*

a living hell   A moribund metaphor (SEE). *hellish; impossible; infernal; insufferable; insupportable; intolerable; painful; plutonic; stygian; sulfurous; unbearable; uncomfortable; unendurable; unpleasant.* The force and colorfulness of this metaphor is no longer evident. An uncommonly used word — such as *insupportable, plutonic, sulfurous* or *stygian* — is often more potent and captivating than a commonly used metaphor. ■ He's made my life *a living hell* for a month. REPLACE WITH *hellish.* SEE ALSO *hell on earth.*

a living legend

all and sundry   A dimwitted redundancy (SEE). *all; everybody; everyone; everything.* SEE ALSO *various and sundry.*

all bets (deals) are off

all dressed up and no place to go   An infantile phrase (SEE).

all ears   A moribund metaphor (SEE). *attentive; heedful; listening; paying attention; paying heed.*

(as) all get-out   *consumedly; exceedingly; extraordinarily; extremely; greatly; hugely; immensely; intensely; mightily; prodigiously; very.* ■ He was funny *as all get-out.* REPLACE WITH *extremely funny.*

all hell broke loose   A moribund metaphor (SEE).

all in a day's work

all in good time   *before long; directly; eventually; in time; later; one day; presently; quickly; shortly; sometime; soon.*

all of the above   An infantile phrase (SEE). ■ Are you looking for a companion or are you not. *All of the above.* SEE ALSO *none of the above.*

(it's) all or nothing

all-out war

all over the lot (map)   A moribund metaphor (SEE).

all roads lead to Rome   A moribund metaphor (SEE).

all rolled into one   *admixture; amalgam; blend; combination; mix; mixture.*

all's fair in love and war   A popular prescription (SEE).

all's well that end's well   A popular prescription (SEE).

all systems (are) go   A moribund metaphor (SEE).

all that glitters isn't gold   A popular prescription (SEE).

(and) all that jazz   A grammatical gimmick (SEE). ■ He tells me what to

do and all that jazz. DELETE *and all that jazz.*

all the world's a stage   A moribund metaphor (SEE).

all (other) things being equal

all things considered

all (good) things must end   A popular prescription (SEE).

all thumbs   A moribund metaphor (SEE). *awkward; blundering; bumbling; bungling; clumsy; gawky; gauche; inapt; inept; lubberly; maladroit; uncouth; ungainly; unhandy; unskillful; unwieldy.*

all-time record   A dimwitted redundancy (SEE). *record.* ■ Anyone who spent time skiing here this past winter would be happy to find the boycott has resulted in an *all-time record* number of skiers. DELETE *all-time.* SEE ALSO *record-breaking; record-high.*

all to the good   A moribund metaphor (SEE). *adequate; advantageous; beneficial; satisfactory; sufficient.*

(from) all walks of life   A moribund metaphor (SEE).

all wet   A moribund metaphor (SEE). *amiss; astray; deceived; deluded; erring; erroneous; fallacious; false; faulty; inaccurate; incorrect; in error; misguided; misinformed; misled; mistaken; not correct; not right; wrong.* ■ Whoever told you that alcohol is less of a problem than drugs is *all wet.* REPLACE WITH *mistaken.*

all wool and a yard wide   A moribund metaphor (SEE). *actual; authen-*

tic; earnest; genuine; heartfelt; honest; legitimate; pure; real; sincere; sterling; true; unadulterated; unalloyed; veritable.

all work and no play

all work and no play makes Jack a dull boy   A popular prescription (SEE).

along the lines of   A dimwitted redundancy (SEE). *akin to; close to; like; resembling; similar to; such as.* ■ It's generally safe to ask people in the field if they've ever heard of anything *along the lines of* your idea. USE *similar to.*

a long time coming

(take) a look see   This phrase is one of the new illiteracies. Expressions like *a good read, a must have,* and *a look see* are favored today by the "illiterati" — smart, articulate people who find it fashionable to speak unintelligibly. SEE ALSO *a good read; a must have; a must read; a must see; an entertaining read.*

a losing battle   A moribund metaphor (SEE).

a lot of times   A dimwitted redundancy (SEE). *frequently; often.* ■ *A lot of times* people have a tendency to think that others are controlling their destiny. USE *Often.*

a love-hate relationship   ■ Americans have *a love-hate relationship* with vice.

a (the) majority (of)   A torpid term (SEE). *Almost all, many, most, and nearly all.* This phrase and others like

it — *a large majority; an overwhelming majority; the vast majority* — are indispensable to those who luxuriate in circumlocutory language. ■ *The vast majority* of those people don't receive death sentences. REPLACE WITH *Most.* ■ Within two years, *the overwhelming majority of* Americans will have health coverage. REPLACE WITH *nearly all.* ■ *A large majority of* the participatory lenders have now joined the major banks in supporting our plan. REPLACE WITH *Almost all.*

a man's home is his castle   A popular prescription (SEE).

a marriage made in heaven   A suspect superlative (SEE).

a marriage of convenience

(it's) a matter of life and death   *critical; crucial; essential; imperative; important; necessary; pressing; urgent; vital.*

amazing   An overworked word (SEE). *astonishing; astounding; extraordinary; marvelous; outstanding; remarkable; spectacular; wonderful; wondrous.*

a menace to society

(as) American as apple pie   An insipid simile (SEE moribund metaphors). *all-American; decent; good; honorable; moral; proper; pure; right; straight; upright; virtuous; wholesome.*

America's sweetheart   A moribund metaphor (SEE).

amidst   An archaism (SEE). *amid; among.*

a mile a minute   A moribund metaphor (SEE). *apace; briskly; expeditiously; fast; hastily; hurriedly; posthaste; quickly; rapidly; speedily; swiftly; wingedly.*

a million miles away   A moribund metaphor (SEE). *absent; absentminded; absorbed; abstracted; bemused; captivated; daydreaming; detached; distracted; distrait; dreamy; engrossed; enraptured; faraway; fascinated; immersed; inattentive; lost; mesmerized; oblivious; preoccupied; rapt; spellbound.*

(has) a mind like a sieve   An insipid simile (SEE moribund metaphors). *forgetful; heedless; inattentive; neglectful; negligent; oblivious; remiss; thoughtless; unmindful; unthinking.*

a miss is as good as a mile   A popular prescription (SEE).

(9:00) A.M. . . . (in the) morning   A dimwitted redundancy (SEE). *(9:00) A.M.; (in the) morning.* ■ Monday's events can be defined to occur from 8 A.M. Monday *morning* to 8 A.M. Tuesday *morning.* DELETE *morning.* ■ This *morning* at 9:35 A.M. a violent clash took place between prisoners. DELETE A.M.

amongst   An archaism (SEE). *among.* ■ There are six children *amongst* us. USE *among.*

a month of Sundays   A moribund metaphor (SEE).

a mountain of   A moribund metaphor (SEE). SEE ALSO *a barrage of.*

ample opportunity   ■ Systems for governing police provided *ample opportunity* for outside control and influence. REPLACE WITH *opportunities.*

a multitude of sins   ■ In polite, carefully chosen words, the auditors take management to task for *a multitude of sins.*

a (absolute) must   *critical; crucial; essential; imperative; important; indispensable; necessary; needed; required.* ■ Prior experience writing user and technical documentation in the computer field is *a must.* REPLACE WITH *necessary.* ■ It is not *an absolute must* to read this part in order to use the second half of the book. REPLACE WITH *essential.* SEE ALSO *a must have; a must see; a (definite) plus.*

a must have   SEE ALSO *(take) a look see; a (absolute) must; a must see; a (definite) plus.*

a must read   SEE ALSO *a good read; (take) a look see; an entertaining read.*

a must see   SEE ALSO *(take) a look see; a (absolute) must; a must have; a (definite) plus.*

(do) an about-face   A moribund metaphor (SEE).

an accident waiting to happen

analyze to death   *analyze; anatomize; dissect; examine; inspect; investigate; scrutinize; study.* SEE ALSO *to death.*

an amazing person   A suspect superlative (SEE). *An amazing person* is so only in the eyes of another who, we can be confident, is not. SEE ALSO *a beautiful person.*

an apple a day keeps the doctor away   A popular prescription (SEE).

an army of   A moribund metaphor (SEE). SEE ALSO *a barrage of.*

an arrow in the heart   A moribund metaphor (SEE).

a national disgrace

an avalanche of   A moribund metaphor (SEE). ■ His antics on the court spawned *an avalanche of* imitators. SEE ALSO *a barrage of.*

(that's) ancient history   *aged; ancient; antediluvian; antique; archaic; elderly; history; hoary; old; past; patriarchal; prehistoric; seasoned; superannuated; venerable.*

and all   A grammatical gimmick (SEE). ■ We're going to look at all these nice buildings *and all.* DELETE *and all.* SEE ALSO *and all like that; and everything (else); and everything like that; and stuff; and (or) stuff like that; and things; and (or) things like that.*

and all like that   A grammatical gimmick (SEE). ■ We went to different agencies for help *and all like that.* DELETE *and all like that.* ■ He caught me off guard by asking for my name and address *and all like that.* DELETE *and all like that.* SEE ALSO *and all; and everything (else); and everything like that; and stuff; and (or) stuff like that; and things; and (or) things like that.*

and etc. (et cetera)   A dimwitted redundancy (SEE). *and so forth; and so on; and the like; etc.* ■ We bought the generic-brand products *and et cetera.* USE *and the like.*

and everything (else)   A grammatical gimmick (SEE). ■ We're responsible for this baby *and everything else.* DELETE *and everything else.* ■ You guys fight *and everything,* but she really does love you. DELETE *and everything.* SEE ALSO *and all; and all like that; and everything like that; and stuff; and (or) stuff like that; and things; and (or) things like that.*

and everything like that   A grammatical gimmick (SEE). ■ They adopted that way of speaking *and everything like that.* DELETE *and everything like that.* ■ Don't you feel cheap and used *and everything like that?* DELETE *and everything like that.* SEE ALSO *and all; and all like that; and everything (else); and stuff; and (or) stuff like that; and things; and (or) things like that.*

and I don't mean maybe   An infantile phrase (SEE).

and never the twain shall meet

and/or   A dimwitted redundancy (SEE). *and; or.* ■ Implant dentistry can be an effective alternative to dentures *and/or* missing teeth. USE *or.* ■ But computers may make both more attractive than the alternatives adopted by those who have abandoned wives *and/or* children by failing to meet their financial obligations. USE *and.*

and so on, and so forth   A grammatical gimmick (SEE). ■ I'm more interested in films about human relationships *and so on, and so forth.* DELETE *and so on, and so forth.* SEE ALSO *blah, blah, blah; et cetera, et cetera.*

and stuff   A grammatical gimmick (SEE). ■ His legs had black bruises on them *and stuff*. DELETE *and stuff*. ■ The customers are really nice people; they're friends *and stuff*. DELETE *and stuff*. SEE ALSO *and all; and all like that; and everything (else); and everything like that; and (or) stuff like that; and things; and (or) things like that*.

and (or) stuff like that   A grammatical gimmick (SEE). ■ I love women — the way they look *and stuff like that*. DELETE *and stuff like that*. ■ People shouldn't shoot others over money or things *or stuff like that*. DELETE *or stuff like that*. SEE ALSO *and all; and all like that; and everything (else); and everything like that; and stuff; and things; and (or) things like that*.

and that kind of thing   A grammatical gimmick (SEE). ■ He's a changed man; he's learned to read and write *and that kind of thing*. DELETE *and that kind of thing*. ■ I was working on getting the house settled *and that kind of thing*. DELETE *and that kind of thing*. SEE ALSO *and that sort of thing; and that type of thing*.

and that sort of thing   A grammatical gimmick (SEE). ■ I enjoy walking in the park *and that sort of thing*. DELETE *and that sort of thing*. SEE ALSO *and that kind of thing; and that type of thing*.

and that type of thing   A grammatical gimmick (SEE). ■ I like interesting conversation and interacting *and that type of thing*. DELETE *and that type of thing*. SEE ALSO *and that kind of thing; and that sort of thing*.

and things   A grammatical gimmick (SEE). ■ They wanted him to go for a bike ride *and things*. DELETE *and things*. ■ We got invited to a lot of Hollywood parties *and things*. DELETE *and things*. SEE ALSO *and all; and all like that; and everything (else); and everything like that; and stuff; and (or) stuff like that; and (or) things like that*.

and (or) things like that   A grammatical gimmick (SEE). ■ I was upset because my mother went through two divorces *and things like that*. DELETE *and things like that*. ■ As a big man, they look at you as big and healthy *and things like that*. DELETE *and things like that*. SEE ALSO *and all; and all like that; and everything (else); and everything like that; and stuff; and (or) stuff like that; and things*.

and this and that   A grammatical gimmick (SEE). ■ He told me how much he cared for me *and this and that*. DELETE *and this and that*. SEE ALSO *and this, that and the other (thing)*.

and this, that and the other (thing)   A grammatical gimmick (SEE). ■ She would say to me, you've got the best of both worlds, you're special, you're loved, *and this, that and the other thing*. DELETE *and this, that and the other thing*. SEE ALSO *and this and that*.

and what do (I) get (for it)?

an easy task   *apparent; basic; clear; clear-cut; conspicuous; distinct; easily done; easy; effortless; elementary; evident; explicit; facile; limpid; lucid; manifest; obvious; patent; pellucid; plain; simple; simplicity itself; simplistic; straightforward; translucent; transparent; unambiguous; uncomplex; uncomplicated; understandable; unequivocal; unmistakable*.

an embarrassment of riches
A moribund metaphor (SEE). ■ It's a city with *an embarrassment of riches*.

an emotional roller coaster
A moribund metaphor (SEE).

an encouraging word

an entertaining read ■ Tom Wolfe's *Bonfire of the Vanities* is *an enormously entertaining read*. REPLACE WITH *enormously entertaining*. SEE ALSO *a good read; (take) a look see; a must read*.

a (whole) new ballgame A moribund metaphor (SEE).

a new lease on life A moribund metaphor (SEE). *animated; energized; enlivened; inspired; inspirited; invigorated; refreshed; reinvigorated; rejuvenated; revitalized; revived; roused; stimulated; stirred; vitalized.*

a new low (point)

a new wrinkle A moribund metaphor (SEE).

an explosion of A moribund metaphor (SEE). SEE ALSO *a barrage of*.

an eye for an eye (and a tooth for a tooth) A popular prescription (SEE).

angel of mercy A moribund metaphor (SEE).

an idea whose time has come ■ The good-news section is *an idea whose time has come*.

(it's) a nightmare A moribund metaphor (SEE). How impoverished our imaginations are. Nightmares ought to be terrifying, but this metaphor—so popular has it become—is hopelessly tame. *It was a nightmare* instills in us as little compassion as it does interest; it makes us yawn rather than yell. No longer is there terror to it.

Though an incident might well be *agonizing, alarming, appalling, awful, disgusting, disquieting, distressing, disturbing, dreadful, excruciating, frightening, frightful, ghastly, grisly, gruesome, harrowing, hideous, horrendous, horrible, horrid, horrific, horrifying, monstrous, nauseating, nightmarish, petrifying, repellent, repulsive, revolting, shocking, sickening, terrifying, tormenting, traumatic*, saying *it was a nightmare* makes it sound as though it were no more than an annoyance, no more than a mere inconvenience.

It was a nightmare, the metaphor, has hardly the force of a sweet dream. ■ It was *a nightmare*. REPLACE WITH *ghastly*. ■ If the birth mother shows up, it's *a nightmare* for the adopting mother. REPLACE WITH *disquieting*. SEE ALSO *(every person's) worst nightmare*.

an inspiration to us all How inspirational could anyone have been when he is described with such an uninspired expression? ■ He's been *an inspiration to us all*.

an ocean of A moribund metaphor (SEE). SEE ALSO *a barrage of*.

a nodding acquaintance A moribund metaphor (SEE).

an old hand A moribund metaphor (SEE). *able; adept; apt; capable; competent; deft; dexterous; experienced; expert;*

practiced; proficient; seasoned; skilled; skillful; veteran.

anon An archaism (SEE).
1. *at another time; later.*
2. *shortly; soon.*
3. *at once; immediately.*

an open-and-shut case *apparent; clear; evident; open; plain; straightforward; unambiguous; uncomplex; uncomplicated.*

an open book A moribund metaphor (SEE).
1. *apparent; clear; clear-cut; crystalline; evident; explicit; limpid; lucid; manifest; obvious; open; patent; pellucid; plain; translucent; transparent; unambiguous; uncomplex; uncomplicated; understandable; unequivocal; unmistakable.*
2. *aboveboard; artless; blunt; candid; direct; forthright; frank; genuine; guileless; honest; ingenuous; naive; sincere; straightforward; truthful; veracious; veridical.*

an open question A dimwitted redundancy (SEE). *a question; debatable; disputable; moot; open; questionable; uncertain; unclear; undecided; undetermined; unknown; unsettled; unsure.* ■ Whether it's still possible for us to complete the project by next season is *an open question* at this point. USE *unknown.*

an orgy of A moribund metaphor (SEE). SEE ALSO *a barrage of.*

another day, another dollar A popular prescription (SEE).

an ounce of prevention is worth a

pound of cure A popular prescription (SEE).

ants in (his) pants A moribund metaphor (SEE). *aflame; agitated; animated; anxious; eager; ebullient; effervescent; enthusiastic; excitable; excited; fervent; fervid; fidgety; frantic; frenzied; impassioned; impatient; jittery; jumpy; lively; nervous; restive; restless; skittish; spirited.*

a number (of) A torpid term (SEE). This phrase along with so many others like it — *a considerable number of, a fair number of, a good number of, a large number of, a vast number of* — is preferred by all who shun specificity or don't precisely know what it is they speak of. ■ You can use the computer to discover students who are making *a large number of* mistakes. REPLACE WITH *many.* ■ *A good number* of troops have arrived in Moscow. REPLACE WITH *Hundreds.* ■ *An overwhelming number of* the participatory lenders have now joined the major banks in supporting our plan. REPLACE WITH *Almost all.* SEE ALSO *a sufficient number (of).*

(face) an uneasy future

an uphill battle (fight) A moribund metaphor (SEE).

anxious telephone calls

any and all A dimwitted redundancy (SEE). *all; any.* ■ *Any and all* accidental needle sticks must be reported to the physician at once. USE *All.* ■ We welcome *any and all* comments and suggestions regarding this project. USE *any.*

anyhow

anyhow   A grammatical gimmick (SEE). ■ *Anyhow*, we got the divorce in 1992. DELETE *Anyhow*. SEE ALSO *anyway*.

any port in a storm   A moribund metaphor (SEE).

anything and everything   A dimwitted redundancy (SEE). *anything; everything.* ■ A deadbeat is generally defined as a person dedicated to getting *anything and everything* possible for nothing. USE *anything* or *everything*.

anything for a laugh   A plebeian sentiment (SEE).

anything (everything) is possible A popular prescription (SEE).

any time soon   ■ The worsening condition of the economy has significantly affected our workload, and we don't foresee an upswing *any time soon*.

anyway   A grammatical gimmick (SEE). ■ But *anyway*, I'll talk to you later in the week. DELETE *anyway*. ■ So *anyway*, I just wanted to verify that with you. DELETE *anyway*. SEE ALSO *anyhow*.

a (taste) of things to come

a pack of lies

a pain in the ass (rear)   A moribund metaphor (SEE). *affliction; annoyance; bane; bother; burden; curse; difficulty; inconvenience; irritant; irritation; load; nuisance; ordeal; pain; pest; plague; problem; torment; tribulation; trouble; vexation; weight; worry.*

a pain in the neck   A moribund metaphor (SEE). *affliction; annoyance; bane; bother; burden; curse; difficulty; inconvenience; irritant; irritation; load; nuisance; ordeal; pain; pest; plague; problem; torment; tribulation; trouble; vexation; weight; worry.*

a paragon of (beauty)

a penny for your thoughts

a penny saved is a penny earned A popular prescription (SEE).

(I'm) a perfectionist   A suspect superlative (SEE). SEE ALSO *I'm not perfect (you know); nobody's perfect.*

a picture is worth a thousand words   A popular prescription (SEE).

a place for everything and everything in its place   A popular prescription (SEE).

a (definite) plus   *advantage; allure; allurement; appeal; asset; attraction; benefit; enticement; inducement; lure; value.* ■ Process control experience is *a definite plus*. REPLACE WITH *an asset*. ■ Its location and accessibility to our members are *a definite plus*. REPLACE WITH *a lure*.

(he's) a poet but (he) doesn't know it   An infantile phrase (SEE).

a point in time   A dimwitted redundancy (SEE). *a time.* ■ There comes *a point in time* when we all pass into adulthood. USE *a time*.

(I) apologize for any inconvenience

18

a poor thing but my own

(exact) a pound of flesh A moribund metaphor (SEE).

appearances can be deceiving A popular prescription (SEE).

appear (arrive) on the scene *appear; arise; come forth; emerge; occur; originate; present itself; rise; surface; turn up.* ■ TTAPS first *appeared on the scene* in 1983 with a paper in *Science* on the global atmospheric consequences of nuclear war. REPLACE WITH *emerged.*

apple polisher A moribund metaphor (SEE). *apparatchik; bootlicker; fawner; flatterer; flunky; follower; lackey; minion; stooge; sycophant; toady; yes-man.*

apples and oranges A moribund metaphor (SEE).

apply the brakes on A moribund metaphor (SEE). *arrest; cease; check; conclude; derail; discontinue; end; halt; stop; suspend; terminate.*

(I) appreciate (it) An overworked word (SEE).
1. *grateful for; thankful for; thank you.*
2. *admire; cherish; esteem; prize; relish; treasure; value.*
■ We *appreciate* your help. REPLACE WITH *are grateful for.* ■ We *appreciate you* being here. REPLACE WITH *thank you for.* ■ I *appreciate* every letter that I have received. REPLACE WITH *treasure.* SEE ALSO *common courtesy.*

(an) approach An overworked word (SEE). For example: *band-aid approach; carrot-and-stick approach; com-* *monsense approach; hands-on approach; holistic approach; shotgun approach; surefire approach; team approach; upbeat approach.*

(take) appropriate action A torpid term (SEE).

a pretty picture A moribund metaphor (SEE).

April showers bring May flowers A popular prescription (SEE).

a prince among men A suspect superlative (SEE).

a promise is a promise A quack equation (SEE).

(only) a question of time

a quick study A moribund metaphor (SEE).

a race against time

a race to the finish (line) A moribund metaphor (SEE).

a raw deal

a ray of hope A moribund metaphor (SEE).

a ray of sunshine A moribund metaphor (SEE).

archaisms There are many rare and wonderful words that we would do well to become familiar with—words that would revitalize us for our revitalizing them—words like *bedizen; bootless; caliginous; compleat; cotquean; ensorcell; hebdomadal; helpmeet; logorrhea; quondam; wont.*

Archaisms, however—words like *albeit; amidst; amongst; behoove; betwixt; ergo; forsooth; perchance; sans; save; thence; to wit; unbeknownst; verily; whence; wherein; whereon; wherewith; whilst*—are hopelessly withered words that deserve to be forgotten.

People who use them may not say much that is memorable. SEE ALSO *foreignisms*.

area of expertise A suspect superlative (SEE). *area; business; calling; craft; field; forte; job; line; métier; occupation; profession; specialty; strength; trade; vocation.*

(seems like) a reasonable request

(we) aren't going to take it anymore A popular prescription (SEE).

(things) aren't what they used to be

a rising tide of A moribund metaphor (SEE). ■ The report found in the nation's public schools *a rising tide of* mediocrity. SEE ALSO *a barrage of.*

armed and dangerous An inescapable pair (SEE).

armed (themselves) to the teeth A moribund metaphor (SEE).

a rogue's gallery of A moribund metaphor (SEE).

a rolling stone gathers no moss A popular prescription (SEE).

a romp through A moribund metaphor (SEE). This phrase is a favorite of dimwitted film critics and book reviewers.

a roof over (their) heads *asylum; cover; harbor; harborage; haven; housing; lodging; protection; refuge; retreat; safety; sanctuary; shelter.*

a rose by any other name (would smell as sweet) A popular prescription (SEE).

a rose is a rose (is a rose) A quack equation (SEE).

around about A dimwitted redundancy (SEE). *about; around.* ■ Let's meet *around about* noon. USE *about* or *around.*

a round peg in a square hole A moribund metaphor (SEE). *curiosity; deviant; eccentric; iconoclast; individual; individualist; maverick; misfit; nonconformist; oddball; oddity; renegade; undesirable.*

(work) around the clock *always; ceaselessly; constantly; continually; continuously; endlessly; eternally; everlastingly; evermore; forever; forevermore; frequently; interminably; nonstop; permanently; perpetually; persistently; recurrently; regularly; repeatedly; unceasingly; unremittingly.*

(just; right) around the corner A moribund metaphor (SEE). *approaching; at hand; close; close by; coming; forthcoming; imminent; impending; near; nearby; vicinal.*

art is long, and life is short A popular prescription (SEE).

a rule is a rule A quack equation (SEE).

a run for (his) money A moribund metaphor (SEE).

a sadder but wiser man

as a man sows so shall he reap
A popular prescription (SEE).

as a matter of fact A dimwitted redundancy (SEE). *actually; indeed; in fact; in faith; in reality; in truth; truly.* ■ *As a matter of fact,* children get disappointed when they grow up to find the adult's prescription didn't match the real world. USE *In truth.*

as a result of A dimwitted redundancy (SEE). *after; because of; by; due to; following; for; from; in; out of; owing to; through; with.* ■ *As a result of* this letter, ten of us did not attend the wedding. USE *Because of.*

a sea of A moribund metaphor (SEE). ■ He was surrounded by *a sea of* concerned women. DELETE *a sea of.* SEE ALSO *a barrage of.*

as far as ... (goes; is concerned) A dimwitted redundancy (SEE). *about; as for; as to; concerning; for; in; of; on; over; regarding; respecting; to; toward; with.* ■ *As far as* improvements *go,* you'd have a battle. USE *As for.* ■ *As far as* those bargains *are concerned,* attempts to place measures on the table would be regressive and an illegal act. USE *Concerning.* SEE ALSO *where ... is concerned.*

as far as the eye can see

as good as it gets

(he's) a shadow of (his) former self A moribund metaphor (SEE).

ashes to ashes (dust to dust) A moribund metaphor (SEE).

a shot in the arm A moribund metaphor (SEE). *boost; encouragement; fillip; goad; impetus; impulse; incentive; incitation; incitement; inducement; jolt; motivation; motive; prod; provocation; push; shove; spur; stimulus; thrust; urge.* ■ Their success will give *a shot in the arm* to the rest of the economy. REPLACE WITH *a thrust.*

a shot in the dark A moribund metaphor (SEE). *appraisal; assessment; assumption; conjecture; estimate; estimation; guess; hypothesis; impression; opinion; presumption; speculation; supposition; surmise.*

(breathe; heave) a sigh of relief ■ After holding its breath for days, the city finally exhaled *a sigh of relief.*

a sight for sore eyes A moribund metaphor (SEE).

a sight to behold

a significant part (portion; proportion) A dimwitted redundancy (SEE). *a good (great) deal; a good (great) many; almost all; many; most; much; nearly all.* ■ Many programmers spend *a significant portion* of their working day maintaining software. USE *a good deal.* SEE ALSO *a substantial part (portion; proportion).*

a sign of the times

a simple task *apparent; basic; clear; clear-cut; conspicuous; distinct; easily done; easy; effortless; elementary; evident; explicit; facile; limpid; lucid; manifest; obvious; patent; pellucid; plain; simple; simplicity itself; simplistic; straightforward; translucent; transparent; unambiguous; uncomplex; uncom-*

plicated; understandable; unequivocal; unmistakable. ■ Identifying opinion leaders is not *a simple task* since they tend to be product specific and differ over time. REPLACE WITH *easy*.

a sinking ship   A moribund metaphor (SEE).

a sin of omission

a sin of omission and (as well as) commission

a sitting duck   A moribund metaphor (SEE).

(like) asking for the moon   An insipid simile (SEE moribund metaphors).

(she's) asking for trouble

ask me no questions and I'll tell you no lies   A popular prescription (SEE).

a slap in the face   A moribund metaphor (SEE). *abuse; affront; contempt; contumely; derision; disdain; impertinence; indignity; insult; offense; outrage; rebuff; rebuke; rejection; scorn; slight; slur; sneer; snub.*

a slap on the wrist   A moribund metaphor (SEE). *admonish; animadvert; berate; castigate; censure; chasten; chastise; chide; condemn; criticize; denounce; denunciate; discipline; impugn; objurgate; punish; rebuke; remonstrate; reprehend; reprimand; reproach; reprobate; reprove; revile; scold; upbraid; vituperate; warn.*

asleep at the switch   A moribund metaphor (SEE).

1. *careless; forgetful; heedless; inattentive; neglectful; negligent; oblivious; remiss; slack; thoughtless; unmindful; unthinking.*
2. *asleep; daydreaming.*

asleep at the wheel   A moribund metaphor (SEE).
1. *careless; forgetful; heedless; inattentive; neglectful; negligent; oblivious; remiss; slack; thoughtless; unmindful; unthinking.*
2. *asleep; daydreaming.*

a slow boat to China (nowhere)   A moribund metaphor (SEE).

as luck would have it   *by chance; coincidentally; luckily.*

a small army of   A moribund metaphor (SEE). ■ *A small army of* labor leaders came to Washington for a final assault against the agreement. SEE ALSO *a barrage of.*

(cost) a small fortune

(as) (wholesome) as mom and apple pie   An insipid simile (SEE moribund metaphors). *decent; ethical; exemplary; good; honest; honorable; just; moral; pure; righteous; straight; upright; virtuous; wholesome.*

(like) a soap opera   An insipid simile (SEE moribund metaphors).

a soft touch   A moribund metaphor (SEE).

a sometime thing   *erratic; fitful; haphazard; inconsistent; intermittent; irregular; occasional; random; sometime; spasmodic; sporadic; unpredictable.*

a sorry sight

a spate of   A moribund metaphor (SEE). ■ The legislation was proposed in response to *a spate of* violent incidents. SEE ALSO *a barrage of.*

a special place in (my) heart

a square peg in a round hole A moribund metaphor (SEE). *curiosity; deviant; eccentric; iconoclast; individual; individualist; maverick; misfit; nonconformist; oddball; oddity; renegade; undesirable.*

as ready as (I'll) ever be

as (you) sow, so shall (you) reap A popular prescription (SEE).

a step backward   *backset; reversal; setback.*

a step forward   *advancement; betterment; development; furtherance; growth; headway; improvement; progress.* ■ This is *a step forward* for us all. REPLACE WITH *betterment.*

For some writers, *a step forward* isn't positive enough: ■ Although the IFS interface is *a positive step forward* for DOS, it remains in a sort of twilight zone. REPLACE WITH *an advancement.* SEE ALSO *a step (forward) in the right direction; go forward; move forward; move (forward) in the right direction; proceed forward.*

a step (forward) in the right direction   A torpid term (SEE). *advancement; betterment; development; furtherance; growth; headway; improvement; progress.* ■ Incentives to attract and retain nurses would be *a step in the right direction.* REPLACE WITH *an improve-*

ment. SEE ALSO *a step forward; go forward; move forward; move (forward) in the right direction; proceed forward.*

as the cliché (saying) goes

as the crow flies   A moribund metaphor (SEE). *directly; lineally; linearly; straight.*

(as) (vain) as the day is long   An insipid simile (SEE moribund metaphors).

a stitch in time saves nine   A popular prescription (SEE).

a stone's throw (away)   A moribund metaphor (SEE). *accessible; at hand; close; close by; handy; near; nearby; neighboring; vicinal.*

a storm of   A moribund metaphor (SEE). SEE ALSO *a barrage of.*

as to whether (why)   A dimwitted redundancy (SEE). *whether.* ■ It is uncertain *as to whether* such a determination can ever be made. DELETE *as to.*

a stroll (walk) in the park   A moribund metaphor (SEE).
1. *easily done; easy; effortless; elementary; facile; simple; simplicity itself; simplistic; straightforward; uncomplex; uncomplicated.*
2. *agreeable; beguiling; charming; delightful; enchanting; engaging; enjoyable; fun; glorious; gratifying; inviting; joyful; joyous; pleasant; pleasing; pleasurable.* ■ Building high-rise buildings, dams and bridges isn't exactly *a walk in the park.* REPLACE WITH *simple.*

a substantial part (portion; proportion)   A   dimwitted   redundancy

(SEE). *a good (great) deal; a good (great) many; almost all; many; most; much; nearly all.* ■ It is unconscionable that *a substantial proportion* of our population does not have adequate access to health care. USE *much.* ■ I assume that Boston will be eligible for *a substantial portion* of the distressed communities fund. USE *a good deal.* SEE ALSO *a significant part (portion; proportion).*

a sufficient number (of)   A dimwitted redundancy (SEE). *enough.* ■ Effective groups contain *a sufficient number of* members to ensure good interaction. USE *enough.* SEE ALSO *a number (of).*

a sure bet (thing)   *assured; certain; sure.*

(even) as we speak   *at present; currently; (just; right) now; presently.* ■ The team is having a pep rally on campus *as we speak.* REPLACE WITH *now.* ■ Are your forces, *even as we speak*, looking for him in a military way? REPLACE WITH *currently.*

as you make your bed, so you must lie on it   A popular prescription (SEE).

at a crossroad   A moribund metaphor (SEE).

at a fast (good) clip   A moribund metaphor (SEE). *apace; briskly; expeditiously; fast; hastily; hurriedly; posthaste; quickly; rapidly; speedily; swiftly; wingedly.*

a tale never loses in the telling   A popular prescription (SEE).

at a loss   *baffled; befuddled; bewil-dered; confounded; confused; disconcerted; mixed up; muddled; nonplussed; perplexed; puzzled.*

at a loss for words   *astonished; dumb; dumbfounded; flabbergasted; mum; mute; quiet; reticent; shocked; silent; speechless; still; stunned; taciturn.*

at a low ebb   A moribund metaphor (SEE).

at arm's length   A moribund metaphor (SEE).

at a snail's pace   A moribund metaphor (SEE). *deliberately; laggardly; lazily; leisurely; slothfully; very slowly; snail-paced; unhurriedly.*

at (my) beck and call   *accepting; accommodating; acquiescent; complacent; complaisant; compliant; cowed; deferential; docile; dutiful; obedient; passive; prostrate; resigned; submissive; subservient; tolerant; tractable; yielding.*

at death's door   A moribund metaphor (SEE). *decaying; declining; deteriorating; disintegrating; dying; ebbing; expiring; fading; failing; near death; sinking; waning.*

at each other's throats   A moribund metaphor (SEE). *arguing; battling; bickering; brawling; clashing; disagreeing; fighting; quarreling; squabbling; wrangling.*

at (my) fingertips   A moribund metaphor (SEE). 1. *recall; recollect; remember; think of.* 2. *accessible; at hand; close; close by; handy; near; nearby; neighboring; vicinal.*

at (the) first blush

a thankless task

a thing of beauty is a joy forever
A popular prescription (SEE).

a thing of the past
1. *ceased; completed; concluded; dead; deceased; defunct; departed; done; ended; exanimate; expired; extinct; extinguished; finished; gone; inanimate; lifeless; no more; over; perished; stopped; terminated.* ■ All agree that the days of students being able to work their way through college are *a thing of the past.* REPLACE WITH *over.*
2. *antediluvian; antiquated; archaic; dead; obsolescent; obsolete; old; old-fashioned; outdated; outmoded; out of date; out of fashion; passé; superannuated.* ■ The eight-hour day has become *a thing of the past.* REPLACE WITH *obsolete.*

a tidal wave of   A moribund metaphor (SEE). ■ There's just *a tidal wave of* vital information that gets delivered by telephone. SEE ALSO *a barrage of.*

a tip of the hat   A moribund metaphor (SEE).

at loggerheads   A moribund metaphor (SEE). *arguing; battling; bickering; brawling; clashing; disagreeing; disputing; fighting; quarreling; squabbling; wrangling.*

at long last   *at length; finally; ultimately.*

at loose ends   A moribund metaphor (SEE).
1. *confused; disorganized; drifting; faltering; in between; irresolute; loose;*
shaky; swaying; tottering; uncertain; undecided; unfixed; unresolved; unsettled; unsteady; unsure; vacillating; wavering; wobbly.
2. *bored; idle; inactive; unemployed; unoccupied.*

at one fell swoop   A moribund metaphor (SEE).

a torrent of   A moribund metaphor (SEE). SEE ALSO *a barrage of.*

a tough call

at peace with the world

a trouble shared is a trouble halved   A popular prescription (SEE).

(all) at sea   A moribund metaphor (SEE). *baffled; befuddled; bewildered; confounded; confused; disconcerted; lost; mixed up; muddled; nonplussed; perplexed; puzzled.*

at sixes and sevens   A moribund metaphor (SEE).
1. *baffled; bewildered; confused; muddled; perplexed; uncertain.*
2. *disarranged; disorganized; entangled; jumbled; in disarray; in disorder; tangled.*

attack (it) head on

attack (them) on all fronts

(pay) attention to detail

at that time   A dimwitted redundancy (SEE). This phrase and several others like it, including *at that juncture in life, at that moment in our national life, at that point in time, at that stage in the history of my life, at that time in our history*, mean no more than *then* and ought not to be used for them. ■ I wasn't happy with what I was doing *at that juncture in life*. USE *then*. ■ DFSMS did not include any cost input parameters *at that point in time*. USE *then*. SEE ALSO *at this time*.

at the breaking point A moribund metaphor (SEE).

at the crack of dawn A moribund metaphor (SEE). *very early*.

(stand) at the crossroads of history A moribund metaphor (SEE).

at (on) the cutting edge A moribund metaphor (SEE). ■ Although his research activities have placed him *on the cutting edge* of his field, Blanchflower is one of Dartmouth's most scintillating instructors.

at the drop of a hat A moribund metaphor (SEE). *at once; directly; forthwith; immediately; instantly; momentarily; promptly; right away; straightaway; summarily; without delay*.

at the eleventh hour A moribund metaphor (SEE). *late*.

at the end of (my) rope (tether) A moribund metaphor (SEE).

at the helm A moribund metaphor (SEE). *in charge; in control*.

at the top of (his) game A moribund metaphor (SEE).

at the top of (my) lungs *blaringly; boisterously; boomingly; deafeningly;* *earsplittingly; loudly; noisily; obstreperously; resoundingly; roaringly; stentorianly; thunderingly; thunderously; tumultuously; vociferously*.

at (behind) the wheel A moribund metaphor (SEE). *in charge; in control*.

at this time A dimwitted redundancy (SEE). This phrase and several others like it, including *at the present time, at this juncture in life, at this moment in our national life, at this point in time, at this stage in the history of my life, at this time in our history*, mean no more than *at present, now, today*, or *yet* and ought not to be used for them. ■ We don't see any significant breakthroughs *at this juncture*. USE *now*. ■ What can she do to help you *at this stage of the game?* USE *now*. ■ *At this point in the current time*, the conditions for an agreement have not been met. USE *At present*. The conditions for an agreement have not *yet* been met. SEE ALSO *at that time*.

attitude An overworked word (SEE). For example: *attitude problem; holier-than-thou attitude; patronizing attitude; superior attitude; wait-and-see attitude*.

attributable to the fact that A dimwitted redundancy (SEE). *because; considering; for; in that; since*. SEE ALSO *due to the fact that; owing to the fact that*.

a tug of war A moribund metaphor (SEE). ■ There's *a tug of war* between people who like the economy and people who are afraid.

a turn on A moribund metaphor (SEE). *animating; arousing; bracing;*

enlivening; exciting; exhilarating; inspiring; inspiriting; invigorating; provoking; refreshing; rousing; stimulating; vivifying.

at (his) wit's end   A moribund metaphor (SEE).

audible (inaudible) to the ear
A dimwitted redundancy (SEE). *audible (inaudible).* SEE ALSO *visible (invisible) to the eye.*

au naturel   A foreignism (SEE). *bare; disrobed; naked; nude; stripped; unclothed; uncovered; undressed.*

(your) average Joe   A moribund metaphor (SEE). *average; common; commonplace; conventional; customary; everyday; familiar; mediocre; middling; normal; ordinary; quotidian; regular; standard; typical; unexceptional; unremarkable; usual.*

avid reader   An inescapable pair (SEE). An *avid reader* suggests someone who reads little more than mysteries, gothic novels, and self-help books.

These are people whose avidity is more for how many books they read than it is for any meaning in books — people, that is, who prefer counting to reading.

avoid (it) like the plague   An insipid simile (SEE moribund metaphors).
1. *abhor; abominate; detest; hate; loathe.*
2. *recoil from; shrink from; shun; spurn.*
■ Your clients will probably either love

Los Angeles or *avoid it like the plague.* REPLACE WITH *loathe it.*

a walking, talking   An infantile phrase (SEE).

a watched pot never boils   A popular prescription (SEE).

a watchful eye   A moribund metaphor (SEE).

awesome   An overworked word (SEE). Like *awful* and *terrific*, the word *awesome* has been made ridiculous by those who are bent on using it solely in its most popular sense.
Awesome means *awe-inspiring, majestic,* or *terrifying,* but of late it most often merely means *fantastic* or *great* (SEE). SEE ALSO *awful; terrific.*

awful   An overworked word (SEE). *Awful* means *awe-inspiring* or *terrifying,* but of late, it means no more than *very bad* or *unpleasant.* SEE ALSO *awesome; terrific.*

a woman's place is in the home
A popular prescription (SEE).

a woman's work is never done
A popular prescription (SEE).

a (whole new) world of   A moribund metaphor (SEE). ■ Mail merge can make your word processor more useful and can open up *a whole new world of* power. SEE ALSO *a barrage of.*

ax (axe) to grind   A moribund metaphor (SEE). *animosity; bitterness; enmity; grievance; grudge; hostility; indignation; ill will; offense; rancor; resentment; spite; umbrage.*

B

babe in the woods   A moribund metaphor (SEE). *adolescent; artless; callow; green; guileless; immature; inexperienced; inexpert; ingenuous; innocent; juvenile; naive; raw; simple; undeveloped; unfledged; unskilled; unskillful; unsophisticated; untaught; untrained; unworldly; young; youthful.*

back (up) against the wall
A moribund metaphor (SEE). *catch; corner; enmesh; ensnare; entangle; entrap; net; snare; trap.*

(meanwhile) back at the ranch
A moribund metaphor (SEE).

back in the saddle (again)   A moribund metaphor (SEE).

(get) back in the swing of things

back into a corner   A moribund metaphor (SEE). *catch; corner; enmesh; ensnare; entangle; entrap; net; snare; trap.*

(get) back on (his) feet   A moribund metaphor (SEE). *ameliorate; amend; come round; convalesce; gain strength; get better; heal; improve; look up; meliorate; mend; rally; recover; recuperate; refresh; regain strength; renew; revive; strengthen.* ■ Even the

construction industry is starting to *get back on its feet*. REPLACE WITH *recover*.

back on track   A moribund metaphor (SEE).

back to basics   ■ Banks and savings and loans are getting *back to basics* and concentrating on home mortgages.

(get) back to reality

back to square one   A moribund metaphor (SEE).

(go) back to the drawing board
A moribund metaphor (SEE). ■ Beware of protracted and angry discussions; they are usually a sign that there is not enough support for the idea, and you should go *back to the drawing board*.

back to the salt mines   A moribund metaphor (SEE).

back to the wall   A moribund metaphor (SEE).
1. *at risk; endangered; hard-pressed; imperiled; in a bind; in a fix; in a jam; in a predicament; in a quandary; in danger; in difficulty; in jeopardy; in peril; in trouble; jeopardized.*
2. *at bay; caught; cornered; enmeshed;*

ensnared; entangled; entrapped; netted; snared; trapped.

back up (their) words with actions

bad apple   A moribund metaphor (SEE). *brute; degenerate; fiend; knave; lout; rake; rascal; rogue; ruffian; scamp; scoundrel; villain.*

bad blood (between them)
A moribund metaphor (SEE). *abhorrence; anger; animosity; antipathy; aversion; detestation; enmity; hate; hatred; hostility; ill will; loathing; malice; malignity; rancor; repugnance; revulsion; venom; virulence.*

bad egg   A moribund metaphor (SEE). *brute; degenerate; fiend; knave; lout; rake; rascal; rogue; ruffian; scamp; scoundrel; villain.*

badge of courage (honor)   A moribund metaphor (SEE).

bad news travels fast

bag and baggage   An inescapable pair (SEE).
1. *accouterments; baggage; bags; belongings; cases; effects; encumbrances; equipment; gear; impedimenta; luggage; portmanteaus; possessions; property; sacks; satchels; stuff; suitcases; supplies; things.*
2. *altogether; completely; entirely; fully; thoroughly; totally; utterly; wholly.*

bag of bones   A moribund metaphor (SEE). *attenuated; bony; emaciated; gaunt; lank; lanky; lean; narrow; railthin; scraggy; scrawny; skeletal; skinny; slender; slight; slim; spare; spindly; svelte; thin; trim; wispy.*

bag (bagful) of tricks   A moribund metaphor (SEE).

baker's dozen   *thirteen.*

balancing act

(as) bald as a baby's backside   An insipid simile (SEE moribund metaphors). *alopecic; bald; bald-headed; baldpated; glabrous; hairless; depilated; pilgarlic; smooth; tonsured.*

(as) bald as a billiard ball   An insipid simile (SEE moribund metaphors). *alopecic; bald; bald-headed; baldpated; glabrous; hairless; depilated; pilgarlic; smooth; tonsured.*

bald is beautiful   A quack equation (SEE).

ball of fire   A moribund metaphor (SEE). *active; animated; ardent; dynamic; emotional; energetic; impassioned; intense; lively; passionate; spirited; sprightly; vigorous; vital; vivacious.*

ballpark figure   A moribund metaphor (SEE). *appraisal; assessment; estimate; estimation; guess; idea; impression; opinion; sense.* ■ Can you give me a *ballpark figure* of how much you made last year? REPLACE WITH *idea.*

bang for (your) buck   *quality; value; worth.*

banging (my) head against the wall   A moribund metaphor (SEE).

banker's hours

baptism of fire   A moribund metaphor (SEE).

bare-bones (budget)   A moribund metaphor (SEE).

bare essentials (necessities)   An inescapable pair (SEE).

barefaced (bold-faced) lie   An inescapable pair (SEE).

bare minimum

bare (her) soul

bargaining chip   A moribund metaphor (SEE).

(her) bark is worse than (her) bite   A moribund metaphor (SEE).

bark up the wrong tree   A moribund metaphor (SEE). *amiss; astray; deceived; deluded; erring; erroneous; fallacious; false; faulty; inaccurate; incorrect; in error; misguided; misinformed; misled; mistaken; not correct; not right; wrong.*

barrel of laughs   A moribund metaphor (SEE).

barring any unforeseen circumstances (problems)

basically   An overworked word (SEE). ■ *Basically*, the program is designed to operate with the same skills used when doing the exercise with a pencil and paper. DELETE *Basically*. ■ If the man wants custody, he must prove the woman to be *basically* unfit. DELETE *basically*. ■ The rest of the day will be *basically* partly cloudy. DELETE *basically*. ■ What *basically* began as an experiment to determine whether a family-type YMCA would survive quickly evolved into a challenge to

serve a very enthusiastic community. DELETE *basically*. ■ *Basically*, the next step is adding the molasses. DELETE *Basically*.

basic (and) fundamental   A dimwitted redundancy (SEE). *basic; fundamental.*

basic principle   An inescapable pair (SEE). ■ Whether or not you are aware of it, there are basic principles of human interaction. DELETE basic.

basis in fact (reality)   A dimwitted redundancy (SEE). *basis; fact; reality; truth; veracity.* ■ The June 2 editorial that describes the final, wheezy stages of the movement to eliminate cigarettes has no *basis in fact*. USE *basis*. ■ To see whether such beliefs have any *basis in fact*, five different brands of fruit cocktail were chosen. USE *veracity*.

basket case   A moribund metaphor (SEE).

bask in the glow of

bask in the limelight

bathed in tears   A moribund metaphor (SEE).

(has) bats in (his) belfry   A moribund metaphor (SEE). *batty; cracked; crazy; daft; demented; deranged; fey; goofy; insane; lunatic; mad; maniacal; neurotic; nuts; nutty; psychotic; raving; squirrelly; touched; unbalanced; unhinged; unsound; wacky; zany.*

batten down the hatches   A moribund metaphor (SEE).

batting a thousand   A moribund metaphor (SEE).

(good) batting average   A moribund metaphor (SEE).

battle for the hearts and minds

battle lines are being drawn A moribund metaphor (SEE).

battle of the bulge

(please) be advised that   An ineffectual phrase (SEE). ■ *Please be advised that* some of the ads in this category may require a fee for services or processing. DELETE *Please be advised that.* ■ *Please be advised that* the valuation below is proposed and not final. DELETE *Please be advised that.* SEE ALSO *(please) be informed that; this is to inform you that.*

be-all and end-all   *acme; ideal; perfection; quintessence; ultimate.*

beat about (around) the bush A moribund metaphor (SEE). *avoid; dodge; double-talk; equivocate; evade; fence; hedge; palter; prevaricate; quibble; shuffle; sidestep; tergiversate; waffle.*

beat a path to (your door)

beat a (hasty) retreat   *abscond; clear out; decamp; depart; desert; disappear; escape; exit; flee; fly; go; go away; leave; move on; part; pull out; quit; retire; retreat; run away; take flight; take off; vacate; vanish; withdraw.*

beat (them) at (their) own game

beat (his) brains out   A moribund metaphor (SEE).

1. *assail; assault; attack; batter; beat; cudgel; flagellate; flog; hit; lambaste; lash; lick; mangle; pound; pummel; strike; thrash; trounce.*
2. *annihilate; assassinate; butcher; destroy; exterminate; kill; massacre; murder; slaughter; slay.*
3. *beat; conquer; crush; defeat; outdo; overcome; overpower; overwhelm; prevail; quell; rout; succeed; triumph; trounce; vanquish; win.*
4. *attempt; drudge; endeavor; essay; exert; grind; grub; labor; slave; strain; strive; struggle; sweat; toil; travail; try; work.*

beat (them) hands down   A moribund metaphor (SEE). *beat; conquer; crush; defeat; outdo; overcome; overpower; overwhelm; prevail; quell; rout; succeed; triumph; trounce; vanquish; win.*

(like) beating (flogging) a dead horse   An insipid simile (SEE moribund metaphors). *barren; bootless; effete; feckless; feeble; fruitless; futile; impotent; inadequate; inconsequential; inconsiderable; ineffective; ineffectual; infertile; insignificant; inutile; meaningless; meritless; nugatory; null; of no value; pointless; powerless; profitless; redundant; sterile; superfluous; trifling; trivial; unavailing; unimportant; unnecessary; unproductive; unprofitable; unserviceable; unworthy; useless; vain; valueless; weak; worthless.*

beat (it) into the ground   A moribund metaphor (SEE). *debilitate; deplete; drain; empty; enervate; exhaust; fatigue; overdo; overwork; sap; tire; wear out; weary.*

beat the bushes   A moribund metaphor (SEE). *hunt; look for; quest; ran-*

sack; rummage; scour; search; seek.

beat the (living) daylights out of
A moribund metaphor (SEE).
1. *assail; assault; attack; batter; beat; cudgel; flagellate; flog; hit; lambaste; lash; lick; mangle; pound; pummel; strike; thrash; trounce.*
2. *beat; conquer; crush; defeat; outdo; overcome; overpower; overwhelm; prevail; quell; rout; succeed; triumph; trounce; vanquish; win.*
3. *castigate; chastise; discipline; penalize; punish.*

beat the drum   A moribund metaphor (SEE). *advertise; announce; broadcast; proclaim; promote; promulgate; publicize; publish; trumpet.*

beat the stuffing out of   A moribund metaphor (SEE).
1. *assail; assault; attack; batter; beat; cudgel; flagellate; flog; hit; lambaste; lash; lick; mangle; pound; pummel; strike; thrash; trounce.*
2. *beat; conquer; crush; defeat; outdo; overcome; overpower; overwhelm; prevail; quell; rout; succeed; triumph; trounce; vanquish; win.*

beat to a pulp   A moribund metaphor (SEE).
1. *assail; assault; attack; batter; beat; cudgel; flagellate; flog; hit; lambaste; lash; lick; mangle; pound; pummel; strike; thrash; trounce.*
2. *beat; conquer; crush; defeat; outdo; overcome; overpower; overwhelm; prevail; quell; rout; succeed; triumph; trounce; vanquish; win.*

beat to death
1. *annihilate; assassinate; butcher; destroy; exterminate; kill; massacre; murder; slaughter; slay.*

2. *debilitate; deplete; drain; empty; enervate; exhaust; fatigue; overdo; overwork; sap; tire; wear out; weary.* SEE ALSO *to death.*

beat (him) to the punch   A moribund metaphor (SEE).

beautiful baby   An inescapable pair (SEE).

beauty and the beast   A moribund metaphor (SEE).

beauty is in the eye of the beholder   A popular prescription (SEE).

because (that's why)   An infantile phrase (SEE). ■ Why did you hit him? *Because.* SEE ALSO *it just happened.*

because of the fact that   A dimwitted redundancy (SEE). *because; considering; for; in that; since.* ■ I married him only *because of the fact that* his family has money. USE *because.* SEE ALSO *by virtue of the fact that; considering the fact that; given the fact that; in view of the fact that.*

because why?   An infantile phrase (SEE). ■ They were afraid of him, too. *Because why?* DELETE *Because.*

(no) bed of roses   A moribund metaphor (SEE). *agreeable; ambrosial; beguiling; celestial; charming; delectable; delicious; delightful; divine; enchanting; engaging; enjoyable; fun; glorious; gratifying; heavenly; inviting; joyful; joyous; luscious; pleasant; pleasing; pleasurable.*

(she's) been around the block (and back)   A moribund metaphor (SEE).

1. *adult; aged; aging; elderly; full-grown; hoary; hoary-headed; mature; old; worn.*
2. *able; adept; apt; capable; competent; deft; dexterous; experienced; expert; practiced; proficient; seasoned; skilled; skillful; veteran.*

before (you) can say (Jack Robinson)   A moribund metaphor (SEE). *at once; directly; forthwith; immediately; instantly; momentarily; promptly; right away; straightaway; summarily; without delay.*

before it's too late

before (you) know it   *before long; directly; eventually; in time; later; one day; presently; quickly; shortly; sometime; soon.*

beg, borrow or steal   A moribund metaphor (SEE).

beggars can't be choosers   A popular prescription (SEE).

begin (start) a new chapter (in my life)   A moribund metaphor (SEE).

behind (me) all the way   *back; support.*

behind closed doors   A moribund metaphor (SEE). *clandestinely; confidentially; covertly; furtively; in private; in secret; mysteriously; privately; secludedly; secretly; slyly; stealthily; surreptitiously; undercover.*

behind every successful man stands a woman   A popular prescription (SEE).

behind the eight ball   A moribund

metaphor (SEE). *at risk; endangered; hard-pressed; imperiled; in a bind; in a fix; in a jam; in a predicament; in a quandary; in danger; in difficulty; in jeopardy; in peril; in trouble; jeopardized.*

(work) behind the scenes   *clandestinely; confidentially; covertly; furtively; in private; in secret; mysteriously; privately; secludedly; secretly; slyly; stealthily; surreptitiously; undercover.*

behind the times   *antediluvian; antiquated; archaic; dead; obsolescent; obsolete; old; old-fashioned; outdated; outmoded; out of date; out of fashion; passé; superannuated.*

behoove   An archaism (SEE).
1. *be advantageous for; benefit; be worthwhile to.*
2. *be necessary for; be proper for.*

(please) be informed that   An ineffectual phrase (SEE). ■ *Please be informed that* your wife has retained my office in the matter of her petition for a divorce. DELETE *Please be informed that.* ■ If you are running a version of Almanac earlier than 3.0, *please be informed that* the format of the desktop data files has been changed. DELETE *please be informed that.* SEE ALSO *(please) be advised that; this is to inform you that.*

(like) being run over (getting hit) by a (Mack) truck   An insipid simile (SEE moribund metaphors). *atomized; crushed; dashed; demolished; depressed; desolate; destroyed; devastated; obliterated; overcome; overpowered; overwhelmed; prostrate; ravaged; ruined; shattered; undone; upset.*

believe it or not

(I'll) believe it when (I) see it

bells and whistles   A moribund metaphor (SEE).

below par   A moribund metaphor (SEE). *inferior; poor; second-class; second-rate; shoddy; subordinate; substandard.*

(hit) below the belt   A moribund metaphor (SEE). *dishonorable; foul; inequitable; unconscientious; underhanded; unethical; unfair; unjust; unprincipled; unscrupulous; unsportsmanlike.*

belt-tightening (measures)   A moribund metaphor (SEE).

bend (my) ear   A moribund metaphor (SEE).

bend over backward(s)   A moribund metaphor (SEE). *aim; attempt; endeavor; essay; exert; labor; strain; strive; struggle; toil; try hard; undertake; work at.* ■ If anything, he will have to *bend over backward* to not appear to be showing favoritism. REPLACE WITH *struggle.*

beneath contempt   An inescapable pair (SEE).

benevolent dictator

be nice   A plebeian sentiment (SEE). "*Be nice,*" we so often are admonished. Or "if you can't say something nice, don't say anything." There can be no complaint with being agreeable when agreeability is warranted, but to soporifically accept niceness as a

virtue, untarnished and true, is utterly benighted.

To be capable of expressing anger and indignation is thwarted by our society's placing a premium on politeness.

Let us not, of course, be rude gratuitously, nor seek to be singular for its own sake, nor foolish or fantastic for the quick cachet. Do, however, let us become more concerned with giving fuller expression to ourselves.

We do possibly irreparable harm to ourselves when we, to avoid unpleasantness, fail to show another how we truly feel. Unknown to ourselves and unknowable to others we homunculi are, for anonymity is won when anger is lost. SEE ALSO *if you can't say something nice, don't say anything; I'm sorry.*

(suffer from) benign neglect

be still my heart

(even the) best laid plans

best of the bunch (lot)   *best; brightest; choice; choicest; elite; excellent; finest; first-class; first-rate; foremost; greatest; highest; matchless; outstanding; paramount; peerless; preeminent; premium; prominent; select; superior; superlative; top; unequaled; unexcelled; unmatched; unrivaled; unsurpassed.*

bestselling author   A suspect superlative (SEE). *Best-selling authors*, of course, are often responsible for the worst-written books. SEE ALSO *a good read; a must read; an entertaining read.*

bet (your) bottom dollar (life)
■ I would have *bet my bottom dollar* that this would not have happened.

be that as it may A dimwitted redundancy (SEE). *all the same; even so; just the same; still; yet.* ■ *Be that as it may,* my editors do not tell me what to write, and I would not presume to tell them how to put out the paper. REPLACE WITH *Even so.*

(I'll) be there with bells on A moribund metaphor (SEE).

(my) better half An infantile phrase (SEE). *consort; helpmate; helpmeet; husband; mate; spouse; wife.*

better late than never A popular prescription (SEE).

better luck next time

better safe than sorry A popular prescription (SEE).

(it's) better than nothing A popular prescription (SEE).

bet the farm (ranch) (on) A moribund metaphor (SEE).

between a rock and a hard place A moribund metaphor (SEE). *at risk; endangered; hard-pressed; imperiled; in a bind; in a dilemma; in a fix; in a jam; in a predicament; in a quandary; in danger; in difficulty; in jeopardy; in peril; in trouble; jeopardized.*

between Scylla and Charybdis A moribund metaphor (SEE). *at risk; endangered; hard-pressed; imperiled; in a bind; in a dilemma; in a fix; in a jam; in a predicament; in a quandary; in danger; in difficulty; in jeopardy; in peril; in trouble; jeopardized.*

between the devil and the deep

blue sea A moribund metaphor (SEE). *at risk; endangered; hard-pressed; imperiled; in a bind; in a dilemma; in a fix; in a jam; in a predicament; in a quandary; in danger; in difficulty; in jeopardy; in peril; in trouble; jeopardized.*

between you and me and the (four walls) A moribund metaphor (SEE). *confidentially; in confidence; in private; in secret; private; privately; secretly.*

betwixt An archaism (SEE). *between.*

betwixt and between An inescapable pair (SEE). *divided; drifting; faltering; in between; irresolute; loose; shaky; swaying; torn; tottering; uncertain; undecided; unfixed; unresolved; unsettled; unsteady; unsure; vacillating; wavering; wobbly.*

beware of Greeks bearing gifts A popular prescription (SEE).

beyond (without) a shadow of a doubt A moribund metaphor (SEE). *absolutely; conclusively; decidedly; definitely; incontrovertibly; indisputably; indubitably; irrefragably; irrefutably; positively; unconditionally; uncontestably; undeniably; undoubtedly; unequivocally; unmistakably; unquestionably.*

beyond the call of duty ■ A lot of talented teachers go way *beyond the call of duty.*

beyond the pale *improper; inappropriate; unacceptable; unreasonable; unseemly; unsuitable; unthinkable.*

beyond (my) wildest dreams

astonishing; astounding; beyond belief; beyond comprehension; breathtaking; extraordinary; fabulous; fantastic; implausible; inconceivable; incredible; marvelous; miraculous; outlandish; overwhelming; prodigious; sensational; spectacular; unbelievable; unimaginable; unthinkable; wonderful.

bide (my) time

(as) **big as a house**   An insipid simile (SEE moribund metaphors). *big; brobdingnagian; colossal; enormous; gargantuan; giant; gigantic; grand; great; huge; immense; large; massive; monstrous; prodigious; tremendous; vast.*

(as) **big as life**   An insipid simile (SEE moribund metaphors).

big blow

Big Brother   A moribund metaphor (SEE).

big bucks

big cheese   A moribund metaphor (SEE).
1. *administrator; boss; brass; chief; commander; director; executive; foreman; head; headman; leader; manager; master; (high) muckamuck; officer; official; overseer; president; principal; superintendent; supervisor.*
2. *aristocrat; dignitary; eminence; lord; luminary; magnate; mogul; notable; patrician; personage; ruler; sovereign; worthy.*

big deal   *appreciable; central; climacteric; consequential; considerable; critical; crucial; essential; grave; major; material; important; meaningful; mo-*mentous; pivotal; pregnant; principal; serious; significant; substantial; vital; weighty.*

big fish in a small pond   A moribund metaphor (SEE).

bigger is better   A quack equation (SEE).

bigger isn't necessarily better   A popular prescription (SEE).

big gun   A moribund metaphor (SEE).
1. *administrator; boss; brass; chief; commander; director; executive; foreman; head; headman; leader; manager; master; (high) muckamuck; officer; official; overseer; president; principal; superintendent; supervisor.*
2. *aristocrat; dignitary; eminence; lord; luminary; magnate; mogul; notable; patrician; personage; ruler; sovereign; worthy.*

big shot   A moribund metaphor (SEE).
1. *administrator; boss; brass; chief; commander; director; executive; foreman; head; headman; leader; manager; master; (high) muckamuck; officer; official; overseer; president; principal; superintendent; supervisor.*
2. *aristocrat; dignitary; eminence; lord; luminary; magnate; mogul; notable; patrician; personage; ruler; sovereign; worthy.*

big-ticket (item)

big wheel   A moribund metaphor (SEE).
1. *administrator; boss; brass; chief; commander; director; executive; foreman; head; headman; leader; manager;*

master; (high) muckamuck; officer; official; overseer; president; principal; superintendent; supervisor.

2. *aristocrat; dignitary; eminence; lord; luminary; magnate; mogul; notable; patrician; personage; ruler; sovereign; worthy.*

bird's-eye view A moribund metaphor (SEE). *outline; overview; profile; review; sketch; summary; survey.*

birds of a feather (flock together) A popular prescription (SEE).

bite (my) head off A moribund metaphor (SEE). *admonish; animadvert; berate; castigate; censure; chasten; chastise; chide; condemn; criticize; denounce; denunciate; discipline; excoriate; fulminate against; imprecate; impugn; inveigh against; objurgate; punish; rebuke; remonstrate; reprehend; reprimand; reproach; reprobate; reprove; revile; scold; swear at; upbraid; vituperate; warn.*

bite off more than (he) can chew A moribund metaphor (SEE). ■ Even in private circles, there is concern that the government has *bitten off more than it can chew*.

bite the bullet A moribund metaphor (SEE).

bite the dust A moribund metaphor (SEE).
1. *decease; depart; die; expire; extinguish; pass away; pass on; perish; terminate.*
2. *be beaten; be conquered; be crushed; be defeated; be outdone; be overcome; be overpowered; be overwhelmed; be quelled; be routed; be trounced; be vanquished.*

3. *cease; close; complete; conclude; derail; desist; discontinue; end; finish; halt; quit; settle; stop; terminate.*
4. *be unsuccessful; bomb; break down; collapse; fail; fall short; falter; fizzle; flop; fold; founder; mess up; miscarry; not succeed; stumble; topple.*

(they) bite the hand that feeds (them) A moribund metaphor (SEE). *unappreciative; ungrateful; unthankful.*

bite your tongue A moribund metaphor (SEE).

(he) bit off more than (he) can chew A moribund metaphor (SEE).

bits and pieces An inescapable pair (SEE). *bits; chunks; crumbs; fragments; modicums; morsels; nuggets; particles; pieces; scraps; segments; shreds; snips; snippets; specks.*

bitter acrimony An inescapable pair (SEE).

(as) black as coal An insipid simile (SEE moribund metaphors). *black; blackish; caliginous; dark; ebony; ecchymotic; fuliginous; inky; jet; nigrescent; nigritudinous; raven; sable; swarthy; tenebrific; tenebrous.*

(as) black as pitch An insipid simile (SEE moribund metaphors). *black; blackish; caliginous; dark; ebony; ecchymotic; fuliginous; inky; jet; nigrescent; nigritudinous; raven; sable; swarthy; tenebrific; tenebrous.*

(as) black as the ace of spades An insipid simile (SEE moribund metaphors). *black; blackish; caliginous; dark; ebony; ecchymotic; fuliginous;*

inky; jet; nigrescent; nigritudinous; raven; sable; swarthy; tenebrific; tenebrous.

black sheep (of the family)
A moribund metaphor (SEE). *curiosity; deviant; eccentric; extremist; iconoclast; individual; individualist; maverick; misfit; nonconformist; oddball; oddity; renegade; undesirable.*

blah, blah, blah
A grammatical gimmick (SEE). ■ He told me, I want you to come out here; I miss you; *blah, blah, blah.* DELETE *blah, blah, blah.* SEE ALSO *and so on, and so forth; et cetera, et cetera.*

blame the messenger

blanket of snow

blast from the past
An infantile phrase (SEE).

blatant lie
An inescapable pair (SEE).

blessed event
An infantile phrase (SEE).
1. *baby; infant; newborn.*
2. *birth; childbearing; childbirth; parturition.*

blessed with (has) the gift of gab
An infantile phrase (SEE). *babbling; blathering; chatty; facile; fluent; garrulous; glib; jabbering; logorrheic; longwinded; loquacious; prolix; talkative; verbose; voluble; windy.*

blessing in disguise

(as) blind as a bat
An insipid simile (SEE moribund metaphors).
1. *blind; eyeless; purblind; sightless; unseeing; unsighted; visionless.*
2. *addlebrained; addlepated; bovine; cretinous; dense; dull; fatuous; fat-witted; half-witted; harebrained; hebetudinous; idiotic; ignorant; imbecilic; incogitant; insensate; mindless; moronic; muddled; nescient; obtuse; phlegmatic; slow; slow-witted; sluggish; thick; torpid; undiscerning; unintelligent; vacuous; witless.*

blind faith
An inescapable pair (SEE).

blithering idiot
An inescapable pair (SEE).

blondes have more fun
An infantile phrase (SEE).

bloodcurdling scream (yell)
An inescapable pair (SEE).

blood is thicker than water
A popular prescription (SEE).

blood, sweat and tears
A moribund metaphor (SEE). *assiduity; diligence; discipline; drudgery; effort; endeavor; exertion; grind; hard work; industry; labor; persistence; slavery; strain; struggle; sweat; toil; travail; work.* ■ However unautobiographical or fictional a book is, it still comes out by hard work, by *blood, sweat and tears.*

blow a fuse
A moribund metaphor (SEE). *bellow; bluster; clamor; explode; fulminate; fume; holler; howl; rage; rant; rave; roar; scream; shout; storm; thunder; vociferate; yell.*

blow a gasket
A moribund metaphor (SEE). *bellow; bluster; clamor; explode; fulminate; fume; holler; howl; rage; rant; rave; roar; scream; shout; storm; thunder; vociferate; yell.*

blow away
1. *annihilate; assassinate; butcher; destroy; exterminate; kill; massacre; murder; slaughter; slay.*
2. *amaze; astonish; astound; awe; dazzle; dumbfound; flabbergast; overpower; overwhelm; shock; startle; stun; stupefy; surprise.*

blow by blow   A moribund metaphor (SEE).

blow hot and cold   A moribund metaphor (SEE).
1. *ambivalent; divided; indecisive; irresolute; torn; uncertain; uncommitted; undecided; unsure.*
2. *capricious; changeable; erratic; fickle; fitful; flighty; fluctuating; haphazard; inconsistent; inconstant; intermittent; irregular; mercurial; occasional; random; sometime; spasmodic; sporadic; unpredictable; unsettled; unstable; unsteady; vacillating; volatile; wavering; wayward.*

blow (my) mind   A moribund metaphor (SEE). *amaze; astonish; astound; awe; dazzle; dumbfound; flabbergast; overpower; overwhelm; shock; startle; stun; stupefy; surprise.*

blow off steam   A moribund metaphor (SEE).
1. *bellow; bluster; clamor; complain; explode; fulminate; fume; holler; howl; object; protest; rage; rant; rave; roar; scream; shout; storm; thunder; vociferate; yell.*
2. *be merry; carouse; carry on; celebrate; frolic; party; play; revel; riot; roister; rollick; romp; skylark.*

blow on the cue ball   A moribund metaphor (SEE).

blow (things) out of proportion
elaborate; embellish; embroider; enhance; enlarge; exaggerate; hyperbolize; inflate; magnify; overdo; overreact; overstress; overstate; strain; stretch.

blow (them) out of the water
A moribund metaphor (SEE).
1. *annihilate; assassinate; butcher; destroy; exterminate; kill; massacre; murder; slaughter; slay.*
2. *beat; conquer; crush; defeat; outdo; overcome; overpower; overwhelm; prevail; quell; rout; succeed; triumph; trounce; vanquish; win.*

blow (your) own horn   A moribund metaphor (SEE). *acclaim; applaud; bluster; boast; brag; celebrate; cheer; commend; compliment; congratulate; crow; extol; flatter; gloat; hail; honor; laud; praise; puff; salute; self-congratulate; strut; swagger.*

blow smoke   A moribund metaphor (SEE). *adumbrate; becloud; befog; camouflage; cloak; cloud; conceal; cover; disguise; dissemble; enshroud; harbor; hide; keep secret; mask; objuscate; obscure; overshadow; screen; shroud; suppress; veil; withhold.*

blow (his) stack   A moribund metaphor (SEE). *bellow; bluster; clamor; explode; fulminate; fume; holler; howl; rage; rant; rave; roar; scream; shout; storm; thunder; vociferate; yell.*

blow the whistle (on)   A moribund metaphor (SEE).
1. *bare; betray; disclose; divulge; expose; give away; reveal; show; tell; uncover; unveil.* ■ He *blew the whistle on* company corruption. REPLACE WITH *exposed.*
2. *betray; deliver up; inform on; turn in.*

blow to bits   *annihilate; assassinate; butcher; demolish; destroy; devastate; eradicate; exterminate; kill; massacre; murder; obliterate; pulverize; rack; ravage; raze; ruin; shatter; slaughter; slay; smash; undo; wrack; wreck.*

blow (my) top   A moribund metaphor (SEE). *bellow; bluster; clamor; explode; fulminate; fume; holler; howl; rage; rant; rave; roar; scream; shout; storm; thunder; vociferate; yell.*

blow to smithereens   *annihilate; assassinate; butcher; demolish; destroy; devastate; eradicate; exterminate; kill; massacre; murder; obliterate; pulverize; rack; ravage; raze; ruin; shatter; slaughter; slay; smash; undo; wrack; wreck.*

blow (this thing) wide open

(until) (I'm) blue in the face
A moribund metaphor (SEE).
1. *angry; annoyed; enraged; exasperated; furious; incensed; infuriated; irate; irked; irritated; mad; raging; wrathful.*
2. *beat; bushed; debilitated; depleted; exhausted; fatigued; fed up; spent; tired; wearied; weary; worn out.*

blue-ribbon commission (committee; panel)   A suspect superlative (SEE).

blushing bride

boil down to

(as) bold as brass   An insipid simile (SEE moribund metaphors). *audacious; bold; brash; brass; brassy; brazen; cheeky; forward; impertinent; impudent; insolent; outrageous; saucy; shameless; unabashed.*

bold, new frontier

bone of contention   A moribund metaphor (SEE).

bone to pick   A moribund metaphor (SEE). *animosity; bitterness; enmity; grievance; grudge; hostility; indignation; ill will; offense; rancor; resentment; spite; umbrage.*

(cite) book, chapter and verse
A moribund metaphor (SEE).

book of woes   A moribund metaphor (SEE).

boom and bust

bore the pants off (me)   *annoy; bore; discourage; disgust; exasperate; exhaust; fatigue; irk; irritate; sicken; tire; wear out; weary.*

bore to death (extinction)   *annoy; bore; discourage; disgust; exasperate; exhaust; fatigue; irk; irritate; sicken; tire; wear out; weary.* SEE ALSO *to death.*

bore to tears   *annoy; bore; discourage; disgust; exasperate; exhaust; fatigue; irk; irritate; sicken; tire; wear out; weary.*

born again

born to the purple   A moribund metaphor (SEE).

born under a lucky star   A moribund metaphor (SEE). *advantageous; auspicious; blessed; charmed; enchanted; favored; felicitous; flourishing; fortuitous; fortunate; golden; happy; in luck; lucky; propitious; prosperous; successful; thriving.*

born with a silver spoon in (his) mouth A moribund metaphor (SEE). *advantageous; auspicious; blessed; charmed; enchanted; favored; felicitous; flourishing; fortuitous; fortunate; golden; happy; in luck; lucky; propitious; prosperous; successful; thriving.*

bottomless pit A moribund metaphor (SEE). *abyss; Hades; hell; inferno; netherworld; perdition.*

(the) bottom line An overworked word (SEE).
1. *conclusion; consequence; culmination; decision; denouement; effect; end; outcome; result; upshot.*
2. *crux; essence; key; keynote; main point; salient point.*
    This is a bottomlessly ordinary term, people bewitched by words that have a trace of technicality to them are inclined to use it. In striving to sound technical, they manage to sound only typical. ■ The *bottom line* is that America can compete if the politicians are kept out of the picture. REPLACE WITH *upshot*. ■ The *bottom line* is that both kinds of water are generally safe. REPLACE WITH *conclusion*. ■ The *bottom line* is you get what you pay for. REPLACE WITH *main point*. ■ The *bottom line* for parents: choose gifts carefully. REPLACE WITH *keynote*. SEE ALSO *feedback; input; interface; output; parameters*.

bottom of the barrel A moribund metaphor (SEE).
1. *alluvium; debris; deposit; detritus; dregs; grounds; lees; precipitate; remains; residue; residuum; sediment; settlings; silt; wash.*
2. *close; completion; conclusion; end; ending; finale; finish; termination.*
3. *bums; deadbeats; derelicts; duds; failures; flobs; hobos; losers; pariahs; rabble; renegades; riffraff; scum; tramps; vagabonds; vagrants; washouts.*

bound and determined An inescapable pair (SEE). *bent on; determined; resolute; resolved.*

bow and scrape *bootlick; bow; crawl; cringe; crouch; fawn; grovel; kowtow; slaver; stoop; toady; truckle.*

bowels of the earth

box into a corner A moribund metaphor (SEE).

boys will be boys

brain drain An infantile phrase (SEE).

brains over brawn

brave new world (of)

bread and butter A moribund metaphor (SEE).
1. *food; keep; livelihood; living; subsistence; support; sustenance.*
2. *mainstay.*
    ■ Now it's a real *bread-and-butter* issue; many of the people I see spend more on drugs than they do on food.

breadth and depth An inescapable pair (SEE). *ambit; area; breadth; compass; degree; extent; field; magnitude; range; reach; scope; sphere; sweep.*

break (his) back A moribund metaphor (SEE). *attempt; drudge; endeavor; essay; exert; grind; grub; labor; slave; strain; strive; struggle; sweat; toil; travail; try; work.*

break down (the) barriers
A moribund metaphor (SEE).

breaking point

break (my) neck   A moribund metaphor (SEE). *attempt; drudge; endeavor; essay; exert; grind; grub; labor; slave; strain; strive; struggle; sweat; toil; travail; try; work.*

break out of the mold   A moribund metaphor (SEE).

(it) breaks (my) heart   A moribund metaphor (SEE). *desolate; disappoint; discourage; dishearten; dispirit; distress; sadden.*

break the bank   A moribund metaphor (SEE). *bankrupt; deplete; drain; exhaust; impoverish; pauperize; ruin.*

break the ice   A moribund metaphor (SEE).

breathe easier (easily)

breathe (new) life into   A moribund metaphor (SEE). *animate; arouse; enliven; exhilarate; inspire; inspirit; invigorate; revivify; spur; stimulate; vitalize; vivify.* ■ The Citizens for Limited Taxation petition would block school reform at the very time it is needed most to *breathe life into* our public schools. REPLACE WITH *invigorate.*

breathing room

breathless anticipation   An inescapable pair (SEE).

breathtaking view

breeze on through

bridge the gap

bright and early   An inescapable pair (SEE). *early.*

(as) bright as a (new) button   An insipid simile (SEE moribund metaphors).
1. *beaming; bright; brilliant; burnished; dazzling; effulgent; gleaming; glistening; glittering; glossy; incandescent; luminous; lustrous; radiant; resplendent; shiny; sparkling.*
2. *able; adroit; alert; apt; astute; bright; brilliant; capable; clever; competent; discerning; enlightened; insightful; intelligent; judicious; keen; knowledgeable; learned; logical; luminous; perceptive; perspicacious; quick; quick-witted; rational; reasonable; sagacious; sage; sapient; sensible; sharp; shrewd; smart; sound; understanding; wise.*

(as) bright as a new penny   An insipid simile (SEE moribund metaphors).
1. *beaming; bright; brilliant; burnished; dazzling; effulgent; gleaming; glistening; glittering; glossy; incandescent; luminous; lustrous; radiant; resplendent; shiny; sparkling.*
2. *able; adroit; alert; apt; astute; bright; brilliant; capable; clever; competent; discerning; enlightened; insightful; intelligent; judicious; keen; knowledgeable; learned; logical; luminous; perceptive; perspicacious; quick; quick-witted; rational; reasonable; sagacious; sage; sapient; sensible; sharp; shrewd; smart; sound; understanding; wise.*

(as) bright as a new pin   An insipid simile (SEE moribund metaphors).
1. *beaming; bright; brilliant; burnished; dazzling; effulgent; gleaming; glistening; glittering; glossy; incandescent; lu-*

minous; lustrous; radiant; resplendent; shiny; sparkling.

2. *able; adroit; alert; apt; astute; bright; brilliant; capable; clever; competent; discerning; enlightened; insightful; intelligent; judicious; keen; knowledgeable; learned; logical; luminous; perceptive; perspicacious; quick; quick-witted; rational; reasonable; sagacious; sage; sapient; sensible; sharp; shrewd; smart; sound; understanding; wise.*

(she) brightens up a room
■ When she walks into a room, *she brightens up the room.*

bright-eyed and bushy-tailed
A moribund metaphor (SEE). *active; adroit; alert; alive; animated; dynamic; energetic; frisky; hearty; lively; nimble; peppy; perky; quick; ready; spirited; sprightly; spry; vibrant; vigorous; vivacious.*

bright future   A suspect superlative (SEE).

bring (take) (him) down a notch (peg)   A moribund metaphor (SEE). *abase; chasten; debase; decrease; deflate; degrade; demean; depreciate; depress; diminish; disgrace; dishonor; embarrass; humble; humiliate; lower; mortify; puncture; shame.*

bring (her) down from (her) high horse   A moribund metaphor (SEE). *abase; chasten; debase; decrease; deflate; degrade; demean; depreciate; depress; diminish; disgrace; dishonor; embarrass; humble; humiliate; lower; mortify; puncture; shame.*

bring down the house   A moribund metaphor (SEE).

bring home the bacon   A moribund metaphor (SEE).

bring to a close (a halt; an end; a stop)   A dimwitted redundancy (SEE). *cease; close; complete; conclude; derail; discontinue; end; finish; halt; settle; stop.* ■ We are pleased to be able *to bring* this longstanding litigation *to a close.* USE *to conclude.* SEE ALSO *come to a close (a halt; an end; a stop); grind to a halt.*

bring to a head   *cap; climax; conclude; consummate; crest; crown; culminate; peak.*

bring (come) to closure
1. *cease; close; complete; conclude; discontinue; end; finish; halt; stop.*
2. *conclude; decide; determine; establish; resolve; settle.*

bring (them) to (their) knees
A moribund metaphor (SEE). *beat; conquer; cow; cripple; crush; defeat; disable; dispirit; enervate; enfeeble; humble; incapacitate; lame; make helpless; neutralize; oppress; overcome; overpower; overrun; overthrow; overwhelm; repress; subdue; subjugate; suppress; vanquish.*
■ A network of computers was *brought to its knees* by something out of our control that seemed to live in and even infect the system. REPLACE WITH *vanquished.*

bring to the table   A moribund metaphor (SEE). ■ What you have to *bring to the table* is the simple ability to listen to your kids.

bring up the rear   *endmost; hindmost; last.*

broad-based support

broken promises

brought it home to (me) A moribund metaphor (SEE).

(as) brown as a berry An insipid simile (SEE moribund metaphors). *beige; bronze; bronzed; brown; burnished; chestnut; copper; coppery; ecru; fawn; mahogany; ocherous; russet; sienna; sun-tanned; tan; tanned; tawny.*

(win) brownie points A moribund metaphor (SEE).

bruised ego

brutally honest An inescapable pair (SEE).

brute force An inescapable pair (SEE).

bucket of bolts A moribund metaphor (SEE).

buck the trend

budding genius

build a better mousetrap (and the world will beat a path to your door) A popular prescription (SEE).

build bridges A moribund metaphor (SEE).

build bridges where there are walls A moribund metaphor (SEE).

build castles in Spain (the air) A moribund metaphor (SEE). *brood; daydream; dream; fantasize; imagine; meditate; muse; reflect.*

building blocks of A moribund metaphor (SEE).

build to a fever pitch

bump in the road A moribund metaphor (SEE). *bar; barrier; block; blockage; check; deterrent; difficulty; encumbrance; handicap; hindrance; hurdle; impediment; interference; obstacle; obstruction.*

bumpy road (ahead) A moribund metaphor (SEE).

bunch of baloney A moribund metaphor (SEE). *balderdash; baloney; nonsense; rubbish.*

bundle of nerves A moribund metaphor (SEE). *agitated; anxious; eager; edgy; excitable; excited; fidgety; frantic; ill at ease; jittery; jumpy; nervous; on edge; restive; restless; skittish; uncomfortable; uneasy.*

burn a hole in (my) pocket A moribund metaphor (SEE).

burn (your) bridges (behind) (you) A moribund metaphor (SEE).

burning desire An inescapable pair (SEE).

burning issue (question)

(it) burns (me) up A moribund metaphor (SEE). *acerbate; anger; annoy; bother; bristle; chafe; enrage; incense; inflame; infuriate; irk; irritate; madden; miff; provoke; rile; vex.*

burn the candle at both ends A moribund metaphor (SEE).
1. *drudge; grind; grub; labor; slave; strain; strive; struggle; sweat; toil; travail; work hard.*
2. *debilitate; drain; empty; enervate; ex-*

haust; fatigue; overdo; overwork; sap; tire; wear out; weary.
3. *be merry; carouse; carry on; celebrate; frolic; party; play; revel; riot; roister; rollick; romp; skylark.*

burn the midnight oil   A moribund metaphor (SEE). *drudge; grind; grub; labor; slave; strain; strive; struggle; sweat; toil; travail; work hard; work long hours.* ■ We are indebted to our wives and families for their patience while we *burned the midnight oil.* RE-PLACE WITH *worked long hours.*

burr under (his) saddle   A moribund metaphor (SEE). *affliction; annoyance; bane; bother; burden; curse; difficulty; inconvenience; irritant; irritation; load; nuisance; ordeal; pain; pest; plague; problem; torment; tribulation; trouble; vexation; weight; worry.*

bursting at the seams   A moribund metaphor (SEE).
1. *aflame; agitated; animated; anxious; eager; ebullient; effervescent; enthusiastic; excitable; excited; fervent; fervid; frantic; frenzied; impassioned; impatient; lively; restless; spirited.*
2. *abounding; brimful; brimming; bursting; chock-full; congested; crammed; crowded; dense; filled; full; gorged; jammed; jam-packed; overcrowded; overfilled; overflowing; packed; replete; saturated; stuffed; swarming; teeming.*

burst on (onto) the scene   *appear; arise; come forth; emerge; occur; originate; present itself; rise; surface; turn up.*

bury the hatchet   A moribund metaphor (SEE). *make peace.*

business as usual   A torpid term (SEE). ■ All too many male-dominated workplaces still are doing *business as usual* and denying women equal pay and benefits. ■ In simple terms, it means *business as usual*; specifically, all business will be conducted today as it was yesterday. SEE ALSO *politics as usual.*

business is booming

business is business   A quack equation (SEE).

busman's holiday

bust (my) ass   A moribund metaphor (SEE). *attempt; drudge; endeavor; essay; exert; grind; grub; labor; slave; strain; strive; struggle; sweat; toil; travail; try; work.*

bustle with activity

(as) busy as a beaver   An insipid simile (SEE moribund metaphors). *assiduous; busy; diligent; grinding; hardworking; indefatigable; industrious; inexhaustible; sedulous; slaving; tireless; toiling; unflagging; unrelenting; untiring.*

(as) busy as a bee   An insipid simile (SEE moribund metaphors). *assiduous; busy; diligent; grinding; hardworking; indefatigable; industrious; inexhaustible; sedulous; slaving; tireless; toiling; unflagging; unrelenting; untiring.*

(there) but for the grace of God (go I)

butterflies in (her) stomach
A moribund metaphor (SEE).
1. *agitated; anxious; eager; edgy; excit-*

able; excited; fidgety; frantic; ill at ease; jittery; jumpy; nervous; on edge; restive; restless; skittish; uncomfortable; uneasy.
2. *nauseated; nauseous; queasy; sick; squeamish.*

butter (them) up   *acclaim; applaud; celebrate; commend; compliment; extol; flatter; laud; praise.*

butter wouldn't melt in (her) mouth   A moribund metaphor (SEE).

button (zip) your lip   A moribund metaphor (SEE). *be silent; be still; hush; keep quiet; quiet; silence.*

buy a pig in a poke   A moribund metaphor (SEE).

buy into   *accept; believe; hold; support.*

buy the farm   A moribund metaphor (SEE). *cease to exist; depart; die; expire; pass away; pass on; perish.*

buy time   *defer; delay; hold off; hold up; postpone; put aside; put off; set aside; shelve; suspend; table; waive.*

by a hair's breadth   A moribund metaphor (SEE). *barely; by a little; hardly; just; merely; narrowly; only just; scarcely.*

(won) by a landslide   A moribund metaphor (SEE).

by a long shot

by and large   *chiefly; commonly; generally; largely; mainly; most; mostly; normally; typically; usually.*

by any (no) stretch of the imagination

by (his) bootstraps   A moribund metaphor (SEE).

by fits and starts   *erratically; fitfully; intermittently; irregularly; randomly; spasmodically; sporadically.*

bygone era

by hook or (by) crook   A moribund metaphor (SEE). *somehow; someway.*

(growing) by leaps and bounds   *abruptly; apace; briskly; fast; hastily; hurriedly; posthaste; promptly; quickly; rapidly; rashly; speedily; straightaway; swiftly; wingedly.*

(go) by the boards   A moribund metaphor (SEE). *abandoned; discarded; forfeited; gone; ignored; lost; over; passed; vanished.*

(go) by the book   ■ She's done everything *by the book*. REPLACE WITH *correctly*. ■ The Senate president does things *by the book*, and most people don't realize this. REPLACE WITH *according to the rules*.

by the dawn's early light   *very early.*

by the same token   A dimwitted redundancy (SEE). *also; and; as well; besides; beyond that (this); even; further; furthermore; in addition; likewise; moreover; more than that (this); similarly; still more; too; what is more.*

by the seat of (his) pants   A moribund metaphor (SEE).

by the skin of (his) teeth   A moribund metaphor (SEE). *barely; by a little; hardly; just; merely; narrowly; only just; scarcely.*

by the sweat of (his) brow
A moribund metaphor (SEE). *arduously; backbreakingly; burdensomely; exhaustingly; fatiguingly; gruelingly; laboriously; onerously; strenuously; toilfully; toilsomely; toughly; wearisomely; with difficulty.*

by virtue of the fact that   A dimwitted redundancy (SEE). *because; considering; for; in that; since.* ■ There are a lot of people who expect too little *by virtue of the fact that* that's all they've known. USE *because.* SEE ALSO *because of the fact that; considering the fact that; given the fact that; in view of the fact that.*

C

calculated risk

call a halt (an end; a stop) to
A dimwitted redundancy (SEE). *cease; close; complete; conclude; derail; discontinue; end; finish; halt; settle; stop.* ■ Let's *call a halt to* this insanity. USE *end.* SEE ALSO *put a halt (an end; a stop) to.*

call a spade a spade   A moribund metaphor (SEE).

called (me) every name in the book

call into question   A dimwitted redundancy (SEE). *challenge; contradict; dispute; doubt; question.*

call it a day   *cease; complete; conclude; desist; discontinue; end; finish; halt; quit; stop; terminate.*

call it quits   *cease; complete; conclude; desist; discontinue; end; finish; halt; quit; stop; terminate.*

call off the dogs   A moribund metaphor (SEE).

call (out) on the carpet   A moribund metaphor (SEE). *admonish; animadvert; berate; castigate; censure; chasten; chastise; chide; condemn; criticize; denounce; denunciate; discipline; excoriate; fulminate against; imprecate; impugn; inveigh against; objurgate; punish; rebuke; remonstrate; reprehend; reprimand; reproach; reprobate; reprove; revile; scold; swear at; upbraid; vituperate; warn.*

callow youth   An inescapable pair (SEE). *adolescent; artless; callow; green; guileless; immature; inexperienced; inexpert; ingenuous; innocent; juvenile; naive; raw; simple; undeveloped; unfledged; unskilled; unskillful; unsophisticated; untaught; untrained; unworldly; young; youthful.*

call the plays   A moribund metaphor (SEE). *administer; boss; choose; command; control; decide; determine; dictate; direct; dominate; govern; in charge; in command; in control; manage; manipulate; master; order; overpower; oversee; predominate; prevail; reign over; rule; superintend.*

call the shots   A moribund metaphor (SEE). *administer; boss; choose; command; control; decide; determine; dictate; direct; dominate; govern; in charge; in command; in control; manage; manipulate; master; order; overpower; oversee; predominate; prevail; reign over; rule; superintend.*

calm, cool and collected   An infantile phrase (SEE). *at ease; calm; collected; composed; controlled; cool; imperturbable; insouciant; nonchalant; placid; poised; relaxed; sedate; self-possessed; serene; tranquil; unemotional; unperturbed; unruffled.* ■ She seemed so *calm, cool and collected* in the interview. USE *calm.*

(we) came, (we) saw, (we) conquered   An infantile phrase (SEE).

(she) can do no wrong

candor and frankness   An inescapable pair (SEE). *candor; frankness; honesty; openness; sincerity; truth; truthfulness; veracity.*

can I ask (tell) you something?   An ineffectual phrase (SEE). ■ *Can I tell you something?* I don't really like to go out. DELETE *Can I tell you something?* ■ *Can I ask you something?* Do you want me to give you a check so you can take care of that? DELETE *Can I ask you something?* SEE ALSO *let me ask you something.*

(you) can make a difference
A popular prescription (SEE).

(I) cannot in good conscious

(I) can take it or leave it   *apathetic; cool; halfhearted; indifferent; insouciant; languid; laodicean; lukewarm; nonchalant; tepid; unenthusiastic.*

(I) can't believe (my) ears

(I) can't believe (my) eyes

(you) can't be too careful

(I) can't complain   *all right; average; fair; fine; good; mediocre; not bad; passable; pretty good; tolerable; well.*

(I) can't get a word in edgewise

(you) can't have your cake and eat it too   A popular prescription (SEE).

(we) can't help you if you don't want to be helped   A popular prescription (SEE).

can't hit the broad side of a barn

(you) can't put it into words

(he) can't see beyond (the end of) (his) nose   A moribund metaphor (SEE).
1. *blind; eyeless; purblind; shortsighted; sightless; unseeing; unsighted; visionless.*
2. *addlebrained; addlepated; bovine; cretinous; dense; dull; fatuous; fat-witted; half-witted; harebrained; hebetudinous; idiotic; ignorant; imbecilic; incogitant; insensate; mindless; moronic; muddled; nescient; obtuse; phlegmatic; slow; slow-witted; sluggish; thick; torpid; undiscerning; unintelligent; vacuous; witless.*

can't see the forest for the trees
A moribund metaphor (SEE).

(they) can't take that away from (me)

captain of industry   *administrator; boss; brass; chief; commander; director; executive; foreman; head; headman; leader; manager; master; (high) muckamuck; officer; official; overseer; owner; president; principal; proprietor; superintendent; supervisor.*

capture the attention of   *absorb; attract; beguile; bewitch; captivate; charm; enamor; engage; engross; enrapture; enthrall; entice; entrance; fascinate; mesmerize; occupy.* ■ The civil rights struggle *captured the attention of* the entire nation. REPLACE WITH *captivated.*

capture the imagination of

card up (his) sleeve   A moribund metaphor (SEE).

carefully orchestrated

carnival atmosphere

(like) carrying coals to Newcastle   An insipid simile (SEE moribund metaphors). *barren; bootless; effete; feckless; feeble; fruitless; futile; impotent; inadequate; inconsequential; inconsiderable; ineffective; ineffectual; infertile; insignificant; inutile; meaningless; meritless; nugatory; null; of no value; pointless; powerless; profitless; redundant; sterile; superfluous; trifling; trivial; unavailing; unimportant; unnecessary; unproductive; unprofitable; unserviceable; unworthy; useless; vain; valueless; weak; worthless.*

carry (his) own weight   A moribund metaphor (SEE).

carry the ball   A moribund metaphor (SEE).

carry the day

carry the weight of the world on (my) shoulders   A moribund metaphor (SEE).

carte blanche   A foreignism (SEE).

carve out a niche

case closed

cash in (their) chips   A moribund metaphor (SEE). *cease to exist; decease; depart; die; expire; pass away; pass on; perish.*

cash in on

cash on the barrel   A moribund metaphor (SEE).

cast in (our) lot with   A moribund metaphor (SEE). *ally; collaborate; comply; concur; conspire; cooperate; join; unite; work together.*

cast (fixed) in stone   A moribund metaphor (SEE). *eternal; everlasting; firm; immutable; invariable; irreversible; irrevocable; permanent; rigid; stable; unalterable; unchangeable; unchanging.* ■ The state's census count is not yet *fixed in stone.* REPLACE WITH *immutable.*

cast into the pot   A moribund metaphor (SEE).

castles in Spain (the air)   A moribund metaphor (SEE). *apparition; caprice; chimera; delusion; dream; fanciful idea; fancy; fantasty; fluff; frivolity; hallucination; illusion; imagination; maggot; mirage; phantasm; vagary; vision; whim; whimsy.*

cast (his) net   A moribund metaphor (SEE).

cast of characters

cast of thousands

cast (your) pearls before swine
A moribund metaphor (SEE).

cast the first stone A moribund metaphor (SEE).

catalyst for change ■ These are the young people who will be the *catalysts for change* in their own communities in the coming decades.

catch as catch can A moribund metaphor (SEE).
1. *aimless; irregular; uncontrolled; unplanned.*
2. *by any means; however possible.*

catch forty winks A moribund metaphor (SEE). *doze; go to bed; nap; rest; retire; sleep; slumber.*

catch the wave A moribund metaphor (SEE).

catch (him) with (his) pants down A moribund metaphor (SEE).

cat's got (your) tongue A moribund metaphor (SEE).

caught in the act

caught in the crossfire A moribund metaphor (SEE).

caught in the middle

caught off guard

caught red-handed A moribund metaphor (SEE).

caught with (her) hand in the cookie jar A moribund metaphor (SEE).

(no) cause for alarm

cause for celebration

cause for concern

cause tongues to wag

cautiously optimistic A torpid term (SEE). *confident; encouraged; heartened; hopeful; optimistic; sanguine. Optimistic* is a perfectly vigorous word, but modified by *cautiously* or *guardedly* it becomes valueless. ■ The retailer was *cautiously optimistic* about its latest report. DELETE *cautiously.* ■ When I realized that CBS was interested, I became *cautiously optimistic.* REPLACE WITH *hopeful.* SEE ALSO *guardedly optimistic.*

cease and desist An inescapable pair (SEE). *cease; desist; end; halt; stop.*

celebrity A suspect superlative (SEE). As the most popular books are sometimes the least worthy of being read, so the most public people are sometimes the least worthy of being known.

If we must acknowledge these *celebrities*, let us better understand them for who they are. All dictionary definitions of *celebrity* should include: 1. a mediocrity; a vulgarian; a coxcomb. 2. a scantly talented person who through shameless self-aggrandizement and utter inanity becomes widely known. SEE ALSO *the rich and famous.*

center around A dimwitted redundancy (SEE). *center on.* ■ Concern will *center around* military governments. USE *center on.*

center of attention   A suspect superlative (SEE). *cynosure.* People who seek to be the *center of attention* are forever peripheral to themselves.

(take) center stage   A moribund metaphor (SEE).

c'est la vie   A foreignism (SEE). To this popular French expression of resignation, there are more than a few English-language equivalents. SEE ALSO *such is life; that's how (the way) it goes; that's how (the way) the ball bounces; that's how (the way) the cookie crumbles; that's life; that's life in the big city; that's show biz; what are you going to do; what can you do.*

chain of events

chalk it up to experience   A popular prescription (SEE).

champing (chomping) at the bit   A moribund metaphor (SEE). *anxious; ardent; avid; craving; desiring; desirous; eager; enthusiastic; fervent; fervid; frantic; frenzied; impassioned; impatient; intent; itching; keen; longing; pining; ready; vehement; yearning; zealous.*

(one) chance in a million

change of heart

change of pace

change of scenery

change (her) tune

changing of the guard   A moribund metaphor (SEE).

charity begins at home   A popular prescription (SEE).

chart a new course   A moribund metaphor (SEE).

cheap shot   A moribund metaphor (SEE).

checkered career

cheek by jowl   A moribund metaphor (SEE). *attached; close; inseparable; intimate; side by side.*

chew (her) out   A moribund metaphor (SEE). *admonish; animadvert; berate; castigate; censure; chasten; chastise; chide; condemn; criticize; denounce; denunciate; discipline; excoriate; fulminate against; imprecate; impugn; inveigh against; objurgate; punish; rebuke; remonstrate; reprehend; reprimand; reproach; reprobate; reprove; revile; scold; swear at; upbraid; vituperate; warn.*

chew the cud   A moribund metaphor (SEE). *brood; cerebrate; cogitate; consider; contemplate; deliberate; excogitate; meditate; ponder; reflect; ruminate; think.*

chew the fat (rag)   A moribund metaphor (SEE). *babble; chat; chatter; confabulate; converse; gossip; jabber; palaver; prate; prattle; rattle; talk.*

(that's) chicken feed   A moribund metaphor (SEE). *frivolous; immaterial; inconsequential; inconsiderable; inferior; insignificant; minor; negligible; niggling; nugatory; petty; secondary; trifling; trivial; unimportant; worthless.*

chicken-or-egg (question)   A moribund metaphor (SEE).

chickens have come home to

roost A moribund metaphor (SEE).

children of all ages

children should be seen and not heard A popular prescription (SEE).

(that's) child's play A moribund metaphor (SEE). *apparent; basic; clear; clear-cut; conspicuous; distinct; easily done; easy; effortless; elementary; evident; explicit; facile; limpid; lucid; manifest; obvious; patent; pellucid; plain; simple; simplicity itself; simplistic; straightforward; translucent; transparent; unambiguous; uncomplex; uncomplicated; understandable; unequivocal; unmistakable.*

chilled to the bone (marrow) A moribund metaphor (SEE). *algid; arctic; brumal; chilly; cold; cool; freezing; frigid; frosty; frozen; gelid; glacial; hibernal; hyperborean; ice-cold; icy; nippy; polar; rimy; wintry.*

chink in (his) armor A moribund metaphor (SEE). *defect; deficiency; disadvantage; failing; fault; flaw; foible; fragility; frailness; frailty; handicap; limitation; shortcoming; susceptibility; susceptibleness; vulnerability; vulnerableness; weakness.*

chip off the old block A moribund metaphor (SEE).

chip on (her) shoulder A moribund metaphor (SEE). *animosity; bitterness; enmity; grievance; grudge; hostility; indignation; ill will; offense; rancor; resentment; spite; umbrage.*

chock full (of) *abounding; brimful; brimming; bursting; congested; crammed; crowded; dense; filled; full; gorged; jammed; jam-packed; overcrowded; overfilled; overflowing; packed; replete; saturated; stuffed; swarming; teeming.*

chosen few

chrome dome An infantile phrase (SEE). *alopecic; bald; bald-headed; baldpated; glabrous; hairless; depilated; pilgarlic; smooth; tonsured.*

Cinderella story A moribund metaphor (SEE).

claim to fame

clarion call

class A suspect superlative (SEE). *Class* is a word whose meaning has deteriorated over time. The antithesis of culture, *class* is a quality possessed by those who have neither elegance nor grace nor poise nor polish. Here's a description of a woman that no discerning man would ever wish to meet: ■ I am a shapely and petite, 31-year-old, exquisitely feminine, *classy* lady. SEE ALSO *lady; gentleman.*

class act

(as) clean as a hound's tooth An insipid simile (SEE moribund metaphors). *antiseptic; clean; cleansed; disinfected; germ-free; hygienic; immaculate; sanitary; sanitized; scoured; scrubbed; spotless; stainless; sterile; unblemished; unsoiled; unspotted; unsullied; untarnished; washed.*

(as) clean as a whistle An insipid simile (SEE moribund metaphors). *antiseptic; clean; cleansed; disinfected; germ-free; hygienic; immaculate; sani-*

tary; sanitized; scoured; scrubbed; spotless; stainless; sterile; unblemished; unsoiled; unspotted; unsullied; untarnished; washed.

clean bill of health *blooming; doing well; energetic; fit; flourishing; good; hale; hardy; healthful; healthy; hearty; robust; sound; strong; vigorous; well; well-off.*

cleanliness is next to godliness A popular prescription (SEE).

clean slate

clean sweep

clean up (its) act

clear a (major) hurdle A moribund metaphor (SEE). ▪ The proposed sale and redevelopment of Lafayette Place *cleared a final hurdle* yesterday.

(as) clear as a bell An insipid simile (SEE moribund metaphors). *audible; clarion; clear; distinct; plain; pure; sharp.*

(as) clear as crystal An insipid simile (SEE moribund metaphors). *apparent; basic; clear; clear-cut; conspicuous; crystalline; distinct; easily done; easy; effortless; elementary; evident; explicit; facile; limpid; lucid; manifest; obvious; patent; pellucid; plain; simple; simplicity itself; simplistic; straightforward; translucent; transparent; unambiguous; uncomplex; uncomplicated; understandable; unequivocal; unmistakable.*

(as) clear as day An insipid simile (SEE moribund metaphors). *apparent; basic; clear; clear-cut; conspicuous;*

crystalline; distinct; easily done; easy; effortless; elementary; evident; explicit; facile; limpid; lucid; manifest; obvious; patent; pellucid; plain; simple; simplicity itself; simplistic; straightforward; translucent; transparent; unambiguous; uncomplex; uncomplicated; understandable; unequivocal; unmistakable.

(as) clear as mud An insipid simile (SEE moribund metaphors). *ambiguous; blurred; blurry; cloudy; dim; fuzzy; hazy; indistinct; muddy; murky; nebulous; obfuscatory; obscure; opaque; unclear; vague.*

clear sailing A moribund metaphor (SEE). *apparent; basic; clear; clear-cut; conspicuous; distinct; easily done; easy; effortless; elementary; evident; explicit; facile; limpid; lucid; manifest; obvious; patent; pellucid; plain; simple; simplicity itself; simplistic; straightforward; translucent; transparent; unambiguous; uncomplex; uncomplicated; understandable; unequivocal; unmistakable.*

clear the air A moribund metaphor (SEE).

clear the decks A moribund metaphor (SEE).

clear the way (for)

climate of opinion

climbing the walls A moribund metaphor (SEE). *agitated; anxious; eager; edgy; excitable; excited; fidgety; frantic; ill at ease; jittery; jumpy; nervous; on edge; restive; restless; skittish; uncomfortable; uneasy.*

climb (move up) the ladder (of success) A moribund metaphor (SEE).

advance; flourish; progress; prosper; rise; succeed.

clinging vine   A moribund metaphor (SEE). *clinging; dependent; subject; subordinate; subservient.*

cling like a limpet   An insipid simile (SEE moribund metaphors). *adhere; affix; attach; bind; cleave; cling; cohere; connect; fasten; fuse; hitch; hold; join; stick.*

cling to hope

clip (her) wings   A moribund metaphor (SEE). *abase; chasten; debase; decrease; deflate; degrade; demean; depreciate; depress; diminish; disgrace; dishonor; embarrass; humble; humiliate; lower; mortify; puncture; shame.*

cloak and dagger   A moribund metaphor (SEE).

close (near) at hand   *accessible; at hand; close; close by; handy; near; nearby; neighboring; vicinal.*

close brush with death

close but no cigar   An infantile phrase (SEE).

close encounter   An infantile phrase. (SEE).

closely allied   An inescapable pair (SEE).

closely guarded (held) secret

close scrutiny   An inescapable pair (SEE).

close (shut) the door on (to)

A moribund metaphor (SEE). *ban; banish; bar; block; disallow; dismiss; eliminate; exclude; hinder; ignore; impede; obstruct; preclude; prevent; prohibit; proscribe; reject; rule out.*

(hold) close to the chest (vest)
A moribund metaphor (SEE).

clothes make the man   A popular prescription (SEE).

clutch at straws   A moribund metaphor (SEE).

cock-and-bull story   A moribund metaphor (SEE).

cockeyed optimist

cock of the walk   A moribund metaphor (SEE). *administrator; boss; brass; chief; commander; director; executive; foreman; head; headman; leader; magnate; manager; master; mogul; (high) muckamuck; notable; officer; official; overseer; patrician; personage; president; principal; ruler; superintendent; supervisor.*

cog in the wheel   A moribund metaphor (SEE). *aide; apparatchik; assistant; cog; dependent; drudge; flunky; helper; hireling; inferior; junior; minion; secondary; servant; slave; subaltern; subordinate; underling; vassal.*

cold and calculating   An inescapable pair (SEE).

(as) cold as a witch's tit   An insipid simile (SEE moribund metaphors). *algid; arctic; brumal; chilly; cold; cool; freezing; frigid; frosty; frozen; gelid; glacial; hibernal; hyperborean; ice-cold; icy; nippy; polar; rimy; wintry.*

(as) cold as ice   An insipid simile (SEE moribund metaphors). *algid; arctic; brumal; chilly; cold; cool; freezing; frigid; frosty; frozen; gelid; glacial; hibernal; hyperborean; ice-cold; icy; nippy; polar; rimy; wintry.*

(as) cold as marble   An insipid simile (SEE moribund metaphors). *algid; arctic; brumal; chilly; cold; cool; freezing; frigid; frosty; frozen; gelid; glacial; hibernal; hyperborean; ice-cold; icy; nippy; polar; rimy; wintry.*

cold comfort

cold enough to freeze the balls off a brass monkey   A moribund metaphor (SEE). *algid; arctic; brumal; chilly; cold; cool; freezing; frigid; frosty; frozen; gelid; glacial; hibernal; hyperborean; ice-cold; icy; nippy; polar; rimy; wintry.*

cold fish   A moribund metaphor (SEE). *apathetic; callous; chilly; cold; cool; detached; dispassionate; distant; emotionless; frigid; hard; hardhearted; harsh; heartless; hostile; icy; impassive; indifferent; passionless; pitiless; reserved; unconcerned; unemotional; unfeeling; unfriendly; unresponsive.*

cold hands, warm heart

cold, hard reality

cold turkey   A moribund metaphor (SEE).

collaborate together   A dimwitted redundancy (SEE). *collaborate.* ■ Staff from the American and European sides *collaborate together* to make the journey and the home stay a rewarding experience. DELETE *together.*

collect dust   A moribund metaphor (SEE).

collision course

combine together   A dimwitted redundancy (SEE). *combine.* ■ The box isolates the various internal state processes, which *combined together*, show the state of the buyer. DELETE *together.*

come and go   ■ Presidents of network news divisions *come and go.*

come around   *agree; consent; feel as (we) do; support (us); think as (I) think.* ■ We believe that in the end the public is going to *come around.* REPLACE WITH *support us.*

come back to haunt (her)

come clean   *acknowledge; admit; affirm; allow; avow; concede; confess; disclose; divulge; expose; grant; own; reveal; tell; uncover; unveil.*

come forward (with)   *advance; broach; introduce; offer; present; propose; propound; submit; suggest; tender.* ■ Nobody has *come forward with* a good argument for any way to create more jobs and raise the incomes of working people without expanding trade. REPLACE WITH *proposed.* SEE ALSO *put forward.*

come full circle   A moribund metaphor (SEE).

come hell or high water   A moribund metaphor (SEE). *no matter what; regardless.*

come home to roost   A moribund

metaphor (SEE). ■ Many bankers are now seeing their old-fashioned greed *come home to roost.*

come in from the cold A moribund metaphor (SEE). ■ Alternative medicine is *coming in from the cold.* RE-PLACE WITH *gaining respectability.*

come in out of the rain A moribund metaphor (SEE).

come in through the back door A moribund metaphor (SEE).

come into (its) own

come knocking (on my door) A moribund metaphor (SEE).

come off without a hitch

come on like gangbusters An insipid simile (SEE moribund metaphors).

come on strong
1. *assertive; commanding; dynamic; emphatic; energetic; forceful; intense; mighty; potent; powerful; strong; vehement; vigorous; virile.*
2. *authoritarian; authoritative; autocratic; bossy; despotic; dictatorial; dogmatic; domineering; imperious; iron-handed; lordly; overbearing; peremptory; tyrannical.*

come out in the wash A moribund metaphor (SEE).

come out of left field A moribund metaphor (SEE).

come out of the closet A moribund metaphor (SEE).

come (crawl) out of the woodwork A moribund metaphor (SEE).

come out (up) smelling like a rose An insipid simile (SEE moribund metaphors).

come out swinging A moribund metaphor (SEE). *aggressive; antagonistic; battling; bellicose; belligerent; combative; fighting; militant; pugnacious; truculent; warlike.*

comes along once in a lifetime

comes (goes) with the territory (turf) A moribund metaphor (SEE). ■ He must understand that these questions *go with the territory.*

come to a boil A moribund metaphor (SEE). *cap; climax; conclude; consummate; crest; crown; culminate; peak.*

come to a close (a halt; an end; a stop) A dimwitted redundancy (SEE). *cease; close; complete; conclude; derail; discontinue; end; finish; halt; settle; stop.* ■ The days of easy credit, strong liquidity and speculation are *coming to a close.* USE *ending.* SEE ALSO *bring to a close (a halt; an end; a stop); grind to a halt.*

come to (find) a happy medium A moribund metaphor (SEE). *compromise.*

come to a head A moribund metaphor (SEE). *cap; climax; conclude; consummate; crest; crown; culminate; peak.*

come to blows *battle; brawl; clash; fight; grapple; jostle; make war; scuffle;*

skirmish; tussle; war; wrestle.

come to find out   *ascertain; determine; discern; discover; find out; learn; realize.*

come to grips with   *accept; comprehend; cope with; deal with; face; handle; struggle with; understand.*

come to mind

come to pass   *befall; come about; happen; occur; result; take place.*

come to roost on   A moribund metaphor (SEE).

come to terms with   *accept; comprehend; cope with; deal with; face; handle; struggle with; understand.*

come to the end of the line (road)
A moribund metaphor (SEE).

come to the rescue

come to think of it

come up empty

come up roses   A moribund metaphor (SEE).

(as) comfortable as an old shoe
An insipid simile (SEE moribund metaphors). *comfortable; cosy; habitable; homey; inhabitable; livable; safe; snug.*

comfort zone

comic relief

coming apart at the seams
A moribund metaphor (SEE). ■ How do you hold it together at work when

your life is *coming apart at the seams?*
REPLACE WITH *unraveling.*

comings and goings

(as) common as dirt   An insipid simile (SEE moribund metaphors). *average; basic; common; commonplace; customary; everyday; normal; omnipresent; ordinary; prevalent; quotidian; regular; standard; typical; ubiquitous; unexceptional; universal; unremarkable; usual; widespread.*

common courtesy   If this expression is not heard as often as it once was, it's because courtesy is today not so common.
   Genuine expressions of courtesy such as *please* and *thank you* (SEE) and *you're welcome* have been virtually usurped by glib ones such as *have a nice day* and *I appreciate it* and *no problem.*
   The worsening of our words reflects the dissolution of our selves. SEE ALSO *have a good (nice) day (evening); (I) appreciate (it); no problem.*

common denominator   ■ Based on interviews, there appear to be several *common denominators* to successful performance among European and Japanese multinationals.

(find) common ground

common misconception

common sense dictates   ■ Doesn't *common sense dictate* that it is time for some management changes?

common thread

communication skills   A torpid

term (SEE). People who use this ponderous expression apparently do not know what it is to speak and write well. ■ It was irrelevant to the 35-year-old single mother of two who was taking the class in order to improve her *communication skills* to get a better paying job.

compare and contrast   A dimwitted redundancy (SEE). *compare; contrast.* ■ Competition is essential to enable consumers to *compare and contrast* alternatives. USE *compare* or *contrast.*

(as) compared to what?   An infantile phrase (SEE). SEE ALSO *it's all relative; (as) opposed to what?.*

comparing apples to oranges   A moribund metaphor (SEE).

compelling reason

competitive edge

complete and utter   A dimwitted redundancy (SEE). *absolute; compleat; complete; consummate; deadly; outright; perfect; thorough; thoroughgoing; total; unmitigated; unqualified; utter.* ■ She may be my boss, but she is also a *complete and utter* fool. USE *complete.*

component part   A dimwitted redundancy (SEE). *component; part.* ■ Denial is a *component part* of dying. USE *component* or *part.*

comrades in arms   A moribund metaphor (SEE).

concerned citizen

concerted effort   An inescapable pair (SEE).

condign punishment   An inescapable pair (SEE).

confirm or deny   ■ The military officials refused to *confirm or deny* the ocean plan.

connect together   A dimwitted redundancy (SEE). *connect.* ■ The next step was to *connect* these systems *together* into a system called APRS. DELETE *together.*

connubial rites   An infantile phrase (SEE).

consciousness raising

consensus of opinion   A dimwitted redundancy (SEE). *consensus.* ■ The *consensus of opinion* is that newspaper endorsements are momentum builders. USE *consensus.*

considering the fact that   A dimwitted redundancy (SEE). *because; considering; for; in that; since; when.* ■ I don't see how you can say you're not a prostitute *considering the fact that* you are paid for your time. USE *when.* SEE ALSO *because of the fact that; by virtue of the fact that; given the fact that; in view of the fact that.*

consign to oblivion

conspicuous by (his) absence   ■ If I didn't sing about what I was going through, it would have been *conspicuous by its absence.*

conspicuous consumption

conspicuously absent

conspiracy of silence

constant reminder

constructive criticism

contact   An overworked word (SEE). *ask; call; inform; phone; query; question; reach; speak to; talk to; tell; write to.*

continue on   A dimwitted redundancy (SEE). *continue.* ■ We're going to *continue on* with more of this. DELETE *on.*

continuing refrain   An inescapable pair (SEE).

continuing saga

contradiction in terms   *contradiction; discrepancy; incongruity; inconsistency; oxymoron.*

contrary to popular belief (opinion)   ■ *Contrary to popular opinion,* a strong dollar does not attract foreign investment to U.S. stocks but to U.S. bonds.

conventional wisdom   *Conventional wisdom* is hardly more than what the majority believes, expects, says, does or values; thus, it is usually a synonym for either *common sense* or *bad sense.*
　　Today, we could profit mightily from some unconventional wisdom, from ideas startling or strange.

conversation piece   A plebeian sentiment (SEE). This is an annoying little term. That people might need an object whose purpose is mainly to stimulate conversation reveals just how infertile, just how fallow, our minds are.

convicted felon   A dimwitted redundancy (SEE). *felon.* ■ You were a deputy sheriff and now you're a *convicted felon?* DELETE *convicted.*

cook (his) goose   A moribund metaphor (SEE).

cook the books   A moribund metaphor (SEE).

(as) cool as a cucumber   An insipid simile (SEE moribund metaphors). *at ease; calm; collected; composed; controlled; cool; imperturbable; insouciant; nonchalant; placid; poised; relaxed; sedate; self-possessed; serene; tranquil; unemotional; unperturbed; unruffled.*

cool customer   *at ease; calm; collected; composed; controlled; cool; imperturbable; insouciant; nonchalant; placid; poised; relaxed; sedate; self-possessed; serene; tranquil; unemotional; unperturbed; unruffled.*

cool (your) heels   A moribund metaphor (SEE). *be patient; hold on; wait.*

cooling-off period

coon's age   A moribund metaphor (SEE).

cooperate together   A dimwitted redundancy (SEE). *cooperate.* ■ It's important that we *cooperate together* in order to resolve our problems. DELETE *together.*

(take) corrective action   A torpid term (SEE).

correct me if I'm wrong

cost (me) an arm and a leg

A moribund metaphor (SEE). *costly; dear; expensive; high-priced; precious; priceless; valuable.*

cost a pretty penny   A moribund metaphor (SEE). *costly; dear; expensive; high-priced; precious; priceless; valuable.*

couch potato

cough up   *pay; hand over.* ■ Wealthy Japanese guests would be happy to *cough up* $176,000 per person for a stay in a hotel floating 281 miles above Earth. REPLACE WITH *pay.*

(it) could be worse

could not be further from the truth

could not be reached for comment

(we) could sell tickets

(I) could (should) write a book
A plebian sentiment (SEE). ■ *I could write a book* about this, but who has the time? SEE ALSO *(you) should write a book.*

count (your) blessings   *be grateful; be thankful.*

course of action   A dimwitted redundancy (SEE). *action; course; direction; intention; method; move; plan; policy; procedure; route; scheme; strategy.*

court of public opinion

cover all the bases   A moribund metaphor (SEE).

cover a lot of ground   A moribund metaphor (SEE).

cover (his) tracks   A moribund metaphor (SEE).

cowardly lion   A moribund metaphor (SEE).

crack the whip   A moribund metaphor (SEE).

cramp (my) style

crap shoot   A moribund metaphor (SEE).

(as) crazy as a coot   An insipid simile (SEE moribund metaphors). *batty; cracked; crazy; daft; demented; deranged; fey; goofy; insane; lunatic; mad; maniacal; neurotic; nuts; nutty; psychotic; raving; squirrelly; touched; unbalanced; unhinged; unsound; wacky; zany.*

(as) crazy as a loon   An insipid simile (SEE moribund metaphors). *batty; cracked; crazy; daft; demented; deranged; fey; goofy; insane; lunatic; mad; maniacal; neurotic; nuts; nutty; psychotic; raving; squirrelly; touched; unbalanced; unhinged; unsound; wacky; zany.*

crazy in love

crazy like a fox   An insipid simile (SEE moribund metaphors). *artful; cagey; clever; conniving; crafty; cunning; foxy; guileful; shifty; shrewd; sly; smart; subtle; tricky; wily.*

create a stir

creature comforts

credibility gap

crème de la crème   A foreignism (SEE). *best; brightest; choice; choicest; elite; excellent; finest; first-class; first-rate; foremost; greatest; highest; matchless; outstanding; paramount; peerless; preeminent; premium; prominent; select; superior; superlative; top; unequaled; unexcelled; unmatched; unrivaled; unsurpassed.*

cries and whispers

crisis   An overworked word (SEE). We have a "crisis" for all occurrences. For example: *career crisis; crisis in the making; crisis in values; crisis of confidence; crisis proportions; crisis situation; crisis stage; current crisis; economic crisis; educational crisis; energy crisis; extinction crisis; family crisis; financial crisis; fiscal crisis; identity crisis; midlife crisis; moral crisis; mounting crisis; national crisis; political crisis;* and even, incomprehensibly, *severe crisis.*

Surely, some of these crises are less than that. The terms we use to characterize events and emotions largely decide how we react to them. SEE ALSO *devastate.*

critical juncture

(shed) crocodile tears   A moribund metaphor (SEE).

(as) crooked as a dog's hind legs   An insipid simile (SEE moribund metaphors).

(as) cross as a bear   An insipid simile (SEE moribund metaphors). *angry; bad-tempered; bilious; cantankerous; choleric; churlish; crabby; cranky; cross; curmudgeonly; disagreeable; dyspeptic; grouchy; gruff; grumpy; ill-humored; ill-tempered; irascible; irritable; mad; peevish; petulant; quarrelsome; short-tempered; splenetic; surly; testy; vexed.*

cross (my) fingers   A moribund metaphor (SEE). *hope for; pray for; think positively; wish.*

cross (my) heart and hope to die   A moribund metaphor (SEE). *affirm; asseverate; assert; attest; aver; avow; declare; pledge; promise; swear; testify; vow; warrant.*

(we'll) cross that bridge when (we) come to it   A moribund metaphor (SEE).

cross the line   A moribund metaphor (SEE).

cross the Rubicon   A moribund metaphor (SEE).

cross to bear   A moribund metaphor (SEE). *affliction; burden; charge; cross; difficulty; encumbrance; hardship; hindrance; impediment; load; obstacle; obstruction; onus; oppression; ordeal; problem; trial; trouble; weight.*

crowning achievement

crown jewels   A moribund metaphor (SEE).

cruel and unusual punishment

cruel hoax

crush like a bug   An insipid simile (SEE moribund metaphors).
1. *annihilate; assassinate; butcher; destroy; exterminate; kill; massacre; murder; slaughter; slay.*
2. *beat; conquer; crush; defeat; outdo;*

overcome; overpower; overwhelm; prevail; quell; rout; succeed; triumph; trounce; vanquish; win.

cry for help

cry like a baby   An insipid simile (SEE moribund metaphors).

cry over spilt milk   A moribund metaphor (SEE). *lament; mourn; sulk.*

crystal clear   *apparent; basic; clear; clear-cut; conspicuous; crystalline; distinct; easily done; easy; effortless; elementary; evident; explicit; facile; limpid; lucid; manifest; obvious; patent; pellucid; plain; simple; simplicity itself; simplistic; straightforward; translucent; transparent; unambiguous; uncomplex; uncomplicated; understandable; unequivocal; unmistakable.* ■ What seems *crystal clear* to you and perhaps to others, is not all that obvious to me. REPLACE WITH *obvious*.

cry (say) uncle   A moribund metaphor (SEE). *abdicate; accede; acquiesce; bow; capitulate; cede; concede; give in; give up; quit; relinquish; retreat; submit; succumb; surrender; yield.*

cry wolf   A moribund metaphor (SEE).

curiosity killed the cat   A popular prescription. (SEE)

curl up with a (good) book

curry favor

curse a blue streak   A moribund metaphor (SEE). *anathematize; blaspheme; condemn; curse; cuss; damn; de-file; desecrate; excoriate; execrate; fulminate; imprecate; swear at.*

cushion the blow   A moribund metaphor (SEE). ■ We think that will help *cushion the blow* for some people.

cut and dried (dry)   A moribund metaphor (SEE).
1. *common; commonplace; customary; everyday; normal; ordinary; quotidian; regular; routine; standard; typical; usual.*
2. *banal; bland; boring; deadly; dry; dull; flat; humdrum; insipid; jejune; lifeless; mediocre; monotonous; prosaic; stale; tedious; tiresome; unexciting; uninteresting; vapid.*

cut a rug   A moribund metaphor (SEE). *dance.*

(as) cute as a button   An insipid simile (SEE moribund metaphors). *appealing; attractive; beautiful; becoming; captivating; comely; cute; dazzling; exquisite; fair; fetching; good-looking; gorgeous; handsome; lovely; nice-looking; pleasing; pretty; pulchritudinous; radiant; ravishing; seemly; stunning.*

cut (them) off at the pass   A moribund metaphor (SEE).

cut off (my) nose to spite (my) face   A moribund metaphor (SEE).

cut (its) own throat   A moribund metaphor (SEE).

cut (her) teeth on   A moribund metaphor (SEE).

cut the legs out from under   A moribund metaphor (SEE).

cut the mustard   A moribund metaphor (SEE). *able; accomplished; adept; adequate; capable; competent; deft; equal to; equipped; fitted; measure up; proficient; qualified; skilled; skillful; suited.*

cutthroat competition   An inescapable pair (SEE).

cut through red tape   A moribund metaphor (SEE).

cutting edge   A moribund metaphor (SEE).

cut (costs) to the bone   A moribund metaphor (SEE).

cut to the chase

cut (stung) to the quick   A moribund metaphor (SEE). *affront; crush; dash; devastate; hurt; injure; insult; offend; outrage; shatter; slight; upset; wound.*

cut (it) with a knife   A moribund metaphor (SEE).

D

daddy's little girl

damage control

damaged goods   A moribund metaphor (SEE).

(he's) damned if (he) does and damned if (he) doesn't

damn with faint praise

damsel in distress

dance the night away

dance up a storm   A moribund metaphor (SEE).

dancing in the aisles (streets)

dangerous liaison

dangerous precedent

dare to be different

dark recesses (of her mind)

dashed hopes

(her) day in court   A moribund metaphor (SEE).

day in (and) day out   *always; ceaselessly; constantly; continually; continuously; daily; diurnally; endlessly; eternally; everlastingly; evermore; every day; forever; forevermore; frequently; interminably; nonstop; permanently; perpetually; persistently; recurrently; regularly; repeatedly; unceasingly; unremittingly.*

day in the sun   A moribund metaphor (SEE).

day of reckoning

(their) days are numbered

days of glory

days of wine and roses   A moribund metaphor (SEE).

dead and buried   A moribund metaphor (SEE). *ceased; completed; concluded; dead; deceased; defunct; departed; done; ended; exanimate; expired; extinct; extinguished; finished; gone; inanimate; lifeless; no more; over; perished; stopped; terminated.*

dead and gone   *ceased; completed; concluded; dead; deceased; defunct; departed; done; ended; exanimate; expired; extinct; extinguished; finished; gone;*

inanimate; lifeless; no more; over; perished; stopped; terminated.

(as) dead as a dodo An insipid simile (SEE moribund metaphors).
1. *ceased; completed; concluded; dead; deceased; defunct; departed; done; ended; exanimate; expired; extinct; extinguished; finished; gone; inanimate; lifeless; no more; over; perished; stopped; terminated.*
2. *antediluvian; antiquated; archaic; dead; obsolescent; obsolete; old; old-fashioned; outdated; outmoded; out of date; out of fashion; passé; superannuated.*
3. *debilitated; exhausted; fatigued; played out; spent; tired; worn out.*

(as) dead as a doornail An insipid simile (SEE moribund metaphors).
1. *ceased; completed; concluded; dead; deceased; defunct; departed; done; ended; exanimate; expired; extinct; extinguished; finished; gone; inanimate; lifeless; no more; over; perished; stopped; terminated.*
2. *antediluvian; antiquated; archaic; dead; obsolescent; obsolete; old; old-fashioned; outdated; outmoded; out of date; out of fashion; passé; superannuated.*
3. *debilitated; exhausted; fatigued; played out; spent; tired; worn out.*

dead body A dimwitted redundancy (SEE). *body.* ■ Their car was abandoned on a bridge, and *dead bodies* were nowhere to be found. DELETE *dead.*

dead duck A moribund metaphor (SEE).

dead-end job

deader than a doornail A moribund metaphor (SEE).

1. *ceased; completed; concluded; dead; deceased; defunct; departed; done; ended; exanimate; expired; extinct; extinguished; finished; gone; inanimate; lifeless; no more; over; perished; stopped; terminated.*
2. *antediluvian; antiquated; archaic; dead; obsolescent; obsolete; old; old-fashioned; outdated; outmoded; out of date; out of fashion; passé; superannuated.*
3. *debilitated; exhausted; fatigued; played out; spent; tired; worn out.*

dead giveaway

dead in the water A moribund metaphor (SEE). *dead; dormant; dull; inactive; inanimate; indolent; inert; inoperative; languid; latent; lethargic; lifeless; listless; motionless; phlegmatic; quiescent; quiet; sluggish; stagnant; static; stationary; still; torpid.* ■ The civil rights impulse from the 1960s is *dead in the water.* REPLACE WITH *listless.*

dead last *endmost; hindmost; last.*

dead on arrival A moribund metaphor (SEE).

dead on (her) feet A moribund metaphor (SEE). *beat; bushed; debilitated; depleted; drained; enervated; exhausted; fatigued; sapped; spent; tired; weary; worn out.*

dead ringer A moribund metaphor (SEE).

dead serious An inescapable pair (SEE).

dead to the world A moribund metaphor (SEE). *anesthetized; asleep; comatose; dozing; insensible; napping;*

oblivious; sleeping; soporiferous; soporific; stuporous; unconscious.

(as) deaf as a post   An insipid simile (SEE moribund metaphors).
1. *deaf; unhearing.*
2. *heedless; inattentive; oblivious; unmindful.*

deaf, dumb and blind

deal a (crushing; devastating; major; serious) blow to   ■ Falling real estate values, the stock market crash, and changes in the rules under which S&Ls operate *dealt crushing blows to* the bank's success.

(like) death warmed over   An insipid simile (SEE moribund metaphors). *anemic; ashen; blanched; bloodless; cadaverous; colorless; deathlike; doughy; haggard; pale; pallid; pasty; peaked; sallow; sickly; wan; whitish.*

debt of gratitude

declare war (on)   A moribund metaphor (SEE).

deep, dark secret

deepen the wound   A moribund metaphor (SEE).

deeper in (into) the hole   A moribund metaphor (SEE).

deeply regret   An inescapable pair (SEE).

(has) deep pockets   A moribund metaphor (SEE). *affluent; moneyed; opulent; prosperous; rich; wealthy; well-off; well-to-do.*

deep six   (*v*) A moribund metaphor (SEE). *discard; eliminate; get rid of; jettison; reject; throw away; toss out.*

definitely   An overworked word (SEE). So popular is this word that we might well marvel at the assuredness of those who use it. But of course the overuse of *definitely* bespeaks carelessness more than it does confidence. SEE ALSO *absolutely; most assuredly; most (very) definitely.*

definitive guide

degree   A torpid term (SEE). Beware of the word *degree*. It—and the many phrases in which it is found—should be excised from almost all of our speech and writing. Though phrases in which *degree* appears are omnipresent—especially among academicians and businesspeople—this is no testimony to the word's value. No sentence is made more compelling by the use of this word and its diffuse phrases. ■ I believe he has *a very high degree* of integrity and takes extreme pride in his workmanship. REPLACE WITH *a good deal.* ■ Increased employee morale would require *a lesser degree of* accuracy. REPLACE WITH *less.* ■ Their hopes are based, *to a large degree*, on signs that business activity is pulling out of its recent slowdown. REPLACE WITH *largely.* ■ *To a larger degree* than was expected, these economically stunted nations can count on help from the twelve-nation organization. REPLACE WITH *More.* ■ Another realm in which schools of choice can and do differ is *the degree to which* the staff and parents are involved in the day-to-day operations of the school. REPLACE WITH *how much.* SEE ALSO *extent.*

déjà vu   A foreignism (SEE).

déjà vu all over again   An infantile phrase (SEE). ■ The police served him with a restraining order; it was *déjà vu all over again*.

delicate balance   An inescapable pair (SEE).

delve deeply

demo   ■ Let's *demo* a few cost savings here and there. REPLACE WITH *demonstrate*. SEE ALSO *info; recap*.

demon rum   A moribund metaphor (SEE). *alcohol; liquor.*

den of iniquity   A moribund metaphor (SEE).

den of thieves   A moribund metaphor (SEE).

depths of depression (despair)

describes (fits) (her) to a T

(he) deserves a medal

(he) deserves what (he) gets

desperately seeking

desperate measures

despite (in spite of) or (maybe; perhaps) because of (the fact that)
■ I did all the prepartum and postpartum workouts, but (*despite or maybe because of* this) I still got a bad back after my first daughter was born. ■ *In spite of or, perhaps, because of the fact that* we humans are normally vision experts at a very young age, we have little intuition about how vision develops or how we accomplish seeing.

despite the fact that   A dimwitted redundancy (SEE). *although; but; even if; even though; still; though; yet.* ■ Long a critic of exorbitant executive salaries, he agreed to a 4.7 percent raise, *despite the fact that* his company's profits doubled. USE *even though*. ■ *Despite the fact that* no serious adverse effects have been found, there are still risks. USE *Although*. SEE ALSO *in spite of the fact that; regardless of the fact that*.

details are sketchy

devastate   An overworked word (SEE). We can hardly wonder why so many of us are so easily *devastated*. This word is pervasive. Rarely are we *upset*, rarely are we *flustered*. If only we would use more measured terms, we might feel less weak and woundable.

Consider these terms, all more moderate: *agitated; bothered; crestfallen; despondent; disappointed; discomposed; disconsolate; distressed; disturbed; downcast; downhearted; flustered; heartbroken; heartsick; perturbed; ruffled; unsettled; upset.* ■ When Glen was transferred to a city one hundred miles away, I was *devastated*. USE *heartbroken*.

But if devastation it is, here are other terms that might relieve us of our reliance on this one: *atomized; crushed; demolished; desolate; destroyed; distraught; obliterated; overcome; overpowered; overwhelmed; prostrate; ravaged; ruined; shattered; undone.* ■ Dean and Jenna were *devastated* when she lost their baby. USE *shattered*. SEE ALSO *crisis*.

develop steam   A moribund metaphor (SEE).

devil's disciple   A moribund metaphor (SEE).

devil to pay   A moribund metaphor (SEE).

diametrically opposed   An inescapable pair (SEE).

(he) did not die in vain

didn't bat (blink) an eye

didn't miss a beat   A moribund metaphor (SEE).

(they) didn't see it coming

(we) did the best (we) could (knew how)

die laughing   A moribund metaphor (SEE).

die on the vine   A moribund metaphor (SEE).

different strokes for different folks   A popular prescription (SEE).

difficult task   An inescapable pair (SEE).

digging (your) own grave   A moribund metaphor (SEE).

dig in (his) heels   A moribund metaphor (SEE). *be adamant; be balky; be bullheaded; be cantankerous; be contrary; be contumacious; be determined; be dogged; be firm; be headstrong; be inflexible; be intractable; be mulish; be obdurate; be obstinate; be ornery; be per-* *verse; be refractory; be resistant; be resolute; be resolved; be rigid; be stubborn; be unyielding; be willful.*

dimwitted redundancies
Witticisms are the work of few words; dimwitticisms, the toil of many.

Reckless writers and slipshod speakers use many words where few would do: *advance planning; at this time; consensus of opinion; dead body; due to the fact that; first and foremost; free gift; just recently; in advance of; in and of itself; in spite of the fact that; in terms of; make a determination; on a . . . basis; on the part of; past experience; period of time; (the) reason (why) is because; refer back; the single best (most); until such time as.* Yet for all the words, their expression is but impoverished; more words do not necessarily signify more meaning.

Life is measured by its meaning, and a good deal of that meaning is inherent in the words we use. If so many of our words are superfluous—and thus do not signify—so much of our life is, ineluctably, meaningless.

In the end, we are no more superfluous than are the words we use. SEE ALSO *inescapable pairs.*

dire consequences

dire straits

dirt cheap   A moribund metaphor (SEE). *cheap; economical; inexpensive; low-cost; low-priced; not costly.*

dirty pool   A moribund metaphor (SEE).

disappear (vanish) into thin air
disappear; disperse; dissolve; evaporate; fade; vanish; vaporize.

disappear (vanish) without a trace *disappear; disperse; dissolve; evaporate; fade; vanish; vaporize.*

dismal failure An inescapable pair (SEE).

distinct possibility

divide and conquer

divine intervention An inescapable pair (SEE).

do a disappearing act A moribund metaphor (SEE). *abscond; clear out; decamp; depart; desert; disappear; escape; exit; flee; fly; go; go away; leave; move on; part; pull out; quit; retire; retreat; run away; take flight; take off; vacate; vanish; withdraw.*

do a hatchet job on A moribund metaphor (SEE). *asperse; badmouth; belittle; besmirch; bespatter; blacken; calumniate; defame; defile; denigrate; denounce; depreciate; deride; disparage; impugn; insult; libel; malign; profane; revile; scandalize; slander; slur; smear; sully; taint; traduce; vilify; vitiate.*

do a job on A moribund metaphor (SEE).
1. *blight; cripple; damage; deface; disable; disfigure; harm; hurt; impair; incapacitate; injure; lame; maim; mar; mess up; rack; ruin; sabotage; spoil; subvert; undermine; vitiate; wrack; wreck.*
2. *agitate; bother; disquiet; distress; disturb; fluster; jar; jolt; pain; perturb; ruffle; shake; trouble; unsettle; upset; wound.*

do all (everything) in (my) power
■ I believe that Cashbuild has *done ev-erything in its power* to cope with the changing South American environment.

do a number on

do as I say, not as I do A popular prescription (SEE).

doctor, lawyer, Indian chief A moribund metaphor (SEE).

dodge the bullet A moribund metaphor (SEE).

(it) doesn't amount to a hill of beans A moribund metaphor (SEE). *barren; bootless; effete; feckless; feeble; fruitless; futile; impotent; inadequate; inconsequential; inconsiderable; ineffective; ineffectual; infertile; insignificant; inutile; meaningless; meritless; nugatory; null; of no value; pointless; powerless; profitless; sterile; trifling; trivial; unavailing; unimportant; unproductive; unprofitable; unserviceable; unworthy; useless; vain; valueless; weak; worthless.*

doesn't have a clue *addlebrained; addleheaded; addlepated; Boeotian; bovine; brainless; clueless; cretinous; dense; dim-witted; doltish; dull; dumb; dunderheaded; empty-headed; fatuous; fat-witted; harebrained; hebetudinous; ignorant; imbecilic; incognitant; insensate; ludicrous; mindless; moronic; muddled; nescient; obtuse; oxlike; phlegmatic; slow-witted; sluggish; stupid; torpid; unaware; unintelligent; unknowing; vacuous; witless.*

doesn't have an enemy in the world

(he) doesn't have a prayer

doesn't have two nickels to rub together   A moribund metaphor (SEE). *broke; destitute; distressed; impecunious; impoverished; indigent; insolvent; needy; penniless; poor; poverty-stricken; underprivileged.*

doesn't hold water   A moribund metaphor (SEE). *baseless; captious; casuistic; casuistical; erroneous; fallacious; false; faulty; flawed; groundless; illogical; inaccurate; incorrect; invalid; irrational; jesuitic; jesuitical; mistaken; nonsensical; non sequitur; paralogistic; senseless; sophistic; sophistical; specious; spurious; unfounded; unreasonable; unsound; untenable; untrue; unveracious; wrong.*

doesn't know enough to come in out of the rain   A moribund metaphor (SEE). *addlebrained; addleheaded; addlepated; Boeotian; bovine; brainless; clueless; cretinous; dense; dim-witted; doltish; dull; dumb; dunderheaded; empty-headed; fatuous; fat-witted; harebrained; hebetudinous; ignorant; imbecilic; incogitant; insensate; ludicrous; mindless; moronic; muddled; nescient; obtuse; oxlike; phlegmatic; slow-witted; sluggish; stupid; torpid; unaware; unintelligent; unknowing; vacuous; witless.*

doesn't know (me) from Adam (Eve)

doesn't stand a chance

dog and pony show   A moribund metaphor (SEE).

dog days (of summer)   A moribund metaphor (SEE).

dog-eat-dog   A moribund metaphor (SEE). *barbarous; bloodthirsty; brutal; cold-blooded; compassionless; cruel; cutthroat; feral; ferocious; fierce; hard; hard-hearted; harsh; heartless; implacable; inexorable; inhuman; merciless; murderous; rancorous; relentless; ruthless; savage; uncompassionate; unmerciful; unrelenting; vicious; virulent; wild.*

(I'm) doing this for (your) own good

dollars and sense   An infantile phrase (SEE).

dollars to doughnuts

don't be a stranger

don't count your chickens before they're hatched   A popular prescription (SEE).

don't cry over spilled milk   A popular prescription (SEE).

don't do (me) any favors

don't do anything I wouldn't do   A popular prescription (SEE).

don't get me wrong   An infantile phrase (SEE). ■ I'm not trying to condone what I've done. *Don't get me wrong.* REPLACE WITH *Don't misunderstand me.* SEE ALSO *I hear you.*

don't give up the ship   A popular prescription (SEE).

don't hold (your) breath   A moribund metaphor (SEE).

don't kid yourself

don't knock it until you try it

A popular prescription (SEE).

don't know (her) from a hole in the wall

don't look now, but

don't rock the boat   A moribund metaphor (SEE).

don't say I didn't tell (warn) you

don't see eye to eye   A moribund metaphor (SEE). *clash; conflict; differ; disagree; think differently.*

don't start anything you can't finish   A popular prescription (SEE).

doom and gloom   An inescapable pair (SEE).

doomed to disappointment

do or die   A popular prescription (SEE).

do's and don'ts   *canon; codes; conventions; conventionality; customs; decorum; directives; etiquette; formula; formulary; law; manners; policy; precepts; protocol; proprieties; regulations; rules; standards.*

do tell

do their (own) thing

dot the i's and cross the t's
A moribund metaphor (SEE). *careful; conscientious; exact; exacting; fastidious; finical; finicky; fussy; meticulous; nice; painstaking; particular; picky; precise; punctilious; scrupulous; thorough.*

double-edged sword   A moribund metaphor (SEE).

double trouble

doubting Thomas   A moribund metaphor (SEE).

(get) down and dirty

down and out   A moribund metaphor (SEE).

down at the heels   A moribund metaphor (SEE).
1. *dowdy; frowzy; ragged; run-down; seedy; shabby; slipshod; sloppy; slovenly; tattered; threadbare; unkempt; untidy; worn.*
2. *broke; destitute; distressed; impecunious; impoverished; indigent; insolvent; needy; penniless; poor; poverty-stricken; underprivileged.*

down for the count   A moribund metaphor (SEE).

down in the mouth   A moribund metaphor (SEE). *aggrieved; blue; cheerless; dejected; demoralized; depressed; despondent; disconsolate; discouraged; disheartened; dismal; dispirited; doleful; downcast; downhearted; dreary; forlorn; funereal; gloomy; glum; grieved; low; melancholy; miserable; mournful; plaintive; sad; sorrowful; unhappy; woeful.*

(go) down the drain   A moribund metaphor (SEE). *break down; collapse; deteriorate; die; disappear; disintegrate; disperse; issipate; dissolve; evaporate; fade; fail; finish; forfeit; go; lose; pass; scatter; vanish.* ■ Without new revenue, our schools will *go down the drain.* REPLACE WITH *collapse.*

down the hatch A moribund metaphor (SEE). *drink; gulp; guzzle; imbibe; quaff; swallow.*

(later on) down the line (path; pike; road) A dimwitted redundancy (SEE). *at length; before long; eventually; from now; in time; later; ultimately.* ∎ Even though this knowledge might not seem essential right now, it just might prove invaluable *down the line.* REPLACE WITH *later.* ∎ Two players will be added to the team *later, some months down the road.* REPLACE WITH *some months later.* ∎ *Later on down the line,* we did in fact marry. REPLACE WITH *Eventually.*

down the primrose path A moribund metaphor (SEE).

(go) down the tubes A moribund metaphor (SEE). *break down; collapse; disintegrate; fail; fall short; flop; founder; miscarry; topple.* ∎ Her article points out a major reason why our country is *going down the tubes.* REPLACE WITH *foundering.*

down to earth A moribund metaphor (SEE). *artless; common; earthly; everyday; genuine; guileless; mortal; mundane; natural; normal; plain; secular; staid; temporal; unaffected; unassuming; unpretentious; worldly.*

(come) down to the wire A moribund metaphor (SEE).

drag (their) feet A moribund metaphor (SEE). *arrest; balk; block; bridle; check; dawdle; defer; delay; detain; encumber; hamper; hinder; hold up; impede; inhibit; obstruct; postpone; put off; retard; stall; stay; suspend.*

drag kicking and screaming A moribund metaphor (SEE).

drag through the mud A moribund metaphor (SEE). *asperse; badmouth; belittle; besmirch; bespatter; blacken; calumniate; defame; defile; denigrate; denounce; depreciate; deride; disparage; impugn; insult; libel; malign; profane; revile; scandalize; slander; slur; smear; sully; taint; traduce; vilify; vitiate.*

dramatic turn of events

(take) drastic action

draw a bead on A moribund metaphor (SEE).

draw a veil over A moribund metaphor (SEE). *adumbrate; becloud; befog; camouflage; cloak; cloud; conceal; cover; dissemble; disguise; enshroud; harbor; hide; keep secret; mask; obfuscate; obscure; overshadow; screen; shroud; suppress; veil; withhold.*

draw fire (from) A moribund metaphor (SEE).

draw in (his) horns A moribund metaphor (SEE). *back away; back down; back off; retreat; withdraw.*

draw in the reins A moribund metaphor (SEE). *bridle; check; curb; curtail; halt; restrain; stall; stay; stop.*

draw the line (at) A moribund metaphor (SEE).

draw the long bow A moribund metaphor (SEE). *elaborate; embellish; embroider; enhance; enlarge; exaggerate; hyperbolize; inflate; magnify;*

overdo; overreact; overstress; overstate; strain; stretch.

dredge up dirt   A moribund metaphor (SEE).

dressed (fit) to kill   A moribund metaphor (SEE).

dressed (up) to the nines   A moribund metaphor (SEE).

dribs and drabs   An inescapable pair (SEE). *bits; chunks; crumbs; fragments; modicums; morsels; nuggets; particles; pieces; scraps; segments; shreds; snips; snippets; specks.*

drink like a fish   An insipid simile (SEE moribund metaphors).

drive a hard bargain

drive a wedge between   A moribund metaphor (SEE).

drive (me) bananas (crazy; nuts)
A moribund metaphor (SEE). *annoy; badger; bedevil; bother; chafe; distress; disturb; gall; grate; harass; harry; hassle; heckle; hector; hound; irk; irritate; nag; nettle; persecute; pester; plague; provoke; rankle; tease; torment; vex.*

drive (the point) home

drive (me) to drink   A moribund metaphor (SEE). *annoy; badger; bedevil; bother; chafe; distress; disturb; gall; grate; harass; harry; hassle; heckle; hector; hound; irk; irritate; nag; nettle; persecute; pester; plague; provoke; rankle; tease; torment; vex.*

drive (me) up the wall   A moribund metaphor (SEE). *annoy; badger;*

bedevil; bother; chafe; distress; disturb; gall; grate; harass; harry; hassle; heckle; hector; hound; irk; irritate; nag; nettle; persecute; pester; plague; provoke; rankle; tease; torment; vex.

driving force   A dimwitted redundancy (SEE). *drive; energy; force; impetus; motivation; power.*

drop (me) a line   *write.*

drop-dead gorgeous

drop like a hot potato   An insipid simile (SEE moribund metaphors). *abandon; abdicate; desert; discard; ditch; drop; forgo; forsake; get rid of; give up; jettison; leave; quit; reject; relinquish; renounce; surrender; throw away; toss out; yield.*

drop like flies   An insipid simile (SEE moribund metaphors).

drop off the face of the earth
A moribund metaphor (SEE). *disappear; vanish.*

drop precipitously

drop the ball   A moribund metaphor (SEE).

drum up business

(as) drunk as a skunk   An insipid simile (SEE moribund metaphors). *besotted; crapulous; drunk; inebriated; intoxicated; sodden; stupefied; tipsy.*

(as) dry as a bone   An insipid simile (SEE moribund metaphors). *arid; dehydrated; desiccated; droughty; dry; exsiccated; parched; sear; shriveled; thirsty; wilted; withered.*

(as) dry as dust An insipid simile (SEE moribund metaphors). *banal; barren; bland; boring; deadly; dreary; dry; dull; flat; humdrum; inanimate; insipid; jejune; lifeless; mediocre; monotonous; prosaic; routine; spiritless; stale; tedious; tiresome; unexciting; uninteresting; vapid; wearisome.*

dubious distinction An inescapable pair (SEE).

duck soup A moribund metaphor (SEE). *easily done; easy; effortless; elementary; facile; simple; simplicity itself; simplistic; straightforward; uncomplex; uncomplicated.*

due to circumstances beyond (our) control Of those who use this phrase, we may remark that they speak as ungrammatically as they act ungenuinely.

Due to, most often, should be *because of* or *owing to*, and only the similarly disingenuous would believe that *circumstances beyond our control* is an explanation rather than an evasion.

Those who express themselves badly are less credible than those who express themselves well. SEE ALSO *due to popular demand.*

due to popular demand There is with this phrase, as with *due to circumstances beyond (our) control* (SEE), the same solecism and a similar suspicion.

due to the fact that A dimwitted redundancy (SEE). *because; considering; for; in that; since.* ■ Requirements continue to decrease slowly *due to the fact that* activity generally decreases with age. USE *since.* ■ Could this be *due to the fact that* it is undecidable?

USE *because.* SEE ALSO *attributable to the fact that; owing to the fact that.*

(as) dull as dishwater An insipid simile (SEE moribund metaphors). 1. *addlebrained; addlepated; bovine; cretinous; dense; dull; fatuous; fat-witted; half-witted; harebrained; hebetudinous; idiotic; ignorant; imbecilic; incogitant; insensate; mindless; moronic; muddled; nescient; obtuse; phlegmatic; slow; slow-witted; sluggish; thick; torpid; undiscerning; unintelligent; vacuous; witless.* 2. *banal; barren; bland; boring; deadly; dreary; dry; dull; flat; humdrum; inanimate; insipid; jejune; lifeless; mediocre; monotonous; prosaic; routine; spiritless; stale; tedious; tiresome; unexciting; uninteresting; vapid; wearisome.*

during (in; over) the course of A dimwitted redundancy (SEE). *during; in; over; throughout.* ■ *In the course of* a 30-minute conversation, she spoke about her married life and her plans for the future. USE *During.* ■ *Over the course of* a woman's life, she may experience a kaleidoscope of health concerns. USE *Throughout.*

during the period (time) that A dimwitted redundancy (SEE). *while.* ■ *During the time that* we were with him, he called her several uncomplimentary names. USE *While.*

dyed-in-the-wool A moribund metaphor (SEE). *ardent; constant; devoted; faithful; inflexible; intractable; loyal; refractory; resolute; rigid; staunch; steadfast; unbending; unwavering; unyielding.*

dynamic duo An infantile phrase (SEE).

E

each and every (one)   A dimwitted redundancy (S<small>EE</small>). *all; each; everybody; everyone.* ■ Software developers have changed the way *each and every one* of us does business. U<small>SE</small> *each.*

each one   A dimwitted redundancy (S<small>EE</small>). *each.* ■ The fact that these companies do have to compete for business gives *each one* an incentive to work harder and to lower prices. D<small>E</small>-L<small>ETE</small> *one.* S<small>EE</small> A<small>LSO</small> *either one; neither one.*

each to his own   A popular prescription (S<small>EE</small>).

eagerly await

eagle eye   A moribund metaphor (S<small>EE</small>).

earn (his) stripes   A moribund metaphor (S<small>EE</small>).

easier said than done

easy access

(as) easy as A, B, C (1, 2, 3)   An insipid simile (S<small>EE</small> moribund metaphors). *apparent; basic; clear; clear-cut; conspicuous; distinct; easily done; easy; effortless; elementary; evident; explicit;* *facile; limpid; lucid; manifest; obvious; patent; pellucid; plain; simple; simplicity itself; simplistic; straightforward; translucent; transparent; unambiguous; uncomplex; uncomplicated; understandable; unequivocal; unmistakable.*

(as) easy as pie   An insipid simile (S<small>EE</small> moribund metaphors). *apparent; basic; clear; clear-cut; conspicuous; distinct; easily done; easy; effortless; elementary; evident; explicit; facile; limpid; lucid; manifest; obvious; patent; pellucid; plain; simple; simplicity itself; simplistic; straightforward; translucent; transparent; unambiguous; uncomplex; uncomplicated; understandable; unequivocal; unmistakable.*

easy come, easy go

(no) easy way out   ■ What we have to understand is that there is no *easy way out.*

eat crow   A moribund metaphor (S<small>EE</small>). *abase; chasten; debase; degrade; demean; disgrace; dishonor; embarrass; humble; humiliate; lower; mortify; shame.*

eat dirt   A moribund metaphor (S<small>EE</small>). *abase; chasten; debase; degrade; demean; disgrace; dishonor; embarrass;*

humble; humiliate; lower; mortify; shame.

eat, drink and be merry A popular prescription (SEE).

eat, drink and be merry, for tomorrow we (may) die A popular prescription (SEE).

eat (my) hat

eat (your) heart out A moribund metaphor (SEE). *ache; agonize; grieve; hurt; lament; mourn; pine; sorrow; suffer; worry.*

eat (live) high off (on) the hog A moribund metaphor (SEE). *epicureanly; extravagantly; lavishly; lushly; luxuriantly; opulently; prodigally; profusely; sumptuously; very well.*

eat humble pie A moribund metaphor (SEE). *abase; chasten; debase; degrade; demean; disgrace; dishonor; embarrass; humble; humiliate; lower; mortify; shame.*

eat like a bird An insipid simile (SEE moribund metaphors).

eat like a horse An insipid simile (SEE moribund metaphors). *esurient; famished; gluttonous; greedy; hungry; insatiable; omnivorous; ravenous; starved; starving; voracious.*

eat out of (the palms of) (her) hands A moribund metaphor (SEE). *administer; boss; command; control; dictate; direct; dominate; domineer; govern; in charge; in control; in command; manage; manipulate; master; misuse; order; overpower; oversee; predominate;*

prevail; reign over; rule; superintend; tyrannize; use.

eat (me) out of house and home A moribund metaphor (SEE). *esurient; famished; gluttonous; greedy; hungry; insatiable; omnivorous; ravenous; starved; starving; voracious.*

eat (her) words A moribund metaphor (SEE).

ebb and flow ■ Optimists try to attribute a linear progression to the *ebb and flow* of history.

educated guess

effect An overworked word (SEE). For example: *chilling effect; cumulative effect; domino effect; dramatic effect; negative effect; snowball effect; sobering effect; trickle-down effect.* ■ LeBlanc's lawyers say that would *have a chilling effect on* fraud lawsuits brought by government employees. REPLACE WITH *discourage.* ■ You can learn how to free yourself from the *destructive effects* of negative people in your workplace. REPLACE WITH *detriment.* SEE ALSO *has an effect on.*

effective and efficient An inescapable pair (SEE). Dimwitted businesspeople, in particular, seem unable to use the word *effective* without also using the synonymic *efficient.* ■ For these methods, more *effective and efficient* methods are available. REPLACE WITH *effective* or *efficient.* ■ More than an audit, the study should evaluate the *efficiency and effectiveness* of social services and public works. REPLACE WITH *effectiveness* or *efficiency.* ■ The work place should be a safe environment where one can *effectively and efficiently* perform required duties. REPLACE WITH *effectively* or *efficiently*.

effective immediately

effectuate   A torpid term (SEE). *bring about; carry out; cause; do; effect; execute; occasion.* SEE ALSO *eventuate.*

egg on (my) face   A moribund metaphor (SEE). *abashed; ashamed; chagrined; confused; discomfited; discomposed; disconcerted; embarrassed; flustered; humbled; humiliated; mortified; nonplussed; perplexed; red-faced; shamed; shamefaced; sheepish; upset.*

egregious error   An inescapable pair (SEE).

either one   A dimwitted redundancy (SEE). *either.* ▪ He doesn't care about *either one* of you. DELETE *one*. SEE ALSO *each one; neither one.*

elegant English   We all know far too well how to speak and write everyday English, but few of us know how to speak and write elegant English. And as there are occasions for everyday English, so there are occasions for elegant English — for English that is expressed with music as well as meaning, with style as well as substance.

The difference between everyday English and elegant English is the difference between manikin — the least manly of men — and man — the most memorable of men.

It is time we aspire to becoming who we were meant to be. It is time we aspire to expressing ourselves well. But, lamentably, where one person sees a goal — bright, beautiful, magnificent — another person sees a

gargoyle — ugly, repellent, grotesque.

Elegant English is grammatically correct English, it is uncommon or forgotten English, it is British English. In all instances, elegant English is English rarely heard, English seldom seen.

Grammatically correct English:

The grammatically correct *It is I* is elegant, and the grammatically incorrect *It is me* is not. ▪ *It was her* who spoke to me that way. USE *It was she.* ▪ He knew it was *her*, but she didn't know it was *him*. USE *she; he.*

The omnipresent *like* is everyday, whereas *as, as if* and *as though* are elegant. ▪ He felt *like* he had been cheated by the system. USE *as though.* ▪ *Like* I was saying, he didn't know what the circumstances were. USE *As.*

Elegant is *graduated from* or *was graduated from*; everyday is *graduated.* ▪ Even before *graduating* college, Hughes had published two books of poetry. USE *graduating from* or *he was graduated from.* ▪ I *graduated* one of the finest medical schools in the country. USE *graduated from* or *was graduated from.*

How come is everyday English, and *how has it come about that* or *how is it that* is elegant. ▪ *How come* you are not supporting my candidacy? USE *How is it that.* ▪ *How come* everyone else is wrong and you are right? USE *How has it come about that.*

Me neither, that makes two of us and *you're not the only one* are everyday; *neither do I, no more do I* and *nor do I* elegant. ▪ I no longer trust her. *You're not the only one.* USE *Neither do I, Nor do I,* or *No more do I.* ▪ I myself know nothing about the subject. *Me neither.* USE *Neither do I, Nor do I,* or *No more do I.*

Likewise or *likewise, I'm sure* in the

following examples is everyday, even ignorant; the alternatives are not. ■ I'm so happy to have met you. *Likewise, I'm sure.* USE *And I, to have met you.* ■ I enjoy meeting intelligent people. *Likewise.* USE *As I do.*

Uncommon or forgotten English:

A lot, very and *very much* are hopelessly everyday expressions; *enormously, hugely, immensely, mightily, monstrously* and *prodigiously* are not. ■ I won't pretend I don't like her; I do—*a lot.* USE *prodigiously.* ■ We are *very* proud of her. USE *enormously.*

All right, O.K. and *whatever* are everyday, but *(just) as you like, (just) as you please* and *very well* are elegant. ■ I think I'll stay here for the night. *O.K.* USE *Just as you please.* ■ I'm supposed to say that, not you. *Whatever.* USE *Very well.*

Phrases like *aren't I? aren't you?* and *wasn't I?* are everyday, but *am I not? are you not?* and *was I not?* are elegant. ■ *Aren't I* going with you next week? USE *Am I not.* ■ He was right, *wasn't he?* USE *was he not.*

Everyday are words like *awful, bad, horrible* and *terrible.* Elegant are words like *abominable, dreadful, frightful, ghastly, hideous, insufferable, intolerable, monstrous, unspeakable* and *unutterable.* ■ What a *terrible* place this city of yours is. USE *monstrous.* ■ This peach pie looks *horrible.* USE *frightful.*

The fact that is everyday, and the largely forgotten *that* elegant. ■ *The fact that* they declared bankruptcy means little to me if not to you. USE *That.* ■ Yes, *the fact that* she behaved like an imbecile did influence any interest we might have had in befriending her. USE *that.*

Similarly, *in order that* and *so that* are everyday, but *that* is elegant. ■ We spoke to her sternly *in order that* she

might learn from her mistakes. USE *that.* ■ *In order that* we might profit from our experience, he had us write an essay on what we learned from it. USE *That.*

Words like *absolutely, completely, definitely, entirely, quite* and *totally* are everyday; *itself* is elegant. ■ She was *absolutely lovely.* USE *loveliness itself.* ■ Throughout the whole affair, he was *completely kind.* USE *kindness itself.*

Exceedingly, extremely, so, terribly and *very* are everyday; *in the extreme* and *too* are not. ■ It's *very* lovely. USE *too.* ■ I found his book *extremely confusing.* USE *confusing in the extreme.*

I don't believe so, I don't think so and *no (I don't)* are everyday; *I think not* is elegant. ■ Would you like to walk along with us? Thanks, but *I don't think so.* USE *I think not.* ■ Do you have any other questions for our guest? *No.* USE *I think not.*

British English:

Phrases such as *am I to?* are elegant, but *shall I?* or *will I?* is everyday. ■ What *will I* do with her? USE *am I to.* ■ Then *shall I* never see you again? USE *am I to.*

Anyway and *anyhow, nevertheless* and *nonetheless* are everyday; *all the same* and *just the same* are elegant. ■ Thanks, *anyway.* USE *all the same.* ■ *Nevertheless,* I believe she is responsible for our failure. USE *Just the same.*

Everyday are *(that's) correct, (most) definitely, I agree, (you're) right, sure;* elegant are *exactly so, just so, precisely so, quite right, quite so.* ■ August is hardly the time to visit Paris. *That's right.* USE *Quite right.* ■ She is the wisest person I know. *Most definitely.* USE *Exactly so.*

Immediately, right away, in a minute and the like are everyday; *directly* is elegant. ■ She'll be down *in a minute.* USE *directly.* ■ We must leave *right away.* USE *directly.*

Expressions like *that's correct, you're right* and *yes, she has* are everyday. Expressions like *I am* and *she has* are elegant. ■ Is it really your birthday today? *That's right.* USE *It is.* ■ Are we there already? *Yes.* USE *We are.*

A phrase such as *do you have* is everyday next to the elegant *have you.* ■ *Do I have* time to take a shower? USE *Have I.* ■ *Do you have* anything to drink? USE *Have you.*

An understood *you* is decidedly everyday; the plainly stated *do* is not. ■ We had a little adventure last night. Oh, *tell* me all about it. USE *do tell.* ■ *Leave* me alone. USE *Do leave.*

About "elegant-sounding" words such as *albeit* (SEE), *beauteous, demise, epistle, ere* (SEE), *perchance* (SEE), *peruse, repast, sans* (SEE), *save* (SEE) and *thrice* — many of which are *archaisms* (SEE) — there is, of course, nothing elegant. SEE ALSO *everyday English; uneducated English.*

(an) element   A torpid term (SEE). ■ Proper validation is *an* essential *element.* DELETE *an element.* ■ Black turnout was especially low, and that was *a* key *element* to her victory. DELETE *a element.* SEE ALSO *(a) factor.*

element of surprise

elevate to an art form   ■ He would add to the gridlock, then compound the people's frustrations by *elevating* the blame game *to an art form.*

eligible bachelor

emotional high

emotionally charged

emotionally distraught

emotions are running high

empty gesture

empty promises

empty void   A dimwitted redundancy (SEE). *emptiness; void.* ■ I know that without me around my mother got lonely and just needed someone to fill the *empty void.* USE *emptiness* or *void.*

enclosed herein (herewith) A dimwitted redundancy (SEE). *enclosed; here.* ■ *Enclosed herein* is the complete manuscript. USE *Here* or *Enclosed.*

enclosed please find   A dimwitted redundancy (SEE). *enclosed is; here is.* ■ *Enclosed please find* materials you might find useful prior to your arrival. USE *Enclosed are.* ■ *Enclosed please find* a listing of single family properties available for purchase by eligible buyers. USE *Here is.*

endangered species   ■ We all recognize that the nuclear family is an *endangered species.*

ending (weeks) of speculation

end of the line   *close; completion; conclusion; culmination; consummation; end; ending; finale; finish; fulfillment; termination.*

end on a high note   A moribund metaphor (SEE).

end result   A dimwitted redundancy (SEE). *result.* ■ The *end result* should be that all mothers and fathers would pay what they can afford. DELETE *end*.

enjoy it while it lasts

enough is enough   A quack equation (SEE).

enough said

equally as   A dimwitted redundancy (SEE). *as; equally*. ■ *Equally as* important, this program provides comprehensive preventive coverage. USE *As* or *Equally*.

equal to the task   *able; accomplished; adept; adequate; capable; competent; deft; equal to; equipped; fitted; measure up; proficient; qualified; skilled; skillful; suited*.

ere   An archaism (SEE). *before*. ■ So I avoided the hole and assumed it might likely be June *ere* it was patched. USE *before*.

ergo   An archaism (SEE). *consequently; hence; therefore*.

err on the side of (caution)

establishment   A torpid term (SEE). *business; club; company; firm; outlet; shop; store*. ■ You should park close to the entrance of the *establishment* where you are shopping. REPLACE WITH *store*.

etc., etc. (et cetera, et cetera)   A grammatical gimmick (SEE). ■ I'm very outgoing and adaptable, *et cetera, et cetera*. DELETE *et cetera, et cetera*. ■ She told me he was everything she was looking for, *et cetera, et cetera*. DELETE *et cetera, et cetera*. SEE ALSO *blah, blah, blah; and so on, and so forth*.

eternal optimist

et tu, Brute   A foreignism (SEE).

even-Steven   An infantile phrase (SEE).

even the score   A moribund metaphor (SEE).

eventuate   A torpid term (SEE). *befall; come about; end; happen; occur; result; take place*. SEE ALSO *effectuate*.

ever and anon   An archaism (SEE). *now and then; occasionally*.

everybody and (his) brother (mother)   *all; everybody; everyone*. ■ *Everybody and their mother* is on line today. REPLACE WITH *Everybody*.

everybody loves a winner

everybody's different   A popular prescription (SEE).

everybody talks about the weather, but nobody does anything about it.   An infantile phrase (SEE).

every cloud has a silver lining   A popular prescription (SEE).

everyday English   Surely the least effective speakers and writers use the most dimwitticisms. The more dimwitticisms are found in a person's speech and writing, the more dull, the more everyday, the person.

Everyday English is the language of a commonplace populace.

Nonetheless, there is a certain adoration of the everyday, a certain homage to homunculi that neither the elegant nor the uneducated will ever likely realize.

Everyday speakers and writers use the first of the following expressions instead of the second: *between (you) and (I)* instead of *between (you) and (me)*. ■ That is probably one of the differences *between my dad and I.* USE *between my dad and me.* ■ *Between you and I*—this is strictly *between you and I*—she wants to marry me. USE *between you and me.*

can't help but instead of *can't help -ing*. ■ I *can't help but think* that she knew about it all along. USE *can't help thinking.* ■ I *couldn't help but overhear.* USE *couldn't help overhearing.*

could care less instead of *couldn't care less*. ■ Although they have heard about the conflict on the news, they quite frankly *could care less* about it. USE *couldn't care less.*

good instead of *well*. ■ He did *good* last night. USE *well.* ■ He helps me to do *good* in school. USE *well.*

hopefully instead of *I am hopeful, I hope, it is to be hoped,* or *let us hope*. ■ *Hopefully,* the low rates will encourage people to buy. USE *Let's hope.* ■ We need the rain, so *hopefully* we'll get some soon. USE *I hope.*

like instead of *as*. ■ I decided to put on a mask, *like* many people do. USE *as.* ■ We're doing it in an orderly way, *like* it's been done before. USE *as.*

like instead of *as if* or *as though*. ■ It's *like* she has to protect him from criticism, shield him from the world. USE *as if.* ■ It was *like* my life had ended. USE *as though.*

(my)self instead of *(me)*. ■ How about *yourself?* USE *you.* ■ She told my sister and *myself* that she was pregnant by him. USE *me.*

the reason (why) is because instead of *because* or *the reason is (that)*. ■ The *reason* some individuals take supplements *is because* they feel the RDAs recommend intakes that prevent deficiency diseases. DELETE *The reason . . . is.* ■ *The reason* I didn't graduate *is because* I had to work. DELETE *because.*

where instead of *that*. ■ I saw on TV *where* he was awarded a prize. USE *that.* ■ I read *where* your neighbor was sentenced for soliciting sex. USE *that.*

which instead of, for instance, *and*. ■ I've told them it's not a good book for children, *which* it isn't. USE *and.* ■ I have to call every time to see if my free time will be convenient for her, *which* it always is. USE *and.*

-wise words instead of actual words. ■ I've been very successful *businesswise.* USE *in business.* ■ *Burialwise,* I don't feel they're responsible enough to take care of *my wishes.* USE *my burial wishes.*

Everyday speakers and writers also tend to confuse the meanings of words and to use words incorrectly.

Aggravate does not mean *annoy* or *irritate*; it means *to make worse.* ■ I get really *aggravated* when people tell me I can't do something. USE *irritated.*

Alternate does not mean *alternative*; it means *occurring or acting by turns.* ■ I do have the ability to be fascinated with *alternate* opinions. USE *alternative.*

Disinterested does not mean *uninterested* or *indifferent*; it means *impartial* or *unbiased.* ■ He made it clear to us that he was *disinterested* in our proposal. USE *uninterested.* ■ Within the culture, this demonstrates attentiveness and agreement rather than rejection, disinterest or disagreement. USE *indifference.*

Enormity does not mean *enormousness*; it means *great wickedness* or *out-*

rageousness. ■ Let me try to give you some idea of the *enormity* of this crowd. USE *hugeness.* ■ When she realized the *enormity* of her accomplishment, her emotions overcame her. USE *enormousness.*

Inflammable does not mean *nonflammable* or *noncombustible*; it means *flammable* or *ignitable.* ■ All bedsheets must be made of *inflammable* material. USE *nonflammable.*

Literally does not mean *figuratively* or *metaphorically*; it means *actually* or *in fact.* ■ Today, our 29,000-square-foot facility is *literally* bursting at the seams! DELETE *literally.* ■ When her sister left, he just *literally* fell apart. DELETE *literally.*

Transpire does not mean *happen* or *occur*; it means *become known* or *leak out.* ■ I think that explains what *transpired* between us. USE *happened.* ■ The police officer is the principal source of information on what *transpired* during the encounter. USE *occurred.*

No person—whatever his stature—can be called compleat if he customarily uses these everyday, dimwitted expressions.

Indeed, much everyday English is uneducated English. The language pullulates with people who hover between the everyday and the uneducated. SEE ALSO *elegant English; uneducated English.*

every effort is being made   This phrase serves to disarm people as it dismisses them. SEE ALSO *that's interesting; that's nice.*

every little bit helps

every man for himself

every mother's son

every nook and cranny   A moribund metaphor (SEE). *all around; all over; all through; everyplace; everywhere; throughout.*

everyone under the sun   *all; everybody; everyone.*

everyone who's anyone

every reason to believe

every single (solitary)   A dimwitted redundancy (SEE). *every.* ■ *Every single solitary* night we see people dying. USE *Every.*

every step of the way
1. *always; ceaselessly; constantly; continually; continuously; endlessly; eternally; everlastingly; evermore; forever; forevermore; frequently; interminably; nonstop; permanently; perpetually; persistently; recurrently; regularly; repeatedly; unceasingly; unremittingly.*
2. *all during; all over; all through; everywhere; throughout.*

everything but the kitchen sink   A moribund metaphor (SEE). *aggregate; all; all things; entirety; everything; gross; lot; sum; total; totality; whole.*

everything happens for a reason   A popular prescription (SEE).

everything's coming up roses   A moribund metaphor (SEE).

everything under the sun   *all; all things; everything.* ■ I tried *everything under the sun* to get her to shape up.

everything will turn out for the

best A popular prescription (SEE).

everything you always wanted to know about . . . but were afraid to ask An infantile phrase (SEE).

every time (you) turn around *always; ceaselessly; constantly; continually; continuously; endlessly; eternally; everlastingly; evermore; forever; forevermore; interminably; permanently; perpetually; persistently; unceasingly; unremittingly.*

every Tom, Dick and Harry
A moribund metaphor (SEE). *all; citizenry; commonage; commonalty; common people; crowd; everybody; everyone; herd; hoi polloi; masses; mob; multitude; plebians; populace; proletariat; public; rabble.*

every trick in the book ■ They're pulling *every trick in the book* to keep this amendment off the 1992 ballot.

excellence An overworked word (SEE). The word is overworked and the concept undervalued. Too much, today, passes for *excellence*. Too much of our work is shoddy, too much of our wisdom, suspect, too much of our worth, unsure. ■ With your help, we will continue that tradition of *excellence*. SEE ALSO *pursue (strive for) excellence*.

except for the grace of God (go I)

excess baggage A moribund metaphor (SEE).

excess verbiage A dimwitted redundancy (SEE). *verbiage.*

exciting opportunity

excruciating pain An inescapable pair (SEE). ■ This medication was initially prescribed to soothe the *excruciating pain* I was suffering.

excuse me? An infantile phrase (SEE). No longer exclusively a polite way of signifying that you did not hear what a person has said, *excuse me* is also an impolite way of signifying that you did not like what a person has said. With an autocratic intonation, the person expresses hostility to what he hears. This phrase is particularly loathsome, for those who use it dare not be openly angry or upset; they try to disguise their anger and arrogance behind a mantle of mannerliness. SEE ALSO *I'm sorry; thank you.*

excuse (pardon) the pun

exercise in futility

expand (your) horizons

expert opinion A suspect superlative (SEE).

expletive deleted An infantile phrase (SEE).

explore every avenue A moribund metaphor (SEE).

express (concern) A torpid term (SEE). Phrases like *express concern, express doubt, express opposition, express thanks* make any sentence instantly sodden. ■ Officials *express concern* about the slow pace of economic growth. REPLACE WITH *worry*. ■ House Democrats continue to *express anger* about the state's ethics and campaign finance laws. REPLACE WITH *fume*. ■ I want to *express my appreciation to* all of you who have lent us a hand in this endeavor. REPLACE WITH *thank*. SEE ALSO *voice (concern)*.

extend (hold out) the olive branch   A moribund metaphor (SEE). *peace offering*.

extent   A torpid term (SEE). Like *degree*, the word *extent*, along with the phrases in which it is found, is best avoided.

These are lifeless expressions, and it is listless people who use them. ■ In some cases, they've been transformed *to such an extent* that you can no longer recognize them. REPLACE WITH *so much*. ■ The study said that women, *to a greater extent* than men, manage by personal interactions with their subordinates. REPLACE WITH *more*. ■ Resources are always used *to the optimum extent*. REPLACE WITH *optimumly*. ■ Sooner or later, we will see *to what extent* the central banks are

prepared to back up words with actions. REPLACE WITH *how far*. ■ *The extent to which* these practices are seen as flowing in one direction, down from headquarters to subsidiaries, may influence *the extent to which* these practices are adopted and *to what extent* the behavior, beliefs and values of the corporate culture are incorporated or even complied with. REPLACE WITH *How much, how much* and *how much*. SEE ALSO *degree*.

extenuating circumstances   An inescapable pair (SEE).

extraordinary measure

(his) eyes are bigger than (his) stomach   A moribund metaphor (SEE).

eyes are the windows of the soul   A moribund metaphor (SEE).

eyewitness accounts

fabulous An overworked word (SEE). As still another synonym for *very good* or *extremely pleasing*, *fabulous* is indeed overused. In its sense of *hard to believe* or *astounding*, it is now and again used, and in its sense of *like a fable* or *legendary*, it is woefully unused.

face an uncertain future

(let's) face (the) facts

face the music A moribund metaphor (SEE).

face up to reality

fact is stranger than fiction

(a) factor A torpid term (SEE). ■ I think the TV show *was a contributing factor* to this tragedy. REPLACE WITH *contributed*. ■ They thought the biggest problem we were dealing with was *a jealousy factor*. REPLACE WITH *jealousy*. ■ The *key factor in* the decline appears to be the Irish-American voter's willingness to vote for candidates from other ethnic groups. REPLACE WITH *key to*. SEE ALSO *(an) element*.

factor into the equation

facts and figures An inescapable pair (SEE).

facts and information A dimwitted redundancy (SEE). *data; facts; information*.

fade from the picture

fade into the sunset A moribund metaphor (SEE). *disappear; disperse; dissolve; evaporate; fade; vanish; vaporize*.

fade into the woodwork A moribund metaphor (SEE). *disappear; disperse; dissolve; evaporate; fade; vanish; vaporize*.

fading fast *beat; bushed; drowsy; exhausted; fatigued; sleepy; spent; tired; weary; worn out*.

fail to materialize

fair and equitable An inescapable pair (SEE). *equitable; fair; just*. ■ The key to maintaining that system is ensuring that you are treated *fairly and equitably*. REPLACE WITH *equitably* or *fairly*.

fair and square An inescapable pair (SEE). *aboveboard; creditable; equitable;*

fair; honest; honorable; just; lawful; legitimate; open; proper; reputable; respectable; right; square; straightforward; upright; veracious; veridical.

fair game   A moribund metaphor (SEE).

fair is fair   A quack equation (SEE).

fair shake

fair share   *allocation; allotment; allowance; amount; apportionment; dole; lot; measure; part; piece; portion; quota; ration; share.* ■ We are setting out to get our *fair share* of the residential real estate mortgage business.

fair to middling   A dimwitted redundancy (SEE). *average; common; fair; mediocre; middling; moderate; ordinary; passable; tolerable.*

fait accompli   A foreignism (SEE).

fall between (through) the cracks   A moribund metaphor (SEE).

fall by the wayside   A moribund metaphor (SEE). *abate; cease to be; diminish; disappear; dissolve; dwindle; fade; go away; recede; vanish.* ■ Social class distinctions have mostly *fallen by the wayside*, and scientists are now more likely to admit the collective nature of research. REPLACE WITH *disappeared.*

fall flat on (its) face   A moribund metaphor (SEE). *be unsuccessful; blunder; bomb; break down; bungle; collapse; fail; fall short; falter; fizzle; flop; fold; founder; mess up; miscarry; not succeed; stumble; topple.* ■ Some professional

investors are betting the company will *fall flat on its face.* REPLACE WITH *fail.*

fall from grace   *collapse; decline; downfall; failure; fall; misadventure; misfortune; offense; peccadillo; ruin; sin; transgression; wrongdoing.*

fall hopelessly behind

fall in (into) line (place)   A moribund metaphor (SEE). *abide by; accede; accommodate; accord; acquiesce; adapt; adhere to; agree; behave; comply; concur; conform; correspond; follow; harmonize; heed; mind; obey; observe; submit; yield.*

fall into (my) lap   A moribund metaphor (SEE).

fall on deaf ears   A moribund metaphor (SEE). *disregard; ignore.*

fall on hard times

fall out of favor

fall (all) over each other

fall through the cracks   A moribund metaphor (SEE). *discount; disregard; elide; ignore; leave out; miss; neglect; omit; overlook; slight.*

false sense of security

fame and fortune   A suspect superlative (SEE). SEE ALSO *the rich and famous.*

(has a) familiar ring

fancy meeting you here

fan (fuel) the fire (flames)
A moribund metaphor (SEE). *activate;*

agitate; animate; arouse; awaken; encourage; enkindle; enliven; exacerbate; excite; feed; foment; ignite; impassion; incite; inflame; intensify; invigorate; make worse; nourish; prod; provoke; rejuvenate; revitalize; revive; rouse; shake up; stimulate; stir up; vitalize; worsen.

far and away   A dimwitted redundancy (SEE). *by far; much.*

far and wide   An inescapable pair (SEE). *all around; all over; all through; everyplace; everywhere; extensively; throughout.*

far be it from me to

far from the maddening (madding) crowd

far-reaching consequences (implications)   An inescapable pair (SEE).

farthest reaches

fashion statement   A plebeian sentiment (SEE). Making a *fashion statement* is the concern of those who have yet to fashion for themselves a sense of identity. Their habiliments interest them more than does their humanity.

People so intent on being fashionable make only misstatements. They but blither.

fast and furious   An inescapable pair (SEE).

fast approaching

(as) fast as (her) legs can carry (her)   An insipid simile (SEE moribund metaphors). *abruptly; apace; at once; briskly; directly; expeditiously;* fast; forthwith; hastily; hurriedly; immediately; instantaneously; instantly; posthaste; promptly; quickly; rapidly; rashly; right away; speedily; straightaway; swiftly; wingedly.

fast buck

fasten your seat belts   A moribund metaphor (SEE).

faster than a speeding bullet, (more powerful than a locomotive, able to leap tall buildings at a single bound)   An infantile phrase (SEE).

fast track   A moribund metaphor (SEE).

fast trigger finger   A moribund metaphor (SEE).

fatal attraction

fatal flaw

(as) fat as a cow   An insipid simile (SEE moribund metaphors). *ample; big; bulky; chubby; chunky; colossal; corpulent; dumpy; enormous; fat; flabby; fleshy; gigantic; heavy; hefty; huge; immense; large; mammoth; massive; obese; plump; portly; pudgy; rotund; round; squat; stocky; stout.*

(as) fat as a pig   An insipid simile (SEE moribund metaphors). *ample; big; bulky; chubby; chunky; colossal; corpulent; dumpy; enormous; fat; flabby; fleshy; gigantic; heavy; hefty; huge; immense; large; mammoth; massive; obese; plump; portly; pudgy; rotund; round; squat; stocky; stout.*

fat cat   A moribund metaphor (SEE).

fat chance

fateful day

fear and trembling   An inescapable pair (SEE). *alarm; anxiety; apprehension; consternation; dismay; dread; fear; foreboding; fright; horror; panic; terror; trembling; trepidation.*

feast or famine   An inescapable pair (SEE).

feather (their) nest   A moribund metaphor (SEE). ■ He repeatedly denied allegations that he used his three years at the Denver-based thrift to *feather his own nest.*

feed (you) a line   *deceive; dissemble; distort; equivocate; falsify; fib; lie; misconstrue; mislead; misrepresent; pervert; prevaricate.*

feedback   A torpid term (SEE). *answers; data; feelings; ideas; information; recommendations; replies; responses; suggestions; thoughts; views.* ■ Your *feedback helps* us continually improve. REPLACE WITH *suggestions help.* ■ And as *feedback is* obtained, it is the duty of the firm's leaders to convey it to all members of the firm. REPLACE WITH *ideas are.* SEE ALSO *(the) bottom line; input; interface; output; parameters.*

feeding frenzy

feeling no pain   A moribund metaphor (SEE). *besotted; crapulous; drunk; inebriated; intoxicated; sodden; stupefied; tipsy.*

feeling (his) oats   A moribund metaphor (SEE). *active; alive; animated; dy-*

namic; energetic; frisky; hearty; indefatigable; inexhaustible; lively; peppy; spirited; sprightly; spry; tireless; unflagging; vibrant; vigorous; vivacious.

(I) feel it in (my) bones

feel the heat   A moribund metaphor (SEE).

feel the pinch   A moribund metaphor (SEE).

ferret out the truth

fertile ground   A moribund metaphor (SEE).

few and far between   *exiguous; limited; inadequate; infrequent; meager; rare; scant; scanty; scarce; sparse; uncommon; unusual.* ■ Role models are *few and far between* in those groups. REPLACE WITH *scarce.*

(every) fiber of (his) being

fiddle while Rome burns   A moribund metaphor (SEE).

field of battle   A moribund metaphor (SEE).

fierce determination to win

fight a losing battle   A moribund metaphor (SEE).

fight fire with fire   A moribund metaphor (SEE).

fighting chance   ■ But I now think we have a *fighting chance* to bring it back to life.

fight like cats and dogs   An insipid

simile (SEE moribund metaphors).
1. *altercate; argue; disagree; dispute; feud; fight; quarrel; spat; squabble; wrangle.*
2. *battle; brawl; clash; fight; grapple; jostle; make war; scuffle; skirmish; tussle; war; wrestle.*

fight the good fight

fight to stay afloat

fight to the death (finish)

figment of (his) imagination

figure on *anticipate; calculate; count; estimate; expect; plan on.*

filled to bursting (overflowing) *abounding; brimful; brimming; bursting; chock-full; congested; crammed; crowded; dense; filled; full; gorged; jammed; jam-packed; overcrowded; overfilled; overflowing; packed; replete; saturated; stuffed; swarming; teeming.*

filled to the brim A moribund metaphor (SEE). *abounding; brimful; brimming; bursting; chock-full; congested; crammed; crowded; dense; filled; full; gorged; jammed; jam-packed; overcrowded; overfilled; overflowing; packed; replete; saturated; stuffed; swarming; teeming.*

filled with anticipation

fill in the blanks An infantile phrase (SEE).

fill (his) shoes A moribund metaphor (SEE).

fill the bill A moribund metaphor (SEE).

fill to capacity A dimwitted redundancy (SEE). *fill.* ■ Our free public facilities are *filled to capacity*, and there are long waiting lists for some programs. USE *filled.*

filthy lucre A moribund metaphor (SEE).

filthy rich

final and irrevocable An inescapable pair (SEE). *final; firm; irrevocable; unalterable.*

final chapter A moribund metaphor (SEE). *close; completion; conclusion; consummation; culmination; denouement; end; ending; finale; finish; termination.*

final culmination A dimwitted redundancy (SEE). *culmination.* ■ Owning a farm was the *final culmination* of all our efforts. DELETE *final.*

final decision A dimwitted redundancy (SEE). *decision.* ■ That's one of the things we have under consideration, but no *final decision* has been made. DELETE *final.*

finalize A torpid term (SEE). *complete; conclude; consummate; end; execute; finish; fulfill; make final; terminate.* ■ Delays in *finalizing* the state budget and its allocations to cities and towns make a special town meeting necessary. REPLACE WITH *completing.* SEE ALSO *utilize.*

financial setback

finders keepers, losers weepers An infantile phrase (SEE).

(like) finding (looking for) a needle in a haystack An insipid simile (SEE moribund metaphors).

find (some) middle ground A moribund metaphor (SEE). *compromise.*

fine and dandy An inescapable pair (SEE). *all right; excellent; fine; good; O.K.; well.* SEE ALSO *well and good.*

fine line A moribund metaphor (SEE). ■ There is a very *fine line* between vision and delusion.

(their) finest hour

fingers on the pulse of A moribund metaphor (SEE).

finishing touches

fire and brimstone A moribund metaphor (SEE).

fire (launch) a salvo A moribund metaphor (SEE).

(all) fired (hopped, psyched) up *afire; anxious; ardent; burning; eager; enthusiastic; excited; fanatic; fanatical; fervent; fervid; fiery; impassioned; inflamed; intense; keen; passionate; pervervid; vehement; zealous.*

firm commitment

firmly establish An inescapable pair (SEE). Adverbs often modify other words needlessly. Here, *firmly* is superfluous, for *establish* means "to make firm." ■ The play *firmly established* him as a dramatist. DELETE *firmly.*

first and foremost A dimwitted re-

dundancy (SEE). *chief; chiefly; first; foremost; initial; initially; main; mainly; most important; mostly; primarily; primary; principal; principally.* ■ *First and foremost* these people must have a commitment to public service. USE *Most important.* SEE ALSO *first and most important.*

first and most important A dimwitted redundancy (SEE). *chief; chiefly; first; foremost; initial; initially; main; mainly; most important; mostly; primarily; primary; principal; principally.* SEE ALSO *first and foremost.*

first begin (start) A dimwitted redundancy (SEE). *begin; start.* ■ When we *first started* exploring the idea, we didn't even know if it was possible to do. DELETE *first.*

first line of defense A moribund metaphor (SEE).

first of all A dimwitted redundancy (SEE). *first.* ■ *First of all*, I am delighted about our progress in that area. USE *First.* SEE ALSO *second of all.*

first priority A torpid term (SEE). ■ When people are house searching, their *first priority* is the town's public schools. REPLACE WITH *principal consideration.* SEE ALSO *number-one priority; top priority.*

first things first

fish or cut bait A moribund metaphor (SEE).

(other) fish to fry A moribund metaphor (SEE).

(as) fit as a fiddle An insipid simile

(SEE moribund metaphors). *athletic;
beefy; brawny; energetic; fit; good; hale;
hardy; healthful; healthy; hearty; husky;
lanky; lean; manly; muscular; powerful;
robust; shapely; sinewy; slender; solid;
sound; stalwart; stout; strong; sturdy;
thin; trim; vigorous; virile; well; well-
built.*

fit for a king A moribund metaphor
(SEE).

fits (him) to a T A moribund metaphor (SEE).

fitting and proper An inescapable
pair (SEE). *appropriate; apt; befitting;
felicitous; fit; fitting; happy; meet;
proper; right; seemly; suitable; suited.*
■ And it is generally regarded as *fitting
and proper* for women to do this. RE-
PLACE WITH *fitting*.

fit to be tied A moribund metaphor
(SEE). *angry; cross; enraged; fuming;
furious; incensed; indignant; infuriated; irate; mad; outraged; raging;
wrathful.*

fix (her) wagon A moribund metaphor (SEE).
1. *castigate; censure; chasten; chastise;
chide; criticize; discipline; penalize;
punish; rebuke; reprove; scold.*
2. *spank.*

flaming inferno An infantile phrase
(SEE).

flash in the pan A moribund metaphor (SEE).

(as) flat as a board An insipid simile (SEE moribund metaphors). *even;
flat; flush; horizontal; level; plane;
smooth.*

(as) flat as a pancake An insipid
simile (SEE moribund metaphors).
*even; flat; flush; horizontal; level; plane;
smooth.*

flat on (his) back A moribund metaphor (SEE). *afflicted; ailing; crippled;
debilitated; defenseless; disabled; diseased; feeble; fragile; helpless; ill; inca-
pacitated; indisposed; infirm; not (feeling) well; sick; sickly; unhealthy;
unwell; valetudinarian; weak.*

flattery will get you everywhere

flattery will get you nowhere

(one) fleeting moment

(my) (own) flesh and blood
A moribund metaphor (SEE).
1. *brother; child; daughter; father; kin;
mother; parent; relative; sibling; sister;
son.*
2. *depth; reality; substance.*

flight of fancy *caprice; chimera;
crotchet; daydream; delusion; dream;
fancy; fantasy; hallucination; humor; illusion; imagination; notion; phantasm;
vagary; whim; whimsy.*

flip (her) lid A moribund metaphor
(SEE). *bellow; bluster; clamor; explode;
fulminate; fume; holler; howl; rage;
rant; rave; roar; scream; shout; storm;
thunder; vociferate; yell.*

flip side (of the coin) A moribund
metaphor (SEE).

(whatever) floats your boat
A moribund metaphor (SEE).

flotsam and jetsam An inescapable pair (SEE).

1. *debris; litter; rack; refuse; rubbish; rubble; wrack; wreckage.*
2. *bits; fragments; modicums; odds and ends; particles; pieces; remnants; scraps; shreds; snippets; trifles.*
3. *itinerants; rovers; tramps; vagabonds; vagrants; wanderers.*

flowing with milk and honey A moribund metaphor (SEE).

fly (too) close to the sun A moribund metaphor (SEE). *chance; dare; endanger; gamble; hazard; imperil; jeopardize; make bold; peril; risk; venture.*

flying by the seat of (his) pants A moribund metaphor (SEE).

flying high A moribund metaphor (SEE).
1. *advantageous; auspicious; blessed; charmed; enchanted; favored; felicitous; flourishing; fortuitous; fortunate; golden; happy; in luck; lucky; propitious; prosperous; successful; thriving.*
2. *blissful; blithe; buoyant; cheerful; delighted; ecstatic; elated; enraptured; euphoric; exalted; excited; exhilarated; exultant; gay; glad; gleeful; good-humored; happy; intoxicated; jolly; jovial; joyful; joyous; jubilant; merry; mirthful; overjoyed; pleased; rapturous; thrilled.*

fly in the face of *challenge; contradict; defy; dispute; disregard.* ■ This is nonsensical and *flies in the face of* history and basic economic principles. REPLACE WITH *contradicts.*

fly in the ointment A moribund metaphor (SEE). *bar; barrier; block; blockage; catch; check; deterrent; difficulty; encumbrance; handicap; hindrance; hitch; hurdle; impediment; in-*terference; obstacle; obstruction; rub; snag.*

fly off the handle A moribund metaphor (SEE). *bellow; bluster; clamor; explode; fulminate; fume; holler; howl; rage; rant; rave; roar; scream; shout; storm; thunder; vociferate; yell.*

fly the coop A moribund metaphor (SEE). *abscond; clear out; decamp; depart; desert; disappear; escape; exit; flee; fly; go; go away; leave; move on; part; pull out; quit; retire; retreat; run away; take flight; take off; vacate; vanish; withdraw.*

foaming (frothing) at the mouth A moribund metaphor (SEE). *angry; berserk; convulsive; crazed; delirious; demented; demoniac; deranged; enraged; feral; ferocious; fierce; frantic; frenzied; fuming; furious; hysterical; infuriated; in hysterics; insane; incensed; irate; mad; maddened; maniacal; murderous; possessed; rabid; raging; ranting; raving; savage; seething; wild; wrathful.*

focus attention (concentration) on A dimwitted redundancy (SEE). *concentrate on; focus on.* ■ Microsoft has always *focused its attention on* software products and software standards. USE *focused on.* ■ It is hardly magic to *focus concentration on* success instead of failure. USE *concentrate on.* SEE ALSO *focus effort (energy) on.*

focus effort (energy) on A dimwitted redundancy (SEE). *concentrate on; focus on.* ■ This downsizing will cut our expenses and allow us to *focus our efforts on* serving our customers. USE *focus on.* ■ Owners can *focus their energy on* expanding the business to a point where it can function outside of a "nurtured" environment. USE *focus on*. SEE ALSO *focus attention (concentration) on*.

focus in on A dimwitted redundancy (SEE). *focus on*. ■ I have to *focus in on* what I want to accomplish. DELETE *in*.

fold (their) tent A moribund metaphor (SEE). *abscond; clear out; decamp; depart; desert; disappear; escape; exit; flee; fly; go; go away; leave; move on; part; pull out; quit; retire; retreat; run away; take flight; take off; vacate; vanish; withdraw*.

follow in (her) footsteps A moribund metaphor (SEE).

follow suit A moribund metaphor (SEE). *copy; do as much; follow; imitate; mimic*. ■ NYNEX is expected to *follow suit* in the near future. REPLACE WITH *do as much*. ■ When American Airlines slashed fares, TWA *followed suit*. REPLACE WITH *did as much*.

follow the crowd A moribund metaphor (SEE). *abide by; accede; accommodate; accord; acquiesce; adapt; adhere to; agree; behave; comply; concur; conform; correspond; follow; harmonize; heed; mind; obey; observe; submit; yield*.

follow to the letter *accurately; correctly; exactly; precisely; rightly; strictly*.

follow your instincts A popular prescription (SEE).

food for thought A moribund metaphor (SEE). SEE ALSO *(it's) something to think about*.

food for worms A moribund metaphor (SEE). *dead; deceased; defunct; departed; exanimate; expired; extinct; extinguished; finished; gone; inanimate; lifeless; no more; perished; terminated*.

fools rush in where angels fear to tread

footloose and fancy free *at liberty; autonomous; free; independent; self-reliant; unattached; unbound; unconfined; unconstrained; unencumbered; unentangled; unfettered; uninhibited; unrestrained; unrestricted; unshackled; untied*.

footnote to history

footprints in the sands of time A moribund metaphor (SEE).

foot the bill

for a limited time (only)

for all intents and purposes A dimwitted redundancy (SEE). *effectively; essentially; in effect; in essence; practically; virtually*. ■ *For all intents and purposes*, the civil rights acts of 1964 and 1965 signified the demise of official segregation in the United States. USE *In effect*. SEE ALSO *for all practical purposes; to all intents and purposes; to all practical purposes*.

for all practical purposes A dimwitted redundancy (SEE). *effectively; essentially; in effect; in essence; practically; virtually*. ■ Services are, *for all practical purposes*, sold as products to end users, so the distinction between services and goods is artificial at best. USE *essentially*. SEE ALSO *for all intents and purposes; to all intents and pur-*

poses; *to all practical purposes*.

for better or worse

foregone conclusion   An inescapable pair (SEE).

foreignisms   Expressions such as *ad infinitum, ad nauseam, crème de la crème, fait accompli, in loco parentis, je ne sais quoi, joie de vivre, mea culpa, mirabile dictu, modus vivendi, ne plus ultra, non compos mentis, par excellence, persona non grata, quid pro quo, raison d'être, sine qua non, très, verboten* and *vive la différence* are, of course, perfectly good foreign words and phrases, but when used by English-speaking people, they are simply tiresome. SEE ALSO *archaisms*.

forever and a day   *always; ceaselessly; constantly; continually; continuously; endlessly; eternally; everlastingly; evermore; forever; forevermore; immortally; indefinitely; interminably; permanently; perpetually; persistently; unceasingly; unremittingly*.

for every action there's an equal and opposite reaction   A popular prescription (SEE).

for every negative there is a positive   A popular prescription (SEE).

for everything there is a season   A popular prescription (SEE).

forewarn   A dimwitted redundancy (SEE). *warn*. ■ *Forewarn* your clients that they might be stared at by locals. USE *Warn*. SEE ALSO *advance warning; warn in advance*.

forewarned is forearmed   A quack equation (SEE).

for free   A dimwitted redundancy (SEE). *free*.

for generations to come

(let's) forget the whole thing

forgive and forget   A popular prescription (SEE).

(throw in) for good measure

fork in the road   A moribund metaphor (SEE).

fork (it) over   *pay; hand over*.

formative years   *adolescence; childhood; immaturity; juvenility*.

formidable foe

for no apparent reason

for services rendered

forsooth   An archaism (SEE). *actually; indeed; in fact; in faith; in reality; in truth; truly*.

(it's) for the birds   A moribund metaphor (SEE).
1. *absurd; asinine; childish; comical; farcical; fatuous; flighty; foolhardy; foolish; frivolous; giddy; idiotic; immature; inane; laughable; ludicrous; nonsensical; preposterous; ridiculous; senseless; silly*.
2. *barren; bootless; effete; feckless; feeble; fruitless; futile; impotent; inadequate; inconsequential; inconsiderable; ineffective; ineffectual; infertile; insignificant; inutile; meaningless; meritless; nugatory; null; of no value; pointless; powerless; profitless; sterile; trifling; trivial; unavailing; unimportant;*

unproductive; unprofitable; unservice-able; unworthy; useless; vain; valueless; weak; worthless.

for the duration

for the (simple) fact that   A dimwitted redundancy (SEE). *because; considering; for; in that; since.* ▪ Women received some assistance in the colonial period *for the simple fact that* American Protestants strongly favored "peaceable" and intact families. USE *because.* SEE ALSO *for the (simple) reason that.*

for the life of me

for the most part   A dimwitted redundancy (SEE). *almost all; chiefly; commonly; generally; greatly; in general; largely; mainly; most; mostly; most often; much; nearly all; normally; overall; typically; usually.* ▪ The search for solutions to these crises has focused *for the most part* on the legal system. USE *largely.*

for (with) the purpose of (-ing)
A dimwitted redundancy (SEE). *for (-ing); so as to; to.* ▪ These analyses have been used *for the purpose of criticizing* the shortcomings of Western management. USE *for criticizing* or *to criticize.*

for the (simple) reason that
A dimwitted redundancy (SEE). *because; considering; for; in that; since.* ▪ Polls dominate political discourse *for the simple reason that* "Everyone else has an opinion; the pollster has a fact." USE *because.* SEE ALSO *for the (simple) fact that.*

for the record

for the umpteenth time

for what(ever) it's worth

for your information   An ineffectual phrase (SEE). ▪ *For your information,* he loves me, and I love him. DELETE *For your information.*

fought (me) all the way

foul up (gum up; screw up) the works   A moribund metaphor (SEE). 1. *agitate; confuse; disorder; disorganize; disquiet; disrupt; disturb; fluster; jar; jinx; jolt; jumble; mix up; muddle; perturb; rattle; ruffle; shake up; stir up; unnerve; unsettle; upset.*
2. *blight; cripple; damage; disable; harm; hurt; impair; incapacitate; lame; mar; mess up; rack; ruin; sabotage; spoil; subvert; undermine; vitiate; wrack; wreck.*

fragile hold on

frame of reference

fraught with danger   *dangerous; hazardous; ominous; perilous; precarious; risky.*

fraught with difficulty   *arduous; backbreaking; burdensome; difficult; exhausting; fatiguing; hard; herculean; laborious; not easy; onerous; severe; strenuous; toilful; toilsome; tough; trying; wearisome.*

fraught with meaning   *meaningful; pregnant; significant.*

free and easy   *casual; carefree; easygoing; informal; insouciant; lighthearted; nonchalant; relaxed; untroubled.*

free and gratis   An infantile phrase (SEE). *free.*

(as) free as a bird   An insipid simile (SEE moribund metaphors). *autonomous; free; independent; self-reliant; unattached; unbound; unconfined; unconstrained; unencumbered; unentangled; unfettered; uninhibited; unrestrained; unrestricted; unshackled; untied.*

(as) free as the wind   An insipid simile (SEE moribund metaphors). *autonomous; free; independent; self-reliant; unattached; unbound; unconfined; unconstrained; unencumbered; unentangled; unfettered; uninhibited; unrestrained; unrestricted; unshackled; untied.*

free exchange of ideas   ■ There was a *free exchange of ideas* about the best ways to teach.

free gift   A dimwitted redundancy (SEE). *gift.* ■ With every renewal, you will receive a *free gift.* DELETE *free.*

free lunch   A moribund metaphor (SEE).

free rein   A moribund metaphor (SEE).

free ride   A moribund metaphor (SEE).

freezing cold   An inescapable pair (SEE). *algid; arctic; brumal; chilly; cold; cool; freezing; frigid; frosty; frozen; gelid; glacial; hibernal; hyperborean; ice-cold; icy; nippy; polar; rimy; wintry.*

frenzied pace

(as) fresh as a daisy   An insipid simile (SEE moribund metaphors). *active; alive; animated; blooming; dynamic; energetic; fresh; healthy; hearty; lively; peppy; refreshed; rested; rosey; ruddy; spirited; sprightly; spry; vibrant; vigorous; vivacious.*

fret and fume   An inescapable pair (SEE).

friend and foe alike

friend for life

friendly advice

frighten (scare) out of (her) wits   A moribund metaphor (SEE). *alarm; appall; benumb; daunt; frighten; horrify; intimidate; panic; paralyze; petrify; scare; shock; startle; terrify; terrorize.*

from a simmer to a hard boil   A moribund metaphor (SEE).

from A to Z   A moribund metaphor (SEE).
1. *all during; all over; all through; throughout.*
2. *altogether; completely; entirely; fully; perfectly; quite; thoroughly; totally; unreservedly; utterly; wholly.*

(go) from bad to worse

from beginning to end
1. *always; ceaselessly; constantly; continually; continuously; endlessly; eternally; everlastingly; evermore; forever; forevermore; frequently; interminably; nonstop; permanently; perpetually; persistently; recurrently; regularly; repeatedly; unceasingly; unremittingly.*
2. *all during; all over; all through; throughout.*

3. *altogether; completely; entirely; fully; perfectly; quite; thoroughly; totally; unreservedly; utterly; wholly.*

from (the) cradle to (the) grave
A moribund metaphor (SEE).
1. *always; ceaselessly; constantly; continually; continuously; endlessly; eternally; everlastingly; evermore; forever; forevermore; frequently; interminably; nonstop; permanently; perpetually; persistently; recurrently; regularly; repeatedly; unceasingly; unremittingly.*
2. *all during; all over; all through; throughout.*

from day one
from the beginning, from the first, from the start. ■ You have complained about me *from day one*. REPLACE WITH *from the first*.

from dusk to dawn
all day.

from hence
A dimwitted redundancy (SEE). *hence.*

from on high

from pillar to post
A moribund metaphor (SEE).

from rags to riches
A moribund metaphor (SEE).

from soup to nuts
A moribund metaphor (SEE). *all; all things; everything.*

from start to finish
1. *always; ceaselessly; constantly; continually; continuously; endlessly; eternally; everlastingly; evermore; forever; forevermore; frequently; interminably; nonstop; permanently; perpetually; persistently; recurrently; regularly; repeatedly; unceasingly; unremittingly.*

2. *all during; all over; all through; throughout.*

from stem to stern
A moribund metaphor (SEE).
1. *all during; all over; all through; throughout.*
2. *altogether; completely; entirely; fully; perfectly; quite; thoroughly; totally; unreservedly; utterly; wholly.*

from the bottom (depths) of (my) heart
A moribund metaphor (SEE).
earnestly; fervently; genuinely; heartily; honestly; sincerely; unreservedly; wholeheartedly.

from the comfort of your own home

from the frying pan into the fire
A moribund metaphor (SEE).

from the ground up

(straight) from the horses mouth
A moribund metaphor (SEE).

from the sublime to the ridiculous

from the word go
from the beginning, from the first, from the start.

from time immemorial

from top to bottom
1. *all during; all over; all through; throughout.*
2. *altogether; completely; entirely; fully; perfectly; quite; thoroughly; totally; unreservedly; utterly; wholly.*

from whence
A dimwitted redundancy (SEE). *whence.* ■ *From whence* comes your accent? DELETE *From.*

from where (I) sit

front and center

fruits of (their) labor

fuel speculation

fuel the fire of   A moribund metaphor (SEE).

full capacity   A dimwitted redundancy (SEE). *capacity.* ■ Buses are running closer to *full capacity* than at any time since the strike began. DELETE *full.*

full frontal assault   A moribund metaphor (SEE).

full of (herself)   *egocentric; egoistic; egotistic; egotistical; narcissistic; self-absorbed; selfish; solipsistic.*

full of beans   A moribund metaphor (SEE).
1. *active; alive; animated; dynamic; energetic; indefatigable; inexhaustible; lively; peppy; spirited; sprightly; spry; tireless; unflagging; vibrant; vigorous; vivacious.*
2. *amiss; astray; deceived; deluded; erring; erroneous; fallacious; false; faulty; inaccurate; incorrect; in error; misguided; misinformed; misled; mistaken; not correct; not right; wrong.*

full of holes   A moribund metaphor (SEE).
1. *defective; faulty; flawed; impaired; imperfect; marred; tainted.*
2. *baseless; captious; casuistic; casuistical; erroneous; fallacious; false; faulty; flawed; groundless; illogical; inaccurate; incorrect; invalid; irrational; jesuitic; jesuitical; mistaken; nonsensical; non sequitur; paralogistic; senseless; sophistic; sophistical; specious; spurious;*

unfounded; unreasonable; unsound; untenable; untrue; unveracious; wrong.

full of hot air   A moribund metaphor (SEE).
1. *aggrandizing; blustering; boasting; bragging; coloring; crowing; elaborating; embellishing; embroidering; exaggerating; fanfaronading; gloating; hyperbolizing; magnifying; overstating; swaggering.*
2. *amiss; astray; deceived; deluded; erring; erroneous; fallacious; false; faulty; inaccurate; incorrect; in error; misguided; misinformed; misled; mistaken; not correct; not right; wrong.*

full of piss and vinegar   A moribund metaphor (SEE). *active; alive; animated; dynamic; energetic; hearty; indefatigable; inexhaustible; lively; peppy; spirited; sprightly; spry; tireless; unflagging; vibrant; vigorous; vivacious.*

full of vim and vigor   A moribund metaphor (SEE). *active; alive; animated; dynamic; energetic; hearty; indefatigable; inexhaustible; lively; peppy; spirited; sprightly; spry; tireless; unflagging; vibrant; vigorous; vivacious.*

full plate   A moribund metaphor (SEE). *booked; busy; employed; engaged; involved; obligated; occupied.*

full potential   A dimwitted redundancy (SEE). *potential.* ■ Youngsters with talents that range from mathematical to musical are not challenged to work to their *full potential.* DELETE *full.*

(at) full speed (ahead)   A moribund metaphor (SEE). *abruptly; apace; at once; briskly; directly; expeditiously; fast; forthwith; hastily; hurriedly; imme-*

diately; instantaneously; instantly; post-haste; promptly; quickly; rapidly; rashly; right away; speedily; straightaway; swiftly; wingedly.

(at) full steam (ahead) A moribund metaphor (SEE). *abruptly; apace; at once; briskly; directly; expeditiously; fast; forthwith; hastily; hurriedly; immediately; instantaneously; instantly; post-haste; promptly; quickly; rapidly; rashly; right away; speedily; straightaway; swiftly; wingedly.*

fulsome praise An inescapable pair (SEE).

fun in the sun

funny you should ask

G

gain a foothold   A moribund metaphor (SEE).

gainfully employed   *employed; working.*

gain steam   A moribund metaphor (SEE).

gala affair

game of cat and mouse   A moribund metaphor (SEE).

game plan   A moribund metaphor (SEE). *action; course; direction; intention; method; move; plan; policy; procedure; route; scheme; strategy.*

game, set and match   A moribund metaphor (SEE).

garden variety   A moribund metaphor (SEE). *average; common; commonplace; customary; everyday; fair; mediocre; middling; normal; ordinary; passable; plain; quotidian; regular; routine; simple; standard; tolerable; typical; uneventful; unexceptional; unremarkable; usual.*

gather dust   A moribund metaphor (SEE).

gather together   A dimwitted redundancy (SEE). *gather.* ■ This summer's training provided all 1,500 youth an opportunity to *gather together* from around the country and to develop their skills and knowledge. DELETE *together*.

(I) gave (him) the best years of (my) life   A plebeian sentiment (SEE).

gaze into a crystal ball   A moribund metaphor (SEE). *anticipate; augur; divine; envision; forebode; forecast; foreknow; foresee; foretell; predict; prognosticate; prophesy; vaticinate.*

general consensus   A dimwitted redundancy (SEE). *consensus.* ■ The *general consensus* is that house prices have hit bottom. DELETE *general*.

generous to a fault

(as) gentle as a lamb   An insipid simile (SEE moribund metaphors). *affable; agreeable; amiable; amicable; compassionate; friendly; gentle; goodhearted; humane; kind; kindhearted; kindly; personable; pleasant; tender; tolerant.*

gentleman   A suspect superlative

(SEE). Slipshod usage has reduced *gentleman* to a vulgarism. Common or crude people say *gentleman* when *man* would serve; though *gentleman* may sound dignified, it is actually dimwitted. ■ I am seeking a professional *gentleman* with diversified interests. USE *man*. ■ One *gentleman* told me it is a fantasy world and not to believe everything I hear. USE *man*. SEE ALSO *lady*.

get (our) act together   An infantile phrase (SEE). ■ They don't have the luxury of five years to *get their act together*.

get (has) a fix on   *ascertain; assess; comprehend; determine; evaluate; learn; understand.*

get (has) a handle on
1. *cope with; deal with.*
2. *ascertain; assess; comprehend; determine; evaluate; learn; understand.*

get a life   An infantile phrase (SEE).

get an earful   A moribund metaphor (SEE).

get at the root of the problem

get away with murder   A moribund metaphor (SEE).

get (my) back up   A moribund metaphor (SEE). *acerbate; anger; annoy; bother; bristle; chafe; enrage; exasperate; gall; incense; inflame; infuriate; irk; irritate; madden; miff; pique; provoke; rile; vex.*

get (his) dander up   A moribund metaphor (SEE). *acerbate; anger; annoy; bother; bristle; chafe; enrage; exasperate; gall; incense; inflame; infuri-*

ate; irk; irritate; madden; miff; pique; provoke; rile; vex.

get down to brass tacks   A moribund metaphor (SEE).

get down to business

get (your) facts straight

get (their) feet wet   A moribund metaphor (SEE).

get (your) foot in the door   A moribund metaphor (SEE).

get (my) goat   A moribund metaphor (SEE). *acerbate; anger; annoy; bother; bristle; chafe; enrage; incense; inflame; infuriate; irk; irritate; madden; miff; provoke; rile; vex.* ■ "In denial" is one of those politically correct terms that *gets my goat*. REPLACE WITH *infuriates me*.

get (her) hackles up   A moribund metaphor (SEE). *acerbate; anger; annoy; bother; bristle; chafe; enrage; incense; inflame; infuriate; insult; irk; irritate; madden; miff; offend; provoke; rile; vex.*

get (his) head examined

get (your) house in order   A moribund metaphor (SEE).

get in (my) hair   A moribund metaphor (SEE). *annoy; badger; bedevil; bother; chafe; distress; disturb; gall; grate; harass; harry; hassle; heckle; hector; hound; irk; irritate; nag; nettle; persecute; pester; plague; provoke; rankle; tease; torment; vex.*

get in on the ground floor   A moribund metaphor (SEE).

get into the act   A moribund metaphor (SEE).

get in touch with (your) feelings   A popular prescription (SEE).

get (your) licks in

get (their) money's worth

get off (my) back   A moribund metaphor (SEE).

get (it) off (your) chest   A moribund metaphor (SEE). *acknowledge; admit; affirm; allow; avow; concede; confess; disclose; divulge; expose; grant; own; reveal; tell; uncover; unveil.*

get off easy

get off on the wrong foot   A moribund metaphor (SEE).

get off the ground   A moribund metaphor (SEE). *begin; commence; embark; inaugurate; initiate; introduce; launch; originate; start.* ■ Like all true entrepreneurs, they were eager to *get* another project *off the ground.* REPLACE WITH *launch.*

get on (my) nerves   A moribund metaphor (SEE). *annoy; badger; bedevil; bother; chafe; distress; disturb; gall; grate; harass; harry; hassle; heckle; hector; hound; irk; irritate; nag; nettle; persecute; pester; plague; provoke; rankle; tease; torment; vex.*

get on the stick   A moribund metaphor (SEE).

get on with (my) life   A popular prescription (SEE).

get out of Dodge   A moribund metaphor (SEE).

get (it) out of (your) system   A moribund metaphor (SEE). *acknowledge; admit; affirm; allow; avow; concede; confess; disclose; divulge; expose; grant; own; reveal; tell; uncover; unveil.*

get (your) priorities straight   A popular prescription (SEE).

get the ax   A moribund metaphor (SEE). *canned; discharged; dismissed; fired; let go; ousted; released; sacked; terminated.*

get (start) the ball rolling   A moribund metaphor (SEE).

get (give) the bum's rush   A moribund metaphor (SEE). *chuck; eject; expel; fling; throw out.*

(I) get the picture   A moribund metaphor (SEE). *appreciate; apprehend; comprehend; discern; fathom; grasp; know; perceive; realize; recognize; see; understand.*

get the word out

(let's) get this show on the road   A moribund metaphor (SEE). *begin; commence; embark; inaugurate; initiate; launch; originate; start.*

get to the bottom of (this)   ■ I make no pretense about *getting to the bottom of* things.

get to the heart of (the matter)

get under (my) skin   A moribund metaphor (SEE). *acerbate; anger; annoy; bother; bristle; chafe; disturb;*

exasperate; gall; grate; irk; irritate; miff; nettle; provoke; rankle; rile; upset; vex.

get-up-and-go   A moribund metaphor (SEE). *ambition; bounce; dash; drive; dynamism; élan; energy; enthusiasm; initiative; liveliness; motivation; spirit; verve; vigor; vim; vitality; vivacity; zeal.*

(full of) get-up-and-go   A moribund metaphor (SEE). *active; alive; ambitious; animated; dynamic; energetic; enthusiastic; indefatigable; inexhaustible; lively; motivated; peppy; spirited; sprightly; spry; tireless; unflagging; vibrant; vigorous; vivacious.*

get up on the wrong side of the bed   A moribund metaphor (SEE). *bad-tempered; cantankerous; crabby; cranky; cross; disagreeable; grouchy; ill-humored; ill-natured; ill-tempered; irascible; irritable; peevish; petulant; quarrelsome; splenetic; sullen; surly; testy.*

get (her) walking papers   *canned; discharged; dismissed; fired; let go; ousted; released; sacked; terminated.*

get wind of   A moribund metaphor (SEE). *ascertain; become aware of; discover; find out; hear about; learn.*

get (our) wires crossed   A moribund metaphor (SEE).

(it'll) get worse before it gets better   ■ Things will *get worse* at the bank *before they get better.*

gild the lily   A moribund metaphor (SEE).

give (me) a break

give (her) a bum steer   *bamboozle; befool; beguile; betray; bilk; bluff; cheat; con; deceive; defraud; delude; dupe; feint; fool; gyp; hoodwink; lead astray; misdirect; misguide; misinform; mislead; spoof; swindle; trick.*

(I don't) give a damn   *(I don't) care.*

give (her) a dose (taste) of (her) own medicine   A moribund metaphor (SEE).

(don't) give a hoot   *(don't) care.*
■ Americans are supposedly more conscious of their fat and calorie intake, but it seems they *don't give a hoot* when it comes to ice cream. REPLACE WITH *don't care.*

give and take   *collaboration; cooperation; exchange; reciprocity.*

give (them) an inch and (they'll) take a mile   A moribund metaphor (SEE).

give (them) a piece of (his) mind   A moribund metaphor (SEE). *admonish; animadvert; berate; castigate; censure; chasten; chastise; chide; condemn; criticize; denounce; denunciate; discipline; impugn; objurgate; punish; rebuke; remonstrate; reprehend; reprimand; reproach; reprobate; reprove; revile; scold; upbraid; vituperate; warn.*

give (him) a run for (his) money   A moribund metaphor (SEE).

give away the store   A moribund metaphor (SEE).

give (her) a wide berth (to)   A moribund metaphor (SEE). *avoid;*

bypass; circumvent; dodge; elude; evade; shun; sidestep; skirt.

give birth (to)   *bring about; cause; effect; generate; give rise to; inaugurate; initiate; introduce; occasion; produce; provoke; result in.*

give credit where credit is due
A popular prescription (SEE).

give (my) eyeteeth (right arm) for   A moribund metaphor (SEE).

give it a rest
1. *be silent; be still; hush; keep quiet; quiet; silence.*
2. *cease; close; complete; conclude; derail; desist; discontinue; end; finish; halt; quit; settle; stop; terminate.*

give it a shot (whirl)   *aim; attempt; endeavor; essay; exert; labor; strain; strive; struggle; toil; try hard; undertake; work at.*

give it (take) (your) best shot
A moribund metaphor (SEE). *aim; attempt; endeavor; essay; exert; labor; strain; strive; struggle; toil; try hard; undertake; work at.*

give new meaning to

given the fact that   A dimwitted redundancy (SEE). *because; considering; for; in that; since; when.* ■ *Given the fact that* all kibbutz youth were inducted into the army and commingled with tens of thousands of potential mates from outside their kibbutz before they got married, the rate of 200 marriages from within the same kibbutz is far more than could be expected by chance. USE *Since.* SEE ALSO *because of the fact that; by virtue of the*

fact that; considering the fact that; in view of the fact that.

give short shrift to

(it) gives (me) something to do
A plebeian sentiment (SEE). SEE ALSO *(it) keeps (me) busy; (it) keeps (me) out of trouble; (it's) something to do.*

give (him) the back of (my) hand
abuse; affront; disdain; insult; offend; outrage; scorn.

give (him) the benefit of the doubt

give (her) the brush (brush-off)
A moribund metaphor (SEE). *abuse; affront; avoid; disdain; disregard; ignore; insult; neglect; offend; outrage; overlook; rebuff; reject; scorn; shun; sidestep; slight; slur; skirt; sneer; snub; spurn.*

give (him) the business   A moribund metaphor (SEE). *admonish; animadvert; berate; castigate; censure; chasten; chastise; chide; condemn; criticize; denounce; denunciate; discipline; impugn; objurgate; punish; rebuke; remonstrate; reprehend; reprimand; reproach; reprobate; reprove; revile; scold; upbraid; vituperate; warn.*

give (him) the cold shoulder
A moribund metaphor (SEE). *abuse; affront; avoid; disdain; disregard; ignore; insult; neglect; offend; outrage; overlook; rebuff; reject; scorn; shun; sidestep; slight; slur; skirt; sneer; snub; spurn.*

give the devil his due   A moribund metaphor (SEE).

give (him) the runaround   A moribund metaphor (SEE). *avoid; dodge; doubletalk; equivocate; evade; fence;*

hedge; palter; prevaricate; quibble; shuffle; sidestep; tergiversate; waffle.

give (him) the third degree
A moribund metaphor (SEE). *catechize; cross-examine; examine; grill; inquire; interrogate; pump; question; quiz; test.*

give the thumbs down (sign)
A moribund metaphor (SEE). *decline; deny; disallow; disapprove; forbid; nix; prohibit; proscribe; refuse; reject; rule out; say no; turn down; veto.*

give the thumbs up (sign)   A moribund metaphor (SEE). *accredit; affirm; allow; approve; authorize; back; bless; certify; countenance; endorse; favor; permit; ratify; sanction; support.*

give up the ghost   A moribund metaphor (SEE). *cease to exist; decease; depart; die; expire; pass away; pass on; perish.*

(just) glad to be alive

glaring inconsistency   An inescapable pair (SEE).

global village   A moribund metaphor (SEE)

gloom and doom   An inescapable pair (SEE).

glory days

glutton for punishment

go against the grain   A moribund metaphor (SEE). ■ Does the message *go against the grain* of corporate philosophy?

go ahead, make my day   An infantile phrase (SEE).

go all the way

go belly up   A moribund metaphor (SEE). *break down; collapse; disintegrate; fail; fall short; flop; founder; miscarry; topple.* ■ All the biotech startups in the Bioventures portfolio would likely *go belly up* if the veterinary school is shut down. REPLACE WITH *fail.*

God-given talent

God (only) knows why

go downhill   A moribund metaphor (SEE). *decay; decline; degenerate; destroy; deteriorate; disintegrate; ebb; erode; fade; fall off; languish; lessen; plummet; ruin; wane; weaken; wither; worsen.* ■ The bad news is that during the second night, everybody's performance *went downhill.* REPLACE WITH *deteriorated.*

(he) goes   An infantile phrase (SEE). Only the adolescent or the addlebrained prefer this gruesome *goes* to *acknowledge; admit; announce; assert; asseverate; aver; avow; comment; confess; cry; declare; disclose; divulge; exclaim; mention; note; observe; proclaim; pronounce; remark; reveal; say; state; utter.* ■ They say they don't know anything, and then they *go*, "If we hear anything, we'll call you." USE *say.* ■ He walked into the room, and she *goes*, "Guess what?" USE *exclaims.* ■ I asked what do you like about her, and he *went*, "I don't know." USE *confessed.* ■ And then he *goes*, "I don't want to see you any more." USE *announces.*

go for broke

go for it

go for the gold   An infantile phrase
(SEE).

go for the gusto   An infantile phrase
(SEE).

go forward   A torpid term (SEE). *advance; continue; develop; go on; grow;
improve; increase; move on; proceed;
progress.* ■ The way in which this is
drafted will allow those takeovers to
go forward, which would allow for a
greater efficiency and productivity.
REPLACE WITH *proceed.* SEE ALSO *a step
forward; a step (forward) in the right direction; move forward; move (forward)
in the right direction; proceed forward.*

go home empty-handed

going, going, gone   An infantile
phrase (SEE).

going great guns   A moribund metaphor (SEE).

going nowhere

going on (nineteen)   An infantile
phrase (SEE). ■ I'm sixty-nine *going on*
seventy. ■ I've been there five years,
going on six years.

going strong

go into a tailspin   A moribund metaphor (SEE).

go it alone

go kicking and screaming   *antago-
nistically;   defiantly;   disagreeably;
grudgingly; recalcitrantly; reluctantly;*

*renitently; resistantly; resistingly; un-
consentingly; unwillingly.*

golden boy   A moribund metaphor
(SEE).

golden opportunity   An inescapable pair (SEE).

golden years

go (run) like the wind   An insipid
simile (SEE moribund metaphors).
*abruptly; apace; at once; briskly;
directly; expeditiously; fast; forthwith;
hastily; hurriedly; immediately; instantaneously; instantly; posthaste; promptly; quickly; rapidly; rashly; right away;
speedily; straightaway; swiftly; wingedly.*

gone but not forgotten

gone with the wind   A moribund
metaphor (SEE).
1. *dead; disappeared; gone; past; vanished.*
2. *ephemeral; evanescent; fleeting; flitting; fugacious; fugitive; short-lived;
transient; transitory; volatile.*

good and sufficient   An inescapable
pair (SEE). *adequate; good; satisfactory;
sufficient.*

(as) good as gold   An insipid simile
(SEE moribund metaphors). *best; excellent; exceptional; fine; finest; first-class;
first-rate; good; great; superior; superlative.*

good, bad and (or) indifferent
■ We really don't know what the effect
will be; it could be *good, bad or indifferent.*

goodbye to all that

good egg   A moribund metaphor (SEE). *agreeable; decent; ethical; forthright; honest; just; moral; righteous; straight; trustworthy; upright; virtuous.*

good-faith effort

good help is hard to find

good news . . . bad news

good stuff

good things come in small packages   A popular prescription (SEE).

goodwill gesture

go off half-cocked   A moribund metaphor (SEE). *careless; emotional; foolhardy; hasty; headlong; heedless; impulsive; incautious; indiscreet; precipitate; rash; reckless; thoughtless; unmindful; unthinking.*

go off the deep end   A moribund metaphor (SEE). *careless; emotional; foolhardy; hasty; headlong; heedless; impulsive; incautious; indiscreet; precipitate; rash; reckless; thoughtless; unmindful; unthinking.*

goose egg   A moribund metaphor (SEE). *cipher; naught; zero.*

(his) goose is cooked   A moribund metaphor (SEE).

go overboard   A moribund metaphor (SEE). *exaggerate; hyperbolize; overdo; overreact; overstress; overstate.*

go over like a lead balloon   An insipid simile (SEE moribund metaphors).

go over with a fine-toothed comb   A moribund metaphor (SEE). *analyze; canvass; comb; examine; explore; filter; forage; hunt; inspect; investigate; look for; probe; quest; ransack; rummage; scour; scrutinize; search; seek; sieve; sift; winnow.*

go (our) separate ways

go (head) south   A moribund metaphor (SEE). *crash; decline; decrease; descend; dip; drop; ebb; fall; plummet; plunge; recede; sink; slide; slip; subside; topple; tumble.* ■ And it is possible that the market may *go south* before the shares can be offered. REPLACE WITH *fall.*

gospel truth

(we've) got a long way to go

go the extra mile   A moribund metaphor (SEE). ■ Average citizens who regularly *go the extra mile* to make this a better world are everywhere.

go the way of all flesh   A moribund metaphor (SEE). *cease to exist; decease; depart; die; expire; pass away; pass on; perish.*

go the way of the dinosaur
A moribund metaphor (SEE). *become extinct; cease to exist; disappear; vanish.*

go through the ceiling (roof)
A moribund metaphor (SEE). *bellow; bluster; clamor; explode; fulminate; fume; holler; howl; rage; rant; rave; roar; scream; shout; storm; thunder; vociferate; yell.*

go through the mill   A moribund metaphor (SEE).

go through the motions

go through the roof   A moribund metaphor (SEE). *ascend; balloon; billow; bulge; climb; expand; go up; grow; increase; inflate; mount; multiply; rise; skyrocket; soar; surge; swell.* ■ Some people thought it was an extravagance at a time when billings aren't exactly *going through the roof.*

go to bat for   A moribund metaphor (SEE).

go toe to toe with   A moribund metaphor (SEE).

(we) got off on the wrong foot   A moribund metaphor (SEE).

go to (her) head

go to hell in a handbasket   A moribund metaphor (SEE). *decay; decline; degenerate; destroy; deteriorate; disintegrate; ebb; erode; fade; fall off; languish; lessen; plummet; ruin; wane; weaken; wither; worsen.*

go to pieces   *decay; decline; degenerate; destroy; deteriorate; disintegrate; ebb; erode; fade; fall off; languish; lessen; ruin; wane; weaken; wither; worsen.*

go to pot   *decay; decline; degenerate; destroy; deteriorate; disintegrate; ebb; erode; fade; fall off; languish; lessen; ruin; wane; weaken; wither; worsen.*

go to (her) reward   A moribund metaphor (SEE). *cease to exist; decease; depart; die; expire; pass away; pass on; perish.*

go (run) to seed   A moribund metaphor (SEE). *decay; decline; degenerate; deteriorate; devitalize; disintegrate; ebb; erode; fade; fall off; languish; lessen; ruin; wane; weaken; wither; worsen.*

go to the dogs   A moribund metaphor (SEE). *decay; decline; degenerate; destroy; deteriorate; disintegrate; ebb; erode; fade; fall off; languish; lessen; ruin; wane; weaken; wither; worsen.*

go (travel) to the end of the earth

(he) got what (he) deserved (had coming)

go up in flames   A moribund metaphor (SEE). *annihilate; break down; crumble; demolish; destroy; deteriorate; die; disintegrate; dissolve; end; eradicate; exterminate; obliterate; pulverize; rack; ravage; raze; ruin; shatter; smash; undo; wrack; wreck.*

go up (the chimney) in smoke
A moribund metaphor (SEE). *annihilate; break down; crumble; demolish; destroy; deteriorate; die; disintegrate; dissolve; end; eradicate; exterminate; obliterate; pulverize; rack; ravage; raze; ruin; shatter; smash; undo; wrack; wreck.*

go whole hog

go with the flow

(as) graceful as a swan   An insipid simile (SEE moribund metaphors). *agile; graceful; limber; lissome; lithe; lithesome; nimble; supple.*

grace under pressure

grace (us) with (his) presence
■ Most of these essays first appeared in *The New Yorker*, which Liebling *graced with his presence* between 1935 and 1963.

grammatical gimmicks
Quite simply, *and everything* is a babbler's way of describing what he was unable to.

This phrase and so many others like it — such as *and everything like that; and stuff; and (or) things like that; and this and that; anyway; I mean; (and that) kind of thing; or something or other; or whatever; this, that and the other (thing); (and that) type of thing; you had to be there* — are grammatical gimmicks that we use to make up for the misfashioned words that precede them.

These are devices that we resort to whenever we are unable to adequately explain our thoughts, feelings or experiences. Grammatical gimmicks attest to just how dull and dimwitted we have become.

A witticism is the highest form of expression; a dimwitticism, the lowest.

grass-roots (effort)   A moribund metaphor (SEE).

(pure) gravy   A moribund metaphor (SEE).

gravy train   A moribund metaphor (SEE).

gray area

grease the skids   A moribund metaphor (SEE).

great   A suspect superlative. (SEE) That which is called *great* is seldom more than *good*, and that which is *good* is scarcely mentionable.

Great is also, of course, a hugely overworked word (SEE). Consider this laughable sentence: ■ When I think of their golf course, the first word that comes to mind is *great.*

Alternatives to the quotidian *great* include: *consummate; distinguished; eminent; excellent; exceptional; exemplary; exquisite; extraordinary; fine; flawless; grand; ideal; illustrious; impeccable; imposing; impressive; magnificent; marvelous; matchless; perfect; preeminent; remarkable; select; splendid; superb; superior; superlative; supreme; transcendent; wonderful.*

great expectations   A suspect superlative (SEE).

(go) great guns   A moribund metaphor (SEE). ■ Under Field's ownership, the company grew *great guns* pursuing joint ventures and building office parks.

great white way   A moribund metaphor (SEE).

green around the gills   A moribund metaphor (SEE).
1. *afflicted; ailing; diseased; ill; indisposed; infirm; not (feeling) well; sick; sickly; suffering; unhealthy; unsound; unwell; valetudinarian.*
2. *nauseated; nauseous; queasy; sick; squeamish; vomiting.*

(as) green as grass   An insipid simile (SEE moribund metaphors).
1. *aquamarine; emerald; green; greenish; teal; verdant; virescent.*
2. *adolescent; artless; awkward; callow;*

green; guileless; immature; inexperienced; inexpert; ingenuous; innocent; juvenile; naive; raw; simple; undeveloped; unfledged; unseasoned; unskilled; unskillful; unsophisticated; untaught; untrained; unworldly; young; youthful.

green-eyed monster A moribund metaphor (SEE). *envy; jealousy.*

green with envy A moribund metaphor (SEE). *covetous; desirous; envious; grudging; jealous; resentful.*

grim reaper A moribund metaphor (SEE). *death.*

grim reminder

grin and bear it A popular prescription (SEE).

grind to a halt *cease; close; complete; conclude; end; finish; halt; settle; stop.*

grin like a Cheshire cat An insipid simile (SEE moribund metaphors).

grist for the mill A moribund metaphor (SEE).

gross exaggeration An inescapable pair (SEE).

ground swell of support

ground zero A moribund metaphor (SEE).

grow (spread) like a cancer An insipid simile (SEE moribund metaphors). *augment; breed; duplicate; grow; increase; metastasize; multiply; mushroom; procreate; proliferate; propagate; reproduce; snowball; spread; swell.*

(doesn't) grow on trees A moribund metaphor (SEE)

gruesome twosome An infantile phrase (SEE).

guardedly optimistic A torpid term (SEE). *confident; encouraged; heartened; hopeful; optimistic; sanguine.* ■ Firefighters are *guardedly optimistic* that they have the blaze under control. DELETE *guardedly*. SEE ALSO *cautiously optimistic.*

guardian angel A moribund metaphor (SEE).

guessing game

guesstimate An infantile phrase (SEE). *appraisal; assessment; estimate; estimation; guess; impression; opinion.*

guilt trip

(as) guilty as sin An insipid simile (SEE moribund metaphors). *at fault; blamable; blameful; blameworthy; censurable; condemnable; culpable; guilty; in error; reprehensible.*

H

(old) habits die hard

(she) had it coming

hail the conquering hero

hale and hearty   An inescapable pair (SEE). *energetic; fine; fit; good; hale; healthful; healthy; hearty; robust; sound; strong; vigorous; well.*

(anyone with) half a brain   A moribund metaphor (SEE).

half a loaf is better than none   A moribund metaphor (SEE).

half-baked (idea)   A moribund metaphor (SEE). *bad; blemished; defective; deficient; faulty; flawed; ill-conceived; imperfect; inadequate; incomplete; inferior; malformed; poor; unsound.*

half the battle   A moribund metaphor (SEE).

(go at it) hammer and tongs   A moribund metaphor (SEE). *aggressively; dynamically; emphatically; energetically; ferociously; fervently; fiercely; forcefully; frantically; frenziedly; furiously; hard; intensely; intently; mightily; passionately; powerfully; robustly; savagely; spiritedly; strenuously; strongly;* *vehemently; viciously; vigorously; violently; wildly; with vigor.*

hammer home

hand and (in) glove   A moribund metaphor (SEE). *amiable; amicable; attached; brotherly; chummy; close; confidential; devoted; familiar; friendly; inseparable; intimate; loving; thick.*

handed to (her) on a silver platter   A moribund metaphor (SEE).

(goes) hand in hand   A moribund metaphor (SEE). *closely; jointly; together.*

hand over fist   A moribund metaphor (SEE). *apace; briskly; expeditiously; fast; hastily; hurriedly; posthaste; quickly; rapidly; speedily; swiftly; wingedly.*

(my) hands are tied   A moribund metaphor (SEE).

(won) hands down

handsome is as handsome does

handwriting (is) on the wall   A moribund metaphor (SEE). *divination; foreboding; forewarning; indica-*

tion; omen; portent; prediction; premonition; presage; presentiment; sign; signal; warning.

hang (on) by a thread   A moribund metaphor (SEE).

hang fire   A moribund metaphor (SEE).
1. *be delayed; be slow.*
2. *be undecided; be unsettled.*

hang (your) hat on   A moribund metaphor (SEE).

hang (our) head(s) in shame

hang in the balance

hang in there   *carry on; get along; manage; succeed.* ■ Even though profits remain down, most firms are still *hanging in there.* REPLACE WITH *succeeding.* ■ I'm *hanging in there.* REPLACE WITH *managing.*

hang loose

hang on every word   A moribund metaphor (SEE). *attend to; hark; hear; hearken; heed; listen; pay attention; pay heed.*

hang on like grim death   An insipid simile (SEE moribund metaphors).

hang over (our) heads   A moribund metaphor (SEE). *hang over; impend; loom; menace; overhang; overshadow; threaten; tower over.*

hang tough

(these things) happen to other people, not to (me)   A plebeian sentiment (SEE).

(as) happy as a clam (at high tide)   An insipid simile (SEE moribund metaphors). *blissful; blithe; buoyant; cheerful; delighted; ecstatic; elated; enraptured; euphoric; exalted; excited; exhilarated; exultant; gay; glad; gleeful; good-humored; happy; intoxicated; jolly; jovial; joyful; joyous; jubilant; merry; mirthful; overjoyed; pleased; rapturous; thrilled.*

(as) happy as a lark   An insipid simile (SEE moribund metaphors). *blissful; blithe; buoyant; cheerful; delighted; ecstatic; elated; enraptured; euphoric; exalted; excited; exhilarated; exultant; gay; glad; gleeful; good-humored; happy; intoxicated; jolly; jovial; joyful; joyous; jubilant; merry; mirthful; overjoyed; pleased; rapturous; thrilled.*

happy camper   An infantile phrase (SEE). *blissful; blithe; buoyant; cheerful; delighted; ecstatic; elated; enraptured; euphoric; exalted; excited; exhilarated; exultant; gay; glad; gleeful; good-humored; happy; intoxicated; jolly; jovial; joyful; joyous; jubilant; merry; mirthful; overjoyed; pleased; rapturous; thrilled.* ■ The six families who bought into the project, all at full price, are not *happy campers* these days. REPLACE WITH *pleased.*

happy hunting

hard and fast (rule)   *absolute; binding; certain; defined; dogmatic; entrenched; established; exact; exacting; fast; firm; fixed; hard; immutable; inflexible; invariable; permanent; resolute; rigid; set; severe; solid; steadfast; strict; stringent; unalterable; unbending; uncompromising; unyielding.* ■ Events are happening too quickly in Eastern Europe to make *hard and fast* plans at this point. REPLACE WITH *firm.*

(as) hard as a rock An insipid simile (SEE moribund metaphors).
1. *adamantine; firm; granitelike; hard; petrified; rock-hard; rocklike; rocky; solid; steellike; steely; stonelike; stony.*
2. *athletic; beefy; brawny; burly; firm; fit; hale; hardy; hearty; husky; manly; mighty; muscular; powerful; puissant; robust; rugged; sinewy; solid; stalwart; stout; strapping; strong; sturdy; tough; vigorous; virile; well-built.*
3. *constant; dependable; determined; faithful; fast; firm; fixed; inexorable; inflexible; loyal; obdurate; resolute; resolved; rigid; solid; stable; staunch; steadfast; steady; stern; tenacious; unflinching; unwavering; unyielding.*

(as) hard as nails An insipid simile (SEE moribund metaphors).
1. *athletic; beefy; brawny; burly; firm; fit; hale; hardy; hearty; husky; manly; mighty; muscular; powerful; puissant; robust; rugged; sinewy; solid; stalwart; stout; strapping; strong; sturdy; tough; vigorous; virile; well-built.*
2. *constant; dependable; determined; faithful; fast; firm; fixed; inexorable; inflexible; loyal; obdurate; resolute; resolved; rigid; solid; stable; staunch; steadfast; steady; stern; tenacious; unflinching; unwavering; unyielding.*

hard, cold facts

hard-earned money

hard to believe *beyond belief; beyond comprehension; doubtful; dubious; farfetched; implausible; improbable; incomprehensible; inconceivable; incredible; inexplicable; questionable; remote; unbelievable; unimaginable; unlikely; unrealistic.*

hard to pin down

hard to resist

hard to swallow *beyond belief; beyond comprehension; doubtful; dubious; farfetched; implausible; improbable; incomprehensible; inconceivable; incredible; inexplicable; questionable; remote; unbelievable; unimaginable; unlikely; unrealistic.* ■ Some innovations are just a little *hard to swallow.* REPLACE WITH *implausible.*

harsh reality An inescapable pair (SEE).

has a finger in every pie A moribund metaphor (SEE).

(sure) has a funny way of showing it

has a heart as big as all outdoors An insipid simile (SEE moribund metaphors). *beneficent; benevolent; bighearted; compassionate; generous; goodhearted; humane; kind; kindhearted; kindly; sensitive; sympathetic; understanding.*

has a heart of gold A moribund metaphor (SEE). *beneficent; benevolent; bighearted; compassionate; generous; good-hearted; good-natured; humane; kind; kindhearted; kindly; sensitive; sympathetic; understanding.*

has a heart of stone A moribund metaphor (SEE). *apathetic; callous; chilly; cold; cool; detached; dispassionate; distant; emotionless; frigid; hard; hardhearted; harsh; heartless; hostile; icy; impassive; indifferent; passionless; pitiless; reserved; unconcerned; unemo-*

tional; unfeeling; unfriendly; unresponsive.

has an effect on   A dimwitted redundancy (SEE). *acts on; affects; bears on; influences; sways; works on.* ■ That's one of the problems that *has an effect on* everyone's quality of life. USE *affects.* SEE ALSO *effect.*

has an impact on   A dimwitted redundancy (SEE). *acts on; affects; bears on; influences; sways; works on.* ■ That too *had an impact on* the jury. USE *swayed.* SEE ALSO *impact.*

(he) has a passion for life

(she) has (such) a pretty face

has a swelled head   A moribund metaphor (SEE). *arrogant; cavalier; conceited; disdainful; egocentric; egotistic; egotistical; haughty; lofty; narcissistic; pompous; pretentious; proud; self-centered; self-important; self-satisfied; supercilious; superior; vain.*

has both feet on the ground   *businesslike; careful; cautious; circumspect; expedient; judicious; politic; practical; pragmatic; prudent; realistic; reasonable; sensible; utilitarian.*

has cold feet   A moribund metaphor (SEE). *afraid; alarmed; apprehensive; cowardly; craven; diffident; faint-hearted; fearful; frightened; pusillanimous; recreant; scared; timid; timorous; tremulous.*

has (his) hands full   A moribund metaphor (SEE). *booked; busy; employed; engaged; involved; obligated; occupied.*

has (her) heart set on

(she) has it all

has it on reliable authority

(she) hasn't a (jealous) bone in (her) body

(he) hasn't aged a bit

(she) has so much to live for

has the courage of (his) convictions

has the patience of Job   A moribund metaphor (SEE). *accepting; accommodating; acquiescent; complacent; complaisant; compliant; cowed; deferential; docile; dutiful; easy; forbearing; gentle; humble; long-suffering; meek; mild; obedient; passive; patient; prostrate; quiet; reserved; resigned; stoical; submissive; subservient; timid; tolerant; tractable; unassuming; uncomplaining; yielding.*

has the whole (town) talking

has to do with   A dimwitted redundancy (SEE). *concerns; deals with; is about; pertains to; regards; relates to.* ■ The most recent academy committee mission *has to do with* climate-monitoring satellites. USE *concerns.*

has (him) under (her) thumb
A moribund metaphor (SEE). *administer; boss; command; control; dictate; direct; dominate; domineer; govern; in charge; in command; in control; manage; manipulate; master; misuse; order; overpower; oversee; predominate; prevail; reign over; rule; superintend; tyrannize; use.*

(she) has what it takes

has (his) work cut out for (him)

(go) hat in hand   A moribund metaphor (SEE).

have a conniption (fit)   A moribund metaphor (SEE). *bellow; bluster; clamor; explode; fulminate; fume; holler; howl; rage; rant; rave; roar; scream; shout; storm; thunder; vociferate; yell.*

have (make) a go at (it)   *aim; attempt; endeavor; essay; exert; labor; strain; strive; struggle; toil; try; undertake; work at.*

have a good (nice) day (evening)
A plebeian sentiment (SEE). We are dimwitted creatures who find that formulas rather than feelings suit us well enough; indeed, they suit us mightily. How pleasant it is not to have to think of a valid sentiment when a vapid one does so nicely; how effortless to rely on triteness rather than on truth.

Dimwitticisms veil our true feelings and avert our real thoughts. SEE ALSO *common courtesy.*

have a hemorrhage   A moribund metaphor (SEE). *bellow; bluster; clamor; explode; fulminate; fume; holler; howl; rage; rant; rave; roar; scream; shout; storm; thunder; vociferate; yell.*

(they) have it both ways

(I) have more than (I) know what to do with

(you) have not seen anything yet

(we) have only (ourselves) to blame

have (got) to   A dimwitted redundancy (SEE). *should; must.* ■ *I have got to get to work.* USE *must.*

(you) have to learn to walk before (you) can run   A popular prescription (SEE).

(you) have to love (yourself) before (you) can love another   A popular prescription (SEE).

(you) have (your) whole life ahead of (you)

hazardous to your health

hazy, hot and humid

(stand) head and shoulders above (the rest)   A moribund metaphor (SEE). *abler; better; exceptional; greater; higher; more able (accomplished; adept; capable; competent; qualified; skilled; talented); outstanding; standout; superior; superlative.*

head for the hills   A moribund metaphor (SEE). *abscond; clear out; decamp; depart; desert; disappear; escape; exit; flee; fly; go; go away; leave; move on; part; pull out; quit; retire; retreat; run away; take flight; take off; vacate; vanish; withdraw.*

head in the clouds   A moribund metaphor (SEE). *absent; absentminded; absorbed; abstracted; bemused; captivated; daydreaming; detached; distracted; distrait; dreamy; engrossed; enraptured; faraway; fascinated; immersed; inattentive; lost; mesmerized; oblivious; preoccupied; rapt; spellbound.*

head in the clouds and feet on the

ground   A moribund metaphor (SEE).

head into the home stretch
A moribund metaphor (SEE).

head on the block   A moribund metaphor (SEE).

head over heels (in love)   A moribund metaphor (SEE). *altogether; ardently; completely; deeply; earnestly; entirely; fervently; fully; intensely; passionately; perfectly; quite; thoroughly; totally; unreservedly; utterly; wholly; zealously.*

(as) healthy as a horse   An insipid simile (SEE moribund metaphors). *athletic; beefy; brawny; energetic; fine; fit; good; hale; hardy; hearty; healthful; healthy; husky; lanky; lean; manly; muscular; powerful; robust; shapely; sinewy; slender; solid; sound; stalwart; strong; sturdy; thin; trim; vigorous; virile; well; well-built.*

healthy, wealthy and wise

heap dirt (scorn) on   A moribund metaphor (SEE). *asperse; badmouth; belittle; besmirch; bespatter; blacken; calumniate; defame; defile; denigrate; denounce; depreciate; deride; disparage; impugn; insult; libel; malign; profane; revile; scandalize; slander; slur; smear; sully; taint; traduce; vilify; vitiate.*

hear by (via) the grapevine
A moribund metaphor (SEE).

heart and soul   A moribund metaphor (SEE).
1. *altogether; completely; entirely; fully; perfectly; quite; thoroughly; totally; unreservedly; utterly; wholly.*

2. *earnestly; fervently; genuinely; heartily; honestly; sincerely; unreservedly; wholeheartedly.*

heartfelt thanks

(his) heart is in the right place
A moribund metaphor (SEE). *be well-intentioned.*

(you) hear what I'm saying?   An ineffectual phrase (SEE). ■ She's the one who did it, not me. *You hear what I'm saying?* DELETE *You hear what I'm saying?* SEE ALSO *(you) know what I mean? (you) know what I'm saying; (you) know what I'm telling you? (do) you know?.*

(I) hear you   *appreciate; apprehend; comprehend; grasp; see; understand.*

heated argument

heated debate   An inescapable pair (SEE).

heave a sigh of relief

heaven on earth

heaven only knows

heavy duty

hedge (your) bets

heightened awareness

heinous   An overworked word (SEE). Many people use *heinous* even though they have scant sense of what the word means. The popularity of the word attests only to the nescience of those who misuse it.
   Some words that might be used in-

stead of the omnipresent *heinous* are: *abhorrent; abominable; appalling; atrocious; awful; beastly; detestable; disagreeable; disgusting; dreadful; frightening; frightful; ghastly; grisly; gruesome; horrendous; horrible; horrid; horrifying; inhuman; loathesome; obnoxious; odious; offensive; repellent; repugnant; repulsive; revolting; terrible; terrifying; unspeakable; unutterable.*

(been to) hell and back

(through) hell and high water A moribund metaphor (SEE). *adversity; affliction; calamity; catastrophe; difficulty; distress; hardship; misadventure; misfortune; ordeal; trial; tribulation; trouble; woe.*

hell (hellbent)-for-leather A moribund metaphor (SEE). *breakneck; fast; madcap; rash; reckless; wild.* ■ Connors clearly thought that he had more to gain by pursuing his *hell-for-leather* expansion in the region.

hell has no fury like (a woman scorned) An insipid simile (SEE moribund metaphors).

hell on earth A moribund metaphor (SEE). *hellish; impossible; infernal; insufferable; insupportable; intolerable; painful; plutonic; sulfurous; unbearable; uncomfortable; unendurable; unpleasant; stygian.* ■ Being a stepparent is *hell on earth.* REPLACE WITH *hellish.* SEE ALSO *a living hell.*

helpful hints An inescapable pair (SEE).

helpless rage

helps put things in perspective

help (us) to help you

hem and haw An inescapable pair (SEE).

hemorrhage red ink A moribund metaphor (SEE).

(right) here and now An inescapable pair (SEE). *currently; now; nowadays; presently; the present; today.*

. . . here (I) come

here (we) go again

here's the thing An ineffectual phrase (SEE). ■ *Here's the thing,* whoever is mayor must be able to work with the community. DELETE *Here's the thing.* ■ *Here's the thing,* men don't even know that we're different. DELETE *Here's the thing.* SEE ALSO *that's the thing; the thing about (of) it is; the thing is.*

here, there and everywhere *all over; everywhere; omnipresent; ubiquitous.*

here today, gone tomorrow *ephemeral; evanescent; fleeting; flitting; fugacious; fugitive; short-lived; transient; transitory; volatile.* ■ I still love it even though nothing is as *here today, gone tomorrow* as a job in TV. REPLACE WITH *fleeting.*

here to stay *constant; deep-rooted; enduring; entrenched; established; everlasting; fixed; lasting; long-lived; permanent; secure; stable; unending.* ■ They questioned whether ability grouping is *here to stay.* REPLACE WITH *permanent.*

he's (she's) my best friend   A suspect superlative (SEE).

he's (she's) the man (woman) of my dreams

hidden agenda   ■ Convergent thinking lends itself to a *hidden agenda* to maintain the status quo.

hide (their) heads in the sand
A moribund metaphor (SEE). *brush aside; avoid; discount; disregard; dodge; duck; ignore; neglect; omit; pass over; recoil from; shrink from; shun; shy away from; turn away from; withdraw from.*
■ Even when informed of the problem, some denominations are continuing to *hide their heads in the sand.*

(neither) hide nor (or) hair
A moribund metaphor (SEE). *nothing; sign; trace; vestige.*

(left) high and dry   An inescapable pair (SEE). *abandoned; alone; deserted; forgotten; helpless; left; powerless; stranded.*

high and low   An inescapable pair (SEE). *all over; everywhere.*

high and mighty   An inescapable pair (SEE). *arrogant; cavalier; conceited; condescending; contemptuous; despotic; dictatorial; disdainful; dogmatic; domineering; haughty; imperious; insolent; lofty; overbearing; overweening; patronizing; pompous; pretentious; scornful; self-important; supercilious; superior; vainglorious.*

(as) high as a kite   An insipid simile (SEE moribund metaphors).
1. *agitated; aroused; ebullient; effusive; enthused; elated; excitable; excited; ex-*
hilarated; expansive; impassioned; inflamed; overwrought; stimulated.
2. *besotted; crapulous; drunk; inebriated; intoxicated; sodden; stupefied; tipsy.*

high hopes

high (top) man on the totem pole
A moribund metaphor (SEE). *administrator; boss; brass; chief; commander; director; executive; foreman; head; headman; leader; manager; master; (high) muckamuck; officer; official; overseer; president; principal; superintendent; supervisor.*

(give) high marks   A moribund metaphor (SEE).

high on (my) list of priorities

high on the hog   *extravagantly; lavishly; luxuriantly.* A moribund metaphor (SEE). ■ It's the state officials who are living *high on the hog.* REPLACE WITH *extravagantly.*

high-water mark   A moribund metaphor (SEE).

highway robbery   A moribund metaphor (SEE).

highways and byways

high, wide and handsome

hindsight is 20/20   A quack equation (SEE).

hired gun   A moribund metaphor (SEE).

history in the making

hit a home run   A moribund metaphor (SEE). *advance; fare well; flourish; prevail; progress; prosper; succeed; thrive; triumph; win.*

hit (me) between the eyes
A moribund metaphor (SEE). *amaze; astonish; astound; awe; dazzle; dumbfound; flabbergast; overpower; overwhelm; shock; startle; stun; stupefy; surprise.*

hit (rock) bottom   A moribund metaphor (SEE).

hitch (your) wagon to a star
A moribund metaphor (SEE).

hit (close to) home   A moribund metaphor (SEE).

hit (me) like a ton of bricks   An insipid simile (SEE moribund metaphors). *amaze; astonish; astound; awe; dazzle; dumbfound; flabbergast; overpower; overwhelm; shock; startle; stun; stupefy; surprise.*

hit list   A moribund metaphor (SEE).

hit or miss   A moribund metaphor (SEE). *aimless; arbitrary; capricious; casual; erratic; haphazard; incidental; inconsistent; infrequent; irregular; lax; loose; occasional; odd; offhand; random; sporadic; uncontrolled; unplanned.*

hit over the head   A moribund metaphor (SEE).

hit pay dirt   A moribund metaphor (SEE). *flourish; get rich; prevail; prosper; succeed; thrive; triumph; win.*

hit (their) stride   A moribund metaphor (SEE).

hit the ceiling   A moribund metaphor (SEE). *bellow; bluster; clamor; explode; fulminate; fume; holler; howl; rage; rant; rave; roar; scream; shout; storm; thunder; vociferate; yell.*

hit the deck   A moribund metaphor (SEE).

hit the ground running   A moribund metaphor (SEE). ■ I get up in the morning and *hit the ground running.*

hit the hay   A moribund metaphor (SEE). *doze; go to bed; nap; rest; retire; sleep; slumber.*

hit the jackpot   A moribund metaphor (SEE). *flourish; get rich; prevail; prosper; succeed; thrive; triumph; win.*

hit the nail (squarely) on the head   A moribund metaphor (SEE).

hit the road   A moribund metaphor (SEE). *abscond; clear out; decamp; depart; desert; disappear; escape; exit; flee; fly; go; go away; leave; move on; part; pull out; quit; retire; retreat; run away; take flight; take off; vacate; vanish; withdraw.*

hit the roof   A moribund metaphor (SEE). *bellow; bluster; clamor; explode; fulminate; fume; holler; howl; rage; rant; rave; roar; scream; shout; storm; thunder; vociferate; yell.*

hit the sack   A moribund metaphor (SEE). *doze; go to bed; nap; rest; retire; sleep; slumber.*

hit the skids   *decay; decline; degenerate; destroy; deteriorate; disintegrate; ebb; erode; fade; fall off; languish;*

lessen; ruin; wane; weaken; wither; worsen.

hit the streets

hit (him) while (he's) down
A moribund metaphor (See).

(as) hoarse as a crow   An insipid simile (See moribund metaphors). *grating; gravelly; gruff; guttural; harsh; hoarse; rasping; raspy; throaty.*

Hobson's choice   *no choice.*

hoist with (his) own petard
A moribund metaphor (See).

(can't) hold a candle to   A moribund metaphor (See).

hold a gun to   A moribund metaphor (See). *coerce; command; compel; constrain; demand; dictate; force; insist; make; order; pressure; require.*

hold all the cards   A moribund metaphor (See). *administer; boss; command; control; dictate; direct; dominate; govern; in charge; in command; in control; manage; manipulate; master; order; overpower; oversee; predominate; prevail; reign over; rule; superintend.*

hold down the fort   A moribund metaphor (See).

hold (their) feet to the fire
A moribund metaphor (See). *coerce; command; compel; constrain; demand; enforce; force; goad; impel; importune; incite; induce; insist; instigate; make; oblige; press; pressure; prod; push; require; spur; urge.*

hold (your) fire   A moribund metaphor (See).

hold (their) ground   A moribund metaphor (See).
1. *hold fast; stand firm.*
2. *assert; command; decree; dictate; insist; order; require.*

hold (my) hand   A moribund metaphor (See). *accompany; escort; guide.*
■ The intent of this text is to *hold your hand* through the learning process. Replace with *guide you.*

hold out hope

hold over (his) head

hold (their) own

hold the phone   A moribund metaphor (See). *be patient; hold on; pause; slow down; wait.*

hold the purse strings   A moribund metaphor (See). *administer; boss; command; control; dictate; direct; dominate; govern; in charge; in command; in control; manage; manipulate; master; order; overpower; oversee; predominate; prevail; reign over; rule; superintend.*

hold true   A dimwitted redundancy (See). *hold.* ■ What *holds true* for them may not *hold true* for others. Delete *true.*

hold up to ridicule

hold your horses   A moribund metaphor (See). *be patient; calm down; hold on; pause; slow down; wait.*

holy terror

(my) home away from home

home free   A moribund metaphor

(SEE). *guarded; protected; safe; secure; sheltered; shielded; undamaged; unharmed; unhurt; unscathed.*

home is where the heart is
A popular prescription (SEE).

(as) honest as the day is long   An insipid simile (SEE moribund metaphors). *aboveboard; blunt; candid; direct; earnest; faithful; forthright; frank; genuine; honest; reliable; sincere; straightforward; trustworthy; truthful; upright; veracious; veridical.*

honestly and truly   An inescapable pair (SEE). ■ I *honestly and truly* believed he was the best I could hope for. REPLACE WITH *honestly* or *truly.*

honest truth   A dimwitted redundancy (SEE). *honesty; truth.* ■ If you want the *honest truth*, I am in love with him. USE *truth.*

honesty is the best policy   A popular prescription (SEE).

honeymoon is over   A moribund metaphor (SEE).

hook, line and sinker   A moribund metaphor (SEE). *altogether; completely; entirely; fully; perfectly; quite; thoroughly; totally; unreservedly; utterly; wholly.*

hoot and holler   An inescapable pair (SEE). *bay; bawl; bellow; blare; caterwaul; clamor; cry; holler; hoot; howl; roar; screak; scream; screech; shout; shriek; shrill; squawk; squeal; vociferate; wail; whoop; yell; yelp; yowl.*

hope against hope

hope and expect (expectation)
A dimwitted redundancy (SEE). *hope; expect (expectation); trust.* ■ I *hope and expect* you'll be seeing a lot more of this. USE *expect* or *hope.*

hope and pray   An inescapable pair (SEE). ■ I *hope and pray* that in future features of this sort, the *Globe* puts the emphasis where it belongs.

hope for the best   A popular prescription (SEE).

hope for the best but expect (prepare for) the worst   A popular prescription (SEE).

(just) hope (it'll) go away   A popular prescription (SEE).

hopelessly inadequate

hopeless romantic   An inescapable pair (SEE).

hopes and dreams   An inescapable pair (SEE).

hope springs eternal   *confident; encouraged; heartened; hopeful; optimistic; sanguine.*

hopping mad   An inescapable pair (SEE). *agitated; alarmed; angry; annoyed; aroused; choleric; enraged; fierce; fuming; furious; incensed; inflamed; infuriated; irate; irritable; mad; maddened; raging; splenetic.*

hornet's nest   A moribund metaphor (SEE). *complexity; complication; difficulty; dilemma; entanglement; imbroglio; labyrinth; maze; muddle; perplexity; plight; predicament; problem; puzzle; quagmire; tangle.* ■ Senator

Dodd called the jurisdictional issue a *hornet's nest* but said he was ready to tackle it. REPLACE WITH *imbroglio*.

horse of a different (another) color   A moribund metaphor (SEE).

hot air   A moribund metaphor (SEE). *aggrandizement; bluster; boasting; braggadocio; bragging; bravado; crowing; elaboration; embellishment; embroidery; exaggeration; fanfaronade; gasconade; gloating; hyperbole; overstatement; rodomontade; swaggering.*

hot and bothered   An inescapable pair (SEE). *agitated; aroused; bothered; disquieted; disturbed; excited; flustered; perturbed; troubled; upset.*

(as) hot as fire   An insipid simile (SEE moribund metaphors). *aflame; blazing; blistering; boiling; burning; fiery; flaming; heated; hot; ovenlike; roasting; scalding; scorching; searing; simmering; sizzling; steaming; sweltering; torrid; tropical; warm.*

hot commodity

hot little hands

hotly contested

hot (right) off the press

hot on (his) trail

hot potato   A moribund metaphor (SEE).

hot spot   A moribund metaphor (SEE).

hot ticket   A moribund metaphor (SEE).

hot to trot   A moribund metaphor (SEE).
1. *concupiscent; horny; lascivious; lecherous; lewd; libidinous; licentious; lustful; prurient.*
2. *anxious; eager; impatient; ready; willing.*

hot under the collar   A moribund metaphor (SEE). *agitated; alarmed; angry; annoyed; aroused; choleric; enraged; fierce; fuming; furious; incensed; inflamed; infuriated; irate; irritable; mad; maddened; raging; splenetic.*

house of cards   A moribund metaphor (SEE).

how could this have happened?   A plebeian sentiment (SEE).

how did (I) get into this?   A plebeian sentiment (SEE).

how goes it?   An ineffectual phrase (SEE). SEE ALSO *how's it going?; how you doing?*

how much (do) you want to bet?   An infantile phrase (SEE).

how (it) plays

how quickly (soon) they forget

how's it going?   An ineffectual phrase (SEE). SEE ALSO *how goes it?; how you doing?*

how you doing?   An ineffectual phrase (SEE). This phrase — as well as others like it — is uttered by the unalert and inert. We who are conscious, we who are keen say a sincere *hello* when greeting a person. SEE ALSO *how goes it?; how's it going?*

hue and cry   An inescapable pair (SEE). *clamor; din; hubbub; noise; outcry; racket; shout; tumult; uproar.*

huff and puff   An inescapable pair (SEE).
1. *blow; huff; puff.*
2. *bluster; boast; brag; crow; gloat; swagger.*

huge throng   A dimwitted redundancy (SEE). *throng.* ■ A *huge throng* of young people attended the concert. DELETE *huge.*

hugs and kisses   An inescapable pair (SEE).

human interest story

human nature being what it is

humongous   An infantile phrase (SEE). *big; brobdingnagian; colossal; elephantine; enormous; gargantuan; giant; gigantic; grand; great; huge; immense; large; mammoth; massive; monstrous; prodigious; stupendous; titanic; tremendous; vast.* This is a word for buffoons. Any businessperson or politician who uses *humongous*, when a word like *huge* or *monstrous* will do, imperils his professionalism. ■ We were up against a *humongous* insurance company. USE *colossal.* ■ My appetite was *humongous.* USE *enormous.*

(as) hungry as a bear   An insipid simile (SEE moribund metaphors). *esurient; famished; gluttonous; greedy; hungry; insatiable; omnivorous; ravenous; starved; starving; voracious.*

(as) hungry as a horse   An insipid simile (SEE moribund metaphors). *esurient; famished; gluttonous; greedy; hungry; insatiable; omnivorous; ravenous; starved; starving; voracious.*

hunt with the hounds and run with the hares   A moribund metaphor (SEE).

hurdle to clear   A moribund metaphor (SEE). *bar; barrier; block; blockage; check; deterrent; difficulty; encumbrance; handicap; hindrance; hurdle; impediment; interference; obstacle; obstruction.*

hurl insults   A moribund metaphor (SEE).

hurry up and wait

(you're) hurting no one but (yourself)

hustle and bustle   An inescapable pair (SEE). *bustle; commotion; hustle; stir.* ■ Macau presents a restful alternative to the *hustle and bustle* of Hong Kong. REPLACE WITH *bustle* or *hustle.*

I

I am who I am A quack equation (SEE).

I am you A quack equation (SEE). *I am you* is the most "salubrious" equation.

I can't believe I'm telling you this A plebeian sentiment (SEE). *I can't believe I'm telling you this* is a sentiment that only the insensible could ever say. SEE ALSO *I don't know why I'm telling you this*.

I can't believe this is happening

I can't believe what I'm hearing

I can't get no satisfaction An infantile phrase (SEE).

I can't (begin to) tell you

icing on the cake A moribund metaphor (SEE). *bonus; dividend; extra; gift; lagniappe; perquisite; premium.*

I couldn't agree with you more

idle chatter (chitchat) *babble; chatter; chitchat; drivel; gibberish; gossip; jabber; nonsense; palaver; patter; prattle; twaddle.*

idle rich An inescapable pair (SEE).

I don't know ■ New passion is sweet, but after you know someone for a while, it fades. *I don't know.* ■ I know who I am — I have a good sense of that — but I will never know you, or anyone else, as well. *I don't know.*

For a person to conclude his expressed thoughts and views with *I don't know* would nullify all he seemed to know if it weren't that *I don't know* is less an admission of not knowing than it is an apology for presuming to.

I don't know if (whether) I'm coming or going *baffled; befuddled; bewildered; confounded; confused; disconcerted; mixed up; muddled; perplexed; puzzled.*

I don't know, what do you want to do? An infantile phrase (SEE).

I don't know what possessed (me)

I don't know whether to laugh or cry

I don't know why I'm telling you this A plebeian sentiment (SEE). SEE ALSO *I can't believe I'm telling you this*.

I (just) don't think about it   A plebeian sentiment (SEE). Sentiments like this ensure that those who say them are, and will always be, no more than plebeian.

if and when   A dimwitted redundancy (SEE). *if; when.* ■ *If and when* a conflict should arise, it should be taken care of as soon as possible to protect the harmonious environment. USE *if* or *when*. SEE ALSO *if, as and when; when and if; when and whether; when, as and if; whether and when.*

if, as and when   A dimwitted redundancy (SEE). *if; when.* SEE ALSO *if and when; when and if; when, as and if; when and whether; whether and when.*

if at first you don't succeed (try, try again)   A popular prescription (SEE).

if (they) could see me now

if (you're) happy, I'm happy

if I can do it, (anyone) can do it

if I don't laugh, I'll cry

if I had to do it (all) over again

if it ain't (isn't) broke(n), don't fix it   A popular prescription (SEE).

if it feels good, it can't be bad   A popular prescription (SEE).

if it isn't one thing, it's another   A plebeian sentiment (SEE). SEE ALSO *it's one thing after another.*

if it's (not) meant to be, it's (not) meant to be   A popular prescription (SEE).

if it sounds too good to be true, it (probably) is   A popular prescription (SEE).

if looks could kill

if my friends could see me now

if only (we) knew then what (we) know now

if the shoe fits (wear it)   A moribund metaphor (SEE).

if the truth be (were) known (told)   An ineffectual phrase (SEE).

if we can send a man to the moon, we can . . .

if (the) worse (worst) comes to (the) worst

if you can't beat them, join them   A popular prescription (SEE).

if you can't say something nice, don't say anything   A plebeian sentiment (SEE). SEE ALSO *be nice.*

if you can't stand the heat, stay out of the kitchen   A popular prescription (SEE).

if you don't know, I'm not going to tell you   An infantile phrase (SEE).

if you get my drift

if you know what I mean

if you liked . . . , you'll love . . .

if you think . . . , you've got another think coming

if you've seen one, you've seen them all

ignominious retreat

ignorance is bliss   A plebeian sentiment (SEE).

I got to (have to) tell you (something)   An ineffectual phrase (SEE). ■ *I got to tell you,* he was the only person I could discuss my frustrations with. DELETE *I got to tell you.* ■ *I've got to tell you something,* I'm so proud of you. DELETE *I've got to tell you something.* ■ *I have to tell you,* the emerging country rates are up 21 percent. DELETE *I have to tell you.* SEE ALSO *I'll tell you (something); I'll tell you what; I'm telling you; let me tell you (something).*

I hate to say it (but)

I hear you   An infantile phrase (SEE). ■ *I hear you.* REPLACE WITH *I understand.* SEE ALSO *don't get me wrong.*

I just work here   A plebeian sentiment (SEE).

I know the feeling

I'll believe it when I see it

I'll be the first to admit

I'll bet you any amount of money   An infantile phrase (SEE).

ill-gotten gains   An inescapable pair (SEE).

I'll know (it) when I see (it)

I'll tell you (something)   An ineffectual phrase (SEE). ■ You got off easy, *I'll tell you.* DELETE *I'll tell you.* ■ *I'll tell you something,* they look like the greatest team ever. DELETE *I'll tell you something.* SEE ALSO *I got to (have to) tell you (something); I'll tell you what; I'm telling you; let me tell you (something).*

I'll tell you what   An ineffectual phrase (SEE). ■ *I'll tell you what,* let's pause for a commercial and then you can tell us your story. DELETE *I'll tell you what.* ■ *I'll tell you what,* I'm not bitter against women, but I sure judge them quicker now. DELETE *I'll tell you what.* SEE ALSO *I got to (have to) tell you (something); I'll tell you (something); I'm telling you; let me tell you (something).*

I love (him) but I'm not *in* love with (him)   A popular prescription (SEE).

imagine for a moment   ■ To understand the significance of the two EDT modules, *imagine for a moment* that you are dictating a letter to a secretary. REPLACE WITH *imagine.*

I'm bored (he's boring)   A plebeian sentiment (SEE). Being boring is preferable to being bored. The boring are often thoughtful and imaginative; the bored, thoughtless and unimaginative.

   We would do well to shun those who whine about how bored they are or how boring another is. It's they, these bored ones, who in their eternal quest for entertainment and self-oblivion are most suited to causing trouble, courting turmoil and coercing talk. SEE ALSO *(it) keeps (me) busy.*

I mean   A grammatical gimmick (SEE). Elliptical for *what I mean to say,*

I mean is said by those who do not altogether know what they mean to say. ■ Nobody deserves to die like that. *I mean*, he didn't stand a chance. DELETE *I mean*. ■ *I mean*, being in the entertainment field is not easy; *I mean*, I work hard at my job and still have performances to give. DELETE *I mean*.

imitation is the sincerest form of flattery   A popular prescription (SEE).

imminent danger

I'm not going to sit here and . . .

I'm not perfect (you know) A plebeian sentiment (SEE). Even though *(I'm) a perfectionist* is a suspect superlative, meaning that people who proclaim this do not easily disabuse themselves of the notion of being perfect, *I'm not perfect (you know)* is a plebeian sentiment, meaning that people who proclaim this all too easily excuse themselves for being imperfect. ■ I have some deep-seated anger. Hey, *I'm not perfect, you know*. SEE ALSO *(I'm) a perfectionist; nobody's perfect.*

I'm not stupid (you know) A plebeian sentiment (SEE). ■ *I'm not stupid, you know*; I'm twenty-four years old, and I've been around.

impact (on) *(v)* An overworked word (SEE). *act on; affect; bear on; influence; sway; work on.* ■ Let's look at two important trends that may *impact* the future of those languages. USE *influence*. ■ Everybody's district is *impacted* in a different way. USE *affected*. SEE ALSO *has an impact on.*

impending doom

implement An overworked word (SEE). *accomplish; achieve; carry out; complete; execute; fulfill; realize.*

impossible dream

I'm sorry A plebeian sentiment (SEE). No simple apology, the plebeian *I'm sorry* pretends to soothe while it actually scolds. Even though it may seem like an apology — often for something that requires nothing of the sort — *I'm sorry* is said, unapologetically, in a tone of resentment.

Traditionally a woman's emotion — for women have been, more than men, reluctant to express anger, bare and unbounded — resentment more and more of late finds favor with men and women alike.

Some people do indeed know how to *be nice* (SEE). ■ You didn't get fat by eating cheeseburgers, *I'm sorry*. ■ Nine years old is too young to be left alone, *I'm sorry*. ■ I have to disagree. *I'm sorry*. SEE ALSO *excuse me?; thank you.*

I'm telling you An ineffectual phrase (SEE). ■ It has more twists and turns than Route 66, *I'm telling you*. DELETE *I'm telling you*. ■ *I'm telling you*, there are people who take this seriously. DELETE *I'm telling you*. SEE ALSO *I got to (have to) tell you (something); I'll tell you (something); I'll tell you what; let me tell you (something).*

in a bad mood A torpid term (SEE). *angry; annoyed; cheerless; cross; dejected; depressed; despondent; discouraged; dispirited; displeased; downcast; enraged; furious; gloomy; glum; grouchy; irate; irritated; mad; morose;*

peevish; sad; testy; troubled; uneasy; unhappy; upset; vexed; worried. SEE ALSO *negative feelings.*

in a big (major) way   *a great deal; badly; consumedly; enormously; exceedingly; extremely; greatly; hugely; immensely; intensely; largely; mightily; prodigiously; seriously; strongly; very much.* ■ He wants to meet me *in a big way.* REPLACE WITH *very much.* ■ It hurt me *in a big way.* REPLACE WITH *badly.* SEE ALSO *in the worst way.*

in a bind   *at risk; endangered; hardpressed; imperiled; in danger; in difficulty; in jeopardy; in peril; in trouble; jeopardized.*

in (the) absence of   A dimwitted redundancy (SEE). *absent; having no; lacking; minus; missing; not having; with no; without.* ■ *In the absence of* these articulated linkages, changes introduced will be difficult to monitor. USE *Absent.*

in a class by (itself)   *different; exceptional; extraordinary; incomparable; inimitable; matchless; notable; noteworthy; novel; odd; original; peculiar; peerless; remarkable; singular; special; strange; uncommon; unequaled; unexampled; unique; unmatched; unparalleled; unrivaled; unusual; without equal.*

in a dog's age   A moribund metaphor (SEE).

in advance of   A dimwitted redundancy (SEE). *ahead of; before.* ■ *In advance of* introducing our guest, let me tell you why he's here. USE *Before.* SEE ALSO *prior to.*

in a former life

in a (blue) funk   A moribund metaphor (SEE). *aggrieved; blue; cheerless; dejected; demoralized; depressed; despondent; disconsolate; discouraged; disheartened; dismal; dispirited; doleful; downcast; downhearted; dreary; forlorn; funereal; gloomy; glum; grieved; low; melancholy; miserable; mournful; plaintive; sad; sorrowful; unhappy; woeful.*

in a good mood   A torpid term (SEE). *blissful; blithe; buoyant; cheerful; cheery; content; contented; delighted; elated; excited; gay; glad; gleeful; happy; jolly; joyful; joyous; merry; pleased; sanguine; satisfied.* SEE ALSO *positive feelings.*

in a heartbeat   A moribund metaphor (SEE). *abruptly; apace; at once; briskly; directly; expeditiously; fast; forthwith; hastily; hurriedly; immediately; instantaneously; instantly; posthaste; promptly; quickly; rapidly; rashly; right away; speedily; straightaway; swiftly; wingedly.*

in a jam   *at risk; endangered; hardpressed; imperiled; in danger; in difficulty; in jeopardy; in peril; in trouble; jeopardized.*

in a manner of speaking   A dimwitted redundancy (SEE). *as it were; in a sense; in a way; so to speak.* ■ Your contractor is correct *in a manner of speaking.* USE *in a sense.*

in and of itself (themselves)
A dimwitted redundancy (SEE). *as such; in itself (in themselves).* ■ This trend is interesting *in and of itself* but is also quite instructive. USE *in itself.*

■ All the benefits are worthwhile *in and of themselves*, but they have the additional benefit of translating into improved cost efficiency. USE *in themselves*.

in a nutshell   *briefly; concisely; in brief; in short; in sum; succinctly; tersely*.

in any way, shape and (or) form
An infantile phrase (SEE). *at all; in any way; in some way; in the least; somehow; someway*. ■ Do you feel being on television will help you *in any way, shape or form*? USE *somehow*. ■ That control is no longer there, not *in any way, shape or form*. USE *at all*. SEE ALSO *in every way, shape and (or) form; in no way, shape or form*.

in a pickle   *at risk; endangered; hard-pressed; imperiled; in danger; in difficulty; in jeopardy; in peril; in trouble; jeopardized*.

in a pig's eye   A moribund metaphor (SEE). *by no means; in no way; never; no; not at all; not ever; not in any way; not in the least*.

(stuck) in a rut   A moribund metaphor (SEE). *bogged down; caught; cornered; enmeshed; ensnared; entangled; entrapped; netted; mired; snared; stuck; trapped*.

in a state of confusion

in a (constant) state of flux
■ Companies in a highly competitive industry are usually *in a constant state of flux* as they vie for market share. REPLACE WITH *forever in flux*.

in a state of shock

in a timely fashion (manner; way)   A dimwitted redundancy (SEE). *in time; promptly; quickly; rapidly; right away; shortly; soon; speedily; swiftly; timely*. ■ He believes in getting the job done *in a timely fashion* and is very committed to achieving that goal.

in a word   *briefly; concisely; in brief; in short; in sum; succinctly; tersely*.

(off) in a world of (his) own
A moribund metaphor (SEE). *absent; absentminded; absorbed; abstracted; bemused; captivated; daydreaming; detached; distracted; distrait; dreamy; engrossed; enraptured; faraway; fascinated; immersed; inattentive; lost; mesmerized; oblivious; preoccupied; rapt; spellbound*.

in (her) birthday suit   A moribund metaphor (SEE). *bare; disrobed; naked; nude; stripped; unclothed; uncovered; undressed*.

inclement weather   An inescapable pair (SEE).

in close (near) proximity to
A dimwitted redundancy (SEE). *close by; close to; in proximity; near; nearby*. ■ Cities were born out of the desire and necessity of human beings to live and work *in close proximity to* each other. USE *close to*.

in (the) clover   A moribund metaphor (SEE). *affluent; moneyed; opulent; prosperous; rich; wealthy; well-off; well-to-do*.

in cold blood   A moribund metaphor (SEE). *deliberately; intentionally; knowingly; mindfully; on purpose; premeditatively; willfully*.

in connection with A dimwitted redundancy (See). *about; as for; as to; concerning; for; in; of; on; over; regarding; respecting; to; toward; with.* ■ The police wanted to talk to him *in connection with* a fur store robbery. Use *about.* ■ *In connection with* the hiring incidents, this was the first time he denied any wrongdoing. Use *Concerning.*

incontrovertible fact

in (my) corner A moribund metaphor (See).

incredible An overworked word (See).
1. *beyond belief; beyond comprehension; doubtful; dubious; implausible; improbable; incomprehensible; inconceivable; inexplicable; questionable; unfathomable; unimaginable; unthinkable.*
2. *astonishing; astounding; breathtaking; extraordinary; fabulous; fantastic; marvelous; miraculous; overwhelming; prodigious; sensational; spectacular; wonderful.*
   Like the platitudinous *unbelievable*, this word is very much overused.
   We would do well to try to distinguish ourselves through our speech rather than rely on the words and phrases that nearly everyone else uses.
   Those who speak as others speak, inescapably, think as others think. ■ But that someone would shoot a two-year-old child is *incredible*. Replace with *unimaginable*. ■ All these people are *incredibly* brave. Replace with *astonishingly*. See also *unbelievable.*

incumbent upon A torpid term (See). *binding; compelling; compulsory; essential; imperative; mandatory; neces-*

sary; obligatory; required; requisite; urgent.

in (his) cups A moribund metaphor (See). *besotted; crapulous; drunk; inebriated; intoxicated; sodden; stupefied; tipsy.*

incurable romantic

indebtedness A torpid term (See). *debt.*

indelible impression An inescapable pair (See).

in-depth analysis An inescapable pair (See).

indicate A torpid term (See). *Indicate* has usurped almost all words that might be used instead of it.
More exact words include *acknowledge; admit; affirm; allow; announce; assert; avow; betoken; claim; confess; comment; concede; contend; declare; disclose; divulge; expose; feel; hint; hold; imply; insinuate; intimate; maintain; make known; mention; note; point out; profess; remark; reveal; say; show; signal; signify; state; suggest; tell; uncover; unveil.* ■ He *indicated* that he would be fine. Replace with *said.* ■ People have provided us with documents that *indicate* that veterans were exposed. Replace with *reveal.* ■ They have *indicated* that they do not understand the managed competition proposals and don't want to. Replace with *confessed.* ■ Last week's decision of the Federal Reserve Board *indicated* that minority-lending records will be an issue for many years to come. Replace with *signaled.*

individual(s) (*n*) A torpid term

(SEE). *anybody; anyone; everybody; everyone; man; men; people; person; somebody; someone; those; woman; women; you.* ■ This *individual* needs to be stopped. REPLACE WITH *woman.* ■ He seemed like a friendly enough *individual.* REPLACE WITH *person.*

in due course (time) *at length; eventually; in time; ultimately; yet.*

ineffectual phrases Ineffectual phrases are empty phrases; no sentence is made more meaningful by their inclusion: *(please) be advised that; I'll tell you (something); it has come to (my) attention; it is interesting to note (that); (you) know what I'm telling you?; the fact of the matter is; the fact remains; the thing about it is; (I would like) to take this opportunity; what happened (is).*

How a person speaks demonstrates how he thinks. And how he thinks determines how he behaves. A person who speaks ineffectually thinks ineffectually, and a person who thinks ineffectually behaves ineffectually.

Ineffectual phrases add only to our being ineffectual people.

in (his) element

inescapable conclusion

inescapable pairs In an inescapable pair, the first word means much the same as the second or so often accompanies the second that any distinction between them is, in effect, forfeited.

And when two words are treated as though they were one—the plight of every inescapable pair—our keenness is compromised, our discernment endangered: *abject poverty; aid and abet;*

alive and well; basic principle; beautiful baby; bloodcurdling scream; closely allied; cutthroat competition; delicate balance; dubious distinction; effective and efficient; egregious error; extenuating circumstances; far and wide; fulsome praise; hope and pray; hue and cry; inextricably tied; meteoric rise; pleasant surprise; pure and simple; richly deserves; serious reservations; short and sweet; sorely missed; valuable asset.

No longer does every word tell; the words themselves have become witless. SEE ALSO *dimwitted redundancies.*

in every way, shape and (or) form An infantile phrase (SEE). *altogether; completely; entirely; fully; quite; thoroughly; in all ways; in every way; perfectly; totally; unreservedly; utterly; wholly.* ■ He supports her *in every way, shape and form.* USE *thoroughly.* SEE ALSO *in any way, shape and (or) form; in no way, shape or form.*

in excess of A torpid term (SEE). *above; better than; beyond; faster than; greater than; larger than; more than; over; stronger than.* ■ *In excess of* ten candidates wanted to make the town of Andover both their profession and their home. USE *More than.* ■ Police said Mr. Howard was driving *in excess of* ninety miles per hour. USE *faster than.*

in extremis A foreignism (SEE). *decaying; declining; deteriorating; disintegrating; dying; ebbing; expiring; fading; failing; near death; sinking; waning.*

inextricably tied An inescapable pair (SEE). ■ In good times and in bad, our future and our fortunes are *inextricably tied* together.

infantile phrases   Infantile phrases make us doubt the seriousness or sincerity of those who use them, for any thought or feeling in which these expressions are found is likely to be made instantly laughable: *absolutely, positively; all of the above; because (that's why); because why?; (as) compared to what?; (he) goes; going on (nineteen); I'll bet you any amount of money; in the wrong place at the wrong time; it takes one to know one; (tiny) little bit; me, myself and I; me neither; never (not) in a million years; real, live; really and truly; (you) started it; (I) take it back; the feeling's mutual; the (F)-word; (my) whole, entire life; with a capital (A); (sixty-two) years young; (a) zillion(s) (of).*

Also included among these phrases that strike all but the dimwitted as derisory are notorious advertising slogans (*inquiring minds want to know; where's the beef*), song and film titles (*a funny thing happened to me on the way to; I can't get no satisfaction*), and alliterative or rhymed phrases (*a bevy of beauties; chrome dome*).

Infantile phrases are popular among adolescents — and dimwits who still think like them.

in fine fettle   *energetic; fine; fit; good; hale; hardy; healthful; healthy; hearty; robust; sound; strong; vigorous; well.*

info   ■ Do you have any *info* about their proposal? REPLACE WITH *information*. SEE ALSO *demo; recap.*

in for a rude awakening (shock)   ■ The companies that still think the only ones who are going to make it are Caucasian males are *in for a rude awakening.*

in for a (pleasant) surprise   ■ If she had set out to write a story about a spoiled brat, she was *in for a surprise.*

in full flower   A moribund metaphor (SEE).

in full swing   A moribund metaphor (SEE).

(you're) in good company

in harm's way   *exposed; insecure; obnoxious; unguarded; unprotected; unsafe; unsheltered; unshielded; vulnerable.*

in (my) heart of hearts

in high gear   A moribund metaphor (SEE). *abruptly; apace; briskly; directly; expeditiously; fast; hastily; hurriedly; immediately; instantaneously; instantly; posthaste; promptly; quickly; rapidly; rashly; speedily; swiftly; wingedly.*

in hot pursuit

in hot water   A moribund metaphor (SEE). *at risk; endangered; hard-pressed; imperiled; in danger; in difficulty; in jeopardy; in peril; in trouble; jeopardized.*

in (their) hour of need

in (my) humble opinion

in (her) infinite wisdom

in it (this) for the long haul

(not) in it for the money

in its (their) entirety   A torpid

term (SEE). *all; complete; completely; entire; entirely; every; full; fully; whole; wholly.* ■ This would leave Wednesday, either partially or *in its entirety*, for coordination. USE *entirely*.

inject (new) life into   *animate; energize; enliven; inspirit; invigorate; vitalize.*

in less than no time   A moribund metaphor (SEE). *abruptly; apace; at once; briskly; directly; expeditiously; fast; forthwith; hastily; hurriedly; immediately; instantaneously; instantly; posthaste; promptly; quickly; rapidly; rashly; right away; speedily; straightaway; suddenly; swiftly; unexpectedly; wingedly.*

in living color

in loco parentis   A foreignism (SEE).

in (our) midst   A dimwitted redundancy (SEE). *amid; among.* ■ There are growing numbers of crazy people *in our midst.* REPLACE WITH *among us.*

in mint condition

in more ways than one

in nature   A dimwitted redundancy (SEE). ■ He said the diaries are personal *in nature.* DELETE *in nature.* ■ Laws governing freedom to protest politically are obviously political *in nature.* DELETE *in nature.*

(as) innocent as a newborn babe (child)   An insipid simile (SEE moribund metaphors).

innocent bystander   An inescap-

able pair (SEE). A bystander is necessarily innocent.

in nothing (no time) flat   *abruptly; apace; at once; briskly; directly; expeditiously; fast; forthwith; hastily; hurriedly; immediately; instantaneously; instantly; posthaste; promptly; quickly; rapidly; rashly; right away; speedily; straightaway; suddenly; swiftly; unexpectedly; wingedly.*

in no uncertain terms

in no way, shape or form   An infantile phrase (SEE). *by no means; in no way; never; no; not at all; not ever; not in any way; not in the least.* ■ The gas contributed *in no way, shape or form* to the fire. USE *not at all.* ■ *In no way, shape or form* did she resemble a sixty-three-year-old woman. USE *In no way.*

As silly as this phrase is, it is apparently too sober for some people. ■ *In no way, shape, form or fashion* was there any wrongdoing or misappropriation of funds. USE *Never.* SEE ALSO *in any way, shape and (or) form; in every way, shape and (or) form.*

(goes) in one ear and out the other   A moribund metaphor (SEE). *forgetful; heedless; inattentive; neglectful; negligent; oblivious; remiss; thoughtless; unmindful; unthinking.*

in one fell swoop

(get) in on the ground floor   A moribund metaphor (SEE).

in over (my) head   A moribund metaphor (SEE).
1. *overburdened; overextended; over-*

loaded; overwhelmed.
2. *in arrears; in debt.*

in (her) own inimitable way

(he's) in (his) own world   *self-absorbed; self-involved; solipsistic.*

in point of fact   A dimwitted redundancy (SEE). *actually; indeed; in fact; in faith; in reality; in truth; truly.* ■ *In point of fact*, we do all the wrong things, and we have for years. USE *In fact*. ■ *In point of fact*, Krakatoa is west of Java, but east apparently sounded better to Hollywood. USE *Actually*. ■ There aren't, *in point of fact*, one or two buildings; there are two exactly. DELETE *in point of fact*.

input   A torpid term (SEE). *data; feelings; ideas; information; recommendations; suggestions; thoughts; views.* ■ We would appreciate *input* from anyone who has knowledge in the above areas. REPLACE WITH *information*. ■ Of course, discretion must be used in evaluating their *inputs* since sales reps are biased toward lowering prices and pushing volume. REPLACE WITH *suggestions*. SEE ALSO *(the) bottom line; feedback; interface; output; parameters*.

inquiring minds (want to know)
An infantile phrase (SEE).

in rare form

in (with) reference to   A dimwitted redundancy (SEE). *about; as for; as to; concerning; for; in; of; on; over; regarding; respecting; to; toward; with.* ■ *With reference to* the latest attempt to forge statehood for the District of Columbia, I favor our ancestors' concept that the District ought to be an

entity unto itself. USE *As for*.

in (with) regard to   A dimwitted redundancy (SEE). *about; as for; as to; concerning; for; in; of; on; over; regarding; respecting; to; toward; with.* ■ *With regard to* the StataQuest, I am expecting the first six chapters sometime this week. USE *Regarding*.

in (with) respect to   A dimwitted redundancy (SEE). *about; as for; as to; concerning; for; in; of; on; over; regarding; respecting; to; toward; with.* ■ Some history *with respect to* the origins and evolution of the AS/400 will then be discussed. USE *of*.

insane   An overworked word (SEE). *Insane* is overused in its more popular sense of *absurd; comical; extravagant; farcical; foolhardy; foolish; idiotic; illogical; imbecilic; impractical; inane; incongruous; irrational; laughable; ludicrous; moronic; nonsensical; preposterous; ridiculous; senseless; silly; unreasonable.* SEE ALSO *absurd*.

in seventh heaven   A moribund metaphor (SEE). *blissful; blithe; buoyant; cheerful; delighted; ecstatic; elated; enraptured; euphoric; exalted; excited; exhilarated; exultant; gay; glad; gleeful; good-humored; happy; intoxicated; jolly; jovial; joyful; joyous; jubilant; merry; mirthful; overjoyed; pleased; rapturous; thrilled.*

in short order   *abruptly; apace; at once; briskly; directly; expeditiously; fast; forthwith; hastily; hurriedly; immediately; instantaneously; instantly; posthaste; promptly; quickly; rapidly; rashly; right away; speedily; straightaway; swiftly; wingedly.*

in short supply *exiguous; inadequate; meager; rare; scant; scanty; scarce; sparse; uncommon; unusual.*

inside (and) out *altogether; completely; entirely; fully; perfectly; quite; thoroughly; totally; unreservedly; utterly; wholly.*

inspiring sight An inescapable pair (SEE).

in spite of the fact that A dimwitted redundancy (SEE). *although; but; even if; even though; still; though; yet.* ■ This is true *in spite of the fact that* a separate symbol has been designated for input and output operations. USE *even though.* SEE ALSO *despite the fact that; regardless of the fact that.*

in (within) striking distance A moribund metaphor (SEE).

(don't) insult (my) intelligence

integral part An inescapable pair (SEE).

interesting An overworked word (SEE). *absorbing; alluring; amusing; arresting; captivating; charming; curious; diverting; enchanting; engaging; engrossing; entertaining; enticing; exciting; fascinating; gripping; intriguing; invigorating; inviting; pleasing; provocative; refreshing; riveting; spellbinding; stimulating; taking; tantalizing.* Few words are as overworked as this one. It is the dimwitted — those uninteresting to themselves as well as to others — who can think of no synonymous word. SEE ALSO *that's interesting.*

interface A torpid term (SEE). SEE

ALSO *(the) bottom line; feedback; input; output; parameters.*

in terms of A dimwitted redundancy (SEE). This phrase is most often a ponderous replacement for simpler words like *about; as for; as to; concerning; for; in; of; on; regarding; respecting; through; with.* And with some slight thought, the phrase frequently can be pared from a sentence. ■ *In terms of* what women need to know about men, I have learned a lot. USE *Regarding.* ■ A key element *in terms of* quality health care is going to be having the best *in terms of the* education and continuing educational abilities to train the best in this country. USE *of;* DELETE *in terms of the.* ■ For further information, you would want to read outside sources that analyze *your competitors in terms of their products.* USE *your competitors' products.*

intestinal fortitude An infantile phrase (SEE). *boldness; bravery; courage; daring; determination; endurance; firmness; fortitude; grit; guts; hardihood; hardiness; intrepidity; mettle; nerve; perseverance; resolution; resolve; spirit; spunk; stamina; steadfastness; tenacity.* ■ It takes a little luck and a lot of *intestinal fortitude* to break into a game. REPLACE WITH *daring.*

in the altogether *bare; disrobed; naked; nude; stripped; unclothed; uncovered; undressed.*

in the arms of Morpheus A moribund metaphor (SEE). *asleep; dozing; dreaming; napping; sleeping; slumbering; unconscious.*

in the back of (my) mind *subconsciously; subliminally.* ■ I always knew, *in the back of my mind*, that something was bothering him. RE-PLACE WITH *subconsciously*.

(it's) in the bag   A moribund metaphor (SEE). *assured; certain; definite; guaranteed; incontestable; incontrovertible; indisputable; indubitable; positive; secure; sure; unquestionable.*

in the best interest of

in the best sense of the word

in the black   A moribund metaphor (SEE). *debt-free; debtless.*

in the blink of an eye   A moribund metaphor (SEE). *abruptly; apace; at once; briskly; directly; expeditiously; fast; forthwith; hastily; hurriedly; immediately; instantaneously; instantly; posthaste; promptly; quickly; rapidly; rashly; right away; speedily; straightaway; suddenly; swiftly; unexpectedly; wingedly.*

in the buff   *bare; disrobed; naked; nude; stripped; unclothed; uncovered; undressed.*

in the cards   A moribund metaphor (SEE). *apt; certain; destined; fated; foreordained; imminent; impending; liable; likely; possible; probable; ordained; prearranged; predestined; predetermined; sure.*

in the chips   A moribund metaphor (SEE). *affluent; moneyed; opulent; prosperous; rich; wealthy; well-off; well-to-do.*

in the clear
1. *absolved; acquitted; blameless; clear; excused; exonerated; faultless; guiltless; inculpable; innocent; irreproachable;*
unblamable; unblameworthy; vindicated.
2. *guarded; protected; safe; secure; sheltered; shielded.*
3. *debt-free; debtless.*

in the closet   A moribund metaphor (SEE). *clandestine; concealed; confidential; covert; hidden; private; secret; secluded; shrouded; surreptitious; undercover; unspoken; veiled.*

in the cold light of reason   A moribund metaphor (SEE).

in the dark   A moribund metaphor (SEE). *ignorant; incognizant; insensible; nescient; unacquainted; unadvised; unapprised; unaware; unenlightened; unfamiliar; uninformed; unintelligent; unknowing; unschooled; untaught; unversed.* ■ They told me everything; I was never *in the dark*. REPLACE WITH *uninformed*.

in the dead of night   A moribund metaphor (SEE).

in the distant future   A dimwitted redundancy (SEE). *at length; eventually; finally; in the end; in time; later; one day; over the (months); over time; someday; sometime; ultimately; with time.* ■ A similar agreement with Mexico could result in a true North American common market *in the distant future*. USE *one day*. SEE ALSO *in the immediate future; in the near future; in the not-too-distant future.*

in the doghouse   A moribund metaphor (SEE). *in disfavor; in disgrace.*

in the driver's seat   A moribund metaphor (SEE). *administer; boss; command; control; dictate; direct; dominate;*

govern; in charge; in command; in control; manage; manipulate; master; order; overpower; oversee; predominate; prevail; reign over; rule; superintend. ■ Buyers are definitely *in the driver's seat*. REPLACE WITH *in control*.

(down) in the dumps A moribund metaphor (SEE). *aggrieved; blue; cheerless; dejected; demoralized; depressed; despondent; disconsolate; discouraged; disheartened; dismal; dispirited; doleful; downcast; downhearted; dreary; forlorn; funereal; gloomy; glum; grieved; low; melancholy; miserable; mournful; plaintive; sad; sorrowful; unhappy; woeful.*

in the event (that) A dimwitted redundancy (SEE). *if; should.* ■ *In the event* you think I am overreacting, let me call attention to the realities of the contemporary workplace. USE *If* or *Should.*

in the eyes of society (the world)

in the eyes of the beholder

in the final (last) analysis A dimwitted redundancy (SEE). *in the end; ultimately.*

in the first place A dimwitted redundancy (SEE). *first.* ■ *In the first place,* I don't want to, and *in the second place,* I can't afford to. USE *First; second.* SEE ALSO *in the second place.*

in the flesh A moribund metaphor (SEE).
1. *alive.*
2. *in person; present.*

in the heat of battle A moribund metaphor (SEE).

in the heat of the moment A moribund metaphor (SEE).

in the history of the universe (world)

in the immediate future A dimwitted redundancy (SEE). *at once; at present; before long; currently; directly; immediately; in a (week); next (month); now; presently; quickly; shortly; soon; straightaway; this (month).* ■ I will, *in the immediate future,* contact my fellow mayor in New York and ask him to make a decision. USE *this week.* SEE ALSO *in the distant future; in the near future; in the not-too-distant future.*

in (on) the issue (matter; subject) of A dimwitted redundancy (SEE). *about; as for; as to; concerning; for; in; of; on; over; regarding; respecting; to; toward; with.* ■ This state used to be a leader *on the issue of* health reform. USE *in.* ■ *On the matter of* quality in teaching, he proposed a more symbiotic relationship between classroom time and research. USE *As for.*

in the know
1. *able; adept; apt; capable; competent; conversant; deft; dexterous; experienced; expert; familiar; practiced; proficient; seasoned; skilled; skillful; veteran.*
2. *adroit; astute; bright; brilliant; clever; discerning; effective; effectual; efficient; enlightened; insightful; intelligent; judicious; keen; knowledgeable; learned; logical; luminous; perceptive; perspicacious; quick; rational; reasonable; sagacious; sage; sapient; sensible; sharp; shrewd; smart; sound; wise.*

(live) in the lap of luxury A moribund metaphor (SEE). *affluent; mon-*

eyed; opulent; prosperous; rich; wealthy; well-off; well-to-do.

in the limelight

in the line of fire

in (over) the long run (term)
A dimwitted redundancy (SEE). *at length; eventually; finally; in the end; in time; later; long-term; one day; over the (months); over time; someday; sometime; ultimately; with time.* ■ *In the long run*, that may be the most important thing. USE *Over time.* SEE ALSO *in (over) the short run (term).*

in the mainstream

(a legend) in the making

in the market for A moribund metaphor (SEE). *able to afford; desire; looking for; need; ready to buy; require; seeking; want; wish for.*

in the midst of A dimwitted redundancy (SEE). *amid; among; between; encircled by; encompassed by; in; inside; in the middle of; surrounded by.* ■ The United States, *in the midst of* increasing tension over Korea, is softening its tone on China. USE *amid.* ■ My profound conviction is that anytime we are together, Christ is *in the midst of* us. USE *among.*

in the money *affluent; moneyed; opulent; prosperous; rich; wealthy; well-off; well-to-do.*

in the national interest ■ But shorter workweeks, many argue, are *in the national interest.*

in the near future A dimwitted re-dundancy (SEE). *before long; directly; eventually; in time; later; one day; presently; quickly; shortly; sometime; soon.* ■ I'm looking forward to the possibility that you might review my work *in the near future.* USE *soon.* SEE ALSO *in the distant future; in the immediate future; in the not-too-distant future.*

in the neighborhood of A dimwitted redundancy (SEE). *about; around; close to; more or less; near; nearly; or so; roughly; some.* ■ The rebels may have killed *in the neighborhood of* ten people. USE *close to.* SEE ALSO *in the vicinity of.*

in the nick of time

in the not-too-distant future
A dimwitted redundancy (SEE). *before long; directly; eventually; in time; later; one day; presently; quickly; shortly; sometime; soon.* ■ *In the not-too-distant future*, Americans will have the telephone equivalent of a superhighway to every home and business. USE *Before long.* SEE ALSO *in the distant future; in the immediate future; in the near future.*

in the not-too-distant past A dimwitted redundancy (SEE). *before; earlier; formerly; not long ago; once; recently.* ■ *In the not-too-distant past*, women were expected to be home, be nice, be sexy and be quiet. USE *Not long ago.* SEE ALSO *in the past; in the recent past.*

in the offing A moribund metaphor (SEE). *approaching; at hand; close; coming; expected; forthcoming; imminent; impending; near; nearby.*

in the palm of my hand A moribund metaphor (SEE).

in the past   A dimwitted redundancy (SEE). ■ I'm just saying what we did do *in the past*. DELETE *in the past*. ■ We can remember *in the past* when we sometimes had two or three representatives. DELETE *in the past*. SEE ALSO *in the not-too-distant past; in the recent past*.

in the picture   A moribund metaphor (SEE).

in the pink   A moribund metaphor (SEE). *energetic; fine; fit; good; hale; hardy; healthful; healthy; hearty; robust; sound; strong; vigorous; well.*

in the pipeline   A moribund metaphor (SEE).

in the prime of life

in the process of -ing   A dimwitted redundancy (SEE). Even though *in the process of* seems to add significance to what is being said—and to who is saying it—it plainly subtracts from both. ■ The hurricane is *in the process of* making a slow turn to the northeast. DELETE *in the process of*. ■ I'm *in the process of* going on a lot of interviews. DELETE *in the process of*.

in the public eye

in the recent past   A dimwitted redundancy (SEE). *before; earlier; formerly; lately; not long ago; of late; once; recent; recently.* ■ *In the recent past*, such performers were on the fringes of American culture. USE *Recently*. SEE ALSO *in the not-too-distant past; in the past*.

in the red   A moribund metaphor (SEE). *in arrears; in debt.*

in the right place at the right time   An infantile phrase (SEE). SEE ALSO *in the wrong place at the wrong time*.

in the running

in the saddle   A moribund metaphor (SEE). *administer; boss; command; control; dictate; direct; dominate; govern; in charge; in command; in control; manage; manipulate; master; order; overpower; oversee; predominate; prevail; reign over; rule; superintend.*

in the same boat   A moribund metaphor (SEE).

in the second place   A dimwitted redundancy (SEE). *second.* ■ *In the second place*, I sincerely believe that the merger has given it another chance to become the quality institution these students deserve. USE *Second*. SEE ALSO *in the first place*.

in (over) the short run (term)   A dimwitted redundancy (SEE). *at present; before long; currently; directly; eventually; in time; later; next (month); now; one day; presently; quickly; shortly; short-term; sometime; soon; this (month).* ■ I hope we're able to do something about this *in the short term*. USE *soon*. SEE ALSO *in (over) the long run (term)*.

in the soup   A moribund metaphor (SEE). *at risk; endangered; hard-pressed; imperiled; in a bind; in a dilemma; in a fix; in a jam; in a predicament; in a quandary; in danger; in difficulty; in jeopardy; in peril; in trouble; jeopardized.*

in the spirit of the moment (of things)

in the spotlight   A moribund metaphor (SEE).

in the swim   A moribund metaphor (SEE). *absorbed; active; busy; employed; engaged; engrossed; immersed; involved; occupied; preoccupied; wrapped up in.*

in the thick of (it)
1. *amid; among; encircled; encompassed; in the middle; surrounded.*
2. *absorbed; active; busy; employed; engaged; engrossed; immersed; involved; occupied; preoccupied; wrapped up in.*

in the trenches   A moribund metaphor (SEE).

in the twinkling (wink) of an eye
A moribund metaphor (SEE). *abruptly; apace; at once; briskly; directly; expeditiously; fast; forthwith; hastily; hurriedly; immediately; instantaneously; instantly; posthaste; promptly; quickly; rapidly; rashly; right away; speedily; straightaway; suddenly; swiftly; unexpectedly; wingedly.*

in the vicinity of   A dimwitted redundancy (SEE). *about; around; close to; more or less; near; nearly; or so; roughly; some.* ■ The final phase prohibits smoking anywhere *in the vicinity of* the main building's entrance. USE *near*. SEE ALSO *in the neighborhood of*.

in the wake of   A moribund metaphor (SEE). *after; behind; ensuing; following; succeeding.* SEE ALSO *(hot) on the heels of.*

in the wastebasket   A moribund metaphor (SEE). *abandoned; discarded; dismissed; jettisoned; rejected; repudiated; thrown out; tossed out.*

in the way of   A dimwitted redundancy (SEE). ■ They don't think they'll meet much *in the way of* resistance. DELETE *in the way of.* ■ The result is a staggering investment in foreign-oriented training with little *in the way of* return on investment. DELETE *in the way of.* ■ They didn't have much *in the way of* money. DELETE *in the way of.*

in the wee small hours   *very early*

in the whole wide world   An infantile phrase (SEE).

in the works

in the worst (possible) way
a great deal; badly; consumedly; exceedingly; extremely; greatly; hugely; immensely; intensely; mightily; prodigiously; seriously; very much. ■ The Eagles want to win *in the worst way.* REPLACE WITH *very much.* SEE ALSO *in a big way.*

in the wrong place at the wrong time   An infantile phrase (SEE). ■ That little girl was just *in the wrong place at the wrong time.* ■ He's a good kid who was just *in the wrong place at the wrong time.* SEE ALSO *in the right place at the right time.*

in this day and age   *at present; currently; now; presently; these days; today.* ■ In this day and age, we need to train medical students to see beyond the front door of the hospital and to see the broader issues. REPLACE WITH *Today.*

(we're) (all) in this together

intimately involved

in (their) time of need   ■ The ultimate beneficiaries are those who turn to the Clinic *in their time of need.*

in two shakes (of a lamb's tail) A moribund metaphor (SEE). *abruptly; apace; at once; briskly; directly; expeditiously; fast; forthwith; hastily; hurriedly; immediately; instantaneously; instantly; posthaste; promptly; quickly; rapidly; rashly; right away; speedily; straightaway; suddenly; swiftly; unexpectedly; wingedly.*

invest in (our) future

in view of the fact that A dimwitted redundancy (SEE). *because; considering; for; in that; since* ■ *In view of the fact that* you couldn't pay your bills, you became a prostitute? USE *Because.* SEE ALSO *because of the fact that; considering the fact that; by virtue of the fact that; given the fact that.*

involve An overworked word (SEE). *comprehend; comprise; consist of; contain; cover; embody; embrace; encompass; entail; include; incorporate.*

in your dreams

ironclad guarantee

iron (things) out

(too many) irons in the fire A moribund metaphor (SEE).

I shall return An infantile phrase (SEE).

is it just me?

is it me, or is it hot in here?

is nothing sacred?

(that word) is not in (my) vocabulary

(money) isn't everything ■ Price is important, but *price isn't everything.*

isolated An overworked word (SEE). For example: *isolated case; isolated event; isolated incident; isolated instance; isolated occurrence; isolated phenomenon.*

(that's what) it boils down to

it can't be done

it can't hurt

it couldn't have come (happened) at a worse time

it doesn't get any better than this

it doesn't take a rocket scientist to An infantile phrase (SEE).

it goes (works) both ways

it (just) goes to show (you)

it has been brought to (my) attention An ineffectual phrase (SEE). ■ *It has been brought to my attention* that we have no record of your order. REPLACE WITH *I have been told.* SEE ALSO *it has come to (my) attention.*

it has come to (my) attention An ineffectual phrase (SEE). ■ *It has come to our attention* that the number *3* is very popular. REPLACE WITH *We have learned.* SEE ALSO *it has been brought to (my) attention.*

I thought I would die

it is important to note (that) An ineffectual phrase (SEE). ■ *It is important to note that* you can change these settings for any document. DELETE *It is important to note that.* SEE ALSO *it is interesting to note (that); it is significant to note (that).*

it is important to remember (that) An ineffectual phrase (SEE). ■ *It is important to remember that* all three phases are important to your success. DELETE *It is important to remember that.*

it is important to understand (that) An ineffectual phrase (SEE). ■ *It is important to understand that* turning the grid lines on and off changes only the display on the monitor and not the printout. DELETE *It is important to understand that.* SEE ALSO *you have to understand (that).*

it is interesting to note (that) An ineffectual phrase (SEE). ■ *It is interesting to note that* although the sex hormone makes men more subject to baldness than women, it is more acceptable for women to wear wigs. DELETE *It is interesting to note that.* SEE ALSO *it is important to note (that); it is significant to note (that).*

(so) . . . it isn't (even) funny ■ We've got so much overcapacity in the securities business *it isn't funny.* ■ I'm so sick of her *it isn't funny.*

it isn't over till it's over A popular prescription (SEE).

it is significant to note (that) An ineffectual phrase (SEE). ■ *It is significant to note that* the original database has not been altered. DELETE *It is sig-*

nificant to note that. SEE ALSO *it is important to note (that); it is interesting to note (that).*

it is worth noting (that) An ineffectual phrase (SEE). ■ *It is worth noting that* he regarded her as "one of the finest writers of fiction." DELETE *It is worth noting that.*

it just happened An infantile phrase (SEE). As an explanation for how circumstances or incidents unfold, none is more puerile. And though we might excuse children such a sentiment, it is rarely they who express it. ■ It wasn't something I planned; *it just happened.* ■ What can I say? *it just happened.* SEE ALSO *because (that's why); whatever happens happens.*

it makes a world of difference

it makes you (stop and) think A plebeian sentiment (SEE).

it must (should) be mentioned (that) An ineffectual phrase (SEE). ■ *It should be mentioned that* hiperspace is used by authorized programs only. DELETE *It should be mentioned that.*

it must (should) be noted (that) An ineffectual phrase (SEE). ■ *It should be noted that* not all parents require an extensive interview. DELETE *It should be noted that.*

it must (should) be pointed out (that) An ineffectual phrase (SEE). ■ *It should be pointed out that* when you send this type of letter you must follow through with the filing in the court, or it can be looked on as a threat. DELETE *It should be pointed out that.*

it must (should) be realized (that) An ineffectual phrase (SEE). ▪ *It should be realized that* uncoupling is complete when the partners have defined themselves and are defined by others as separate and independent of each other. DELETE *It should be realized that.*

it must (should) be understood (that) An ineffectual phrase (SEE). ▪ *It should be understood that* a quitting concern assumption would be clearly disclosed on the financial statement. DELETE *It should be understood that.*

it never ceases (fails) to amaze me

it never ends A plebeian sentiment (SEE).

it never rains, but it pours A moribund metaphor (SEE).

I told you (so) An infantile phrase (SEE).

it's a bird, it's a plane, (it's Superman) An infantile phrase (SEE).

it's a dirty job, but someone's got to do it A popular prescription (SEE).

it's a dream come true

it's a fact of life

it's a free country An infantile phrase (SEE). Only fettered thinkers argue that *it's a free country.* ▪ If owners of eating establishments want to allow smoking, let them do so—*it's a free country.*

it's a jungle (out there) A moribund metaphor (SEE).

it's all Greek to me An infantile phrase (SEE). *abstract; abstruse; ambiguous; arcane; blurred; blurry; cloudy; confusing; cryptic; deep; dim; esoteric; impenetrable; inaccessible; incoherent; incomprehensible; indecipherable; indistinct; muddy; murky; nebulous; obscure; puzzling; recondite; unclear; unfathomable; unintelligible; vague.*

it's all relative An infantile phrase (SEE). This is a childish, indeed, a dimwitted, response to issues and inquiries that people have no considered response for. With *it's all relative,* a person scampers away from having to think. SEE ALSO *(as) compared to what? (as) opposed to what?*

it's a long story *It's a long story*—cipher for *I don't want to tell you*—is a mannerly expression that we use to thwart the interest of a person in whom we are not interested. SEE ALSO *that's for me to know and you to find out.*

it's always darkest just before dawn A popular prescription (SEE).

it's always something A plebeian sentiment (SEE).

it's a man's world

it's an art A suspect superlative (SEE). ▪ Parallel parking is not easy; *it's an art.*

it's a nice place to visit but I wouldn't want to live there A popular prescription (SEE).

it's anybody's guess

it's a sad day when

it's a small world

it's as simple as that

it's a start

it's a two-way street   A moribund metaphor (SEE).

it's a way of life

it's a whole different ballgame A moribund metaphor (SEE).

it's better than nothing   A popular prescription (SEE).

it's better to have loved and lost than never to have loved at all A popular prescription (SEE).

it's easy when you know how

it seemed like a lifetime   An insipid simile (SEE moribund metaphors).

it seemed like an eternity   An insipid simile (SEE moribund metaphors).

it's enough to drive (a person) to drink

it's got (your) name on it

it's like a death in the family   An insipid simile (SEE moribund metaphors).

it's like losing a member of the family   An insipid simile (SEE moribund metaphors).

it's (your) loss

it's more fun than a barrel of monkeys   A moribund metaphor (SEE).

it's (just) not going to happen

it's not over till (until) it's over A quack equation (SEE).

it's not over till (until) the fat lady sings   An infantile phrase (SEE).

it's not the end of the world

it's not the greatest in the world
1. *average; common; commonplace; customary; everyday; fair; mediocre; middling; normal; ordinary; passable; quotidian; regular; routine; standard; tolerable; typical; uneventful; unexceptional; unremarkable; usual.*
2. *inappreciable; inconsequential; inconsiderable; insignificant; minor; negligible; niggling; petty; trifling; trivial; unimportant; unsubstantial.*

it's not you, it's me

it's (been) one of those days A plebeian sentiment (SEE).

it's one thing after another   A plebeian sentiment (SEE). SEE ALSO *if it isn't one thing, it's another.*

it's only a matter of time

it's only money

it stands to reason (that)   An ineffectual phrase (SEE).

it's (always) the same (old) thing

it's what's inside that counts A popular prescription (SEE).

it takes all kinds   A popular prescription (SEE).

it takes one to know one   An infantile phrase (SEE).

it takes two   A popular prescription (SEE).

it takes two to tango   A popular prescription (SEE).

it was a dark and stormy night   An infantile phrase (SEE).

it was unreal

it will all come out in the wash   A moribund metaphor (SEE).

it won't happen again

it works both ways   A popular prescription (SEE).

(and) I use the term loosely

I've never been so humiliated in all my life

I've never seen anything like it

I wasn't born yesterday

I wouldn't kick (her) out of bed

I wouldn't wish (it) on my worst enemy   ■ I know enough family members, friends and acquaintances who have had cancer to know that *I wouldn't wish it on my worst enemy.*

J

jack of all trades and master of none

(Dr.) Jekyll-(Mr.) Hyde (personality)   A moribund metaphor (See).

je ne sais quoi   A foreignism (See).

John Hancock   A moribund metaphor (See). *signature.*

joie de vivre   A foreignism (See).

join forces   *ally; collaborate; comply; concur; conspire; cooperate; join; unite; work together.*

join the club

join together   A dimwitted redundancy (See). *join.* ■ ASA *joins* a powerful job scheduler *together* with select elements of automated operations to create a unique software system. De-lete *together.*

judge, jury and executioner

judge not, lest you be judged   A popular prescription (See).

juggling act   A moribund metaphor (See).

jump all over   A moribund metaphor (See). *admonish; anathematize; berate; blame; castigate; censure; chastise; chide; condemn; criticize; curse; decry; denounce; execrate; imprecate; inculpate; indict; rebuke; reprimand; reproach; reprove; scold; upbraid.*

jump at the chance

jump down (her) throat   A moribund metaphor (See). *admonish; animadvert; berate; castigate; censure; chasten; chastise; chide; condemn; criticize; denounce; denunciate; discipline; excoriate; fulminate against; imprecate; impugn; inveigh against; objurgate; punish; rebuke; remonstrate; reprehend; reprimand; reproach; reprobate; reprove; revile; scold; swear at; upbraid; vituperate; warn.*

jump from the frying pan into the fire   A moribund metaphor (See).

jumping for (with) joy   A moribund metaphor (See). *blissful; blithe; buoyant; cheerful; delighted; ecstatic; elated; enraptured; euphoric; exalted; excited; exhilarated; exultant; gay; glad; gleeful; good-humored; happy; intoxicated; jolly; jovial; joyful; joyous; jubilant; merry; mirthful; overjoyed; pleased; rapturous; thrilled.*

jumping-off point   A moribund metaphor (SEE).

jump into the fray   ■ A number of political specialists gave her credit for *jumping into the fray* with a specific fiscal plan.

jump on the bandwagon   A moribund metaphor (SEE). ■ Once everyone in an industry has learned about something that works, there's a tendency to *jump on the bandwagon*, and then it no longer works.

jump out of (her) skin   A moribund metaphor (SEE). *be afraid; be alarmed; be apprehensive; be cowardly; be craven; be diffident; be faint-hearted; be fearful; be frightened; be pusillanimous; be recreant; be scared; be terror-stricken; be timid; be timorous; be tremulous.*

jump ship   A moribund metaphor (SEE). *abandon; desert; forsake; leave; quit.*

jump the gun   A moribund metaphor (SEE).

jump through hoops   A moribund metaphor (SEE).

(it's) just a memory

just desserts

just exactly   A dimwitted redundancy (SEE). *exactly; just.* ■ *Just exactly* what do you mean? USE *Just* or *Exactly*.

justice (has) prevailed

(it was) just one of those things

just recently   A dimwitted redundancy (SEE). *just; recently.* ■ I *just recently* completed my bachelor's degree. USE *just* or *recently*.

just say no   A popular prescription (SEE).

just what the doctor ordered   A moribund metaphor (SEE).

just when you thought it was safe to   An infantile phrase (SEE).

K

keep a (the) lid on   A moribund metaphor (SEE).

keep all (your) options open

keep a low profile   A moribund metaphor (SEE).

keep an ear to the ground   A moribund metaphor (SEE). *be alert; be attentive; be awake; be aware; be eagle-eyed; be heedful; be informed; be observant; be vigilant; be wakeful; be watchful.*

keep a stiff upper lip   A moribund metaphor (SEE). *be brave; be courageous; be determined; be resolute.*

keep (them) at arm's length
A moribund metaphor (SEE).

keep a watchful eye on   *be alert; be attentive; be awake; be aware; be eagle-eyed; be heedful; be informed; be observant; be vigilant; be wakeful; be watchful.*

keep body and soul together
A moribund metaphor (SEE). *endure; exist; keep alive; live; manage; subsist; survive.*

keep (your) chin up   A moribund metaphor (SEE). *be brave; be coura-*
geous; be determined; be resolute.

keep (his) cool   *be calm; be composed; be patient; be self-possessed; be tranquil.*

keep (our) distance   *be aloof; be chilly; be cool; be reserved; be standoffish; be unamiable; be unamicable; be uncompanionable; be uncongenial; be unfriendly; be unsociable; be unsocial.*

keep (his) eye on the ball   A moribund metaphor (SEE).
1. *be alert; be attentive; be awake; be aware; be eagle-eyed; be heedful; be observant; be vigilant; be wakeful; be watchful.*
2. *be able; be adroit; be apt; be astute; be bright; be brilliant; be capable; be clever; be competent; be discerning; be effective; be effectual; be efficient; be enlightened; be insightful; be intelligent; be judicious; be keen; be knowledgeable; be learned; be logical; be luminous; be perceptive; be perspicacious; be quick; be rational; be reasonable; be sagacious; be sage; be sapient; be sensible; be sharp; be shrewd; be smart; be sound; be wise.*

keep (your) eyes peeled   A moribund metaphor (SEE). *be alert; be attentive; be awake; be aware; be eagle-eyed;*

149

be heedful; be observant; be vigilant; be wakeful; be watchful.

keep (its) finger on the pulse of
A moribund metaphor (SEE). ■ The Chinese government has been able to *keep its finger on the pulse of* technology acquisition activities.

keep (your) fingers crossed
A moribund metaphor (SEE). *hope for; pray for; think positively; wish.*

keep (me) glued to (my) seat
A moribund metaphor (SEE).

keep (my) head above water
A moribund metaphor (SEE).

keep (your) nose clean   A moribund metaphor (SEE).

keep (your) nose to the grindstone   A popular prescription (SEE). *drudge; grind; grub; labor; slave; strain; strive; struggle; sweat; toil; travail; work hard.*

keep on a short leash   A moribund metaphor (SEE).

keep (your) options open

keep (your) pants (shirt) on
A moribund metaphor (SEE). *be calm; be composed; be patient; be self-possessed; be tranquil; calm down; hold on; wait.*

keep (me) posted

(it) keeps (me) busy   A plebeian sentiment (SEE). SEE ALSO *(he's) boring; (it) gives (me) something to do; (it) keeps (me) out of trouble; (it's) something to do.*

(it) keeps (me) going   A plebeian sentiment (SEE).

keep smiling   A plebeian sentiment (SEE). *Keep smiling* is insisted on by ghoulish brutes who would rob us of our gravity, indeed, steal us from ourselves. SEE ALSO *smile!*

(it) keeps (me) out of trouble
A plebeian sentiment. (SEE) SEE ALSO *(it) gives (me) something to do; (it) keeps (me) busy; (it's) something to do.*

keep the ball rolling   A moribund metaphor (SEE).

keep the faith   A popular prescription (SEE).

keep the home fires burning
A moribund metaphor (SEE).

keep the lines of communication open

keep the wolves at bay   A moribund metaphor (SEE).

keep under (his) hat   A moribund metaphor (SEE). *camouflage; cloak; conceal; cover; disguise; enshroud; harbor; hide; keep secret; mask; screen; shroud; suppress; veil; withhold.*

keep under wraps   A moribund metaphor (SEE). *camouflage; cloak; conceal; cover up; disguise; enshroud; harbor; hide; keep secret; mask; screen; shroud; suppress; veil; withhold.*

keep up appearances   A plebeian sentiment (SEE).

keep up the good work

keep up with the Joneses   A plebeian sentiment (SEE).

kernel of truth

key (major) player

kick the bucket   A moribund metaphor (SEE). *cease to exist; decease; depart; die; expire; pass away; pass on; perish.*

kick the habit

kick up (our) heels   A moribund metaphor (SEE). *be merry; carouse; carry on; cavort; celebrate; frolic; gambol; party; play; revel; riot; roister; rollick; romp; skylark.*

killer instinct

kill the fatted calf   A moribund metaphor (SEE).

kill the goose that lays the golden egg   A moribund metaphor (SEE).

kill two birds with one stone   A moribund metaphor (SEE).

kill (her) with kindness   A moribund metaphor (SEE).

kind (and) gentle   An inescapable pair (SEE). *affable; agreeable; amiable; amicable; compassionate; friendly; gentle; good-hearted; humane; kind; kindhearted; personable; pleasant; tender; tolerant.*

(a). . . kind (sort; type) of thing   A grammatical gimmick (SEE). ■ It was *a* spur-of-the-moment *kind of thing.* DELETE *a . . . kind of thing.* ■ It's *a* very upsetting *sort of thing.* DELETE

a . . . sort of thing. ■ It's difficult to find a person to commit to a long-term relationship *type of thing.* DELETE *type of thing.*

kindred spirit(s)   An inescapable pair (SEE).

king of the hill   A moribund metaphor (SEE).

kiss and make up   A moribund metaphor (SEE).

kiss and tell   A moribund metaphor (SEE).

kiss of death   A moribund metaphor (SEE).

kith and kin   An inescapable pair (SEE). *acquaintances; family; friends; kin; kindred; kinfolk; kinsman; kith; relatives.*

knee-high to a grasshopper   A moribund metaphor (SEE). *diminutive; dwarfish; elfin; elfish; lilliputian; little; miniature; minikin; petite; pygmy; short; small; teeny; tiny.*

knee-jerk reaction   A moribund metaphor (SEE). *automatic; habitual; instinctive; inveterate; mechanical; perfunctory; reflex; spontaneous; unconscious; unthinking.*

knight in shining armor   A moribund metaphor (SEE).

knight in tarnished armor   A moribund metaphor (SEE).

knock-down, drag-out fight
1. *altercation; argument; disagreement; discord; disputation; dispute; feud;*

fight; misunderstanding; quarrel; rift; row; spat; squabble.
2. *battle; brawl; clash; fight; grapple; jostle; make war; scuffle; skirmish; tussle; war; wrestle.*

knock (me) down with a feather
A moribund metaphor (SEE). *amaze; astonish; astound; awe; dazzle; dumbfound; flabbergast; overpower; overwhelm; shock; startle; stun; stupefy; surprise.*

knock for a loop
A moribund metaphor (SEE). *amaze; astonish; astound; awe; dazzle; dumbfound; flabbergast; overpower; overwhelm; shock; startle; stun; stupefy; surprise.*

knock off (his) feet
A moribund metaphor (SEE). *amaze; astonish; astound; awe; dazzle; dumbfound; flabbergast; overpower; overwhelm; shock; startle; stun; stupefy; surprise.*

knock on wood
A moribund metaphor (SEE). *hope for; pray for; think positively; wish.*

knock (himself) out
A moribund metaphor (SEE). *aim; attempt; endeavor; essay; exert; exhaust; labor; strain; strive; struggle; toil; try hard; undertake; work at.*

knock-out punch
A moribund metaphor (SEE).

knock (her) socks off
A moribund metaphor (SEE).
1. *amaze; astonish; astound; awe; dazzle; dumbfound; flabbergast; overpower; overwhelm; shock; startle; stun; stupefy; surprise.*
2. *beat; better; conquer; defeat; exceed; excel; outclass; outdo; outflank; outma-*

neuver; outperform; outplay; overcome; overpower; prevail; rout; succeed; surpass; top; triumph; trounce; vanquish; whip; win.

knock the bottom out of
A moribund metaphor (SEE). *belie; confute; contradict; controvert; counter; debunk; deny; disprove; discredit; dispute; expose; invalidate; negate; rebut; refute; repudiate.*

knock the spots off
A moribund metaphor (SEE). *beat; better; conquer; defeat; exceed; excel; outclass; outdo; outflank; outmaneuver; outperform; outplay; overcome; overpower; prevail; rout; succeed; surpass; top; triumph; trounce; vanquish; whip; win.*

know for a fact
An infantile phrase (SEE). ■ I *know for a fact* that he was there with her. DELETE *for a fact.* ■ I'm sure they do; I *know for a fact* they do. DELETE *for a fact.*

(don't) know from Adam

know (her) in the biblical sense

knowledge is power
A quack equation (SEE).

knows all the angles
1. *able; adept; apt; capable; competent; deft; dexterous; experienced; expert; practiced; proficient; seasoned; skilled; skillful; veteran.*
2. *adroit; astute; bright; brilliant; clever; discerning; effective; effectual; efficient; enlightened; insightful; intelligent; judicious; keen; knowledgeable; learned; logical; luminous; perceptive; perspicacious; quick; rational; reasonable; sagacious; sage; sapient; sensible; sharp; shrewd; smart; sound; wise.*

(you) know something? An ineffectual phrase (SEE). ■ *You know something?* I'm going to do whatever is in my power to end this relationship. DELETE *You know something?* ■ *You know something?* I never loved you either. DELETE *You know something?.* SEE ALSO *(you) know what?*

knows what's what
1. *able; adept; apt; capable; competent; deft; dexterous; experienced; expert; practiced; proficient; seasoned; skilled; skillful; veteran.*
2. *adroit; astute; bright; brilliant; clever; discerning; effective; effectual; efficient; enlightened; insightful; intelligent; judicious; keen; knowledgeable; learned; logical; luminous; perceptive; perspicacious; quick; rational; reasonable; sagacious; sage; sapient; sensible; sharp; shrewd; smart; sound; wise.*

knows which side (her) bread is buttered on A moribund metaphor (SEE).

know thyself A popular prescription (SEE).

(you) know what? An ineffectual phrase (SEE). ■ *You know what?* When we return, you'll meet her mother. DELETE *You know what?* ■ She broke up with me, and *you know what?*, I've got a career now, which is good. DELETE *you know what?* SEE ALSO *(you) know something?*

(you) know what I mean? An in-effectual phrase (SEE). ■ Some people have to work at it more than others. *Know what I mean?* DELETE *Know what I mean?* ■ How can you not be depressed if you don't remember things. *You know what I mean?* DELETE *You know what I mean?* SEE ALSO *(you) hear what I'm saying?; (you) know what I'm saying?; (you) know what I'm telling you?; (do) you know?*

(you) know what I'm saying? An ineffectual phrase (SEE). ■ It was an association that wasn't based on any fact. *You know what I'm saying?* DELETE *You know what I'm saying?* ■ I want a girl that's real. *You know what I'm saying?* DELETE *You know what I'm saying?* SEE ALSO *(you) hear what I'm saying?; (you) know what I mean?; (you) know what I'm telling you?; (do) you know?*

(you) know what I'm telling you? An ineffectual phrase (SEE). ■ I don't know; I can't think of the words. *You know what I'm telling you?* DELETE *You know what I'm telling you?* ■ I like to be with a woman who has the same mindset as I do. *You know what I'm telling you?* DELETE *You know what I'm telling you?* SEE ALSO *(you) hear what I'm saying?; (you) know what I mean?; (you) know what I'm saying?; (do) you know?*

knuckle under A moribund metaphor (SEE). *abdicate; accede; acquiesce; bow; capitulate; cede; concede; give in; give up; quit; relinquish; retreat; submit; succumb; surrender; yield.*

L

lack of A torpid term (SEE). Whatever happened to our negative words, to the prefixes *dis-, il-, im-, in-, ir-, mis-, non-,* and *un-?* No doubt many people say *absence of* or *lack of* because they know so few negative forms of the words that follow these phrases. These people will say *lack of moderation* instead of *immoderation* and *absence of pleasure* instead of *displeasure*.

Others subscribe to society's oral imperative that all things negative be left unsaid. To these people, *lack of respect* is somehow preferable to, and more positive than, *disrespect*. ■ These reports by the media reflect a *lack of sensitivity* to basic human decency. REPLACE WITH *insensitivity*. ■ It was her *lack of judgment* that lost us the sale. REPLACE WITH *misjudgment*. SEE ALSO *absence of; less than (enthusiastic)*.

lady A suspect superlative (SEE). As a gentleman is less than a man, so a *lady* is less than a woman. *Lady* has become a pejorative term. No longer does it suggest a cultured, sophisticated woman; rather, it suggests a woman hopelessly common, forever coarse. ■ If you wanted to sweep one of these *ladies* off her feet, what would you do? REPLACE WITH *women*. ■ I have a question for both of you *ladies*.

DELETE *ladies*. SEE ALSO *class; gentleman*.

lady luck A moribund metaphor (SEE).

landmark agreement (decision)

landslide victory A moribund metaphor (SEE).

larger than life

last but (by) no means least An infantile phrase (SEE).

last but not least An infantile phrase (SEE).

last ditch attempt (effort)

last gasp

last hurrah

lasting An overworked word (SEE). For example: *lasting consequence; lasting contribution; lasting impact; lasting impression; lasting lesson; lasting peace*.

last nail in (his) coffin A moribund metaphor (SEE).

last of the Mohicans   An infantile phrase (SEE).

laughing (my) head off   A moribund metaphor (SEE). *cachinnate; cackle; chortle; chuckle; convulse; guffaw; hoot; howl; laugh; roar; shriek.*

laughing on the outside and crying on the inside

laughter is the best medicine
A popular prescription (SEE).

launching pad (for)   A moribund metaphor (SEE).

launch into a diatribe

laundry list   A moribund metaphor (SEE).

lavishly illustrated   An inescapable pair (SEE).

lavish praise

law of the jungle   A moribund metaphor (SEE).

(don't) lay a finger (hand) on
A moribund metaphor (SEE). *caress; feel; finger; fondle; handle; pat; paw; pet; rub; stroke; touch.*

lay an egg   A moribund metaphor (SEE). *abort; blunder; bomb; fail; fall short; falter; flop; flounder; go wrong; miscarry; not succeed; slip; stumble; trip.*

lay at the feet of   A moribund metaphor (SEE). *accredit to; ascribe to; assign to; associate with; attribute to; blame on; charge to; connect with; correlate to; credit to; equate to; impute to;*

link to; relate to; trace to. ■ It doesn't seem that all this volatility can be *laid at the feet of* foreigners. REPLACE WITH *blamed on.*

lay (your) cards on the table
A moribund metaphor (SEE).

lay down the law   A moribund metaphor (SEE).
1. *assert; command; decree; dictate; insist; order; require.*
2. *admonish; berate; castigate; censure; chastise; chide; condemn; criticize; decry; rebuke; reprimand; reproach; reprove; scold; upbraid.*

lay it on the line   A moribund metaphor (SEE).

lay (spread) it on thick   A moribund metaphor (SEE).
1. *elaborate; embellish; embroider; enhance; enlarge; exaggerate; hyperbolize; inflate; magnify; overdo; overreact; overstress; overstate; strain; stretch.*
2. *acclaim; applaud; celebrate; commend; compliment; congratulate; eulogize; extol; flatter; hail; laud; panegyrize; praise; puff; salute.*

lay (his) life on the line

lay (her) out in lavender   A moribund metaphor (SEE). *admonish; animadvert; berate; castigate; censure; chasten; chastise; chide; condemn; criticize; denounce; denunciate; discipline; excoriate; fulminate against; imprecate; impugn; inveigh against; objurgate; punish; rebuke; remonstrate; reprehend; reprimand; reproach; reprobate; reprove; revile; scold; swear at; upbraid; vituperate; warn.*

lay (roll) out the red carpet

A moribund metaphor (SEE).

lay the groundwork (for) A moribund metaphor (SEE). *arrange; groom; make ready; plan; prepare; prime; ready.*

lead (her) by the nose A moribund metaphor (SEE). *administer; boss; command; control; dictate; direct; dominate; domineer; govern; in charge; in command; in control; manage; manipulate; master; misuse; order; overpower; oversee; predominate; prevail; reign over; rule; superintend; tyrannize; use.*

lead down the garden path A moribund metaphor (SEE). *bamboozle; befool; beguile; bilk; bluff; cheat; con; deceive; defraud; delude; dupe; feint; fool; gyp; hoodwink; lead astray; misdirect; misguide; misinform; mislead; spoof; swindle; trick; victimize.*

leader of the pack

leading contender

leading edge

lead the charge

leak like a sieve An insipid simile (SEE moribund metaphors).

lean and hungry (look) A moribund metaphor (SEE).

lean and mean An inescapable pair (SEE).

leap into the briar patch A moribund metaphor (SEE).

leap of faith

leaps off the page A moribund metaphor (SEE).

learning experience ■ Don't look at the job change as a failure but as a *learning experience.* ■ Our commitment to provide you with the highest-quality *learning experience* has made SkillPath the fastest-growing training company in the world.

learn (my) lesson

learn the hard way

learn the ropes A moribund metaphor (SEE).

leave a bad taste in (my) mouth A moribund metaphor (SEE).

leave holding the bag A moribund metaphor (SEE).

leave in droves

leave (out) in the cold A moribund metaphor (SEE). *abandon; ban; banish; bar; desert; exclude; exile; forsake; ostracize; shut out.*

leave (me) in the dark A moribund metaphor (SEE).

leave (him) in the dust A moribund metaphor (SEE). *beat; better; defeat; exceed; excel; outclass; outdo; outflank; outmaneuver; outperform; outplay; outrank; outsmart; outthink; outwit; overcome; overpower; prevail; rout; surpass; top; triumph; trounce; vanquish; whip; win.*

leave (hanging) in the lurch A moribund metaphor (SEE). *abandon; desert; forsake; leave; quit.* ■ We don't want to *leave* parents *hanging in the lurch.* REPLACE WITH *abandon.*

leave no stone unturned   A moribund metaphor (SEE). *analyze; canvass; comb; examine; explore; filter; forage; hunt; inspect; investigate; look for; probe; quest; ransack; rummage; scour; scrutinize; search; seek; sieve; sift; winnow.*

leaves a little (lot; much) to be desired   ■ In the area of health, the U.S. position *leaves much to be desired.* REPLACE WITH *is sickly.* ■ The plan was great; it was the execution that *left a little to be desired.* REPLACE WITH *was not.*

leave the door (wide) open (for)   A moribund metaphor (SEE). ■ The remainder of the majority *left the door open for* a return to capital punishment.

leave to (her) own devices

leave well enough alone   A popular prescription (SEE).

left-handed compliment

legal eagle

legitimate concern

leg to stand on   A moribund metaphor (SEE).

lend a (helping) hand (to)   A moribund metaphor (SEE). *aid; assist; benefit; favor; help; oblige; succor.* ■ During this holiday season, it is fitting for all of us to be thinking of *lending a helping hand to* those in need. REPLACE WITH *aiding.*

lend an ear   A moribund metaphor (SEE). *attend to; heed; listen; note.*

leopards don't lose their spots   A moribund metaphor (SEE).

less is more   A quack equation (SEE).

lesson to be learned

less than (enthusiastic)   A torpid term (SEE). ■ When Fred told his wife about the unbelievable opportunity, he was shocked at her *less than enthusiastic* response. REPLACE WITH *unenthusiastic.* ■ The response from their neighbors has been *less than hospitable.* REPLACE WITH *inhospitable.* SEE ALSO *absence of; lack of.*

less than meets the eye

let bygones be bygones   A popular prescription (SEE).

let down (their) guard

let go of the past   A popular prescription (SEE).

let (take) (her) hair down   A moribund metaphor (SEE). *be casual; be free; be informal; be loose; be natural; be open; be relaxed; be unbound; be unconfined; be unrestrained; be unrestricted.*

let (him) have it with both barrels   A moribund metaphor (SEE). *admonish; animadvert; berate; castigate; censure; chasten; chastise; chide; condemn; criticize; denounce; denunciate; discipline; excoriate; fulminate against; imprecate; impugn; inveigh against; objurgate; punish; rebuke; remonstrate; reprehend; reprimand; reproach; reprobate; reprove; revile; scold; swear at; upbraid; vituperate; warn.*

let (you) in on a (little) secret

let it all hang out   A moribund metaphor (SEE). *acknowledge; admit; affirm; allow; avow; concede; confess; disclose; divulge; expose; grant; own; reveal; tell; uncover; unveil.*

let it be   A popular prescription (SEE).

let it ride

let me ask you something   An ineffectual phrase (SEE). ■ *Let me ask you something,* is there anything about school that you like? DELETE *Let me ask you something.* ■ *Let me ask you something*: What would you think if I met three women tonight? DELETE *Let me ask you something.* SEE ALSO *can I ask (tell) you something?*

let me count the ways

let me hasten to add

let me tell you (something)   An ineffectual phrase (SEE). ■ This is really class, *let me tell you.* DELETE *let me tell you.* ■ It's been one of those days, *let me tell you.* DELETE *let me tell you.* SEE ALSO *I got to (have to) tell you (something); I'll tell you (something); I'll tell you what; I'm telling you.*

let nature take its course   A popular prescription (SEE).

let (her) off the hook   A moribund metaphor (SEE).

let sleeping dogs lie   A popular prescription (SEE).

let's see the color of your money

let's try and keep it that way

let the cat out of the bag   A moribund metaphor (SEE).

let the chips fall where they may   A moribund metaphor (SEE).

let the good times roll

let there be no mistake   SEE ALSO *make no mistake (about it).*

let the record speak for itself

let the world pass (her) by

let your fingers do the walking   An infantile phrase (SEE).

let your mind run wild   A moribund metaphor (SEE).

level (the) playing field   A moribund metaphor (SEE). ■ The chief aim of the bill is to *level the playing field* so challengers and incumbents will have an equal opportunity to get their message across.

lick (his) chops   A moribund metaphor (SEE).

lick (your) wounds   A moribund metaphor (SEE).

lie like a rug   An insipid simile (SEE moribund metaphors). *deceive; dissemble; distort; equivocate; falsify; fib; lie; misconstrue; mislead; misrepresent; pervert; prevaricate.*

lie low

lie through (his) teeth   *deceive; dissemble; distort; equivocate; falsify; fib;*

lie; misconstrue; mislead; misrepresent; pervert; prevaricate.

life begins at forty A popular prescription (SEE).

life goes on A popular prescription (SEE).

life in a fishbowl A moribund metaphor (SEE).

life in the fast lane A moribund metaphor (SEE).

life is a cabaret A moribund metaphor (SEE).

life is for the living A popular prescription (SEE).

(my) life is not (my) own

life isn't (always) fair A popular prescription (SEE).

life is short A quack equation (SEE).

life, liberty and the pursuit of happiness

(live a) life of luxury *affluent; moneyed; opulent; prosperous; rich; wealthy; well-off; well-to-do.*

(put my) life on the line

lift a finger A moribund metaphor (SEE). *aid; assist; benefit; favor; help; oblige; succor.*

light a fire under A moribund metaphor (SEE). *arouse; awaken; excite; goad; impel; incite; induce; motivate; prompt; provoke; push; rouse; spur;*

stimulate; stir; urge. ■ May the bishops' counsel encourage those husbands already living their words and *light a fire under* those dozing. REPLACE WITH *rouse*.

(as) light as a feather An insipid simile (SEE moribund metaphors). *airy; buoyant; delicate; ethereal; feathery; gaseous; gauzy; gossamer; light; lightweight; slender; slight; thin; vaporous; weightless.*

(as) light as air An insipid simile (SEE moribund metaphors). *airy; buoyant; delicate; ethereal; feathery; gaseous; gauzy; gossamer; light; lightweight; slender; slight; thin; vaporous; weightless.*

light at the end of the tunnel
A moribund metaphor (SEE). ■ When the opportunity arose that he could work for the government, we saw *light at the end of the tunnel*.

lighten the load

lighten up

(she) lights up my life

like An infantile phrase (SEE). A cachet of all who are grievously adolescent, *like* mars the meaning of every sentence in which it is used. ■ Our family is, *like*, very open. DELETE *like*. ■ They lived together for, *like*, twelve years. DELETE *like*. ■ I should, *like*, get up and do something. DELETE *like*.

(know) (her) like a book An insipid simile (SEE moribund metaphors). *altogether; completely; entirely; fully; perfectly; quite; thoroughly; totally; unreservedly; utterly; wholly.*

(works) like a charm   An insipid simile (SEE moribund metaphors). *accurately; exactly; excellently; faultlessly; flawlessly; methodically; perfectly; precisely; regularly; systematically; well.*

like clockwork   An insipid simile (SEE moribund metaphors). *accurately; exactly; excellently; faultlessly; flawlessly; methodically; perfectly; precisely; regularly; systematically; well.*

(spending money) like it was going out of style   An insipid simile (SEE moribund metaphors).

like (a streak of; greased) lightning   A moribund metaphor (SEE). *abruptly; apace; at once; briskly; directly; expeditiously; fast; forthwith; hastily; hurriedly; immediately; instantaneously; instantly; posthaste; promptly; quickly; rapidly; rashly; right away; speedily; straightaway; swiftly; wingedly.*

like nobody's business   *brilliantly; consummately; dazzlingly; excellently; exceptionally; expertly; exquisitely; extraordinarily; fabulously; flawlessly; grandly; magnificently; marvelously; perfectly; remarkably; splendidly; superbly; superlatively; supremely; transcendently; very well; wonderfully; wondrously.* ■ Here was the one and only Kronos Quartet in town again, playing—as always—*like nobody's business.* REPLACE WITH *superbly.*

(just) like old times   An insipid simile (SEE moribund metaphors).

(sounds) like something out of a novel   An insipid simile (SEE moribund metaphors).

(he) likes to hear (himself) talk   *babbling; blathering; chatty; facile; fluent; garrulous; glib; jabbering; logorrheic; long-winded; loquacious; prolix; talkative; verbose; voluble; windy.*

like the back of my hand   An insipid simile (SEE moribund metaphors). *altogether; completely; entirely; fully; perfectly; quite; thoroughly; totally; unreservedly; utterly; wholly.*

like there's no tomorrow

limited only by your imagination

limp into port

line of fire   A moribund metaphor (SEE).

lines are drawn   A moribund metaphor (SEE).

lingering doubt

lining (his) pockets   A moribund metaphor (SEE).

link together   A dimwitted redundancy (SEE). *link.* ■ This business will *link together* the telephone, the television and the computer. DELETE *together.*

(my) lips are sealed   A moribund metaphor (SEE).

liquid refreshment   An infantile phrase (SEE). *beverage; drink; refreshment.*

litany of complaints   A moribund metaphor (SEE).

literary event   A suspect superlative (SEE).

(tiny) little bit   An infantile phrase (SEE).

little did (they) realize

little old lady from Dubuque
A moribund metaphor (SEE). *boor; bumpkin; commoner; common man; common person; conventional person; peasant; pleb; plebeian; vulgarian; yokel.* ■ By the time the contest was over, *little old ladies in Dubuque* could probably discourse on the subject.

lit to the gills   A moribund metaphor (SEE). *besotted; crapulous; drunk; inebriated; intoxicated; sodden; stupefied; tipsy.*

lit up like a Christmas tree   An insipid simile (SEE moribund metaphors).

live a lie

live and breathe for

live and learn   A popular prescription (SEE).

live and let live   A popular prescription (SEE).

live as though each day were your last   A popular prescription (SEE).

live dangerously   A popular prescription (SEE).

live each day to the fullest   A popular prescription (SEE).

live for the moment   A popular prescription (SEE).

live from hand to mouth

live from paycheck to paycheck

live happily ever after   A suspect superlative (SEE).

live in a pigsty   A moribund metaphor (SEE).

(will) live in infamy

live one day at a time   A popular prescription (SEE).

live to a ripe old age

live up to (your) part of the bargain

live wire   A moribund metaphor (SEE).

(learn to) live with it   A popular prescription (SEE).

living, breathing

living proof

loaded for bear   A moribund metaphor (SEE).
1. *eager; prepared; ready; set.*
2. *angry; bad-tempered; bilious; cantankerous; choleric; churlish; crabby; cranky; cross; curmudgeonly; disagreeable; dyspeptic; grouchy; gruff; grumpy; ill-humored; ill-tempered; irascible; irritable; mad; peevish; petulant; quarrelsome; short-tempered; splenetic; surly; testy; vexed.*

lo and behold   An archaism (SEE).

local boy makes good

location, location, location   An infantile phrase (SEE).

lock horns with   A moribund metaphor (SEE). *battle; brawl; clash; fight; grapple; jostle; make war; scuffle; skirmish; tussle; war; wrestle.*

lock, stock and barrel   A moribund metaphor (SEE). *aggregate; all; all things; entirety; everything; gross; lot; sum; total; totality; whole.*

lock (them) up and throw away the key

long and hard   *aggressively; dynamically; emphatically; energetically; ferociously; fervently; fiercely; forcefully; frantically; frenziedly; furiously; hard; intensely; intently; mightily; passionately; powerfully; robustly; savagely; spiritedly; strenuously; strongly; vehemently; viciously; vigorously; violently; wildly; with vigor.* ■ The compromise would be a partial victory for Baybanks, which has fought *long and hard* against the legislation. REPLACE WITH *mightily.*

long, hot summer

long in the tooth   A moribund metaphor (SEE). *aged; aging; ancient; antediluvian; antique; archaic; elderly; hoary; hoary-headed; old; patriarchal; prehistoric; seasoned; superannuated.*

long on (promise) and short on (delivery)

long on talk, short on action

long overdue   An inescapable pair (SEE). ■ This legislation is *long overdue.*

long road ahead   A moribund metaphor (SEE).

long shot   A moribund metaphor (SEE). *doubtful; dubious; farfetched; implausible; improbable; remote; unlikely; unrealistic.*

(don't) look a gift horse in the mouth   A popular prescription (SEE).

(you) look at it as being half empty, but (I) look at it as half full   A popular prescription (SEE).

look before you leap   A popular prescription (SEE).

look down (her) nose (at)   A moribund metaphor (SEE). *contemn; deride; despise; detest; disdain; jeer at; laugh at; mock; ridicule; scoff at; scorn; shun; slight; sneer; snub; spurn.*

looking for all the world like

looking for love in all the wrong places

look (them) in the eye

look into a crystal ball   A moribund metaphor (SEE).

look like a drowned rat   An insipid simile (SEE moribund metaphors). *bedraggled; drenched; dripping; saturated; soaked; sopping; wet.*

(try to) look on the bright side (of things)

look over (their) shoulders

looks aren't everything   A popular prescription (SEE).

(she) looks like a million bucks

An insipid simile (SEE moribund metaphors).

look the other way A moribund metaphor (SEE). *avoid; brush aside; discount; disregard; dodge; duck; ignore; neglect; omit; pass over; recoil from; shrink from; shun; shy away from; turn away from; withdraw from.*

look through rose-colored glasses A moribund metaphor (SEE).

look what (who) the cat dragged in A moribund metaphor (SEE).

look what the tide brought in A moribund metaphor (SEE).

look who's talking An infantile phrase (SEE).

loose cannon A moribund metaphor (SEE).

lose ground A moribund metaphor (SEE).

lose sight of the fact that

lose steam A moribund metaphor (SEE).

lost cause An inescapable pair (SEE).

lost in the shuffle A moribund metaphor (SEE).

lost (his) marbles A moribund metaphor (SEE).

loud and clear An inescapable pair

(SEE). *apparent; audible; clear; conspicuous; definite; distinct; emphatic; evident; explicit; graphic; lucid; manifest; obvious; patent; pellucid; plain; sharp; translucent; transparent; unambiguous; uncomplex; uncomplicated; understandable; unequivocal; unmistakable; vivid.*

love and cherish An inescapable pair (SEE).

love conquers all A popular prescription (SEE).

love is blind A quack equation (SEE).

love it or leave it An infantile phrase (SEE).

love moves mountains A moribund metaphor (SEE).

low blow *dishonorable; foul; inequitable; unconscientious; underhanded; unethical; unfair; unjust; unprincipled; unscrupulous; unsportsmanlike.*

lower the boom on A moribund metaphor (SEE).

lowest common denominator A moribund metaphor (SEE). ■ Instead of disseminating the best in our culture, television too often panders to the *lowest common denominator*. REPLACE WITH *worst*.

low man on the totem pole A moribund metaphor (SEE).

luck of the draw

lust for life

M

(as) mad as a hatter An insipid simile (SEE moribund metaphors). *batty; cracked; crazy; daft; demented; deranged; fey; goofy; insane; lunatic; mad; maniacal; neurotic; nuts; nutty; psychotic; raving; squirrelly; touched; unbalanced; unhinged; unsound; wacky; zany.*

(as) mad as a hornet An insipid simile (SEE moribund metaphors). *angry; berserk; convulsive; crazed; delirious; demented; demoniac; deranged; enraged; feral; ferocious; fierce; frantic; frenzied; fuming; furious; hysterical; infuriated; in hysterics; incensed; insane; irate; mad; maddened; maniacal; murderous; possessed; rabid; raging; ranting; raving; savage; seething; wild; wrathful.*

(as) mad as a March hare An insipid simile (SEE moribund metaphors). *batty; cracked; crazy; daft; demented; deranged; fey; goofy; insane; lunatic; mad; maniacal; neurotic; nuts; nutty; psychotic; raving; squirrelly; touched; unbalanced; unhinged; unsound; wacky; zany.*

(as) mad as a wet hen An insipid simile (SEE moribund metaphors). *angry; berserk; convulsive; crazed; delirious; demented; demoniac; deranged;* *enraged; feral; ferocious; fierce; frantic; frenzied; fuming; furious; hysterical; infuriated; in hysterics; incensed; insane; irate; mad; maddened; maniacal; murderous; possessed; rabid; raging; ranting; raving; savage; seething; wild; wrathful.*

(he) made (me) an offer (I) couldn't refuse ■ We'd still be there today if Bally's hadn't *made us an offer we couldn't refuse.*

(you) made my day A plebeian sentiment (SEE). Often a response to being complimented, *you made my day* appeals to the mass of people who rely on others for their opinion of themselves.

And if they embrace others' approval, so they bow to their criticism.

magic bullet A moribund metaphor (SEE). *answer; solution.*

magnum opus A foreignism (SEE).

major An overworked word (SEE). For example: *major blow; major breakthrough; major commitment; major concern; major consideration; major defeat; major disaster; major new writer; major opportunity; major player; major rami-*

fications; major roadblock; major setback; major thrust.

make a clean breast of *acknowledge; admit; affirm; allow; avow; concede; confess; disclose; divulge; expose; grant; own; reveal; tell; uncover; unveil.*

make a concerted effort *aim; attempt; endeavor; essay; labor; seek; strive; toil; try; undertake; venture; work.* ■ True change will come only when those in power *make a concerted effort* to promote large numbers of women and blacks to high-status jobs. REPLACE WITH *try.*

make a conscious attempt (effort) A dimwitted redundancy (SEE). *aim; attempt; endeavor; essay; labor; seek; strive; toil; try; undertake; venture; work.* ■ We *made a conscious effort* not to do what most companies do. USE *strived.* ■ Wash your hands and *make conscious attempts* not to touch your face, nose and eyes. USE *try.*

make a conscious choice (decision) A dimwitted redundancy (SEE). *Make a conscious choice* means no more than *choose,* and *make a conscious decision* means no more than *decide.* ■ We *made a conscious decision* that this sort of legal terrorism would not affect the way we operate. USE *decided.* ■ They *made a conscious choice* not to have any bedroom scenes in this movie. USE *chose.* SEE ALSO *make an informed choice (decision).*

make a decision A dimwitted redundancy (SEE). *conclude; decide; determine; resolve.* ■ It's difficult to *make a decision* at this time. USE *decide.* ■ If he *made a decision* not to use protec-

tion, he should *make a decision* to support the child. USE *resolved.*

make a dent (in)

make a determination A dimwitted redundancy (SEE). *conclude; decide; determine; resolve.* ■ We want the SJC to look at it and *make a determination* to clearly state what is permissible and impermissible. USE *determine.*

make a difference
1. *be climacteric; be consequential; be considerable; be critical; be crucial; be important; be significant; be vital; count; matter.*
2. *act on; affect; bear on; influence; sway; work on.* ■ She is part of a great tradition in U.S. society, in which ordinary individuals voice their concerns in order to *make a difference* about issues that matter to them. ■ Thank you in advance for your time and assistance; your answers really can *make a difference.*

make a federal case out of A moribund metaphor (SEE). *elaborate; embellish; embroider; enhance; enlarge; exaggerate; hyperbolize; inflate; magnify; overdo; overreact; overstress; overstate; strain; stretch.*

make a getaway *abscond; clear out; decamp; depart; desert; disappear; escape; exit; flee; fly; go; go away; leave; move on; part; pull out; quit; retire; retreat; run away; take flight; take off; vacate; vanish; withdraw.*

make a killing

make all the difference in the world

make a monkey out of   A moribund metaphor (SEE). *abase; chasten; debase; degrade; demean; deride; disgrace; dishonor; dupe; embarrass; humble; humiliate; mock; mortify; ridicule; shame.*

make a mountain out of a molehill   A moribund metaphor (SEE). *elaborate; embellish; embroider; enhance; enlarge; exaggerate; hyperbolize; inflate; magnify; overdo; overreact; overstress; overstate; strain; stretch.*

make an honest woman of her

make an informed choice (decision)   A dimwitted redundancy (SEE). *choose; decide.* SEE ALSO *make a conscious choice (decision).*

make a quick exit   *abscond; clear out; decamp; depart; desert; disappear; escape; exit; flee; fly; go; go away; leave; move on; part; pull out; quit; retire; retreat; run away; take flight; take off; vacate; vanish; withdraw.*

make a silk purse out of a sow's ear   A moribund metaphor (SEE).

make a virtue of necessity

make (my) blood boil   A moribund metaphor (SEE). *acerbate; anger; annoy; bother; bristle; chafe; enrage; incense; inflame; infuriate; irk; irritate; madden; miff; provoke; rile; vex.*

make (both) ends meet   A moribund metaphor (SEE). *economize; endure; exist; live; manage; subsist; survive.* ■ Older people are having a tough enough time trying to *make ends meet.* REPLACE WITH *survive.*

make eyes at   A moribund metaphor (SEE). *flirt.*

make false statements   A dimwitted redundancy (SEE). *lie.* ■ The indictment alleges that he *made false statements* to the FEC and obstructed proceedings. USE *lied.*

make (my) flesh creep   A moribund metaphor (SEE). *alarm; appall; disgust; frighten; horrify; nauseate; panic; repel; repulse; revolt; scare; shock; sicken; startle; terrify.*

make (my) hair stand on end   A moribund metaphor (SEE). *alarm; appall; disgust; frighten; horrify; nauseate; panic; repel; repulse; revolt; scare; shock; sicken; startle; terrify.*

make hay out of   A moribund metaphor (SEE).

make hay while the sun shines   A moribund metaphor (SEE). *capitalize on; exploit; take advantage.*

make heads or tails of   A moribund metaphor (SEE). *appreciate; apprehend; comprehend; discern; fathom; grasp; know; make sense of; perceive; realize; recognize; see; understand.* ■ His failures in punctuation make it almost impossible to *make heads or tails of* his convoluted sentences. REPLACE WITH *understand.*

make it   ■ As far as *making it* in the New York art scene—*making it* fast, that is—it's ninety-nine percent social networking and one percent talent.

make it big   *prevail; succeed; triumph; win.*

make (my) mark (on)   *affect; bear on; influence; sway.* ■ They have certainly *made their mark on* infant fashion. REPLACE WITH *influenced.*

make no bones about it   A moribund metaphor (SEE).

make no mistake (about it)
■ *Make no mistake about it,* if we were to leave, other nations would leave, too, and chaos would resume. SEE ALSO *let there be no mistake.*

make or break

make (his) presence felt

make (yourself) scarce   *abscond; clear out; decamp; depart; desert; disappear; escape; exit; flee; fly; go; go away; leave; move on; part; pull out; quit; retire; retreat; run away; take flight; take off; vacate; vanish; withdraw.*

make (me) see red   A moribund metaphor (SEE). *acerbate; anger; annoy; bother; bristle; chafe; enrage; incense; inflame; infuriate; irk; irritate; madden; miff; provoke; rile; vex.*

make short work of

make (it) stick

(try to) make the best (most) of it
A popular prescription (SEE).

make the feathers (fur) fly
A moribund metaphor (SEE).

make the grade   A moribund metaphor (SEE). *able; accomplished; adept; adequate; capable; competent; deft; equal to; equipped; fitted; measure up; proficient; qualified; skilled; skillful; suited.*

make the most of (it)   *capitalize on; exploit.*

make tracks   *abscond; clear out; decamp; depart; desert; disappear; escape; exit; flee; fly; go; go away; leave; move on; part; pull out; quit; retire; retreat; run away; take flight; take off; vacate; vanish; withdraw.*

make up for lost ground

make up (his) mind   A dimwitted redundancy (SEE). *choose; conclude; decide; determine; pick; resolve; select; settle.*

make waves   A moribund metaphor (SEE).

male chauvinist (pig)

many are called but few are chosen

many moons ago

many of my closest friends (are)
■ *Many of my closest friends* are Italian.

marching orders   A moribund metaphor (SEE).

married to (my) job

mass exodus   A dimwitted redundancy (SEE). *exodus.*

mass hysteria

maybe, maybe not   An infantile phrase (SEE).

maybe yes, maybe no   An infantile phrase (SEE).

may (might) possibly   A dimwitted

redundancy (SEE). *may (might).* ■ I *might possibly* be there when you are. DELETE *possibly.*

may the best (man) win

mea culpa   A foreignism (SEE).

meal ticket   A moribund metaphor (SEE).

meaningful   An overworked word (SEE). So elusive is meaning that we apparently feel as though we must modify scores of words with *meaningful.* For example: *meaningful action; meaningful answers; meaningful change; meaningful dialogue; meaningful discussion; meaningful experience; meaningful friendship; meaningful impact; meaningful reform; meaningful relationship; meaningful response.* SEE ALSO *significant.*

... means never having to say you're sorry   An infantile phrase (SEE).

meat and potatoes   A moribund metaphor (SEE).

(as) meek as a lamb   An insipid simile (SEE moribund metaphors). *accepting; accommodating; acquiescent; complacent; complaisant; compliant; cowed; deferential; docile; dutiful; easy; forbearing; gentle; humble; long-suffering; meek; mild; obedient; passive; patient; prostrate; quiet; reserved; resigned; stoical; submissive; subservient; timid; tolerant; tractable; unassuming; uncomplaining; yielding.*

(as) meek as Moses   An insipid simile (SEE moribund metaphors). *accepting; accommodating; acquiescent;*

complacent; complaisant; compliant; cowed; deferential; docile; dutiful; easy; forbearing; gentle; humble; long-suffering; meek; mild; obedient; passive; patient; prostrate; quiet; reserved; resigned; stoical; submissive; subservient; timid; tolerant; tractable; unassuming; uncomplaining; yielding.

meeting of (the) minds   *accord; accordance; agreement; common view; compatibility; concord; concordance; concurrence; consensus; harmony; unanimity; understanding; unison; unity.* ■ We're talking to him to see if we can have *meeting of minds.* REPLACE WITH *agreement.*

meet (your) match

meet up with   A dimwitted redundancy (SEE). *meet.* ■ I *met up with* my friends at the dance. USE *met.*

meet (his) Waterloo   A moribund metaphor (SEE).

meet with an untimely end

me, myself and I   An infantile phrase (SEE).

mend fences   A moribund metaphor (SEE).

mere mortals

meteoric rise   An inescapable pair (SEE). ■ His approach has struck a chord with the American people, hence his unprecedented and *meteoric rise* to prominence.

method in (his) madness

methodology   A torpid term (SEE).

A favorite among academicians, this polysyllabic word means no more than *method*.

Mickey-Mouse   An infantile phrase (SEE).

microcosm of society

middle-of-the-road   A moribund metaphor (SEE).
1. *average; common; conservative; conventional; everyday; mediocre; middling; normal; ordinary; quotidian; second-rate; standard; traditional; typical; uneventful; unexceptional; unremarkable; usual.*
2. *careful; cautious; circumspect; prudent; safe; wary.*

midsummer madness

might makes right   A popular prescription (SEE).

miles to go before (they) sleep

milk the last drop out of   A moribund metaphor (SEE).

millstone around (my) neck
A moribund metaphor (SEE). *burden; duty; encumbrance; hardship; hindrance; impediment; obligation; obstacle; obstruction; onus; responsibility.*

mind over matter

mind (your) *p*'s and *q*'s   A moribund metaphor (SEE). *be accurate; be careful; be exact; be meticulous; be particular; be precise.*

mindset   An overworked word (SEE). *attitude; bent; bias; cast; disposition; habit; inclination; leaning; out-look; penchant; perspective; point of view; position; predilection; predisposition; prejudice; proclivity; slant; stand; standpoint; temperament; tendency; view; viewpoint; way of thinking.* ■ You don't have these huge organizations built on patronage anymore, but the *mindset* is still there. REPLACE WITH *predisposition.* ■ What we are doing is changing people's *mindset*. REPLACE WITH *views.* ■ The report is critical of the *mindset* of those in charge of the pipeline. REPLACE WITH *attitude.*

mind the store   A moribund metaphor (SEE).

mirabile dictu   A foreignism (SEE).

miscarriage of justice

misery loves company   A popular prescription (SEE).

(they'll be) missed but not forgotten

mission accomplished

mission of mercy

miss the boat   A moribund metaphor (SEE).

mix and mingle   An inescapable pair (SEE). *associate; consort; hobnob; fraternize; keep company; mingle; mix; socialize.*

mixed bag   A moribund metaphor (SEE).

mixed blessing

mixed emotions

moan and groan   An inescapable pair (SEE). *bawl; bemoan; bewail; blubber; cry; groan; moan; snivel; sob; wail; weep; whimper; whine.*

modus operandi   A foreignism (SEE).

modus vivendi   A foreignism (SEE).

moment of truth

Monday morning quarterback (-ing)   A moribund metaphor (SEE).

money can't buy everything
A popular prescription (SEE).

(like) money in the bank   An insipid simile (SEE moribund metaphors).

money is the root of all evil
A popular prescription (SEE).

money (making) machine   A moribund metaphor. (SEE)

money talks   A moribund metaphor (SEE).

money to burn   A moribund metaphor (SEE).

money well spent

monkey on (my) back   A moribund metaphor (SEE). *addiction; fixation; habit; obsession.*

monkey see, monkey do   An infantile phrase (SEE).

mop (wipe) the floor with   A moribund metaphor (SEE).
1. *assail; assault; attack; batter; beat; cudgel; flagellate; flog; hit; lambaste; lash; lick; mangle; pound; pummel; strike; thrash; trample; trounce.*
2. *beat; conquer; crush; defeat; outdo; overcome; overpower; overwhelm; prevail; quell; rout; subdue; succeed; triumph; trounce; vanquish; win.*

more bang for (your) buck

more cheers than jeers

(does) more harm than good

more in sorrow than in anger

more is better   A quack equation (SEE).

more of the same

more power to (them)

more preferable   A dimwitted redundancy (SEE). *preferable.* ■ While the patient is still at risk to hemorrhage during that time, waiting may be *more preferable* to surgery. DELETE *more.*

more sinned against than sinning

more than (they) bargained for

more than meets the eye

more . . . than you could shake a stick at   A moribund metaphor (SEE). *countless; dozens of; hundreds of; incalculable; inestimable; innumerable; many; numerous; scores of; thousands of; untold.* ■ He had *more* women in his life *than you could shake a stick at.* REPLACE WITH *untold.*

moribund metaphors*

Metaphors, like similes, should have the briefest of lives. Their vitality depends on their evanescence.

And yet must we forever endure the dimwitted *(it's) a jungle (out there), an emotional roller coaster, (as) cool as a cucumber, everything but the kitchen sink, leak like a sieve, light at the end of the tunnel, out to lunch, pass like ships in the night, (as) phony as a three-dollar bill, piece of cake, window of opportunity, (every parent's) worst nightmare,* and countless other metaphors that characterize people as dull, everyday speakers and writers, indeed, as platitudinarians? Nothing new do they tell us. Nothing more do they show us.

Moreover, if it weren't for our plethora of metaphors, especially, sports images — *above par, a new ballgame, down for the count, hit a home run, off base, pull no punches, stand on the sidelines, step up to the plate* — and war images — *a call to arms, an uphill battle, draw fire, earn his stripes, first line of defense, in the trenches, on the firing line, take by storm* — dimwitted men and, even, women would be far less able to articulate their thoughts. People would speak and write more haltingly than they already do; their thoughts and feelings more misshapen than they already are.

Metaphors hamper our understanding as often as they help it. They interfere with our understanding not only when we use them singly but

---

*Rather than have a separate section on "insipid similes," I include them here. Since a metaphor can be thought of as a condensed simile (which often uses the word *as* or *like*) and a simile usually can be converted into a metaphor, this does not strike me as taking too much license.

also, and especially, when we use them simultaneously, that is, when we use them together, metaphor on metaphor. Frequently incongruous, these metaphors disfigure any sentence in which they are found. ■ And by last Christmas, for any defense contractor, the dwindling Soviet threat had evolved from *meal ticket* into *writing on the wall.* ■ Our restaurant *cost* me and my wife *an arm and a leg*, but we didn't build it without planning and we certainly wouldn't let it *go down the drain.* ■ Right now, USAir's problem is trying to determine whether this is *a soft landing* for the economy or a recession, and *the jury is still out.*

People rely on metaphors not because they feel it makes their speech and writing more vivid and inviting but because they fail to learn how to express themselves otherwise; they know not the words.

The more of these metaphors that people use, the less effective is their speech and writing. Neither interesting nor persuasive, their expression fatigues us where they thought it would inform us, annoys us where they believed it would amuse us, and benumbs us where they felt it would bestir us.

most assuredly   An infantile phrase (SEE). *assuredly; certainly; decidedly; definitely; positively; surely; undoubtedly; unequivocally; unhesitatingly; unquestionably.* ■ The customer will *most assuredly* notify the maître d' if he or she is expecting someone else. REPLACE WITH *certainly.* SEE ALSO *absolutely; definitely; most (very) definitely.*

most (very) definitely   An infantile phrase (SEE). It is irredeemably dimwitted to say *most definitely* when the more moderate, indeed, the more civilized *I (am), just so, quite right, surely, that's right* or *yes* will do. ■ And you feel your daughter was unjustly treated? *Most definitely.* USE *I do.* ■ So whoever you meet has to accommodate your needs? *Very definitely.* USE *Yes.* ■ So when you're sitting around, you are the only white person there? *Most definitely.* USE *Just so.*

As a synonym for words like *assuredly; certainly; decidedly; definitely; positively; surely; undoubtedly; unequivocally; unhesitatingly; unquestionably;* the phrase *most definitely* verges on infantile. ■ Colder weather is *most definitely* on the way. REPLACE WITH *unquestionably.* ■ Would you do it again? *Most definitely.* REPLACE WITH *Unhesitatingly.* SEE ALSO *absolutely; definitely; most assuredly.*

motivating force   A dimwitted redundancy (SEE). *drive; energy; force; impetus; motivation; power.*

motley crew   An inescapable pair (SEE).

mounting evidence

move forward   A torpid term (SEE). Politicians, in particular, endlessly spout *move forward* and *go forward* and even *proceed forward* — just a few of the fuzzy phrases that politicos depend on. Pellucid words like *advance, continue, develop, go on, grow, improve, move on, proceed* and *progress* seem to completely elude their suspect intellects. ■ I believe it was contact with the United States that has *moved* the process of economic reform *forward*, and hopefully some day will *move* the process of political reform *forward*. REPLACE WITH *advanced* and *advance.*

■ We need to empower the city to *move* it *forward*. REPLACE WITH *improve.* ■ As the company *moves forward*, it's very important that we hold on to those values. REPLACE WITH *grows.*

And here is a truly ludicrous example: ■ As the year *moves forward*, we will see more *forward movement* in global and domestic environmental issues. REPLACE WITH *advances* and *progress.* SEE ALSO *a step forward; a step (forward) in the right direction; go forward; move (forward) in the right direction; proceed forward.*

move heaven and earth   A moribund metaphor (SEE).

move (forward) in the right direction   A torpid term (SEE). *advance; continue; develop; go on; grow; improve; increase; move on; proceed; progress.* ■ I know the company will resolve its problems and *move forward in the right direction.* REPLACE WITH *grow.* ■ All the numbers are looking pretty good and *moving in the right direction.* REPLACE WITH *increasing.*

Often, formulaic phrases like *move in the right direction* are simply bluster, as in this nearly nonsensical sentence: ■ I'm ready, willing and able to bring people together and get everybody *moving in the right direction forward.* SEE ALSO *a step forward; a step (forward) in the right direction; go forward; move forward; proceed forward.*

move it or lose it   An infantile phrase (SEE).

move mountains   A moribund metaphor (SEE).

mover and shaker   A moribund metaphor (SEE).

moving target   A moribund metaphor (SEE).

Mr. Right

(make) much ado about nothing
elaborate; embellish; embroider; enhance; enlarge; exaggerate; hyperbolize; inflate; magnify; overdo; overreact; overstress; overstate; strain; stretch.

much to (their) relief

much to (my) surprise

muck and mire   A moribund metaphor (SEE).

muddy the waters   A moribund metaphor (SEE).

music to (my) ears   A moribund metaphor (SEE).

mutual admiration society   An infantile phrase (SEE).

mutually exclusive   ■ Smoking and good health are *mutually exclusive.*

my (whole) life flashed before me

my sentiments exactly

N

nagging doubts   An inescapable pair (SEE).

nail (their) flag to the mast
A moribund metaphor (SEE).

(like) nailing jelly to the wall   An insipid simile (SEE moribund metaphors).

nail (him) to the wall   A moribund metaphor (SEE).

(as) naked as a jaybird   An insipid simile (SEE moribund metaphors). *bare; disrobed; naked; nude; stripped; unclothed; uncovered; undressed.*

(my) name is mud   A moribund metaphor (SEE).

name of the game   A moribund metaphor (SEE). *basis; center; core; crux; essence; gist; heart; kernel; pith; substance.*

(as) narrow as an arrow   An insipid simile (SEE moribund metaphors). *attenuated; bony; emaciated; gaunt; lank; lanky; lean; narrow; rail-thin; scraggy; scrawny; skeletal; skinny; slender; slight; slim; spare; spindly; svelte; thin; trim; wispy.*

national pastime   A moribund metaphor (SEE). *baseball.*

natural progression of things

near and dear to (my) heart

neat and tidy   An inescapable pair (SEE). *neat; orderly; tidy.*

(as) neat as a pin   An insipid simile (SEE moribund metaphors). *methodical; neat; ordered; orderly; organized; systematic; tidy; trim; well-organized.*

necessary evil   ■ Their staunch refusal to concede that new taxes are, at the least, a *necessary evil*, could shut them out of the budget process altogether.

(a) necessary prerequisite
A dimwitted redundancy (SEE). *necessary; prerequisite.* ■ An understanding of expressions is *a necessary prerequisite* to learning any command language. DELETE *necessary.* ■ The transfer of information is *a necessary prerequisite* for the effective transfer of technology. DELETE *a prerequisite.*

necessary requirement   A dimwitted redundancy (SEE). *necessary; requirement.* ■ Because of the labor problems that we have been having with the police patrolmen's union, we will be unable to meet the *necessary requirements* by the deadline. DELETE *necessary*.

necessity is the mother of invention A popular prescription (SEE).

neck and neck A moribund metaphor (SEE).

(our) neck of the woods *area; community; district; domain; environment; environs; locale; locality; neighborhood; region; vicinity.*

(I) need all the help (I) can get

need(s) and want(s) An inescapable pair (SEE). ■ The economy is tight, but we all continue to have *needs and wants* that must be met.
   The following sentence illustrates just how ridiculous the use of this pair of words can be: ■ Two eight-ounce glasses contain almost 100 percent of the recommended nutrients and minerals your body *needs and wants*. SEE ALSO *want(s) and need(s)*.

(I) need (it) like (I need) a hole in the head An insipid simile (SEE moribund metaphors).

needs no introduction ■ The sexiest man alive *needs no introduction*.

negative (*n*) A torpid term (SEE). *burden; deterrence; deterrent; disadvantage; drawback; encumbrance; frailty; hardship; hindrance; liability; limitation; obstacle; onus; shortcoming; weakness.* ■ I don't see how it's a *negative* to the United States to be supporting a democratic government. REPLACE

WITH *disadvantage*. SEE ALSO *positive*.

negative feelings A torpid term (SEE). This expression tells us how little we listen to how we feel. In our quest for speed and efficiency, we have forfeited our feelings. The niceties of emotion—*anger, animosity, anxiety, despair, displeasure, disquiet, fear, frustration, fury, gloom, grief, guilt, hatred, hostility, ill will, insecurity, malice, melancholy, rage, sadness, shame*, and so on—have been sacrificed to a pointless proficiency. ■ It was reported that IAM headquarters failed to renew a $1 million bond that matured in June, due to their *negative feelings* toward El Al's actions. REPLACE WITH *displeasure*. SEE ALSO *in a bad mood; positive feelings*.

negative impact ■ There are people we avoid at all costs because of their *negative impact* on our state of mind.

neither a borrower nor a lender be A popular prescription (SEE).

neither confirm nor deny
■ American Express officials would *neither confirm nor deny* the existence of the policy.

neither fish nor fowl A moribund metaphor (SEE). *indefinite; indeterminate; indistinct; undefined; undetermined.*

neither here nor there *extraneous; immaterial; impertinent; inapplicable; irrelevant.*

neither one A dimwitted redundancy (SEE). *neither*. ■ *Neither one* of these choices is exclusive of the other.

DELETE *one*. SEE ALSO *each one; either one*.

ne plus ultra   A foreignism (SEE).

nerves of steel   A moribund metaphor (SEE).

nest egg   A moribund metaphor (SEE).

never a dull moment

(she's) never at a loss for words

(I'll) never be the same

never-ending battle

(she) never had a chance

(he) never hurt anybody

never (not) in a million years   An infantile phrase (SEE). ▪ I would never have imagined—*not in a million years*—feeling compelled to come to the defense of that grande dame of the administration, the president's wife. DELETE *not in a million years*.

never (not) in (my) wildest dreams

never say die   A popular prescription (SEE).

never say never   A popular prescription (SEE).

new and improved   A suspect superlative (SEE).

new and innovative   An inescapable pair (SEE). *innovative; new*. ▪ We used some *new and innovative* manu-

facturing techniques. REPLACE WITH *innovative* or *new*.

new breed (of)

new deck (pack) of cards   A moribund metaphor (SEE).

(the) new kid on the block   ▪ Being *the new kid on the block* does not excuse them from their responsibilities.

(like) new wine in old bottles   An insipid simile (SEE moribund metaphors).

next to impossible

nice   An overworked word (SEE). *affable; agreeable; amiable; amicable; companionable; compassionate; congenial; cordial; delightful; friendly; genial; good; good-hearted; humane; kind; kindhearted; likable; neighborly; personable; pleasant; pleasing; sociable; tender; tolerant*.

   The word *nice* we might reserve for its less well-known definitions of *fastidious* and *subtle*.

nice and (hot)

(as) nice as pie   An insipid simile (SEE moribund metaphors). *affable; agreeable; amiable; amicable; companionable; compassionate; congenial; cordial; delightful; friendly; genial; good; good-hearted; humane; kind; kindhearted; likable; neighborly; personable; pleasant; pleasing; sociable; tender; tolerant*.

nice work if you can get it   A plebeian sentiment (SEE).

nickel-and-dime   A moribund metaphor (SEE). ■ The banks were shoveling money into every *nickel-and-dime* developer that walked in.

nickel and dime (him) to death
A moribund metaphor (SEE). SEE ALSO *to death*.

(like) night and day   An insipid simile (SEE moribund metaphors).

nine times out of ten   *commonly; customarily; frequently; generally; most often; normally; often; ordinarily; routinely; usually.*

nip and tuck   A moribund metaphor (SEE).

nip (it) in the bud   A moribund metaphor (SEE). *annul; arrest; balk; block; cancel; check; contain; crush; derail; detain; end; extinguish; foil; frustrate; halt; hinder; impede; neutralize; nullify; obstruct; prevent; quash; quell; repress; restrain; retard; squelch; stall; stay; stifle; stop; subdue; suppress; terminate; thwart.*

nipping at (your) heels   A moribund metaphor (SEE).

no big deal   *inappreciable; inconsequential; inconsiderable; insignificant; minor; negligible; niggling; petty; trifling; trivial; unimportant; unsubstantial.*

nobody but nobody   *nobody; nobody at all; none; no one; no one at all.*

nobody's perfect   A popular prescription (SEE). SEE ALSO *(I'm) a perfectionist; I'm not perfect (you know).*

no comment

no easy task   *arduous; backbreaking; burdensome; difficult; exhausting; fatiguing; hard; herculean; laborious; not easy; onerous; severe; strenuous; toilful; toilsome; tough; trying; wearisome.* ■ Getting this place ready has been *no easy task*. REPLACE WITH *backbreaking*.

no end in sight

no great shakes   A moribund metaphor (SEE).
1. *average; common; commonplace; customary; everyday; fair; mediocre; middling; normal; ordinary; quotidian; passable; regular; routine; standard; tolerable; typical; uneventful; unexceptional; unremarkable; usual.*
2. *inappreciable; inconsequential; inconsiderable; insignificant; minor; negligible; niggling; petty; trifling; trivial; unimportant; unsubstantial.*

no guts, no glory   A popular prescription (SEE).

no holds barred   A moribund metaphor (SEE).

(there's) no honor among thieves

no ifs, ands or buts   An infantile phrase (SEE). SEE ALSO *period*.

no (not a) laughing matter

no longer in the picture

no love lost

no man is an island   A popular prescription (SEE).

no man's land

no more mister nice guy

non compos mentis   A foreignism (SEE). *batty; cracked; crazy; daft; demented; deranged; insane; lunatic; mad; maniacal; neurotic; nuts; nutty; psychotic; raving; squirrelly; touched; unbalanced; unhinged; unsound.*

none of the above   An infantile phrase (SEE). ■ Do you want to talk to me or argue with me? *None of the above.* SEE ALSO *all of the above.*

no news is good news   A quack equation (SEE).

no offense   An infantile phrase (SEE).

(every) nook and cranny   *complexities; details; fine points; intricacies; minutiae; niceties; particulars.* ■ There is lots of time in which to explore the *nooks and crannies* of virtually any topic on AM radio. REPLACE WITH *intricacies.*

no one in (his) right mind

no pain, no gain   A popular prescription (SEE).

no problem
1. *you're welcome.*
2. *not at all; not in the least.*
3. *I'd be glad to; I'd be happy to.*
4. *it's O.K.; that's all right.*
5. *easy; easily; effortlessly; readily.*
■ Thanks very much. *No problem.* USE *You're welcome.* ■ Can you do it? *No problem.* USE *Easily.* SEE ALSO *common courtesy.*

no pun intended   An infantile phrase (SEE).

no relief in sight

no rest for the weary (wicked)

nose out of joint   A moribund metaphor (SEE).
1. *acerbated; angry; annoyed; bothered; cross; displeased; enraged; furious; grouchy; incensed; inflamed; infuriated; irate; irked; irritated; mad; miffed; peeved; provoked; riled; testy; upset; vexed.*
2. *covetous; desirous; envious; grudging; jealous; resentful.*

(it's) no skin off my nose   A moribund metaphor (SEE).

no small feat (task)   *arduous; backbreaking; burdensome; difficult; exhausting; fatiguing; hard; herculean; laborious; not easy; onerous; severe; strenuous; toilful; toilsome; tough; trying; wearisome.*

no stranger to   *acquainted with; familiar with; conversant with.*

no strings attached   A moribund metaphor (SEE).

no sweat   A moribund metaphor (SEE). *easily done; easy; effortless; elementary; facile; simple; simplicity itself; simplistic; straightforward; uncomplex; uncomplicated.*

not a Chinaman's chance   A moribund metaphor (SEE).
1. *doubtful; dubious; farfetched; implausible; improbable; remote; unlikely; unrealistic.*
2. *hopeless; impossible; impracticable;*

impractical; infeasible; unrealizable; unworkable.

not a ghost of a chance A moribund metaphor (SEE).
1. *doubtful; dubious; farfetched; implausible; improbable; remote; unlikely; unrealistic.*
2. *hopeless; impossible; impracticable; impractical; infeasible; unrealizable; unworkable.*

not a hope in hell A moribund metaphor (SEE).
1. *doubtful; dubious; farfetched; implausible; improbable; remote; unlikely; unrealistic.*
2. *hopeless; impossible; impracticable; impractical; infeasible; unrealizable; unworkable.*

not a job for the fainthearted

(you're) not a kid anymore

not all (what) (it's) cracked up to be *deficient; disappointing; discouraging; dissatisfying; inadequate; inapt; incapable; incompetent; ineffective; inferior; insufficient; lacking; unfit; unqualified; unsatisfactory; wanting.*

not a mean bone in (her) body A moribund metaphor (SEE). *affable; agreeable; amiable; amicable; compassionate; friendly; gentle; good-hearted; humane; kind; kindhearted; personable; pleasant; tender; tolerant.*

(and) not a minute (second) too soon

(it's) not a pretty picture (sight)

not a snowball's chance in hell A moribund metaphor (SEE).

1. *doubtful; dubious; farfetched; implausible; improbable; remote; unlikely; unrealistic.*
2. *hopeless; impossible; impracticable; impractical; infeasible; unrealizable; unworkable.*

not by a long shot *by no means; in no way; never; no; not at all; not ever; not in any way; not in the least.*

not by any stretch of the imagination *by no means; in no way; never; no; not at all; not ever; not in any way; not in the least.*

notch in (his) belt A moribund metaphor (SEE).

not (my) cup of tea A moribund metaphor (SEE).

not enough hours in a day

not for all the tea in China A moribund metaphor (SEE).

not for anything in the world A moribund metaphor (SEE).

not for lack of trying

not for love or money A moribund metaphor (SEE).

not for the world A moribund metaphor (SEE).

(has) not gone unnoticed

nothing could be further from the truth
1. *by no means; in no way; never; no; not at all; not ever; nothing of the sort; not in any way; not in the least.*
2. *be amiss; be astray; be deceived; be*

deluded; be erring; be erroneous; be fallacious; be false; be faulty; be inaccurate; be incorrect; be in error; be misguided; be misinformed; be misled; be mistaken; be not correct; be not right; be untrue; be wrong. ■ The premise put forth by the administration that employment must be sacrificed to protect the environment *could not be further from the truth.* REPLACE WITH *is erroneous.*

nothing lasts forever   A popular prescription (SEE).

nothing to sneeze at   A moribund metaphor (SEE). *consequential; considerable; meaningful; momentous; significant; substantial; weighty.* ■ Two hundred thousand jobs is *nothing to sneeze at.* REPLACE WITH *considerable.*

nothing to write home about
A moribund metaphor (SEE).
1. *average; common; commonplace; customary; everyday; fair; mediocre; middling; normal; ordinary; passable; quotidian; regular; standard; tolerable; typical; uneventful; unexceptional; unexciting; unremarkable; usual.*
2. *banal; barren; bland; boring; deadly; dreary; dry; dull; flat; humdrum; inanimate; insipid; jejune; lifeless; mediocre; monotonous; prosaic; routine; spiritless; stale; tedious; tiresome; unexciting; uninteresting; vapid; wearisome.*

nothing ventured, nothing gained   A popular prescription (SEE).

noticeable by (his) absence

noticeably absent

not in (my) backyard

not in (this) lifetime   *by no means; in no way; never; no; not at all; not ever; not in any way; not in the least.*

(that word is) not in (my) vocabulary

not necessarily in that order

not one iota

not on your life   *by no means; in no way; never; no; not at all; not ever; not in any way; not in the least.*

not really   *by no means; in no way; never; no; not at all; not ever; not in any way; not in the least.*

(he's) not taking any chances

(I'm) not that kind of girl

not too tough to take

not to worry

not what (it) used to be   *deficient; disappointing; discouraging; dissatisfying; inadequate; inapt; incapable; incompetent; ineffective; inferior; insufficient; lacking; unfit; unqualified; unsatisfactory; wanting.*

not with a bang but with a (whimper)   An infantile phrase (SEE).

not worth a continental   A moribund metaphor (SEE). *barren; bootless; effete; feckless; feeble; fruitless; futile; impotent; inadequate; inconsequential; inconsiderable; ineffective; ineffectual; infertile; insignificant; inutile; meaningless; meritless; nugatory; null; of no value; pointless; powerless; profitless; sterile; trifling; trivial; unavailing; un-*

important; unproductive; unprofitable; unserviceable; unworthy; useless; vain; valueless; weak; worthless.

not worth a (tinker's) damn

A moribund metaphor (SEE). *barren; bootless; effete; feckless; feeble; fruitless; futile; impotent; inadequate; inconsequential; inconsiderable; ineffective; ineffectual; infertile; insignificant; inutile; meaningless; meritless; nugatory; null; of no value; pointless; powerless; profitless; sterile; trifling; trivial; unavailing; unimportant; unproductive; unprofitable; unserviceable; unworthy; useless; vain; valueless; weak; worthless.*

not worth a plugged nickel

A moribund metaphor (SEE). *barren; bootless; effete; feckless; feeble; fruitless; futile; impotent; inadequate; inconsequential; inconsiderable; ineffective; ineffectual; infertile; insignificant; inutile; meaningless; meritless; nugatory; null; of no value; pointless; powerless; profitless; sterile; trifling; trivial; unavailing; unimportant; unproductive; unprofitable; unserviceable; unworthy; useless; vain; valueless; weak; worthless.*

not worth a straw   A moribund

metaphor (SEE). *barren; bootless; effete; feckless; feeble; fruitless; futile; impotent; inadequate; inconsequential; inconsiderable; ineffective; ineffectual; infertile; insignificant; inutile; meaningless; meritless; nugatory; null; of no value; pointless; powerless; profitless; sterile; trifling; trivial; unavailing; unimportant; unproductive; unprofitable; unserviceable; unworthy; useless; vain; valueless; weak; worthless.*

not worth the paper it's written

(printed) on   A moribund metaphor (SEE). *barren; bootless; effete; feckless; feeble; fruitless; futile; impotent; inadequate; inconsequential; inconsiderable; ineffective; ineffectual; infertile; insignificant; inutile; meaningless; meritless; nugatory; null; of no value; pointless; powerless; profitless; sterile; trifling; trivial; unavailing; unimportant; unproductive; unprofitable; unserviceable; unworthy; useless; vain; valueless; weak; worthless.* ■ I say to you that the governor's budget is *not worth the paper it's written on.* REPLACE WITH *useless.*

(there are) no two ways about it

no use crying over spilt milk

A popular prescription (SEE).

no way   *by no means; in no way;

never; no; not at all; not ever; not in any way; not in the least.*

no way José   *by no means; in no

way; never; no; not at all; not ever; not in any way; not in the least.*

nowhere to go but up

nowhere (else) to turn

now I've heard everything

(it's) now or never

now you see it, now you don't   An

infantile phrase (SEE).

null and void   An inescapable pair

(SEE). *abolished; annulled; canceled; countermanded; invalid; null; nullified; recalled; repealed; rescinded; revoked; void; withdrawn; worthless.* ■ We aren't sure what the terms of the deal are, or what may be expected of them, or what may make them *null and void*. REPLACE WITH *invalid*.

(her) number is up   A moribund metaphor (SEE).

number one (two)   A dimwitted redundancy (SEE). *first (second)*. ■ *Number one*, I don't feel that qualifies her as black. *Number two*, people shouldn't wear their color on their sleeve. REPLACE WITH *First; Second*.

number-one (no. 1) priority A torpid term (SEE). ■ Your satisfaction is our *number-one priority*. REPLACE WITH *main concern*. SEE ALSO *first priority; top priority*.

nuts and bolts   A moribund meta-phor (SEE). *basics; essentials; foundation; fundamentals; principles*. ■ In this text we explore the *nuts and bolts* of radio production. REPLACE WITH *essentials*.

nuttier than a fruitcake   A moribund metaphor (SEE). *batty; cracked; crazy; daft; demented; deranged; fey; goofy; insane; lunatic; mad; maniacal; neurotic; nuts; nutty; psychotic; raving; squirrelly; touched; unbalanced; unhinged; unsound; wacky; zany*.

(as) nutty as a fruitcake   An insipid simile (SEE moribund metaphors). *batty; cracked; crazy; daft; demented; deranged; fey; goofy; insane; lunatic; mad; maniacal; neurotic; nuts; nutty; psychotic; raving; squirrelly; touched; unbalanced; unhinged; unsound; wacky; zany*.

O

object of one's affection *admirer; beau; beloved; boyfriend (girlfriend); companion; darling; dear; flame; infatuate; inamorato (inamorata); lover; paramour; steady; suiter; swain; sweetheart; wooer.* SEE ALSO *significant other.*

obscene An overworked word (SEE). *abhorrent; abominable; accursed; appalling; atrocious; awful; beastly; blasphemous; detestable; disagreeable; disgusting; dreadful; execrable; frightening; frightful; ghastly; grisly; gruesome; hateful; horrendous; horrible; horrid; horrifying; indecent; indelicate; inhuman; insulting; loathesome; monstrous; obnoxious; odious; offensive; repellent; repugnant; repulsive; revolting; tasteless; terrible; terrifying; unspeakable; unutterable; vulgar.* ■ Certain levels of expenditure are *obscene* and do a great injustice to our concept of social justice. REPLACE WITH *offensive.* ■ It's an *obscene* scenario that's being played out. REPLACE WITH *unspeakable.*

obviate the need for A dimwitted redundancy (SEE). *obviate.* ■ If indicated, create a limited-access, safe unit to *obviate the need for* activity restriction. DELETE *the need for.*

oceans of ink A moribund metaphor (SEE).

odd couple

odds are in (his) favor

(disaster) of biblical proportions *colossal; elephantine; enormous; gargantuan; giant; gigantic; great; huge; immense; mammoth; massive; monstrous; prodigious; stupendous; titanic; tremendous; vast.*

off again, on again *capricious; changeable; erratic; fickle; fitful; flighty; fluctuating; haphazard; inconsistent; inconstant; intermittent; irregular; mercurial; occasional; random; sometime; spasmodic; sporadic; unpredictable; unsettled; unstable; unsteady; vacillating; volatile; wavering; wayward.*

off and running A moribund metaphor (SEE).

off base A moribund metaphor (SEE). *amiss; astray; deceived; deluded; erring; erroneous; fallacious; false; faulty; inaccurate; incorrect; in error; misguided; misinformed; misled; mistaken; not correct; not right; wrong.* ■ Given all the uncertainty surrounding the nation's economic future, no one is prepared to say the administration is *off base*. REPLACE WITH *incorrect*.

off (her) rocker   A moribund metaphor (SEE). *batty; cracked; crazy; daft; demented; deranged; fey; goofy; insane; lunatic; mad; maniacal; neurotic; nuts; nutty; psychotic; raving; squirrelly; touched; unbalanced; unhinged; unsound; wacky; zany.*

off the beaten track   A moribund metaphor (SEE). *aberrant; abnormal; anomalistic; anomalous; atypical; bizarre; curious; deviant; different; distinct; distinctive; eccentric; exceptional; extraordinary; fantastic; foreign; grotesque; idiosyncratic; independent; individual; individualistic; irregular; novel; odd; offbeat; original; peculiar; queer; uncommon; unconventional; unexampled; unique; unnatural; unorthodox; unusual.*

off the cuff   A moribund metaphor (SEE). *extemporaneously; extempore; impromptu; improvised; spontaneous; unprepared; unprompted; unrehearsed.*

(go) off the deep end   A moribund metaphor (SEE).

off the hook   A moribund metaphor (SEE).

off the top of (my) head   A moribund metaphor (SEE). *extemporaneously; extempore; impromptu; improvised; spontaneous; unprepared; unprompted; unrehearsed.*

off the wall   A moribund metaphor (SEE). *aberrant; abnormal; anomalistic; anomalous; atypical; bizarre; curious; deviant; different; distinct; distinctive; eccentric; exceptional; extra-*

ordinary; fantastic; foreign; grotesque; idiosyncratic; independent; individual; individualistic; irregular; novel; odd; offbeat; original; peculiar; puzzling; quaint; queer; rare; remarkable; separate; singular; uncommon; unconventional; unexampled; unique; unorthodox; unparalleled; unprecedented; unusual.

off to the races   A moribund metaphor (SEE).

off track   A moribund metaphor (SEE). *amiss; astray; deceived; deluded; erring; erroneous; fallacious; false; faulty; inaccurate; incorrect; in error; misguided; misinformed; misled; mistaken; not correct; not right; wrong.*

oftentimes   A dimwitted redundancy (SEE). *often.* ■ *Oftentimes*, this results in overloading the office staff with the added responsibility of planning the company's meetings and events. USE *Often*.

ofttimes   An archaism (SEE). *frequently; often; repeatedly.*

of two minds   A moribund metaphor (SEE). *ambivalent; confused; divided; indecisive; in doubt; irresolute; neutral; torn; uncertain; uncommitted; undecided; unsure.*

O.K.?   An ineffectual phrase (SEE). To call *O.K.?* an ineffectual phrase is too kind, and any censure that those who use it suffer, condign. ■ I don't have a lot of respect for people who judge others by their skin tone, *O.K.?* DELETE *O.K.?* ■ I have a master's degree, *O.K.?* but if I dress bad or speak bad, I'm treated bad, *O.K.?* DELETE *O.K.?*

old adage A dimwitted redundancy (SEE). *adage.* ■ The *old adage* "The first half of our lives is ruined by our parents and the last half by our children" need not be and should not be. DELETE *old.*

old and decrepit An inescapable pair (SEE).

(as) old as Adam An insipid simile (SEE moribund metaphors). *aged; aging; ancient; antediluvian; antique; archaic; elderly; hoary; hoary-headed; old; patriarchal; prehistoric; seasoned; superannuated; venerable.*

(as) old as the hills An insipid simile (SEE moribund metaphors). *aged; aging; ancient; antediluvian; antique; archaic; elderly; hoary; hoary-headed; old; patriarchal; prehistoric; seasoned; superannuated; venerable.*

(as) old as time An insipid simile (SEE moribund metaphors). *aged; aging; ancient; antediluvian; antique; archaic; elderly; hoary; hoary-headed; old; patriarchal; prehistoric; seasoned; superannuated; venerable.*

old-boy network A moribund metaphor (SEE).

old cliché A dimwitted redundancy (SEE). *cliché.* ■ Working for these guys I feel like the *old cliché* "a cog in the wheel." DELETE *old.*

old enough to know better

older but wiser

old hat A moribund metaphor (SEE).
1. *antediluvian; antiquated; archaic;*

dead; obsolescent; obsolete; old; old-fashioned; outdated; outmoded; out of date; out of fashion; passé; superannuated.
2. *banal; barren; bland; boring; deadly; dreary; dry; dull; flat; humdrum; inanimate; insipid; jejune; lifeless; mediocre; monotonous; prosaic; routine; spiritless; stale; tedious; tiresome; unexciting; uninteresting; vapid; wearisome.*

old maxim A dimwitted redundancy (SEE). *maxim.* ■ A number of studies indicate that, in deciding what punishment is appropriate for different crimes, individuals typically rely on an *old maxim*: Let the punishment fit the crime. DELETE *old.*

old soldiers never die, they just fade away

old wives' tale A moribund metaphor (SEE).

on a . . . basis A dimwitted redundancy (SEE). ■ Meat production is the major use of goats *on a worldwide basis.* USE *worldwide.* ■ I am tortured *on a daily basis.* USE *daily.* ■ I see him for my treatment *on a regular basis.* USE *regularly.* ■ You meet the students *on a weekly basis.* USE *weekly.* ■ We should look at these issues *on a case-by-case basis.* USE *case-by-case.*

on a collision course A moribund metaphor (SEE).

on a different wavelength A moribund metaphor (SEE). *conflict; differ; disagree; disharmonize; feel differently; think unalike.*

on a fool's errand

on again, off again *capricious;*

changeable; erratic; fickle; fitful; flighty; fluctuating; haphazard; inconsistent; inconstant; intermittent; irregular; mercurial; occasional; random; sometime; spasmodic; sporadic; unpredictable; unsettled; unstable; unsteady; vacillating; volatile; wavering; wayward.

on an ego trip

on an equal footing

on an even keel A moribund metaphor (SEE). *balanced; even; firm; fixed; stable; steadfast; steady; unfaltering; unwavering.*

on a ... note A dimwitted redundancy (SEE). ■ *On a personal note*, I would not be all that appalled if my children were to perform well only 99 percent of the time. USE *Personally.*

on a roll *doing well; flourishing; prospering; succeeding; thriving.*

on a scale of 1 to 10 An infantile phrase (SEE).

on a shoestring A moribund metaphor (SEE).

on automatic pilot A moribund metaphor (SEE).

(come) on board A moribund metaphor (SEE). ■ Some doctors are starting to *come on board*, but many haven't a clue what's going on. REPLACE WITH *take alternative medicine seriously.*

on both sides of the fence A moribund metaphor (SEE). *ambivalent; divided; indecisive; in doubt; irresolute; neutral; torn; uncertain; uncommitted; undecided; unsure.*

once and for all

once bitten (burned), twice shy A popular prescription (SEE).

once in a blue moon A moribund metaphor (SEE). *hardly; infrequently; not often; occasionally; rarely; scarcely; seldom; sporadically; uncommonly.*

once in a great while *hardly; infrequently; not often; occasionally; rarely; scarcely; seldom; sporadically; uncommonly.*

once-in-a-lifetime opportunity

once upon a time An infantile phrase (SEE).

on cloud nine A moribund metaphor (SEE). *blissful; blithe; buoyant; cheerful; delighted; ecstatic; elated; enraptured; euphoric; exalted; excited; exhilarated; exultant; gay; glad; gleeful; good-humored; happy; intoxicated; jolly; jovial; joyful; joyous; jubilant; merry; mirthful; overjoyed; pleased; rapturous; thrilled.*

on (the) condition of anonymity

on (our) doorstep A moribund metaphor (SEE).

(the) one and only A dimwitted redundancy (SEE). *one; only; sole.* ■ In the early days of any business, the *one and only* thing you understand is that the customer is king. USE *one* or *only.*

one and the same A dimwitted redundancy (SEE). *identical; one; the same.* ■ Are you saying that submission and competition are *one and the same*? USE *the same.* ■ Some people believe that marketing and advertising are *one and the same*. USE *identical*.

on easy street   A moribund metaphor (SEE). *affluent; moneyed; opulent; prosperous; rich; wealthy; well-off; well-to-do.*

one big, happy family   A suspect superlative (SEE).

one disappointment after another

one foot in and one foot out A moribund metaphor (SEE). *ambivalent; divided; indecisive; irresolute; torn; uncertain; uncommitted; undecided; unsure.*

(put) one foot in front of the other   A moribund metaphor (SEE).

one foot in the grave   A moribund metaphor (SEE). *decaying; declining; deteriorating; disintegrating; dying; ebbing; expiring; fading; failing; moribund; near death; sinking; very ill; waning.*

one for all and all for one

one for the books   A moribund metaphor (SEE). *different; exceptional; extraordinary; incomparable; inimitable; matchless; notable; noteworthy; novel; odd; original; peculiar; peerless; remarkable; singular; special; strange; uncommon; unequaled; unexampled; unique; unmatched; unparalleled; unrivaled; unusual; without equal.*

one good turn deserves another A popular prescription (SEE).

one hundred (100) percent *absolutely; altogether; categorically; completely; entirely; fully; perfectly; positively; quite; thoroughly; totally; unconditionally; unreservedly; utterly; wholly.* ■ I agree with you *one hundred percent*. REPLACE WITH *unreservedly*.

one in a million   *different; exceptional; extraordinary; incomparable; inimitable; matchless; notable; noteworthy; novel; odd; original; peculiar; peerless; remarkable; singular; special; strange; uncommon; unequaled; unexampled; unique; unmatched; unparalleled; unrivaled; unusual; without equal.*

one man's meat is another man's poison   A popular prescription (SEE).

one man's trash is another man's treasure   A popular prescription (SEE).

one of a kind   *different; exceptional; extraordinary; incomparable; inimitable; matchless; notable; noteworthy; novel; odd; original; peculiar; peerless; remarkable; singular; special; strange; uncommon; unequaled; unexampled; unique; unmatched; unparalleled; unrivaled; unusual; without equal.*

one-shot deal

one size fits all   *procrustean*. ■ We do not advocate a *one-size-fits-all* approach in making decisions about how students should be educated. REPLACE WITH *procrustean*.

one step at a time   A popular prescription (SEE).

(well) one thing led to another A grammatical gimmick (SEE).

one-two punch A moribund metaphor (SEE).

one-way street A moribund metaphor (SEE).

one-way ticket to A moribund metaphor (SEE).

on firm (financial) ground A moribund metaphor (SEE).

on God's green earth

ongoing An overworked word (SEE). *Ongoing* has superseded practically all of its synonyms. For example: *ongoing basis; ongoing care; ongoing commitment; ongoing destruction; ongoing discussions; ongoing education; ongoing effort; ongoing investigation; ongoing plan; ongoing process; ongoing program; ongoing relationship; ongoing service; ongoing support.*

Consider these synonyms: *ceaseless; constant; continual; continuing; continuous; endless; enduring; incessant; lifelong; long-lived; nonstop; progressing; unbroken; unceasing; unremitting.* ■ With this new rehabilitation center, patients will no longer have to travel outside the community to receive the *ongoing* care they need. DELETE *ongoing*. ■ Establishing paternity also may force more women into *ongoing* relationships with fathers who are abusive or violent. REPLACE WITH *lifelong*.

(up) on (her) high horse A moribund metaphor (SEE). *arrogant; cavalier; condescending; contemptuous; despotic; dictatorial; disdainful; dogmatic; domineering; haughty; imperious; insolent; lofty; overbearing; overweening; patronizing; pompous; pretentious;* *scornful; self-important; supercilious; superior; vainglorious.*

on hold

on (its) last legs A moribund metaphor (SEE).
1. *decaying; declining; deteriorating; disappearing; disintegrating; dying; ebbing; expiring; fading; failing; moribund; near death; sinking; vanishing; waning.*
2. *beat; bushed; debilitated; depleted; drained; enervated; exhausted; fatigued; sapped; spent; tired; weary; worn out.*
■ The battle for a smoke-free environment is hardly *on its last legs*. REPLACE WITH *moribund*.

(I'm) only human

only the strong survive A popular prescription (SEE).

on (his) part A dimwitted redundancy (SEE). *among; by; for; from; of; -s.* ■ I think this is really irresponsible *on your part*. USE *of you*. ■ I guess this is selfish *on my part*. USE *of me*. SEE ALSO *on the part of*.

on pins and needles A moribund metaphor (SEE). *agitated; anxious; apprehensive; disquieted; distressed; disturbed; edgy; fretful; ill at ease; impatient; in suspense; nervous; on edge; restive; restless; troubled; uneasy; unquiet; unsettled; worried.*

on (her) plate A moribund metaphor (SEE).

on safe ground A moribund metaphor (SEE). *guarded; protected; safe; secure; sheltered; shielded.*

on second thought

on shaky ground   A moribund metaphor (SEE).

on solid ground   A moribund metaphor (SEE).

(right) on target   A moribund metaphor (SEE). *accurate; correct; exact; irrefutable; precise; right; true.* ■ The January 19 editorial identifying the inconsistent, but vociferous, antitax group as "the haters" is *right on target.* REPLACE WITH *irrefutable.*

on tenterhooks   A moribund metaphor (SEE). *agitated; anxious; apprehensive; disquieted; distressed; disturbed; edgy; fretful; ill at ease; impatient; in suspense; nervous; on edge; restive; restless; troubled; uneasy; unquiet; unsettled; worried.*

on the ball   A moribund metaphor (SEE).
1. *alert; attentive; awake; aware; eagle-eyed; heedful; observant; vigilant; wakeful; watchful.*
2. *able; adroit; apt; astute; bright; brilliant; capable; clever; competent; discerning; effective; effectual; efficient; enlightened; insightful; intelligent; judicious; keen; knowledgeable; learned; logical; luminous; perceptive; perspicacious; quick; rational; reasonable; sagacious; sage; sapient; sensible; sharp; shrewd; smart; sound; wise.*

on the blink   *broken; defective; in disrepair; not working; not functioning; out of order.*

(look) on the bright side

(right) on the button   A moribund

metaphor (SEE). *accurate; correct; exact; irrefutable; precise; right; true.*

on the cheap   *cheaply; inexpensively.*

on the chopping block   A moribund metaphor (SEE).

(ride) on the coattails of   A moribund metaphor (SEE).

on the cutting (leading) edge
A moribund metaphor (SEE). *first; forefront; foremost; leading; vanguard.*

on the dot   A moribund metaphor (SEE) *accurate; correct; exact; irrefutable; precise; right; true.*

on the drawing board   A moribund metaphor (SEE). ■ The university now has seven new schools *on the drawing board.*

(luckiest man) on the face of the earth

on the fast track   A moribund metaphor (SEE).

(sit) on the fence   A moribund metaphor (SEE). *ambivalent; divided; impartial; indecisive; irresolute; neutral; torn; uncertain; uncommitted; undecided; unsettled; unsure.*

on the firing line   A moribund metaphor (SEE).

on the fly   A moribund metaphor (SEE).

on the fritz   *broken; defective; in disrepair; not working; not functioning; out of order.*

on the front burner   A moribund metaphor (SEE). ■ Preserving Yellowstone is probably a priority for most Americans, but at the moment it's not *on* anyone's *front burner.*

on the front lines   A moribund metaphor (SEE).

on the go   *absorbed; active; busy; employed; engaged; engrossed; going; immersed; involved; moving; occupied; preoccupied; wrapped up in.*

(hot) on the heels of   A moribund metaphor (SEE). *after; behind; ensuing; following; succeeding.* SEE ALSO *in the wake of.*

on the horizon   A moribund metaphor (SEE).

(caught) on the horns of a dilemma   A moribund metaphor (SEE). *at risk; endangered; hardpressed; imperiled; in a bind; in a dilemma; in a fix; in a jam; in a predicament; in a quandary; in danger; in difficulty; in jeopardy; in peril; in trouble; jeopardized.*

(take it) on the lam   *abscond; clear out; decamp; depart; desert; disappear; escape; exit; flee; fly; go; go away; leave; move on; part; pull out; quit; retire; retreat; run away; take flight; take off; vacate; vanish; withdraw.*

on the level   *aboveboard; creditable; equitable; fair; genuine; honest; honorable; just; lawful; legitimate; open; proper; reputable; respectable; right; sincere; square; straightforward; truthful; upright; veracious; veridical.*

on the loose   A moribund metaphor (SEE). *at large; at liberty; free; loose; unattached; unbound; unconfined; unrestrained; unrestricted.*

on the mend   *ameliorating; amending; coming round; convalescent; convalescing; gaining strength; getting better; healing; improving; looking up; meliorating; mending; rallying; recovering; recuperating; refreshing; renewing; reviving; strengthening.*

(right) on the money   A moribund metaphor (SEE). *accurate; correct; exact; irrefutable; precise; right; true.*

on the nose   A moribund metaphor (SEE). *accurate; correct; exact; irrefutable; precise; right; true.*

on the other hand   *but; in contrast; conversely; however; whereas; yet.*

on the other side of the coin   A moribund metaphor (SEE). *but; in contrast; conversely; however; whereas; yet.* ■ *On the other side of the coin,* if you're astute you can occasionally buy them at big discounts. REPLACE WITH *But.*

on the outside looking in

on the part of   A dimwitted redundancy (SEE). *among; by; for; from; of; -s.* ■ This is not an investigation to uncover bad behavior *on the part of* the board of medicine. USE *by.* ■ We haven't missed any deadlines, but it was mostly because of great effort *on the part of* the staff. USE *from.* ■ *Misconduct on the part of the police* sometimes also violates the criminal law. USE *Police misconduct.* SEE ALSO *on (his) part.*

on the prowl (for)

on the razor's edge   A moribund metaphor (SEE). *at risk; endangered; hard-pressed; imperiled; in danger; in difficulty; in jeopardy; in peril; in trouble; jeopardized.*

on the rebound

(start) on the right foot   A moribund metaphor (SEE). *auspiciously; favorably; positively; propitiously; well.*

on the right track   A moribund metaphor (SEE).

on the road to (success)   A moribund metaphor (SEE).

on the road to recovery   A moribund metaphor (SEE). *ameliorating; amending; coming round; convalescent; convalescing; feeling better; gaining strength; getting better; healing; improving; looking up; meliorating; mending; rallying; recovering; recuperating; refreshing; renewing; reviving; strengthening.* ■ His wife has been ill, but she's *on the road to recovery.* REPLACE WITH *improving.*

on the rocks   A moribund metaphor (SEE). *at risk; endangered; imperiled; in danger; in difficulty; in jeopardy; in peril; in trouble; jeopardized.* ■ Our marriage is *on the rocks.* REPLACE WITH *imperiled.*

on the ropes   A moribund metaphor (SEE).
1. *at risk; endangered; hard-pressed; imperiled; in danger; in difficulty; in jeopardy; in peril; in trouble; jeopardized.*

2. *defenseless; helpless; impotent; powerless.*

on the same wavelength   A moribund metaphor (SEE). *agree; concur; feel similarly; harmonize; match; mesh; think alike.*

on the short list

on the . . . side   A dimwitted redundancy (SEE). ■ Tuesday will be *on the chilly side.* USE *chilly.* ■ She is *on the thin side.* USE *thin.* ■ That means the 550,000 estimate is probably *on the low side.* USE *low.*

on the sly   *clandestinely; confidentially; covertly; furtively; in private; in secret; mysteriously; privately; secludedly; secretly; slyly; stealthily; surreptitiously; undercover.*

on the spot   A moribund metaphor (SEE).
1. *at once; directly; forthwith; immediately; instantly; momentarily; promptly; right away; straightaway; summarily; without delay.*
2. *at risk; endangered; hard-pressed; imperiled; in danger; in difficulty; in jeopardy; in peril; in trouble; jeopardized.*

on the table   A moribund metaphor (SEE). ■ A healthy dialog on value systems when there is no pressing issue *on the table* may help clear the air. REPLACE WITH *before us.* ■ There is nothing that is not *on the table.* REPLACE WITH *being considered.*

(out) on the town   A moribund metaphor (SEE). *be merry; carouse; carry on; celebrate; frolic; party; play;*

revel; riot; roister; rollick; romp; sky-lark.

on the up-and-up   *aboveboard; creditable; equitable; fair; honest; honorable; just; lawful; legitimate; open; proper; reputable; respectable; right; sincere; square; straightforward; upright; veracious; veridical.*

on the upswing

on the warpath   A moribund metaphor (SEE). *aggressive; antagonistic; arguing; argumentative; battling; bellicose; belligerent; bickering; brawling; clashing; combative; contentious; fighting; militant; pugnacious; quarrelsome; querulous; squabbling; truculent; warlike; wrangling.*

on the wings of the wind   A moribund metaphor (SEE). *abruptly; apace; at once; briskly; directly; expeditiously; fast; forthwith; hastily; hurriedly; immediately; instantaneously; instantly; posthaste; promptly; quickly; rapidly; rashly; right away; speedily; straightaway; swiftly; wingedly.*

(start) on the wrong foot   A moribund metaphor (SEE). *adversely; inauspiciously; negatively; unfavorably; unpropitiously.*

on the wrong track   A moribund metaphor (SEE). *amiss; astray; deceived; deluded; erring; erroneous; fallacious; false; faulty; inaccurate; incorrect; in error; misguided; misinformed; misled; mistaken; not correct; not right; wrong.*

(skate) on thin ice   A moribund metaphor (SEE). *chance; dare; endanger; gamble; hazard; imperil; jeopardize;*

make bold; peril; risk; venture.

on (his) toes   A moribund metaphor (SEE). *alert; attentive; awake; aware; heedful; vigilant; wakeful.*

(sitting) on top of the world
A moribund metaphor (SEE).
1. *advantageous; auspicious; blessed; charmed; enchanted; favored; felicitous; flourishing; fortuitous; fortunate; golden; in luck; lucky; propitious; prosperous; successful; thriving.*
2. *blissful; blithe; buoyant; cheerful; delighted; ecstatic; elated; enraptured; euphoric; exalted; excited; exhilarated; exultant; gay; glad; gleeful; good-humored; happy; intoxicated; jolly; jovial; joyful; joyous; jubilant; merry; mirthful; overjoyed; pleased; rapturous; thrilled.*

on track   A moribund metaphor (SEE).

on (his) trail

onward and upward   An inescapable pair (SEE).

open (up) a can of worms   A moribund metaphor (SEE).

open and aboveboard   *aboveboard; creditable; equitable; fair; honest; honorable; just; lawful; legitimate; open; proper; reputable; respectable; right; square; straightforward; upright; veracious; veridical.*

open (up) a Pandora's box   A moribund metaphor (SEE).

open invitation

open the door for (on; to)   A moribund metaphor (SEE). *bring about;*

cause; create; effect; generate; give rise to; inaugurate; initiate; introduce; occasion; produce; provoke; result in. ■ This breakthrough could *open the door to* a wide range of new varieties of important crops. REPLACE WITH *result in.*

open the floodgates   A moribund metaphor (SEE).

operative   A torpid term (SEE). ■ The *operative* point is that the Republican hopes next year don't rest on voters like those who occasionally elected a Richardson or a Leverett Saltonstall. ■ The *operative* philosophy is spelled out early on: Winning is the most important thing in life.

opportunity knocks only once A popular prescription (SEE).

(as) opposed to what?   An infantile phrase (SEE). SEE ALSO *(as) compared to what?; it's all relative.*

opposites attract   A popular prescription (SEE).

or anything   A grammatical gimmick (SEE). ■ I didn't go beat her up, *or anything.* DELETE *or anything.* ■ Not to be rude *or anything*, but I don't think we should talk to each other. DELETE *or anything.* SEE ALSO *or anything like that.*

or anything like that   A grammatical gimmick (SEE). ■ He wasn't my first boyfriend *or anything like that.* DELETE *or anything like that.* ■ He didn't go out and say, "Who goes there?" *or anything like that.* DELETE *or anything like that.* SEE ALSO *or anything.*

or (a; the) lack thereof   ■ He was ousted because the majority of voters believe he didn't do a good job as mayor — not because of his skin color, but because of his merit *or lack thereof.*

or something   A grammatical gimmick (SEE). ■ This is like something I'd wear in third grade, *or something.* DELETE *or something.* ■ It makes you mad when they make them sound like they're vicious people — that if you walk the street, they're going to grab you *or something.* DELETE *or something.* SEE ALSO *or something like that; or something or other.*

or something like that   A grammatical gimmick (SEE). ■ Why couldn't they have shot him in his arm or leg *or something like that*? DELETE *or something like that.* SEE ALSO *or something; or something or other.*

or something or other   A grammatical gimmick (SEE). ■ We might go to the movies *or something or other.* DELETE *or something or other.* SEE ALSO *or something; or something like that.*

or what   A grammatical gimmick (SEE). ■ Did you see an opportunity for escape, or plan it for a long time, *or what*? DELETE *or what.* ■ Was he being vulgar *or what*? DELETE *or what.* ■ Did you make enough money so you can retire *or what*? REPLACE WITH *or not.*

or whatever   A grammatical gimmick (SEE). ■ They say he corrupted my mind *or whatever.* DELETE *or whatever.* ■ Is it a good thing, is it a bad thing, is it useless, *or whatever*? DELETE *or whatever.* ■ She just wants the extra attention, *or whatever.* DELETE *or* *whatever.* ■ You can call this arrogance or way too much self-assurance *or whatever.* DELETE *or whatever.*

or words to that effect   A grammatical gimmick (SEE).

other things being equal

out and out   *absolute; compleat; complete; consummate; deadly; outright; perfect; thorough; thoroughgoing; total; unmitigated; unqualified; utter.*

out at the elbows   A moribund metaphor (SEE).
1. *dowdy; frowzy; ragged; run-down; seedy; shabby; slipshod; sloppy; slovenly; tattered; threadbare; unkempt; untidy; worn.*
2. *broke; destitute; distressed; impecunious; impoverished; indigent; insolvent; needy; penniless; poor; poverty-stricken; underprivileged.*

out for blood   A moribund metaphor (SEE).

out in left field   A moribund metaphor (SEE). *amiss; astray; deceived; deluded; erring; erroneous; fallacious; false; faulty; inaccurate; incorrect; in error; misguided; misinformed; misled; mistaken; not correct; not right; wrong.*

(they're) out in the cold   A moribund metaphor (SEE).

out in the sun too much   A moribund metaphor (SEE). *bewildered; confounded; confused; dazed; mixed up; muddled; perplexed.*

out like a light   An insipid simile (SEE moribund metaphors). *anesthetized; asleep; comatose; dozing; insensible; napping; oblivious; sleeping; soporiferous; soporific; stuporous; unconscious.*

out of a clear blue sky   A moribund metaphor (SEE). *abruptly; immediately; instantly; quickly; rashly; suddenly; unexpectedly.*

out of circulation   A moribund metaphor (SEE).

out of commission
1. *broken; defective; in disrepair; not working; not functioning; out of order.*
2. *afflicted; ailing; diseased; ill; indisposed; infirm; not (feeling) well; sick; sickly; suffering; unhealthy; unsound; unwell; valetudinarian.*

out of (his) element

out of gas   A moribund metaphor (SEE). *beat; bushed; debilitated; depleted; drained; enervated; exhausted; fatigued; sapped; spent; tired; weary; worn out.*

out of (our) hands

out of harm's way   *guarded; protected; safe; secure; sheltered; shielded; undamaged; unharmed; unhurt; unscathed.*

out of it   *ignorant; incognizant; insensible; nescient; unacquainted; unadvised; unapprised; unaware; unenlightened; unfamiliar; uninformed; unintelligent; unknowing; unschooled; untaught; unversed.*

out of kilter
1. *broken; defective; in disrepair; not working; not functioning; out of order.*
2. *lopsided; shaky; unbalanced; unset-*

tled; unsound; unstable; wobbly.

out of sight

out of sight, out of mind

out of step (with)

out of sync
1. *broken; defective; in disrepair; not working; not functioning; out of order.*
2. *lopsided; shaky; unbalanced; unsettled; unsound; unstable; wobbly.*

out of the blue   A moribund metaphor (SEE). *abruptly; immediately; instantly; quickly; rashly; suddenly; unexpectedly.*

out of the frying pan and into the fire   A moribund metaphor (SEE). *aggravate; complicate; exacerbate; heighten; increase; intensify; irritate; make worse; worsen.*

out of the game   A moribund metaphor (SEE).

out of the picture   A moribund metaphor (SEE).

out of the running   A moribund metaphor (SEE). *noncontender; not competing; not contending.*

out of the woods   A moribund metaphor (SEE). *guarded; protected; safe; secure; sheltered; shielded; undamaged; unharmed; unhurt; unscathed.*

out of thin air   A moribund metaphor (SEE).

out of this world   A moribund metaphor (SEE). *consummate; distinguished; eminent; excellent; exceptional;* *exemplary; exquisite; extraordinary; fabulous; fantastic; flawless; grand; great; ideal; illustrious; magnificent; marvelous; matchless; perfect; preeminent; remarkable; splendid; superb; superior; superlative; supreme; transcendent; wonderful; wondrous.*

out of touch (with)

out of whack
1. *broken; defective; in disrepair; not working; not functioning; out of order.*
2. *lopsided; shaky; unbalanced; unsettled; unsound; unstable; wobbly.*

out on a limb   A moribund metaphor (SEE).
1. *at risk; endangered; hard-pressed; imperiled; in a bind; in a dilemma; in a fix; in a jam; in a predicament; in a quandary; in danger; in difficulty; in jeopardy; in peril; in trouble; jeopardized.*
2. *abandoned; alone; assailable; attackable; defenseless; deserted; exposed; forsaken; invadable; obnoxious; penetrable; pregnable; stranded; undefended; unguarded; unprotected; unshielded; vulnerable.*

outpouring of sympathy

output   A torpid term (SEE). SEE ALSO *(the) bottom line; feedback; input; interface; parameters.*

out the window   A moribund metaphor (SEE).
1. *abandoned; discarded; dismissed; jettisoned; rejected; repudiated; thrown out; tossed out.*
2. *dead; disappeared; dissolved; dispersed; evaporated; finished; forfeited; gone; inapplicable; inappropriate; inoperative; insignificant; irrelevant; lost;*

no longer applicable (apply); over; past; scattered; unimportant; vanished. ■ It's just that old rules are *out the window,* like most of last year's assumptions about Europe. REPLACE WITH *inapplicable.*

out to lunch   A moribund metaphor (SEE).
1. *absent-minded; absorbed; abstracted; bemused; daydreaming; distrait; dreamy; faraway; lost; preoccupied.*
2. *forgetful; heedless; inattentive; neglectful; oblivious; unmindful.*
3. *ignorant; incognizant; insensible; nescient; unacquainted; unadvised; unapprised; unaware; unenlightened; unfamiliar; uninformed; unintelligent; unknowing; unschooled; untaught; unversed.*

(put) out to pasture   A moribund metaphor (SEE). ■ Motors Inc. said Joe will be *put out to pasture* when it introduces next year's lineup of vehicles. REPLACE WITH *retired.*

out with the old and in with the new

over a barrel   A moribund metaphor (SEE). *defenseless; helpless; impotent; powerless.*

over and above   *apart from; aside from; besides; beyond; further; furthermore; likewise; more than.* SEE ALSO *above and beyond.*

over and done with   A dimwitted redundancy (SEE). *completed; concluded; done; ended; finished; over; past; through.* ■ But in reality, it is the same old story, one we'd like to think of as *over and done with.* USE *concluded.*

over and over (again)   A dimwitted redundancy (SEE). *frequently; habitually; often; recurrently; regularly; repeatedly.* ■ We use the same words and expressions *over and over again.* USE *habitually.* SEE ALSO *again and again; time and (time) again.*

over (my) dead body   A moribund metaphor (SEE).

overplay (his) hand   A moribund metaphor (SEE).

over the edge   A moribund metaphor (SEE).

over the hill   A moribund metaphor (SEE). *aged; aging; ancient; antediluvian; antique; archaic; elderly; hoary; hoary-headed; old; patriarchal; prehistoric; seasoned; superannuated; venerable.*

over the transom   A moribund metaphor (SEE).

overworked and understaffed   An inescapable pair (SEE).

overworked words   Dimwitted speakers and writers rely on certain words—overworked words like *actively, amazing, basically, definitely, devastate, effect, great, heinous, incredible, interesting, isolated, lasting, major, meaningful, mindset, nice, obscene, ongoing, pretty, really, situation, strange, unbelievable.*

Words, when overworked, diminish the meaning of all they are used to describe. Our statements—whether of fact or of falsehood—our declarations—whether of likes or of dislikes—our assertions—whether of views or of values—are all enfeebled by these tired terms. Nothing we express with overworked words has the force or effectiveness of less habitually spoken, less repeatedly written words.

Moreover, since a person understands little more than what the words he is knowledgeable of convey—a word means only so much—to rely on so few words reveals just how limited a person's understanding of himself, and those about him, is.

Our familiarity with the world expands as our familiarity with words increases. SEE ALSO *torpid terms*.

owing to the fact that   A dimwitted redundancy (SEE). *because; considering; for; in that; since.* ■ *Owing to the fact that* many companies are members of more than one EDI system, it is helpful if they all change in recognizable ways. USE *Since*. SEE ALSO *attributable to the fact that; due to the fact that.*

(he's his) own man   *at liberty; autonomous; free; independent; self-reliant.*

(she's her) own worst enemy

P

pack a punch (wallop) A moribund metaphor (See). *cogent; convincing; dynamic; effective; effectual; emotional; energetic; forceful; gripping; impassioned; inspiring; intense; lively; moving; passionate; persuasive; potent; powerful; strong; vehement; vigorous; vital.*

packed in like sardines An insipid simile (See moribund metaphors). *abounding; brimful; brimming; bursting; chock-full; congested; crammed; crowded; dense; filled; full; gorged; jammed; jam-packed; overcrowded; overfilled; overflowing; packed; replete; saturated; stuffed; swarming; teeming.*

pack to the rafters A moribund metaphor (See). *abounding; brimful; brimming; bursting; chock-full; congested; crammed; crowded; dense; filled; full; gorged; jammed; jam-packed; overcrowded; overfilled; overflowing; packed; replete; saturated; stuffed; swarming; teeming.*

pack up and leave *abscond; clear out; decamp; depart; desert; disappear; escape; exit; flee; fly; go; go away; leave; move on; part; pull out; quit; retire; retreat; run away; take flight; take off; vacate; vanish; withdraw.*

paddle (my) own canoe A moribund metaphor (See). *autonomous; free; independent; self-reliant.*

pain and suffering An inescapable pair (See). *agony; anguish; distress; grief; misery; pain; suffering; torment; worry.*

painfully shy An inescapable pair (See). *afraid; apprehensive; bashful; coy; demure; diffident; distant; fearful; humble; introverted; meek; modest; quiet; reserved; reticent; retiring; sheepish; shrinking; shy; timid; timorous; tremulous; unassuming; unobtrusive; unsociable; unsocial; withdrawn.*

paint a (rosy) picture of A moribund metaphor (See). ■ The document will *paint a dark picture of* the nation's financial system and warn that many large banks are near insolvency.

paint (himself) into a corner A moribund metaphor (See).

paint the town red A moribund metaphor (See). *be merry; carouse; carry on; celebrate; frolic; party; play; revel; riot; roister; rollick; romp; skylark.*

paint with a broad brush A moribund metaphor (See).

pair of (two) twins   A dimwitted redundancy (SEE). *twins.* ■ There were *two twins* at the mall who came up to him and asked him out. DELETE *two.*

(as) pale as a ghost   An insipid simile (SEE moribund metaphors). *anemic; ashen; blanched; bloodless; cadaverous; colorless; deathlike; doughy; haggard; pale; pallid; pasty; peaked; sallow; sickly; wan; whitish.*

pale in comparison   ■ His incentive *pales in comparison* to what most consumers really want.

palpable lie   An inescapable pair (SEE).

Pandora's box (of)   A moribund metaphor (SEE).

pangs of conscience

paper tiger   A moribund metaphor (SEE).

paralyzed with fear

parameters   An overworked word (SEE).
1. *boundary; limit; limitation; perimeter.*
2. *characteristic; factor.* ■ At this time, potential funding *parameters* may change in a variety of ways. REPLACE WITH *characteristics.* SEE ALSO *(the) bottom line; feedback; input; interface; output.*

pardon my French   An infantile phrase (SEE).

par excellence   A foreignism (SEE). *incomparable; preeminent.*

par for the course   A moribund metaphor (SEE). *average; common; commonplace; customary; everyday; mediocre; middling; normal; ordinary; quotidian; regular; routine; standard; typical; uneventful; unexceptional; unremarkable; usual.* ■ That is *par for the course* for foreign businesses here, which have descended upon the Soviet Union much as they descended upon China. REPLACE WITH *normal.*

part and parcel   An inescapable pair (SEE). *component; element; factor; part; portion.*

parting is such sweet sorrow
A popular prescription (SEE).

parting of the ways   A moribund metaphor (SEE). *altercation; argument; conflict; disagreement; discord; disputation; dispute; feud; fight; misunderstanding; quarrel; rift; row; spat; squabble.*

partner in crime   A moribund metaphor (SEE).

part of the landscape   A moribund metaphor (SEE).

pass muster   A moribund metaphor (SEE).

pass the buck

pass the hat

pass the time of day   A moribund metaphor (SEE). *babble; chat; chatter; confabulate; converse; gossip; jabber; palaver; prate; prattle; rattle; talk.*

past experience   A dimwitted redundancy (SEE). *experience.* ■ I know from *past experience* that a lot of you are not going to like what I have to say. DELETE *past*.

past history   A dimwitted redundancy (SEE). *history*. ■ We did not anticipate that the town would attempt to live off its *past history*. DELETE *past*.

past (its) peak

past (his) prime   *aged; aging; ancient; antediluvian; antique; archaic; elderly; hoary; hoary-headed; old; patriarchal; prehistoric; seasoned; superannuated; venerable.*

past the point of no return   A moribund metaphor (SEE).

patently false (and misleading)

patience is a virtue   A popular prescription (SEE).

(as) patient as Job   An insipid simile (SEE moribund metaphors). *accepting; accommodating; acquiescent; complacent; complaisant; compliant; cowed; deferential; docile; dutiful; easy; forbearing; gentle; humble; long-suffering; meek; mild; obedient; passive; patient; prostrate; quiet; reserved; resigned; stoical; submissive; subservient; timid; tolerant; tractable; unassuming; uncomplaining; yielding.*

pat on the back   A moribund metaphor (SEE). *applause; compliment; congratulation; felicitation; honor; praise; recognition; tribute.* ■ The selections are a nice *pat on the back* for our talented staff around the world. REPLACE WITH *compliment*.

pat (myself) on the back   A mori-

bund metaphor (SEE). *acclaim; applaud; celebrate; cheer; commend; compliment; congratulate; extol; flatter; hail; honor; laud; plume; praise; puff; salute; self-congratulate.* ■ After *patting himself on the back*, he incidentally pointed out that many other people may have had something to do with it. REPLACE WITH *congratulating himself*.

pave the way (for)   *arrange; groom; make ready; plan; prepare; prime; ready.*

pay (their) debt to society   A moribund metaphor (SEE).

pay dividends   A moribund metaphor (SEE).

pay (my) dues   A moribund metaphor (SEE).

pay the fiddler (piper)   A moribund metaphor (SEE).

pay the price   A moribund metaphor (SEE).

pay through the nose   A moribund metaphor (SEE). *costly; dear; excessive; exorbitant; expensive; high-priced.*

peace and harmony   A dimwitted redundancy (SEE). *harmony; peace.* ■ I want there to be *peace and harmony* between us. USE *harmony* or *peace*.

peace and quiet   An inescapable pair (SEE). *calm; calmness; composure; equanimity; peace; peacefulness; poise; quiet; quietude; repose; rest; serenity; silence; stillness; tranquillity.*

peace of mind   *calm; calmness; composure; equanimity; peace; peacefulness; poise; quiet; quietude; repose; rest;*

serenity; silence; stillness; tranquillity.

peaches and cream (complexion)
A moribund metaphor (SEE).

peachy keen   An infantile phrase
(SEE).

pea in (my) shoe   A moribund metaphor (SEE). *affliction; annoyance;
bane; bother; burden; curse; difficulty;
inconvenience; irritant; irritation; load;
nuisance; ordeal; pain; pest; plague;
problem; torment; tribulation; trouble;
vexation; weight; worry.*

peaks and valleys   A moribund
metaphor (SEE).

peanut gallery   An infantile phrase
(SEE).

pearls of wisdom   A moribund metaphor (SEE).

pencil pusher   A moribund metaphor (SEE). *assistant; clerk; office
worker; recorder; scribe; secretary;
typist.*

penny wise and pound foolish

people change   A popular prescription (SEE).

**people who live in glass houses
shouldn't throw stones**   A popular
prescription (SEE).

(as) per (your request)   A torpid
term (SEE). ■ Enclosed are chapters
one through six, *as per your request.*
REPLACE WITH *as you requested.* ■ *As
per usual,* he refuses to choose between his chief of staff and his chief of
budget. REPLACE WITH *As usual.*

perception is reality   A quack
equation (SEE). Perception is too often
purblind for there to be much reality
to this quack equation. Still, it is a formula, uttered by mountebanks and
managers alike, that has done much to
disturb the lives and livelihood of
people.

perchance   An archaism (SEE).
1. *conceivably; feasibly; maybe; perhaps;
possibly.*
2. *accidentally; by chance.*

perennially popular   An inescapable pair (SEE).

period   An infantile phrase (SEE).
■ The lesson of the women's movement is clearly that no one makes it
on their own. *Period.* DELETE *period.*
■ I know some professional, single
women who would not date married
men. *Period.* DELETE *period.* SEE ALSO
no ifs, ands or buts.

period of time   A dimwitted redundancy (SEE). *period; time.* ■ I've been
wanting to watch this movie for a long
period of time. USE *time.* ■ Over a considerable *period of time,* this therapy
gradually provides immunization. USE
period.

permanent fixture

personal friend   A suspect superlative (SEE). Since friends are so often
ephemeral, *personal friend* was likely
devised to give more value to the concept of friendship.

Still, a *personal friend* is but a
friend, and a friend, more often than
not, but an acquaintance.

persona non grata   A foreignism
(SEE). *undesirable.*

pet peeve

(as) phony (queer) as a three-dollar bill   An insipid simile (SEE moribund metaphors). *artificial; bogus; counterfeit; ersatz; fake; false; feigned; fictitious; forged; fraudulent; imitation; mock; phony; pseudo; sham; simulated; spurious; synthetic.*

phony baloney   An infantile phrase (SEE). *artificial; bogus; counterfeit; ersatz; fake; false; feigned; fictitious; forged; fraudulent; imitation; mock; phony; pseudo; sham; simulated; spurious; synthetic.*

physically, mentally and emotionally

physician, heal thyself   A popular prescription (SEE).

pick and choose   An inescapable pair (SEE). *choose; cull; decide; determine; elect; pick; select.* ■ For years, we could *pick and choose* where our students worked. USE *select.*

pick (its) bones   A moribund metaphor (SEE).

pick (his) brains   A moribund metaphor (SEE).

pick of the litter   A moribund metaphor (SEE). *best; choice; elite; excellent; finest; first-class; first-rate; foremost; greatest; highest; matchless; outstanding; paramount; peerless; preeminent; premium; prominent; select; superior; superlative; top; unequaled; unexcelled; unmatched; unrivaled; unsurpassed.*

pick up speed   A moribund metaphor (SEE). *accelerate; advance; bestir;*

bustle; hasten; hurry; precipitate; quicken; rush; speed up.

pick up steam   A moribund metaphor (SEE).
1. *accelerate; advance; bestir; bustle; hasten; hurry; precipitate; quicken; rush; speed up.*
2. *advance; awaken; better; expand; flourish; gain; gain strength; grow; heal; improve; increase; pick up; progress; prosper; rally; recover; recuperate; refresh; renew; revive; rouse; strengthen; thrive.*

pick up the pace   A moribund metaphor (SEE). *accelerate; advance; bestir; bustle; hasten; hurry; precipitate; quicken; rush; speed up.*

pick up the pieces   A moribund metaphor (SEE).

pick up where (they) left off

picture if you will

picture perfect   *absolute; beautiful; consummate; excellent; exemplary; exquisite; faultless; flawless; ideal; impeccable; lovely; magnificent; matchless; model; peerless; perfect; pretty; pure; sublime; superb; supreme; transcendent; ultimate; unblemished; unequaled; unexcelled; unrivaled; unsurpassed; untarnished.*

pièce de résistance   A foreignism (SEE).

piece (their) lives back together (again)

(a) piece of cake   A moribund metaphor (SEE). *apparent; basic; clear; clear-cut; conspicuous; distinct; easily done; easy; effortless; elementary; evident; explicit; facile; limpid; lucid; manifest; obvious; patent; pellucid; plain; simple; simplicity itself; simplistic; straightforward; translucent; transparent; unambiguous; uncomplex; uncomplicated; understandable; unequivocal; unmistakable.* ■ While the new rules for claiming the dependent-care credit may sound complicated, they're *a piece of cake* compared with the tax-reporting requirements for parents who have a child-care provider in their homes. REPLACE WITH *simple.*

(a) piece of the action ■ Similar to the U.S. model, it will give companies the capital and technology they need while giving employees a *piece of the action* and establishing a constituency for capitalism.

(a) piece of the pie A moribund metaphor (SEE).

(a) piece of the puzzle A moribund metaphor (SEE).

(a) piece of work A moribund metaphor (SEE). *aberrant; abnormal; anomalistic; anomalous; atypical; bizarre; curious; deviant; different; distinct; distinctive; eccentric; exceptional; extraordinary; fantastic; foreign; grotesque; idiosyncratic; independent; individual; individualistic; irregular; novel; odd; offbeat; original; peculiar; puzzling; quaint; queer; rare; remarkable; separate; singular; uncommon; unconventional; unexampled; unique; unnatural; unorthodox; unparalleled; unprecedented; unusual.*

pie in the sky A moribund metaphor (SEE). *apparition; caprice; chimera; delusion; dream; fanciful idea; fancy; fantasty; fluff; frivolity; hallucination; illusion; imagination; maggot; mirage; phantasm; vagary; vision; whim; whimsy.*

(like) pigs in clover An insipid simile (SEE moribund metaphors).

pillar of society (the church; the community) A suspect superlative (SEE).

pillar (tower) of strength A moribund metaphor (SEE). *constant; dependable; determined; faithful; fast; firm; fixed; inexorable; inflexible; loyal; obdurate; reliable; resolute; resolved; rigid; solid; stable; staunch; steadfast; steady; stern; strong; supportive; tenacious; true; trustworthy; trusty; unflinching; unwavering; unyielding.*

pin (his) ears back A moribund metaphor (SEE).
1. *beat; better; cap; defeat; exceed; excel; outclass; outdo; outflank; outmaneuver; outperform; outplay; outrank; outsmart; outthink; outwit; overcome; overpower; prevail over; surpass; top; triumph over; trounce; whip; win out.*
2. *admonish; animadvert; berate; castigate; censure; chasten; chastise; chide; condemn; criticize; denounce; denunciate; discipline; impugn; objurgate; punish; rebuke; remonstrate; reprehend; reprimand; reproach; reprobate; reprove; revile; scold; upbraid; vituperate; warn.*

pin (her) hopes on

pin the blame on *accuse; blame; censure; charge; condemn; criticize; implicate; incriminate; inculpate; rebuke; reprimand; reproach; reprove; scold.*

pity the poor

places to go, people to see

place the blame on (her) shoulders   A moribund metaphor (SEE). *accuse; blame; censure; charge; condemn; criticize; implicate; incriminate; inculpate; rebuke; reprimand; reproach; reprove; scold.*

plain and simple   An inescapable pair (SEE). *apparent; basic; clear; clear-cut; conspicuous; distinct; easily done; easy; effortless; elementary; evident; explicit; facile; limpid; lucid; manifest; obvious; patent; pellucid; plain; simple; simplicity itself; simplistic; straightforward; translucent; transparent; unambiguous; uncomplex; uncomplicated; understandable; unequivocal; unmistakable.*

(as) plain as a pikestaff   An insipid simile (SEE moribund metaphors). *apparent; basic; clear; clear-cut; conspicuous; distinct; easily done; easy; effortless; elementary; evident; explicit; facile; limpid; lucid; manifest; obvious; patent; pellucid; plain; simple; simplicity itself; simplistic; straightforward; translucent; transparent; unambiguous; uncomplex; uncomplicated; understandable; unequivocal; unmistakable.*

(as) plain as day   An insipid simile (SEE moribund metaphors). *apparent; basic; clear; clear-cut; conspicuous; distinct; easily done; easy; effortless; elementary; evident; explicit; facile; limpid; lucid; manifest; obvious; patent; pellucid; plain; simple; simplicity itself; simplistic; straightforward; translucent; transparent; unambiguous; uncomplex; uncomplicated; understandable; unequivocal; unmistakable.*

(as) plain as the nose on (your) face   An insipid simile (SEE moribund metaphors). *apparent; basic; clear; clear-cut; conspicuous; distinct; easily done; easy; effortless; elementary; evident; explicit; facile; limpid; lucid; manifest; obvious; patent; pellucid; plain; simple; simplicity itself; simplistic; straightforward; translucent; transparent; unambiguous; uncomplex; uncomplicated; understandable; unequivocal; unmistakable.*

plain (smooth) sailing   A moribund metaphor (SEE). *apparent; basic; clear; clear-cut; conspicuous; distinct; easily done; easy; effortless; elementary; evident; explicit; facile; limpid; lucid; manifest; obvious; patent; pellucid; plain; simple; simplicity itself; simplistic; smooth; straightforward; translucent; transparent; unambiguous; uncomplex; uncomplicated; understandable; unequivocal; unmistakable.*

(just) plain stupid   SEE ALSO *stupid.*

plain vanilla   A moribund metaphor (SEE). *basic; common; conservative; conventional; customary; general; normal; ordinary; quotidian; regular; routine; standard; traditional; typical; uncreative; undaring; unimaginative; usual.* ■ He was uninterested in staying now that the bank has been limited to *plain vanilla* banking. REPLACE WITH *basic.*

plan ahead   A dimwitted redundancy (SEE). *plan.* ■ It's important that you *plan ahead* for your retirement. DELETE *ahead.*

plan for the worst, but hope for the best   A popular prescription (SEE).

plan of action A dimwitted redundancy (SEE). *action; course; direction; intention; method; move; plan; policy; procedure; route; scheme; strategy.*

plans and specifications A dimwitted redundancy (SEE). *plans; specifications.* ■ Allowed expenditures include architectural and engineering services and related costs for *plans and specifications* for the renovation. USE *plans* or *specifications.*

plant the seeds of A moribund metaphor (SEE).

play ball A moribund metaphor (SEE). *collaborate; comply; concur; conspire; cooperate; work together.*

play both ends against the middle A moribund metaphor (SEE).

play by the rules

play (your) cards right A moribund metaphor (SEE).

play cat and mouse A moribund metaphor (SEE).

play (his cards) close to the chest (vest) A moribund metaphor (SEE). *be clandestine; be confidential; be covert; be furtive; be mysterious; be private; be secretive; be secret; be sly; be stealthy; be surreptitious.*

play cupid A moribund metaphor (SEE).

play (the) devil's advocate A moribund metaphor (SEE).

play fast and loose (with) A moribund metaphor (SEE).

play games A moribund metaphor (SEE).

play hardball A moribund metaphor (SEE). ■ Hospitals that have set up risk management aren't really *playing hardball* with the doctors causing those risks in hospitals.

play hard to get A moribund metaphor (SEE).

play hide and seek A moribund metaphor (SEE).

(like) playing Russian roulette An insipid simile (SEE moribund metaphors).

(will it) play in Peoria A moribund metaphor (SEE).

play it by ear A moribund metaphor (SEE). *ad-lib; extemporize; improvise.*

play musical chairs A moribund metaphor (SEE).

play out
1. *carry out; execute; perform; play.*
2. *develop; evolve; unfold.* ■ We will report to you how all this *plays out*. REPLACE WITH *unfolds*.

play possum A moribund metaphor (SEE).

play second fiddle A moribund metaphor (SEE).

play the field A moribund metaphor (SEE).

play the game A moribund metaphor (SEE). *abide by; accommodate;*

accord; acquiesce; adapt; adhere to; agree; behave; comply; concur; conform; correspond; follow; harmonize; heed; mind; obey; observe; submit; yield.

play the same tune   A moribund metaphor (SEE).

play (his) trump card   A moribund metaphor (SEE).

play with fire   A moribund metaphor (SEE). chance; dare; endanger; gamble; hazard; imperil; jeopardize; make bold; peril; risk; venture.

pleasant surprise   An inescapable pair (SEE). ■ Whatever your life insurance needs, you're sure of a *pleasant surprise* when you ask one of our advisors for a quote.

(as) pleased as Punch   An insipid simile (SEE moribund metaphors). blissful; buoyant; cheerful; delighted; elated; excited; gay; glad; gladdened; gleeful; good-humored; gratified; happy; jolly; jovial; joyful; joyous; jubilant; merry; mirthful; pleased; tickled.

pleasingly plump   An inescapable pair (SEE). ample; big; bulky; chubby; chunky; colossal; corpulent; dumpy; enormous; fat; flabby; fleshy; gigantic; heavy; hefty; huge; immense; large; mammoth; massive; obese; plump; portly; pudgy; rotund; round; squat; stocky; stout.

plebeian sentiments   Plebeian sentiments reflect the views and values of the least thoughtful among us: *a little knowledge is a dangerous thing; be nice; (he's) boring; (I) gave (him) the best years of (my) life; (it) gives (me) something to do; (these things) hap-* pen to other people, not to (me); I (just) don't think about it; I just work here; (it) keeps (me) busy; (it's) something to look forward to; you think too much; what can you do; why me?

What's more, these expressions, base as they are, blunt our understanding and quash our creativity. They actually shield us from our thoughts and feelings, from any profound sense of ourselves.

People who use these expressions have not become who they were meant to be. SEE ALSO *popular prescriptions; quack equations.*

plow new ground   A moribund metaphor (SEE).

plus   additionally; also; and; as well; besides; beyond that (this); even; further; furthermore; in addition; likewise; moreover; more than that (this); still more; too; what is more. ■ *Plus*, doctors will have a more practical option for the continued care of their patients. REPLACE WITH *What is more.* ■ *Plus*, the center will also provide new employment opportunities for people. DELETE *Plus*.

(5:00) P.M. ... (in the) afternoon (evening)   A dimwitted redundancy (SEE). *(5:00) P.M.; (in the) afternoon (evening).* ■ The city school legislature was called to order at *2 P.M.* on a Monday *afternoon.* DELETE *afternoon.*

pocket the difference

poetic justice   An inescapable pair (SEE).

poetry in motion   A moribund metaphor (SEE). agile; graceful; limber; lissome; lithe; lithesome; nimble; supple.

point of departure   A moribund metaphor (SEE).

point of no return

point the finger at   A moribund metaphor (SEE). *accuse; blame; censure; charge; condemn; criticize; implicate; incriminate; inculpate; rebuke; reprimand; reproach; reprove; scold.* ■ When the problem is that severe, regulators have to *point the finger at* someone. REPLACE WITH *blame*.

point the finger of blame   A moribund metaphor (SEE). *accuse; blame; censure; charge; condemn; criticize; implicate; incriminate; inculpate; rebuke; reprimand; reproach; reprove; scold.*

poke (her) nose into   A moribund metaphor (SEE). *encroach; entrench; infringe; interfere; intrude; invade; meddle; pry; tamper; trespass.*

political suicide

politics as usual   A torpid term (SEE). ■ People are tired of *politics as usual.* ■ We cannot continue *politics as usual*; we must change the way our state is governed. SEE ALSO *business as usual.*

politics makes strange bedfellows

pomp and circumstance   An inescapable pair (SEE). *array; ceremony; circumstance; dazzle; display; fanfare; grandeur; magnificence; ostentation; pageantry; panoply; parade; pomp; resplendence; ritual; show; spectacle; splendor.*

(as) poor as a churchmouse   An insipid simile (SEE moribund meta-

phors). *broke; destitute; distressed; impecunious; impoverished; indigent; insolvent; needy; penniless; poor; poverty-stricken; underprivileged.*

poor but honest

poor cousin to   ■ Independent TV stations were once viewed as *poor cousins to* networked-owned stations and affiliates.

poor excuse for a (man)

pop the question

popular prescriptions , Popular prescriptions are the platitudes and proverbs by which we live our lives: *absence makes the heart grow fonder; actions speak louder than words; a picture is worth a thousand words; beauty is in the eye of the beholder; better late than never; do as I say, not as I do; forgive and forget; hope for the best but expect the worst; it takes two; keep (your) nose to the grindstone; live and learn; misery loves company; money isn't everything; neither a borrower nor a lender be; take it one day (step) at a time; the best things in life are free; the meek shall inherit the earth; the sooner the better; time flies when you're having fun; two wrongs don't make a right; what goes around, comes around; you can't be all things to all people; you can't have everything.*

These formulas instruct us in how to live our lives. It is these dicta that determine who we are and how we act. They define our moral makeup. Dim-witted speakers and writers depend on prescriptions like these to guide them through life. From the popular or proper course, there is scant deviation. A stray thought is, for them, a gray thought.

Popular prescriptions endure not for their sincerity but for their simplicity. We embrace them because they make all they profess to explain and all they profess to describe seem plain and uncomplicated.

Inexorably, we become as simple as they—we people, we platitudes. SEE ALSO *plebeian sentiments; quack equations*.

portray in a bad light

pose no immediate (imminent) danger (threat) ■ And though the radioactive fuel may *pose no immediate threat*, the canisters continue to deteriorate.

positive (*n*) A torpid term (SEE). *advantage; asset; benefit; gain; strength.* SEE ALSO *negative*.

positive feelings A torpid term (SEE). As the following variety of synonyms shows, *positive feelings* is a pulpous expression that arouses only our inattention: *affection; approval; blissfulness; courage; delectation; delight; ecstasy; fondness; friendliness; friendship; generosity; goodwill; happiness; hope; joy; kindness; lightheartedness; like; liking; love; loyalty; merriment; passion; peace; pleasure; rapture; respect; warmth.* ■ I feel she may have *positive feelings* for me, and I'd like to know for sure. REPLACE WITH *affection*. SEE ALSO *in a good mood; negative feelings*.

positive move (step)

pot of gold A moribund metaphor (SEE).

pound the pavement A moribund metaphor (SEE). *hunt; look for; quest; ransack; rummage; scour; search; seek.*

pouring (down) rain *pouring; raining; storming.*

pour oil on troubled waters A moribund metaphor (SEE). *allay; alleviate; appease; assuage; calm; compose; ease; mitigate; mollify; pacify; palliate; quiet; relieve; soothe; still; tranquilize.*

pour (rub) salt on (our) wounds A moribund metaphor (SEE). *aggravate; complicate; exacerbate; heighten; increase; intensify; irritate; make worse; worsen.*

power breakfast (lunch)

power play

practice makes perfect A popular prescription (SEE).

practice what (you) preach A popular prescription (SEE).

praise (them) to the skies A moribund metaphor (SEE). *acclaim; applaud; celebrate; commend; compliment; congratulate; eulogize; extol; flatter; hail; laud; panegyrize; praise; puff; salute.*

precarious position An inescapable pair (SEE).

precious few (little) An inescapable pair (SEE).

preemptive strike

preferential treatment

preparations are underway

present and accounted for

pretty An overworked word (SEE). *adequately; amply; enough; fairly; moderately; quite; rather; reasonably; somewhat; sufficiently; tolerably.* ■ She's a *pretty* bright woman. REPLACE WITH *reasonably.* ■ How are you? *Pretty* well. REPLACE WITH *Tolerably.*

Often it is best to delete *pretty*, as in the following sentence: ■ He's basically a *pretty* lively individual. DELETE *pretty.*

(as) pretty as a picture An insipid simile (SEE moribund metaphors). *appealing; attractive; beautiful; becoming; captivating; comely; cute; dazzling; exquisite; fair; fetching; good-looking; gorgeous; handsome; lovely; nice-looking; pleasing; pretty; pulchritudinous; radiant; ravishing; seemly; stunning.*

pretty is as pretty does

prevailing sentiment

prevailing winds of A moribund metaphor (SEE).

previous to A torpid term (SEE). *before.* ■ *Previous to* meeting her, I showed no interest in women. REPLACE WITH *Before.*

price breakthrough

price war A moribund metaphor (SEE).

prick (puncture) (his) balloon A moribund metaphor (SEE). *abase; chasten; debase; decrease; deflate; degrade; demean; depreciate; depress; di-*

minish; disgrace; dishonor; embarrass; humble; humiliate; lower; mortify; puncture; shame.

prick up (her) ears A moribund metaphor (SEE). *attend to; hark; hear; hearken; heed; listen; pay attention; pay heed.*

pride and joy An inescapable pair (SEE).

pride goes before a fall

pride of place

prim and proper An inescapable pair (SEE).

primrose path A moribund metaphor (SEE).

prince charming An infantile phrase (SEE).

princely price *costly; dear; excessive; exorbitant; expensive; high-priced.*

prioritize A torpid term (SEE). *arrange; classify; list; order; place; put; rank; rate.* ■ He *prioritizes* this relationship above all his after-high-school plans, such as going to college. REPLACE WITH *ranks.*

prior to A torpid term (SEE). *before.* ■ Select only the cells to be printed *prior to* selecting the Print command. REPLACE WITH *before.* SEE ALSO *in advance of; subsequent to.*

prize(d) possession ■ In an era of spiraling costs, a good indirect cost rate is a *prized possession.*

proactive A torpid term (SEE).

problematic (-al)   A torpid term (SEE).

proceeded to   A torpid term (SEE). ■ The team *proceeded to develop* the recently generated ideas into a concrete curriculum. REPLACE WITH *developed*. ■ He then *proceeded to declare* his undying love for me. REPLACE WITH *declared*.

proceed forward   A torpid term (SEE). *advance; continue; develop; go on; grow; improve; increase; move on; proceed; progress.* ■ Reducing operating losses in this business will give us increased flexibility to *proceed forward* with other endeavors. REPLACE WITH *proceed.* SEE ALSO *a step forward; a step (forward) in the right direction; go forward; move forward; move (forward) in the right direction.*

proceed with caution

profiles in courage

proof positive

(as) proud as a peacock   An insipid simile (SEE moribund metaphors). *arrogant; cavalier; conceited; disdainful; egocentric; egotistic; egotistical; haughty; lofty; pompous; pretentious; proud; narcissistic; self-centered; self-important; self-satisfied; supercilious; superior; vain.*

proud parent   An inescapable pair (SEE).

proven fact

proven track record   A moribund metaphor (SEE).

proving ground   A moribund metaphor (SEE).

public enemy number one   A moribund metaphor (SEE).

pull a fast one   *bamboozle; befool; beguile; bilk; bluff; cheat; con; deceive; defraud; delude; dupe; feint; fool; gyp; hoodwink; lead astray; misdirect; misguide; misinform; mislead; spoof; swindle; trick; victimize.*

pull a rabbit out of the hat   A moribund metaphor (SEE).

(like) pulling teeth   An insipid simile (SEE moribund metaphors). *arduous; backbreaking; burdensome; difficult; exhausting; fatiguing; hard; herculean; laborious; not easy; onerous; severe; strenuous; toilful; toilsome; tough; trying; wearisome.* ■ Getting these people to level with reporters is often *like pulling teeth.* REPLACE WITH *arduous.*

pull (my) leg   A moribund metaphor (SEE). *bamboozle; befool; beguile; bilk; bluff; cheat; con; deceive; defraud; delude; dupe; feint; fool; gyp; hoodwink; jest; joke; kid; lead astray; misdirect; misguide; misinform; mislead; spoof; swindle; tease; trick; trifle with.*

pull no punches   A moribund metaphor (SEE).

pull (it) off   A moribund metaphor (SEE). *accomplish; bring about; do; carry out; perform; succeed.*

pull out all the stops   A moribund metaphor (SEE).

pull (some) strings   A moribund metaphor (SEE).

pull the plug (on)   A moribund metaphor (SEE). *abandon; annul; arrest; cancel; cease; check; conclude; derail; desert; desist; discontinue; end; forsake; halt; invalidate; leave; quit; repeal; rescind; revoke; stop; suspend; terminate; withdraw.* ■ Organizers say they'll *pull the plug* on the parade if a gay and lesbian group is allowed to participate. REPLACE WITH *cancel.*

pull the rug out from under
A moribund metaphor (SEE). *capsize; founder; invert; overset; overthrow; overturn; reverse; sink; tip; topple; tumble; upend; upset.*

pull the wool over (his) eyes
A moribund metaphor (SEE). *bamboozle; befool; beguile; bilk; bluff; cheat; con; deceive; defraud; delude; dupe; feint; fool; gyp; hoodwink; lead astray; misdirect; misguide; misinform; mislead; spoof; swindle; trick; victimize.*

pull (yourself) up by (your) own bootstraps   A moribund metaphor (SEE).

pull up stakes   A moribund metaphor (SEE). *abscond; clear out; decamp; depart; desert; disappear; escape; exit; flee; fly; go; go away; leave; move on; part; pull out; quit; retire; retreat; run away; take flight; take off; vacate; vanish; withdraw.*

pure and simple   An inescapable pair (SEE). *basic; elementary; fundamental; pure; simple; straightforward; uncomplicated.*

(as) pure as the driven snow   An insipid simile (SEE moribund metaphors).
1. *decent; ethical; exemplary; good; honest; honorable; just; moral; pure; righteous; straight; upright; virtuous; wholesome.*
2. *celibate; chaste; immaculate; maidenly; modest; snowy; spotless; stainless; unblemished; unsoiled; untarnished; virgin; virginal; virtuous.*

pursuant to   A torpid term (SEE). *according to; by; following; under.*

pursue (strive for) excellence
A suspect superlative (SEE). ■ *Striving for excellence* is not just a goal but a way of life. ■ The recipients had to prepare brief statements on what inspires them to *strive for excellence.* SEE ALSO *excellence.*

push and shove   An inescapable pair (SEE). *bulldoze; drive; propel; push; shove; thrust.*

(when) push comes to shove
A moribund metaphor (SEE).

pushed (me) to the wall   A moribund metaphor (SEE).
1. *coerced; compelled; constrained; dictated; enforced; enjoined; forced; made; ordered; pressed; pressured; required.*
2. *at bay; caught; cornered; enmeshed; ensnared; entangled; entrapped; netted; snared; trapped.*

push the envelope   A moribund metaphor (SEE).

push the panic button   A moribund metaphor (SEE).

push the right buttons   A moribund metaphor (SEE).

push to the limit

put a bug in (his) ear   A moribund metaphor (SEE). *allude to; clue; connote; cue; hint; imply; indicate; insinuate; intimate; prompt; suggest; tip off.*

put a damper on   A moribund metaphor (SEE). *check; dampen; deaden; depress; discourage; hinder; impede; inhibit; obstruct; repress; restrain.*

put a gun to (my) head   A moribund metaphor (SEE). *coerce; command; compel; constrain; demand; dictate; enforce; enjoin; force; insist; make; order; pressure; require.* ■ Nobody *put a gun to your head.* USE *forced you.*

put a halt (an end; a stop) to
A dimwitted redundancy (SEE). *cease; close; complete; conclude; derail; discontinue; end; finish; halt; settle; stop.* ■ It's time we *put a stop to* all the violence. USE *stop.* SEE ALSO *call a halt (an end; a stop) to.*

put a lid on (it)   A moribund metaphor (SEE).
1. *abandon; arrest; cancel; cease; check; conclude; desert; desist; discontinue; end; forsake; halt; leave; quit; stop; suspend; terminate.*
2. *be silent; be still; hush; keep quiet; quiet; silence.* ■ *Put a lid on it.* REPLACE WITH *Be quiet.*

(don't) put all (your) eggs in one basket   A moribund metaphor (SEE).

put a spin on   A moribund metaphor (SEE).

put (his) best foot forward
A moribund metaphor (SEE).

put (her) cards on the table
A moribund metaphor (SEE).

put (your) finger on   A moribund metaphor (SEE). *detect; discern; discover; distinguish; find; identify; know; locate; make out; note; notice; perceive; pick out; pinpoint; place; point out; recall; recognize; recollect; remember; see; specify; spot; think of.*

put food on the table

put (her) foot down   A moribund metaphor (SEE).
1. *hold fast; stand firm.*
2. *assert; command; decree; dictate; insist; order; require.*

put (his) foot in (his) mouth
A moribund metaphor (SEE).

put forward   *advance; broach; introduce; offer; present; propose; propound; submit; suggest; tender.* ■ There is speculation that he opposed Moynihan's plan so he could *put forward* his own. REPLACE WITH *propose.* SEE ALSO *come forward (with).*

put (his) head in the lion's mouth
A moribund metaphor (SEE). *chance; dare; endanger; gamble; hazard; imperil; jeopardize; make bold; peril; risk; venture.*

put (our) heads together   A moribund metaphor (SEE). *collaborate; conspire; cooperate; work together.*

put (your) house (back) in order
A moribund metaphor (SEE). ■ Ravaged by losses after it lost direction in a period of rapid growth, Phoenix is attempting to *put its house back in order.*

put (him) in bad light   A moribund metaphor (SEE).

put in cold storage   A moribund metaphor (SEE). *defer; delay; forget; hold off; hold up; ignore; pigeonhole; postpone; procrastinate; put aside; put off; set aside; shelve; suspend; table; waive.*

put in motion   *begin; commence; embark; inaugurate; initiate; launch; originate; start; undertake.*

put (her) in (her) place   *abase; chasten; debase; decrease; deflate; degrade; demean; depreciate; depress; diminish; disgrace; dishonor; embarrass; humble; humiliate; lower; mortify; puncture; shame.*

put (yourself) in (her) place   *be sorry for; commiserate; empathize; feel for; feel sorry for; identify with; pity; sympathize; understand.*

put (myself) in (his) shoes   A moribund metaphor (SEE). *be sorry for; commiserate; empathize; feel for; feel sorry for; identify with; pity; sympathize; understand.*

put (your) life on the line   A moribund metaphor (SEE). *chance; dare; endanger; gamble; hazard; imperil; jeopardize; make bold; peril; risk; venture.*

put money on   *bet; gamble; wager.*

put (your) money where (your) mouth is

put (his) neck on the line   A moribund metaphor (SEE). *chance; dare; endanger; gemble; hazard; imperil; jeopardize; make bold; peril; risk; venture.*

put new life into   *animate; energize; enliven; inspire; inspirit; invigorate; refresh; reinvigorate; rejuvenate; revitalize; revive; rouse; stimulate; stir; vitalize.*

put on airs   A moribund metaphor (SEE). *be affected; be arrogant; be haughty; be pretentious; be self-important; be supercilious.*

put (her) on a pedestal   A moribund metaphor (SEE). *adore; cherish; esteem; eulogize; exalt; extol; glorify; honor; idealize; idolize; laud; love; panegyrize; prize; revere; treasure; venerate; worship.*

put one over on (her)   *bamboozle; befool; beguile; bilk; bluff; cheat; con; deceive; defraud; delude; dupe; feint; fool; gyp; hoodwink; lead astray; misdirect; misguide; mislead; spoof; swindle; trick; victimize.*

put on hold   *defer; delay; forget; hold off; hold up; ignore; pigeonhole; postpone; procrastinate; put aside; put off; set aside; shelve; suspend; table; waive.* ■ The agreement had been scheduled to go into effect on Tuesday, after being *put on hold* for thirty days. REPLACE WITH *delayed*.

put on ice   A moribund metaphor (SEE). *defer; delay; forget; hold off; hold up; ignore; pigeonhole; postpone; procrastinate; put aside; put off; set aside; shelve; suspend; table; waive.*

put (them) on notice

put on the back burner   A moribund metaphor (SEE). *defer; delay; forget; hold off; hold up; ignore; pigeonhole; postpone; procrastinate; put aside; put* *off; set aside; shelve; suspend; table; waive.* ■ She understands the necessity of *putting* her own emotional needs *on the back burner* when these would otherwise interfere with her goal. REPLACE WITH *waiving.*

put (us) on the map   A moribund metaphor (SEE). ■ At the time analysts thought Ames was just the tonic Zayre needed, and the deal *put* the thirty-year-old Ames *on the map.*

put (his) pants on one leg at a time   A moribund metaphor (SEE). *average; common; commonplace; conservative; conventional; customary; everyday; mediocre; middling; normal; ordinary; quotidian; regular; routine; standard; traditional; typical; uneventful; unexceptional; unremarkable; usual.*

put pen to paper   *author; compose; indite; inscribe; jot down; pen; scrabble; scratch; scrawl; scribble; scribe; write.*

put (your) shoulder to the wheel   A moribund metaphor (SEE). *drudge; grind; grub; labor; slave; strain; strive; struggle; sweat; toil; travail; work hard.*

put something over on (them)   *bamboozle; befool; beguile; bilk; bluff; cheat; con; deceive; defraud; delude; dupe; feint; fool; gyp; hoodwink; lead astray; misdirect; misguide; mislead; spoof; swindle; trick; victimize.*

put (your) stamp of approval on   A moribund metaphor (SEE). *approve of; authorize; certify; endorse; sanction.* ■ To portray our community as *putting a stamp of approval on* the execution is inaccurate. REPLACE WITH *approving of.*

put that in your pipe and smoke it   A moribund metaphor (SEE).

put the brakes on   A moribund metaphor (SEE). *abandon; arrest; cancel; cease; check; conclude; derail; desert; desist; discontinue; end; forsake; halt; leave; quit; stop; suspend; terminate.* ■ The parent's problems with its retail divisions effectively *put the brakes on* the project and helped stall other downtown projects as well. REPLACE WITH *stopped.*

put the cart before the horse   A moribund metaphor (SEE).

put the (best) face on   A moribund metaphor (SEE). ■ In the aftermath, AT&T management tried to *put the best face on* an embarrassing and costly mix-up.

put the fear of God into (them)   *alarm; appall; benumb; daunt; frighten; horrify; intimidate; panic; paralyze; petrify; scare; shock; startle; terrify; terrorize.*

put the finger on   A moribund metaphor (SEE). *betray; deliver up; inform on; turn in.*

put the finishing touches on   *complete; conclude; consummate; finish.*

put the genie back in the bottle   A moribund metaphor (SEE).

put the kibosh on   A moribund metaphor (SEE). *annul; arrest; balk; block; bridle; cancel; check; derail; detain; end; foil; frustrate; halt; harness; neutralize; nullify; restrain; retard; stall; stay; stop; terminate; thwart.*

put the screws to   A moribund metaphor (SEE). *bulldoze; bully; coerce; compel; constrain; demand; drive; enforce; enjoin; goad; force; impel; incite; intimidate; make; necessitate; obligate; oblige; order; press; pressure; prod; require; threaten; tyrannize; urge.*

put the skids on   A moribund metaphor (SEE). *abandon; arrest; cancel; cease; check; conclude; derail; desert; desist; discontinue; end; forsake; halt; leave; quit; stop; suspend; terminate.*

put through (her) paces   A moribund metaphor (SEE). *catechize; cross-examine; examine; grill; inquire; interrogate; pump; question; quiz; test.*

put through the wringer   A moribund metaphor (SEE). *catechize; cross-examine; examine; grill; inquire; interrogate; pump; question; quiz; test.*

put together the pieces of the puzzle   A moribund metaphor (SEE). *clear up; decipher; disentangle; explain; explicate; figure out; resolve; solve; unravel; untangle; work out.*

put (them) to the test   *catechize; cross-examine; examine; grill; inquire; interrogate; pump; question; quiz; test.*

put two and two together   A moribund metaphor (SEE). *conclude; deduce; gather; infer; reason.*

(like) putty in (my) hands   An insipid simile (SEE moribund metaphors). *accommodating; acquiescent; adaptable; agreeable; amenable; complacent; complaisant; compliant; deferential; docile; ductile; elastic; flexible; malleable; manageable; moldable; obedient; obliging; persuasible; pliant; responsive; submissive; tractable; trained; yielding.*

put up a good fight

put up or shut up   An infantile phrase (SEE).

put words in (her) mouth

quack doctor   *charlatan; dissembler; fake; fraud; impostor; mountebank; phony; pretender; quack.*

quack equations

Quack equations readily explain behavior that the dimwitted otherwise find inexplicable and justify attitudes that they otherwise find unjustifiable: *a deal is a deal; a promise is a promise; a rule is a rule; bald is beautiful; bigger is better; enough is enough; fair is fair; I am you; less is more; more is better; perception is reality; (what's) right is right; seeing is believing; talk is cheap; the law is the law; what happened happened; what's done is done.*

Equally distressing is that there is no end to these false prescriptions. Any word, any concept, can instantly become a quack equation: *alcohol is alcohol; her business is her business; math is math; plastic is plastic; prejudice is prejudice is prejudice; their reasoning is their reasoning.*

Quack equations are much favored by mountebanks and pretenders, by businesspeople and politicians. The more simple the formula, the more palatable it is. SEE ALSO *plebeian sentiments; popular prescriptions.*

qualitative difference

(spend) quality time

quantum leap

queer fish   A moribund metaphor (SEE). *aberrant; abnormal; anomalistic; anomalous; atypical; bizarre; curious; deviant; different; distinct; distinctive; eccentric; exceptional; extraordinary; fantastic; foreign; grotesque; idiosyncratic; independent; individual; individualistic; irregular; novel; odd; offbeat; original; peculiar; puzzling; quaint; queer; rare; remarkable; separate; singular; uncommon; unconventional; unexampled; unique; unnatural; unorthodox; unparalleled; unprecedented; unusual.*

quick and dirty   An inescapable pair (SEE).

quick and easy   ■ Using alcohol or a spray cleaner and paper towels is a *quick and easy* way to spot clean these areas.

(as) quick as a bunny   An insipid simile (SEE moribund metaphors). *brisk; expeditious; fast; fleet; hasty; hurried; immediate; instant; instantaneous; prompt; quick; rapid; speedy; spry; sudden; swift; winged.*

(as) **quick as a flash**   An insipid simile (SEE moribund metaphors). *brisk; expeditious; fast; fleet; hasty; hurried; immediate; instant; instantaneous; prompt; quick; rapid; speedy; spry; sudden; swift; winged.*

(as) **quick as a wink**   An insipid simile (SEE moribund metaphors). *brisk; expeditious; fast; fleet; hasty; hurried; immediate; instant; instantaneous; prompt; quick; rapid; speedy; spry; sudden; swift; winged.*

(as) **quick as lightning**   An insipid simile (SEE moribund metaphors). *brisk; expeditious; fast; fleet; hasty; hurried; immediate; instant; instantaneous; prompt; quick; rapid; speedy; spry; sudden; swift; winged.*

quick fix

quick on the draw   A moribund metaphor (SEE). *fast; fast-acting; quick; rapid; speedy; swift.*

quick to point out

quid pro quo   A foreignism (SEE).

(as) **quiet as a mouse**   An insipid simile (SEE moribund metaphors). *dumb; hushed; motionless; mum; mute; noiseless; quiet; reticent; silent; speechless; stationary; still; subdued; taciturn; unmoving; voiceless; wordless.*

quiet desperation   An inescapable pair (SEE).

quiet diplomacy

quit the scene   *abscond; clear out; decamp; depart; desert; disappear; escape; exit; flee; fly; go; go away; leave; move on; part; pull out; quit; retire; retreat; run away; take flight; take off; vacate; vanish; withdraw.*

quit while (you're) ahead   A popular prescription (SEE).

quote, unquote   An infantile phrase (SEE). *as it were; so-called; so to speak; such as it is.* ■ It's too soon in the *quote, unquote* relationship for that. REPLACE WITH *so-called.* ■ I was referred to them by a friend of mine, *quote, unquote.* REPLACE WITH *as it were.*

R

rack (wrack) and ruin An inescapable pair (SEE).

rack (wrack) (my) brains *endeavor; exert; labor; slave; strain; strive; struggle; toil; try; work.*

radiantly happy An inescapable pair (SEE). *blissful; blithe; buoyant; cheerful; delighted; ecstatic; elated; enraptured; euphoric; exalted; excited; exhilarated; exultant; gay; glad; gleeful; good-humored; happy; intoxicated; jolly; jovial; joyful; joyous; jubilant; merry; mirthful; overjoyed; pleased; rapturous; thrilled.*

rags to riches (story)

raid the cookie jar A moribund metaphor (SEE).

raining cats and dogs A moribund metaphor (SEE). *pouring; raining; storming.*

raining pitchforks A moribund metaphor (SEE). *pouring; raining; storming.*

rain on (your) parade A moribund metaphor (SEE). *blight; cripple; damage; disable; harm; hurt; impair; incapacitate; lame; mar; mess up; rack;* *ruin; sabotage; spoil; subvert; undermine; vitiate; wrack; wreck.*

(come) rain or shine A moribund metaphor (SEE). *no matter what; regardless.*

raise a (red) flag A moribund metaphor (SEE). *alert; apprise; caution; forewarn; inform; notify; signal; warn.*

raise a stink A moribund metaphor (SEE).

raise Cain A moribund metaphor (SEE).
1. *bellow; bluster; clamor; complain; explode; fulminate; fume; holler; howl; object; protest; rage; rant; rave; roar; scream; shout; storm; thunder; vociferate; yell.*
2. *be merry; carouse; carry on; celebrate; frolic; party; play; revel; riot; roister; rollick; romp; skylark.*

raise (some) eyebrows A moribund metaphor (SEE). *amaze; astonish; astound; awe; dumbfound; flabbergast; jar; jolt; shock; start; startle; stun; stupefy; surprise.*

raise hell A moribund metaphor (SEE).
1. *bellow; bluster; clamor; complain;*

explode; fulminate; fume; holler; howl; object; protest; rage; rant; rave; roar; scream; shout; storm; thunder; vociferate; yell.
2. be merry; carouse; carry on; celebrate; frolic; party; play; revel; riot; roister; rollick; romp; skylark.

raise (your) sights

(it) raises more questions than (it) answers ■ This briefing *raises more questions than it answers.*

raise the dead   A moribund metaphor (SEE). *be merry; carouse; carry on; celebrate; frolic; party; play; revel; riot; roister; rollick; romp; skylark.*

raise the hackles   A moribund metaphor (SEE). *acerbate; anger; annoy; bother; bristle; chafe; enrage; incense; inflame; infuriate; insult; irk; irritate; madden; miff; nettle; offend; rile; provoke; vex.*

raise the possibility

raise the roof   A moribund metaphor (SEE).
1. *bellow; bluster; clamor; complain; explode; fulminate; fume; holler; howl; object; protest; rage; rant; rave; roar; scream; shout; storm; thunder; vociferate; yell.*
2. *be merry; carouse; carry on; celebrate; frolic; party; play; revel; riot; roister; rollick; romp; skylark.*

raise the spectre of   ■ The Troika's standard response to all who *raised the spectre of* diminished social services has been insult, invective and ire.

raise the stakes

raison d'être   A foreignism (SEE).

rake (him) over the coals   A moribund metaphor (SEE). *admonish; animadvert; berate; castigate; censure; chasten; chastise; chide; condemn; criticize; denounce; denunciate; discipline; excoriate; fulminate against; imprecate; impugn; inveigh against; objurgate; punish; rebuke; remonstrate; reprehend; reprimand; reproach; reprobate; reprove; revile; scold; swear at; upbraid; vituperate; warn.*

rally 'round the flag   A moribund metaphor (SEE).

rank and file   A moribund metaphor (SEE). *all; citizenry; commonage; commonalty; common people; crowd; everybody; everyone; followers; herd; hoi polloi; laborers; masses; mob; multitude; plebeians; populace; proletariat; public; rabble; workers.*

rank has its privileges

rank right up there   ■ Monet is expected to *rank right up there* with the blockbuster Renoir exhibit of 1985.

rant and rave   An inescapable pair (SEE). *bellow; bluster; clamor; explode; fulminate; fume; holler; howl; rage; rant; rave; roar; scream; shout; storm; thunder; vent; vociferate; yell.*

rapierlike wit   An insipid simile (SEE moribund metaphors).

rara avis   A foreignism (SEE). *aberrant; abnormal; anomalistic; anomalous; atypical; bizarre; curious; deviant; different; distinct; distinctive; eccentric; exceptional; extraordinary; fantastic; foreign; grotesque; idiosyncratic; inde-*

pendent; individual; individualistic; irregular; novel; odd; offbeat; original; peculiar; puzzling; quaint; queer; rare; remarkable; separate; singular; uncommon; unconventional; unexampled; unique; unnatural; unorthodox; unparalleled; unprecedented; unusual.

rarely (seldom) ever A dimwitted redundancy (SEE). *rarely (seldom)*. ■ We are brothers, but we *rarely ever* speak. DELETE *ever*.

rat race A moribund metaphor (SEE).

(like) rats abandoning a ship An insipid simile (SEE moribund metaphors).

rattle the wrong cage A moribund metaphor (SEE).

rave reviews An inescapable pair (SEE).

raving lunatic An inescapable pair (SEE).

reach epidemic proportions
■ The availability of guns on the street has *reached epidemic proportions*.

reach for the sky A moribund metaphor (SEE).

reach out and touch An infantile phrase (SEE).

reach the end of (our) rope
A moribund metaphor (SEE).

read between the lines A moribund metaphor (SEE). *assume; conclude; conjecture; deduce; gather; guess; hypothesize; imagine; infer; presume;*

speculate; suppose; surmise; theorize; venture.

read it and reap An infantile phrase (SEE).

read it and weep An infantile phrase (SEE).

read (her) like a (an open) book
An insipid simile (SEE moribund metaphors).

read my lips An infantile phrase (SEE).

read (him) the riot act A moribund metaphor (SEE). *admonish; animadvert; berate; castigate; censure; chasten; chastise; chide; condemn; criticize; denounce; denunciate; discipline; excoriate; fulminate against; imprecate; impugn; inveigh against; objurgate; punish; rebuke; remonstrate; reprehend; reprimand; reproach; reprobate; reprove; revile; scold; swear at; upbraid; vituperate; warn.*

read with interest

ready, willing and able An infantile phrase (SEE). ■ She described her client as being *ready, willing and able* to testify. REPLACE WITH *willing*. ■ We have a lot of social problems that need to be addressed, and I'm *ready, willing and able* to do that. REPLACE WITH *ready*.

re- again A dimwitted redundancy (SEE). *re-*. ■ I divorced him, and then I *remarried again*. DELETE *again*. ■ We missed the first ten minutes of his talk, so he *repeated* it *again* for us. DELETE *again*. ■ That film will make addicts want to *reexperience* taking crack again. DELETE *again*.

real   An overworked word (SEE). For example: *real contribution; real difference; real obvious; real possibility; real progress; real tragedy.*

reality check   An infantile phrase (SEE).

reality sets in

real, live   An infantile phrase (SEE).

really   An overworked word (SEE). If such an intensive is needed at all, alternatives to the word *really* include *consumedly; enormously; especially; exceedingly; exceptionally; extraordinarily; extremely; genuinely; particularly; remarkably; specially; truly; uncommonly; very.*

   Often, however, such highlighting serves to diminish the believability of our statements. ■ At the *London Review* we take serious pride in our role as one of the *really* significant participants in the international exchange of ideas and information. DELETE *really*. ■ He did a *really* good job of convincing us to buy. DELETE *really*. SEE ALSO *very*.

really?   An infantile phrase (SEE). SEE ALSO *you're kidding; you've got to be kidding.*

really (and) truly   An infantile phrase (SEE). ■ I *really and truly* love being in love. DELETE *really and truly*.

rear (its) ugly head   A moribund metaphor (SEE). ■ That hypocritical axiom, "Do as I say, not as I do" seems to have *reared its ugly head* on the edi-

torial pages of the *Globe* once again.

reasonable facsimile   An inescapable pair (SEE).

(the) reason (why) is because
A dimwitted redundancy (SEE). *because; reason is (that).* ■ One of *the reasons why* people keep this to themselves *is because of* the stigma. USE *the reasons . . . is.*

(the) reason why   A dimwitted redundancy (SEE). *reason.* ■ There is a *reason why* she is the way she is. DELETE *why*. ■ The researchers are not certain as to the *reason why*. DELETE *why.*

recap   ■ For those of you just joining us, let me *recap*. REPLACE WITH *recapitulate*. SEE ALSO *demo; info.*

receive back   A dimwitted redundancy (SEE). *receive.* ■ DPL now communicates with Excel, sending the input values and *receiving back* the output value Profit. DELETE *back.*

recipe for disaster

reckless abandon   An inescapable pair (SEE).

record-breaking   A dimwitted redundancy (SEE). *record.* ■ We'll take a look at some *record-breaking* snowfalls. USE *record*. SEE ALSO *all-time record; record-high.*

record-high   A dimwitted redundancy (SEE). *record.* ■ In Concord, it was a *record-high* 12 degrees. USE *record*. SEE ALSO *all-time record; record-breaking.*

(as) red as a beet An insipid simile (SEE moribund metaphors).

1. *beet-red; blood-red; burgundian; burgundy; cardinal; carmine; cerise; cherry; crimson; fire-engine-red; maroon; purple; purplish; red; reddish; rose; rose-colored; rosey; rubefacient; rubescent; rubicund; rubied; rubiginous; ruby; ruddy; rufescent; rufous; russet; sanguine; sanguineous; scarlet; vermilion; wine; wine-colored.*

2. *abashed; ashamed; blushing; chagrined; confused; discomfited; discomposed; disconcerted; embarrassed; flushed; flustered; mortified; nonplussed; perplexed; red-faced; shamed; shamefaced; sheepish.*

(as) red as a cherry An insipid simile (SEE moribund metaphors).

1. *beet-red; blood-red; burgundian; burgundy; cardinal; carmine; cerise; cherry; crimson; fire-engine-red; maroon; purple; purplish; red; reddish; rose; rose-colored; rosey; rubefacient; rubescent; rubicund; rubied; rubiginous; ruby; ruddy; rufescent; rufous; russet; sanguine; sanguineous; scarlet; vermilion; wine; wine-colored.*

2. *abashed; ashamed; blushing; chagrined; confused; discomfited; discomposed; disconcerted; embarrassed; flushed; flustered; mortified; nonplussed; perplexed; red-faced; shamed; shamefaced; sheepish.*

(as) red as a rose An insipid simile (SEE moribund metaphors).

1. *beet-red; blood-red; burgundian; burgundy; cardinal; carmine; cerise; cherry; crimson; fire-engine-red; maroon; purple; purplish; red; reddish; rose; rose-colored; rosey; rubefacient; rubescent; rubicund; rubied; rubiginous; ruby; ruddy; rufescent; rufous; russet; sanguine; sanguineous; scarlet;*

vermilion; wine; wine-colored.

2. *abashed; ashamed; blushing; chagrined; confused; discomfited; discomposed; disconcerted; embarrassed; flushed; flustered; mortified; nonplussed; perplexed; red-faced; shamed; shamefaced; sheepish.*

(as) red as a ruby An insipid simile (SEE moribund metaphors).

1. *beet-red; blood-red; burgundian; burgundy; cardinal; carmine; cerise; cherry; crimson; fire-engine-red; maroon; purple; purplish; red; reddish; rose; rose-colored; rosey; rubefacient; rubescent; rubicund; rubied; rubiginous; ruby; ruddy; rufescent; rufous; russet; sanguine; sanguineous; scarlet; vermilion; wine; wine-colored.*

2. *abashed; ashamed; blushing; chagrined; confused; discomfited; discomposed; disconcerted; embarrassed; flushed; flustered; mortified; nonplussed; perplexed; red-faced; shamed; shamefaced; sheepish.*

red-carpet treatment A moribund metaphor (SEE).

red herring A moribund metaphor (SEE).

red hot

red in the face A moribund metaphor (SEE). *abashed; ashamed; blushing; chagrined; confused; discomfited; discomposed; disconcerted; embarrassed; flushed; flustered; mortified; nonplused; perplexed; red-faced; shamed; shamefaced; sheepish.*

red-letter day A moribund metaphor (SEE).

redouble (our) efforts

red tape   A moribund metaphor (SEE).

refer back   A dimwitted redundancy (SEE). *refer.* ■ *Refer back* to chapter 4. DELETE *back.*

regardless of the consequences

regardless of the fact that   A dimwitted redundancy (SEE). *although; but; even if; even though; still; though; yet.* ■ *Regardless of the fact that* these products are low in sucrose, they still contain energy from other nutrients. USE *Though.* SEE ALSO *despite the fact that; in spite of the fact that.*

register here to win

(as) regular as clockwork   An insipid simile (SEE moribund metaphors). *cyclic; established; fixed; habitual; periodic; recurrent; recurring; regular; repetitive; rhythmic; rhythmical.*

reign of terror

reinvent the wheel   A moribund metaphor (SEE).

relate back   A dimwitted redundancy (SEE). *relate.* ■ Like the Chicago School, anomie theory *relates back* to the European sociology of the 1800s. DELETE *back.*

relatively speaking

relaxed atmosphere

reliable source

relic of the past   A dimwitted redundancy (SEE). *relic.* ■ The very idea of a single, domestic market has become a *relic of the past.* USE *relic.*

(it) remains to be seen   A torpid term (SEE). This phrase is often a foolish euphemism for *(I) don't know* and similar admissions. ■ So much *remains to be seen.* REPLACE WITH *is unknown.* ■ *It remains to be seen* whether dietary soybeans can protect women against breast cancer. REPLACE WITH *We do not know.* ■ How the French public, fond of both cigarettes and alcohol, will respond *remains to be seen.* REPLACE WITH *is not yet known.* SEE ALSO *your guess is as good as mine.*

remedy the situation   A torpid term (SEE). Like all torpid terms, *remedy the situation* neither moves us nor motivates us; its use virtually ensures that nothing will be righted, nothing remedied.

We will always be more easily persuaded to remedy an ill or a problem or a wrong than a situation. ■ If the decisions actually turn out to hamper civil rights enforcement, obviously I would want to take steps to *remedy the situation.* ■ To *remedy the situation* and make the process fairer, the SEC should require that voting be strictly confidential. SEE ALSO *(a) situation.*

reminisce about the past   A dimwitted redundancy (SEE). *reminisce.* ■ She's now eighty-nine years old and she spends most of her time *reminiscing about the past.* DELETE *about the past.*

remote possibility

remove the cotton from (my) ears   A moribund metaphor (SEE).

renewed vigor

replace back   A dimwitted redundancy (SEE). *replace*. ■ When a change needs to be made, a developer reserves that file from the library, makes the change, and then *replaces* it *back*. DELETE *back*.

reports of (my) death are greatly exaggerated   An infantile phrase (SEE).

represent(s)   A torpid term (SEE). Increasingly, *represents* is being used for a sad, simple *is* (and *represent* for *are*). ■ The budgeted capacity level *represents* the level of expected business activity under normal operating conditions. REPLACE WITH *is*. ■ Newstar and BASYS currently *represent* the major newsroom computer systems in the broadcasting field. REPLACE WITH *are*. ■ Radiosurgery *represents* a major step forward in our ability to treat tumors that previously have been untreatable. REPLACE WITH *is*. ■ I think Ginger, Patty and I *represent* three very hardworking, committed faculty members. REPLACE WITH *are*.

(your) reputation precedes (you)

rest and relaxation   An inescapable pair (SEE). *calm; calmness; leisure; peace; peacefulness; quiet; quietude; relaxation; repose; rest; serenity; stillness; tranquillity*.

(I) rest (my) case

rest on (her) laurels   A moribund metaphor (SEE).

restore back   A dimwitted redundancy (SEE). *restore*. ■ The new Undo feature allows you to *restore* the disk *back* to its original state. DELETE *back*.

return back   A dimwitted redundancy (SEE). *return*. ■ When SEU is exited, the user will be *returned back* to the Programmer Menu. DELETE *back*.

return to normalcy

revenge is sweet   A quack equation (SEE).

revert back   A dimwitted redundancy (SEE). *revert*. ■ Scientists speculate that the rapid spread of the disease may be due to farmland *reverting back* to woodland. DELETE *back*.

revolutionary new product

revolving door policy   A moribund metaphor (SEE).

(neither) rhyme nor (or) reason   A moribund metaphor (SEE). *intelligence; order; reason; sense*.

(as) rich as Croesus   An insipid simile (SEE moribund metaphors). *affluent; moneyed; opulent; prosperous; rich; wealthy; well-off; well-to-do*.

rich beyond (my) wildest dreams

richly deserves   An inescapable pair (SEE). ■ Instead of vilifying him, we should be giving him the encouragement and support he *richly deserves*.

rich man, poor man, beggarman, thief   A moribund metaphor (SEE). ■ It doesn't matter whether you are *rich man, poor man, beggar or thief*, if you are black, there's an artificial ceiling on your ambition.

ride herd on   A moribund metaphor (SEE). *boss; browbeat; brutalize; bully; dictate; domineer; enslave; master; oppress; overpower; reign over; repress; rule; subjugate; suppress; tyrannize.*

ride off into the sunset   A moribund metaphor (SEE).

ride on (her) coattails   A moribund metaphor (SEE).

ride out the storm   A moribund metaphor (SEE).

ride roughshod over   A moribund metaphor (SEE). *boss; browbeat; brutalize; bully; dictate; domineer; enslave; master; oppress; overpower; reign over; repress; rule; subjugate; suppress; tyrannize.*

(as) right as rain   An insipid simile (SEE moribund metaphors).
1. *accurate; correct; exact; irrefutable; precise; right; true.*
2. *fit; good; hale; hardy; healthful; healthy; hearty; robust; sound; strong; well.*

righteous indignation   An inescapable pair (SEE).

(what's) right is right   A quack equation (SEE).

right off the bat   A moribund metaphor (SEE). *abruptly; apace; at once; briskly; directly; expeditiously; fast; forthwith; hastily; hurriedly; immediately; instantaneously; instantly; posthaste; promptly; quickly; rapidly; rashly;*

right away; speedily; straightaway; swiftly; wingedly.

(on the) right track   A moribund metaphor (SEE).

ring a bell   A moribund metaphor (SEE).

ring down the curtin (on)   A moribund metaphor (SEE). *cease; close; complete; conclude; discontinue; end; finish; halt; settle; stop.*

ringing endorsement   An inescapable pair (SEE).

ringing off the hook   A moribund metaphor (SEE).

riot of color

ripe for the kill

ripe for the picking (plucking)

rip (tear) to shreds   A moribund metaphor (SEE). *demolish; destroy; devastate; obliterate; rack; ravage; ruin; shatter; smash; undo; wrack; wreck.*

rise and shine

rise from the ashes   A moribund metaphor (SEE).

rise like a phoenix   An insipid simile (SEE moribund metaphors).

rise to new heights

rise to the occasion

rising star   A moribund metaphor (SEE).

risk life and limb

risky business

rite of passage

road less traveled   A moribund metaphor (SEE).

road to ruin   A moribund metaphor (SEE).

roar (in) like a lion   An insipid simile (SEE moribund metaphors).

rob Peter to pay Paul   A moribund metaphor (SEE).

rock-bottom prices

rock the boat   A moribund metaphor (SEE). *agitate; confuse; disorder; disorganize; disquiet; disrupt; disturb; fluster; jar; jolt; jumble; mess up; mix up; muddle; perturb; rattle; ruffle; shake up; stir up; unnerve; unsettle; upset.*

(positive) role model   *archetype; example; exemplar; good example; good man (woman); guide; hero; ideal; inspiration; model; paragon; prototype.*

roller-coaster (ride)   A moribund metaphor (SEE).

rolling in money   A moribund metaphor (SEE). *affluent; moneyed; opulent; prosperous; rich; wealthy; well-off; well-to-do.*

roll in the aisles   A moribund metaphor (SEE). *cachinnate; cackle; chortle; chuckle; convulse; guffaw; hoot; howl; laugh; roar; shriek.*

roll over

roll over and die

roll up (her) sleeves   A moribund metaphor (SEE).

roll with the punches   A moribund metaphor (SEE).

Rome wasn't built in a day   A popular prescription (SEE).

room for improvement

root cause   A dimwitted redundancy (SEE). *cause; origin; reason; root; source.* ■ It does not truly solve the problem of rising health care costs since it does not address the *root cause* of the problem. REPLACE WITH *root*.

rootin', tootin', shootin'   An infantile phrase (SEE).

rotten apple   A moribund metaphor (SEE). *bastard; blackguard; cad; charlatan; cheater; fake; fraud; impostor; knave; mountebank; phony; pretender; quack; rascal; rogue; scoundrel; swindler; undesirable; villain.*

rotten to the core   A moribund metaphor (SEE). *bad; base; contemptible; corrupt; crooked; deceitful; despicable; dishonest; evil; immoral; iniquitous; malevolent; mean; miserable; nefarious; pernicious; praetorian; rotten; sinister; underhanded; unethical; untrustworthy; venal; vicious; vile; wicked.*

rough and ready   An inescapable pair (SEE).

rough and tumble   A moribund metaphor (SEE). *boisterous; disorderly; raucous; riotous; rough; tempestous;*

tumultuous; turbulent; uproarious; violent; wild.

rough around the edges   A moribund metaphor (SEE).

rousing success   An inescapable pair (SEE).

rub elbows   A moribund metaphor (SEE). *associate; consort; hobnob; fraternize; keep company; mingle; mix; socialize.*

rub (me) the wrong way   A moribund metaphor (SEE). *acerbate; anger; annoy; bother; chafe; disturb; gall; grate; irk; irritate; miff; nettle; provoke; rankle; rile; upset; vex.*

rue the day

(soothe) ruffled feathers   A moribund metaphor (SEE).

rules and regulations   An inescapable pair (SEE). ■ You may have a player who's disappointed, but we're adhering to our *rules and regulations*. REPLACE WITH *regulations* or *rules*.

rules are made to be broken   A popular prescription (SEE).

rule the roost   A moribund metaphor (SEE). *administer; boss; command; control; dictate; direct; dominate; govern; in charge; in command; in control; manage; manipulate; master; order; overpower; oversee; predominate; prevail; reign over; rule; superintend.*

rule with an iron fist (hand)   A moribund metaphor (SEE). *authoritarian; authorative; autocratic; cruel; despotic; dictatorial; dogmatic; domi-*

neering; hard; harsh; imperious; ironhanded; lordly; oppressive; overbearing; peremptory; repressive; rigorous; severe; stern; strict; tough; tyrannical.

rumor has it

run a tight ship   A moribund metaphor (SEE).

run circles around   A moribund metaphor (SEE). *beat; better; cap; defeat; exceed; excel; outclass; outdo; outflank; outmaneuver; outperform; outplay; outrank; outsmart; outthink; out-wit; overcome; overpower; prevail over; surpass; top; triumph over; trounce; whip; win out.*

run for (their) money

run (it) into the ground   A moribund metaphor (SEE).

running on empty   A moribund metaphor (SEE).

running on fumes   A moribund metaphor (SEE).

run off at the mouth   A moribund metaphor (SEE). *babbling; blathering; chatty; facile; fluent; garrulous; glib; jabbering; logorrheic; long-winded; loquacious; prolix; talkative; verbose; voluble; windy.*

run of the mill   A moribund metaphor (SEE). *average; common; commonplace; customary; everyday; fair; mediocre; middling; normal; ordinary; passable; plain; quotidian; regular; routine; simple; standard; tolerable; typical; uneventful; unexceptional; unremarkable; usual.*

run out of steam   A moribund metaphor (SEE). *beat; bushed; debilitated; depleted; drained; enervated; exhausted; fatigued; sapped; spent; tired; weary; worn out.*

run ragged

runs the gamut

(money) runs through (his) fingers   A moribund metaphor (SEE).

run the show   A moribund metaphor (SEE). *administer; boss; command; control; dictate; direct; dominate; govern; in charge; in command; in control; manage; manipulate; master; order; overpower; oversee; predominate; prevail; reign over; rule; superintend.*

run with the ball   A moribund metaphor (SEE).

run with the hare and hunt with the hounds   A moribund metaphor (SEE).

run with the pack   A moribund metaphor (SEE). *abide by; accommodate; accord; acquiesce; adapt; adhere to; agree; behave; comply; concur; conform; correspond; follow; harmonize; heed; mind; obey; observe; submit; yield.*

rush headlong

rush to judgment

S

sacred cow   A moribund metaphor (SEE).

sacred trust

sacrificial lamb   A moribund metaphor (SEE).

sad but true

sad commentary

sadder but wiser

sad to say   *sadly; unhappily.*

safe and sound   An inescapable pair (SEE).

safe bet

safety net   A moribund metaphor (SEE).

sail (too) close to the wind
A moribund metaphor (SEE). *chance; dare; endanger; gamble; hazard; imperil; jeopardize; make bold; peril; risk; venture.*

sail under false colors   A moribund metaphor (SEE). *bamboozle; befool; beguile; belie; bilk; bluff; cheat; color; con; deceive; defraud; delude; disguise; dissemble; dissimulate; dupe; fake; falsify; feign; feint; fool; gyp; hoodwink; lead astray; misdirect; misguide; misinform; mislead; misrepresent; pretend; simulate; spoof; swindle; trick.*

sale of the century

(the) same but different   An infantile phrase (SEE). SEE ALSO *same difference.*

same difference

(the) same old song and dance

(the) same old story

(the) same old thing

sans   An archaism (SEE). *lacking; without.* ■ He has a reckless streak, as revealed in his tendency to go swimming *sans* suit. REPLACE WITH *without a.*

save   An archaism (SEE). *but; except.* ■ The room was quiet during his performance, *save* when he would take a deep breath and let out some of it. REPLACE WITH *except.*

saved by the bell   An infantile phrase (SEE).

save (it) for a rainy day   A moribund metaphor (SEE).

save (his) skin   A moribund metaphor (SEE).

save the best for last

save the day

save your breath   A moribund metaphor (SEE).

saving grace

(he) saw (you) coming

(as) scarce as hen's teeth   An insipid simile (SEE moribund metaphors). *exiguous; inadequate; meager; rare; scant; scanty; scarce; sparse; uncommon; unusual.*

scarcer than hen's teeth   A moribund metaphor (SEE). *exiguous; inadequate; meager; rare; scant; scanty; scarce; sparse; uncommon; unusual.*

scared for life

scare the (living) daylights out of (me)   A moribund metaphor (SEE). *alarm; appall; benumb; daunt; frighten; horrify; intimidate; panic; paralyze; petrify; scare; shock; startle; terrify; terrorize.*

scare the pants off (me)   A moribund metaphor (SEE). *alarm; appall; benumb; daunt; frighten; horrify; intimidate; panic; paralyze; petrify; scare; shock; startle; terrify; terrorize.*

scare to death   A moribund metaphor (SEE). *alarm; appall; benumb; daunt; frighten; horrify; intimidate;* *panic; paralyze; petrify; scare; shock; startle; terrify; terrorize.* SEE ALSO *to death.*

scathing attack

(a) scenario   An overworked word (SEE). ∎ The worst-case *scenario* would be for Question 3 to pass and for Question 5 to fail. DELETE *scenario.* ∎ He believes that putting the question of rent control before the voters will lead to *an absurd scenario.* REPLACE WITH *absurdity.*

school of hard knocks   A moribund metaphor (SEE).

(just) scratch the surface   A moribund metaphor (SEE).

scream and yell   An inescapable pair (SEE). *bay; bawl; bellow; blare; caterwaul; clamor; cry; holler; hoot; howl; roar; screak; scream; screech; shout; shriek; shrill; squawk; squeal; vociferate; wail; whoop; yell; yelp; yowl.* ∎ If parents are *screaming and yelling* at each other, that causes fear in children. REPLACE WITH *screaming* or *yelling.* SEE ALSO *yell and scream.*

scream (yell) bloody murder   A moribund metaphor (SEE). *bay; bawl; bellow; blare; caterwaul; clamor; cry; holler; hoot; howl; roar; screak; scream; screech; shout; shriek; shrill; squawk; squeal; vociferate; wail; whoop; yell; yelp; yowl.*

screech to a halt   A moribund metaphor (SEE). *cease; close; complete; conclude; derail; discontinue; end; finish; halt; settle; stop.* ∎ Work in 535 congressional offices *screeched to a halt.* REPLACE WITH *ceased.*

(get) (his) sea legs

seal (her) fate

seal of approval

second banana   A moribund metaphor (SEE). ■ Murphy's greatest political need is to convince the public that she is a leader and not just the governor's long-suffering *second banana*.

second-class citizen   A moribund metaphor (SEE).

second of all   A dimwitted redundancy (SEE). *second*. ■ *Second of all*, you're going to get hurt if you continue this behavior. USE *Second*. SEE ALSO *first of all*.

second to none   *best; different; exceptional; extraordinary; finest; first; greatest; highest; incomparable; inimitable; matchless; notable; noteworthy; novel; odd; original; outstanding; peculiar; peerless; remarkable; singular; special; strange; superlative; uncommon; unequaled; unexampled; unique; unmatched; unparalleled; unrivaled; unusual; without equal.*

secure in the knowledge that

see eye to eye   A moribund metaphor (SEE). *agree; concur; think alike.* ■ We *see eye to eye* on most all matters. REPLACE WITH *agree*.

seeing is believing   A quack equation (SEE).

(we didn't) see it coming

seek and you shall find   A popular prescription (SEE).

see no evil, hear no evil, speak no evil

see red   A moribund metaphor (SEE). *acerbate; anger; annoy; bother; bristle; chafe; enrage; incense; inflame; infuriate; irk; irritate; madden; miff; provoke; rile; vex.*

see the error of (our) ways

see the light   A moribund metaphor (SEE). *appreciate; apprehend; comprehend; discern; fathom; grasp; know; make sense of; perceive; realize; recognize; see; understand.*

see the light of day   A moribund metaphor (SEE).

seething mass of humanity
A moribund metaphor (SEE).

see (things) with half an eye
A moribund metaphor (SEE).

seige mentality

seize the day

self-fulfilling prophesy   ■ If retailers think negatively and pessimistically about Christmas, it's going to be a *self-fulfilling prophecy*.

sell (him) a bill of goods   A moribund metaphor (SEE). *cheat; deceive; defraud; dupe; fool; lie to; swindle; trick; victimize.* ■ We realize that we've been *sold a bill of goods*. REPLACE WITH *swindled*.

sell (him) down the river   A moribund metaphor (SEE). *betray; deliver up; inform on; turn in.*

selling like hotcakes   An insipid simile (SEE moribund metaphors).

sell (herself) short

send a message (signal)   A torpid term (SEE). This phrase is a favorite of politicians who express themselves neither persuasively nor purposefully.

Rather than use this sluggish phrase, more telling and true would be to use words like *advise; announce; assert; asseverate; aver; contend; declare; disclose; expose; indicate; inform; make clear; make known; maintain; mention; point out; proclaim; reveal; say; show; state; suggest; tell; uncover; unveil.* ■ The patent system that protects new drugs from competition *sends a message* to pharmaceutical companies: If you invest enough money and come up with a hit, you can make a killing. REPLACE WITH *says.* ■ We want to *send a message* that this kind of behavior will not be tolerated. REPLACE WITH *make clear.* ■ The police department *sent out a message* that would not allow such looting to occur again. REPLACE WITH *made it known.* ■ By agreeing to act now, we are *sending a signal* that we do not want this plan to fail. REPLACE WITH *announcing.*

send (throw) good money after bad

send into a tailspin   A moribund metaphor (SEE).

send (me) mixed signals

send (them) packing   *discard; dismiss; discharge.*

send shivers down (my) spine
A moribund metaphor (SEE). *jittery; jumpy; nervous; quivering; shaking;* *shivering; shivery; shuddering; skittish; trembling.*

send shock waves (through)
A moribund metaphor (SEE). *agitate; arouse; astound; bother; confuse; discomfit; disconcert; disquiet; disrupt; disturb; excite; jolt; shock; startle; stimulate; stir; stun; unsettle; upset.* ■ When Swiss pharmaceutical giant Roche Holding Ltd. announced that it would buy 60 percent of Genentech Inc., it *sent shock waves through* the biotechnology community. REPLACE WITH *shocked.*

send up a trial balloon   A moribund metaphor (SEE).

senseless violence

sense of urgency

sent (them) into a tizzy

sent (him) into orbit   A moribund metaphor (SEE).

sent shivers down (through)

separate and distinct   A dimwitted redundancy (SEE). *distinct; separate.* ■ Nor are the stages *separate and distinct*; they may occur at the same time. USE *distinct.*

separate and independent   A dimwitted redundancy (SEE). *independent; separate.* ■ Since the audio and video in an Interactive Multipoint videoconference travel over *separate and independent* paths, the audio must be delayed to synchronize it with the video. USE *separate.*

separate fact from fiction

separate out   A dimwitted redundancy (SEE). *separate*. ■ I don't think you can *separate out* those two things. DELETE *out*.

separate the men from the boys   A moribund metaphor (SEE). *choose; cull; differentiate; discriminate; distinguish; divide; filter; isolate; pick; screen; segregate; select; separate; sieve; sift; sort; strain; weed out; winnow.*

separate the sheep from the goats   A moribund metaphor (SEE). *choose; cull; differentiate; discriminate; distinguish; divide; filter; isolate; pick; screen; segregate; select; separate; sieve; sift; sort; strain; weed out; winnow.*

separate the wheat from the chaff   A moribund metaphor (SEE). *choose; cull; differentiate; discriminate; distinguish; divide; filter; isolate; pick; screen; segregate; select; separate; sieve; sift; sort; strain; weed out; winnow.*

sequence of events

serious reservations   An inescapable pair (SEE).

set in concrete   A moribund metaphor (SEE). *eternal; everlasting; firm; immutable; invariable; irreversible; irrevocable; permanent; rigid; stable; unalterable; unchangeable; unchanging.*

set in (their) ways

set (her) straight

set (her) teeth on edge   A moribund metaphor (SEE).
1. *acerbate; anger; annoy; bristle; chafe; enrage; incense; inflame; infuriate; irk; irritate; madden; miff; nettle; offend;* *rile; provoke; vex.*
2. *agitate; bother; disconcert; disturb; fluster; perturb; unnerve; upset.*

set the record straight   ■ There are a lot of things I can do in my book *to set the record straight.*

set the stage (for)   A moribund metaphor (SEE). *arrange; groom; make ready; plan; prepare; prime; ready.*

set the wheels in motion   A moribund metaphor (SEE).

set the world on fire   A moribund metaphor (SEE).

settle the score   A moribund metaphor (SEE).

set tongues wagging   A moribund metaphor (SEE).

set (myself) up for a fall

set up shop

seventh heaven   A moribund metaphor (SEE).

shaken to its foundations   A moribund metaphor (SEE).

shake, rattle and roll

shake things up

shaking in (his) boots   A moribund metaphor (SEE).
1. *afraid; alarmed; apprehensive; cowardly; craven; diffident; fainthearted; fearful; frightened; pusillanimous; recreant; scared; terror-stricken; timid; timorous; tremulous.*
2. *jittery; jumpy; nervous; quivering;*

shaking; shivering; shivery; shuddering; skittish; trembling.

shaking like a leaf   An insipid simile (SEE moribund metaphors).
1. *jittery; jumpy; nervous; quivering; shaking; shivering; shivery; shuddering; skittish; trembling.*
2. *afraid; cowardly; craven; diffident; fainthearted; fearful; frightened; pusillanimous; recreant; scared; timid; timorous; tremulous.*

shanks' mare   A moribund metaphor (SEE).

shape up or ship out

share and share alike   A popular prescription (SEE).

(as) sharp as a razor   An insipid simile (SEE moribund metaphors). *able; adroit; apt; astute; bright; brilliant; capable; clever; competent; discerning; enlightened; insightful; intelligent; judicious; keen; knowledgeable; learned; logical; luminous; perceptive; perspicacious; quick; rational; reasonable; sagacious; sage; sapient; sensible; sharp; shrewd; smart; sound; understanding; wise.*

(as) sharp as a tack   An insipid simile (SEE moribund metaphors). *able; adroit; apt; astute; bright; brilliant; capable; clever; competent; discerning; enlightened; insightful; intelligent; judicious; keen; knowledgeable; learned; logical; luminous; perceptive; perspicacious; quick; rational; reasonable; sagacious; sage; sapient; sensible; sharp; shrewd; smart; sound; understanding; wise.*

shed (throw) light on   A moribund metaphor (SEE). *clarify; clear up; describe; disentangle; elucidate; enlighten; explain; explicate; illume; illuminate; interpret; make clear; make plain; reveal; simplify.*

shift gears   A moribund metaphor (SEE).

shift into high gear   A moribund metaphor (SEE). ■ The lawyer is *shifting into high gear*, summoning all his persuasive powers for a rhetorical flourish that will dazzle the jury and save his client a multimillion-dollar court award.

ship of fools   A moribund metaphor (SEE).

(like) (two) ships passing in the night   An insipid simile (SEE moribund metaphors).

(my) ship to come in   A moribund metaphor (SEE).

shocked and saddened   (dismayed) These are formulas that people — especially groups — use to express indignation. And, as formulas, the *shock and sadness* hardly ever felt, the *shock and dismay* hardly heartfelt. ■ I was *shocked and saddened* by the news of his death. ■ Shoppers and shop owners were also *shocked and saddened* by Mr. Stuart's suicide. ■ Relatives were *shocked and dismayed* by what they saw today.

shoot down   A moribund metaphor (SEE). *belie; confute; contradict; controvert; counter; debunk; deny; disprove; discredit; dispute; expose; invalidate; negate; rebut; refute; repudiate.*

shoot first and ask questions later

shoot from the hip A moribund metaphor (SEE).

shoot full of holes A moribund metaphor (SEE). *belie; confute; contradict; controvert; counter; debunk; deny; disprove; discredit; dispute; expose; invalidate; negate; rebut; refute; repudiate.*

(like) shooting fish in a barrel An insipid simile (SEE moribund metaphors). *easily done; easy; effortless; elementary; facile; simple; simplicity itself; simplistic; straightforward; uncomplex; uncomplicated.*

shoot the breeze (bull) A moribund metaphor (SEE). *babble; chat; chatter; confabulate; converse; gossip; jabber; palaver; prate; prattle; rattle; talk.* ■ He would come down every couple of weeks just to *shoot the breeze*. REPLACE WITH *chat*.

shoot the messenger A moribund metaphor (SEE).

shoot the works A moribund metaphor (SEE).

shoot to kill A moribund metaphor (SEE).

shop till you drop A moribund metaphor (SEE).

short and sweet An inescapable pair (SEE). *brief; compact; concise; condensed; curt; laconic; pithy; short; succinct; terse.*

short end of the stick A moribund metaphor (SEE).

short on (delivery) and (but) long on (promise) ■ Last summer he proposed a plan for solving the state's fiscal problems that was *short on* specifics *but long on* criticizing business as usual at the State House.

shot heard around the world A moribund metaphor (SEE).

shot (himself) in the foot A moribund metaphor (SEE).

shot to hell A moribund metaphor (SEE).
1. *demolished; destroyed; devastated; obliterated; racked; ruined; shattered; smashed; wracked; wrecked.*
2. *damaged; decayed; decrepit; deteriorated; dilapidated; ragged; shabby; shopworn; tattered; worn.*

shoulder the blame

shoulder the burden (responsibility)

(stand) shoulder to shoulder
A moribund metaphor (SEE). *collaborate; comply; concur; conspire; cooperate; work together.*

(you) should get a medal

(I) should have stayed in bed

shout (it) from the housetops (rooftops) A moribund metaphor (SEE). *advertise; announce; broadcast; proclaim; promulgate; publicize; publish; trumpet.*

shove down (their) throats
A moribund metaphor (SEE). *bulldoze; bully; coerce; compel; constrain; demand; drive; enforce; enjoin; force;*

goad; impel; incite; intimidate; make; necessitate; obligate; oblige; order; press; pressure; prod; require; threaten; tyrannize; urge.

show me a . . . and I'll show you a . . . ■ *Show me a* person who's lived a normal, conventional life, *and I'll show you a* dullard.

show (their) stuff

show (your) true colors

shred of evidence ■ There was not a *shred of evidence* to support his contentions.

shrinking violet A moribund metaphor (SEE).

shudder to think

shut (his) eyes to A moribund metaphor (SEE). *avoid; brush aside; discount; disregard; dodge; duck; ignore; neglect; omit; pass over; recoil from; shrink from; shun; shy away from; turn away from; withdraw from.*

sick and tired (of) An inescapable pair (SEE).
1. *annoyed; bored; discouraged; disgusted; exasperated; exhausted; fatigued; fed up; impatient; irked; irritated; sick; sickened; tired; wearied; weary.*
2. *cloyed; glutted; gorged; jaded; sated; satiated; surfeited.* ■ I'm *sick and tired* of seeing the welfare bashing in the newspaper. REPLACE WITH *weary.*

(as) sick as a dog An insipid simile (SEE moribund metaphors).
1. *afflicted; ailing; diseased; ill; indisposed; infirm; not (feeling) well; sick;* sickly; suffering; unhealthy; unsound; unwell; valetudinarian.
2. *nauseated; nauseous; queasy; sick; squeamish; vomiting.*

sick to death *annoyed; bored; discouraged; disgusted; exasperated; exhausted; fatigued; fed up; impatient; irked; irritated; sick; sickened; tired; wearied; weary.* SEE ALSO *to death.*

(her) side of the story

signed, sealed and delivered A moribund metaphor (SEE). *completed; concluded; consummated; ended; executed; finished; fulfilled; made final; terminated.*

significant An overworked word (SEE). For example: *significant development; significant effect; significant impact; significant progress.* SEE ALSO *meaningful.*

significant other A torpid term (SEE). *admirer; beau; beloved; boyfriend (girlfriend); companion; confidant; darling; dear; familiar; flame; friend; infatuate; inamorato (inamorata); intimate; lover; paramour; partner; steady; suiter; swain; sweetheart; wooer.*
  This is a loathsome expression—doubtlessly the creation of someone bereft of sensibility and subtlety. ■ My *significant other* is always calling me a spoilsport because I won't compromise on things. REPLACE WITH *lover.* SEE ALSO *object of one's affection.*

sign of encouragement

sign off on *approve; authorize; certify; endorse; sanction.*

sign of the times

silence is golden   A quack equation (SEE).

(as) silent as the dead   An insipid simile (SEE moribund metaphors). *dumb; hushed; mum; mute; noiseless; quiet; reticent; silent; speechless; still; taciturn; voiceless; wordless.*

(as) silly as a goose   An insipid simile (SEE moribund metaphors). *absurd; asinine; childish; comical; farcical; fatuous; flighty; foolhardy; foolish; frivolous; giddy; idiotic; immature; inane; laughable; ludicrous; nonsensical; ridiculous; senseless; silly.*

silver lining   A moribund metaphor (SEE).

simple pleasures

simultaneously at the same time   A dimwitted redundancy (SEE). *at the same time; simultaneously.* ■ This machine does four welds *simultaneously at the same time.* USE *at the same time* or *simultaneously.* SEE ALSO *while at the same time.*

sine qua non   A foreignism (SEE). *essential; indispensable.*

sing (whistle) a different tune   A moribund metaphor (SEE).

sing for (her) supper   A moribund metaphor (SEE).

single best (most)   A dimwitted redundancy (SEE). *best (most).* ■ The *single most* important problem is discrimination among one another. DELETE *single.* ■ Good records are the *single best* way to avoid having deductions disallowed in the event you are

audited. DELETE *single.* ■ The *single biggest* issue is the cost of upgrading a substandard system. DELETE *single.*

sing like a bird   An insipid simile (SEE moribund metaphors).

sing (his) praises   *acclaim; applaud; celebrate; commend; compliment; congratulate; eulogize; extol; flatter; hail; laud; panegyrize; praise; puff; salute.*

sink or swim   A moribund metaphor (SEE).

sink (their) teeth into   A moribund metaphor (SEE).

sink to a new low

sit idly by   ■ We didn't want to *sit idly by* and wait for the commission to issue its findings.

sit on (her) duff   A moribund metaphor (SEE). *be idle; be inactive; be lazy; be unemployed; be unoccupied; dally; dawdle; loaf; loiter; loll; lounge; relax; repose; rest; tarry; unwind.*

sit on (their) hands   A moribund metaphor (SEE).

sit tight   A moribund metaphor (SEE). *be patient; hold on; wait.*

sitting on a gold mine   A moribund metaphor (SEE).

sitting pretty   *advantageous; auspicious; blessed; charmed; enchanted; favored; felicitous; flourishing; fortuitous; fortunate; golden; in luck; lucky; propitious; prosperous; successful; thriving.*

(a) situation   An overworked word

(SEE). For example: *crisis situation; difficult situation; life-threatening situation; push-pull situation; no-lose situation; no-win situation; open-ended situation; problematic situation; sad situation; tragic situation; win-win situation.* ■ It's really *a* pathetic *situation.* DELETE *a situation.* ■ If there is an emergency *situation*, then that person can exit as well. DELETE *situation.* ■ It's nice to be *in a situation where you are* recognized for the work you're doing. DELETE *in a situation where you are.* ■ The network approach *is a win-win situation for* all involved. REPLACE WITH *benefits.* SEE ALSO *remedy the situation.*

sit up and take notice

(it's) six of one, half dozen of the other   *either; either way; it doesn't matter; no matter.*

six ways to Sunday

skate on thin ice   A moribund metaphor (SEE). *chance; dare; endanger; gamble; hazard; imperil; jeopardize; make bold; peril; risk; venture.*

skeletons in the closet   A moribund metaphor (SEE).

skin and bones   A moribund metaphor (SEE). *attenuated; bony; emaciated; gaunt; lank; lanky; lean; narrow; rail-thin; scraggy; scrawny; skeletal; skinny; slender; slight; slim; spare; spindly; svelte; thin; trim; wispy.*

sleep like a log   An insipid simile (SEE moribund metaphors). *doze; nap; rest; sleep; slumber.*

sleep like a top   An insipid simile

(SEE moribund metaphors). *doze; nap; rest; sleep; slumber.*

sleep the sleep of the just   A moribund metaphor (SEE).

slice of life   A moribund metaphor (SEE).

slice of the pie   A moribund metaphor (SEE).

slim and trim   An inescapable pair (SEE). *attenuated; bony; emaciated; gaunt; lank; lanky; lean; narrow; rail-thin; scraggy; scrawny; skeletal; skinny; slender; slight; slim; spare; spindly; svelte; thin; trim; wispy.*

slim pickings

slings and arrows   A moribund metaphor (SEE).

(as) slippery as an eel   An insipid simile (SEE moribund metaphors).
1. *elusive; ephemeral; evanescent; evasive; fleeting; fugitive; passing; slippery; volatile.*
2. *crafty; cunning; deceitful; dishonest; foxy; shifty; slick; tricky; wily.*

slippery slope   A moribund metaphor (SEE).

slip through (our) fingers   A moribund metaphor (SEE).

slip through the cracks   A moribund metaphor (SEE). *discount; disregard; elide; ignore; leave out; miss; neglect; omit; overlook; slight.*

slow and steady wins the race   A popular prescription (SEE).

(as) slow as molasses (in January)   An insipid simile (SEE moribund metaphors). *crawling; dallying; dawdling; deliberate; dilatory; faltering; hesitant; laggardly; lagging; leisurely; methodical; plodding; procrastinating; slothful; slow; slow-paced; sluggardly; sluggish; snaillike; systematic; tardy; tortoiselike; unhurried.*

slow(ly) but sure(ly)   An inescapable pair (SEE).

slower than molasses (in January)   A moribund metaphor (SEE). *crawling; dallying; dawdling; deliberate; dilatory; faltering; hesitant; laggardly; lagging; leisurely; methodical; plodding; procrastinating; slothful; slow; slow-paced; sluggardly; sluggish; snaillike; systematic; tardy; tortoiselike; unhurried.*

slow to deliver

smack dab in the middle of   An infantile phrase (SEE). ■ It puts readers *smack dab in the middle of* the action.

small comfort

small potatoes   A moribund metaphor (SEE).

small price to pay

small wonder

(as) smart as a whip   An insipid simile (SEE moribund metaphors). *able; adroit; alert; apt; astute; bright; brilliant; capable; clever; competent; discerning; enlightened; intelligent; judicious; keen; knowledgeable; learned; logical; luminous; perceptive; perspicacious; quick; quick-witted; rational; rea-*sonable; sagacious; sage; sapient; sensible; sharp; shrewd; smart; sound; understanding; wise.

smart cookie   A moribund metaphor (SEE). *able; adroit; apt; astute; bright; brilliant; capable; clever; competent; discerning; enlightened; intelligent; judicious; keen; knowledgeable; learned; logical; luminous; perceptive; perspicacious; quick; rational; reasonable; sagacious; sage; sapient; sensible; sharp; shrewd; smart; sound; understanding; wise.*

smash hit

smashing success

smash to bits (smithereens)   *annihilate; assassinate; butcher; demolish; destroy; devastate; eradicate; exterminate; kill; massacre; murder; obliterate; pulverize; rack; ravage; raze; ruin; shatter; slaughter; slay; smash; undo; wrack; wreck.*

smell a rat   A moribund metaphor (SEE).

smell fishy   A moribund metaphor (SEE). *doubtful; dubious; questionable; shady; shaky; suspect; suspicious.*

smell (stink) to high heaven
A moribund metaphor (SEE). *reek; smell; stink.*

smile!   A plebeian sentiment (SEE). SEE ALSO *keep smiling.*

smoke and mirrors   A moribund metaphor (SEE). *artfulness; artifice; chicanery; cover-up; cozenage; craftiness; cunning; deceit; deceiving; deception; dissembling; dissimulation;*

duplicity; feigning; fraud; guile; pretense; shamming; trickery; wile.

smokes like a chimney   An insipid simile (SEE moribund metaphors).

smoking gun   A moribund metaphor (SEE).

(as) smooth as glass   An insipid simile (SEE moribund metaphors).
1. *burnished; even; glassy; glossy; greasy; lustrous; oily; polished; satiny; silky; sleek; slick; slippery; smooth; velvety.*
2. *apparent; basic; clear; clear-cut; conspicuous; distinct; easily done; easy; effortless; elementary; evident; explicit; facile; limpid; lucid; manifest; obvious; patent; pellucid; plain; simple; simplicity itself; simplistic; smooth; straightforward; translucent; transparent; unambiguous; uncomplex; uncomplicated; understandable; unequivocal; unmistakable.*

(as) smooth as silk   An insipid simile (SEE moribund metaphors).
1. *burnished; even; glassy; glossy; greasy; lustrous; oily; polished; satiny; silky; sleek; slick; slippery; smooth; velvety.*
2. *apparent; basic; clear; clear-cut; conspicuous; distinct; easily done; easy; effortless; elementary; evident; explicit; facile; limpid; lucid; manifest; obvious; patent; pellucid; plain; simple; simplicity itself; simplistic; smooth; straightforward; translucent; transparent; unambiguous; uncomplex; uncomplicated; understandable; unequivocal; unmistakable.*

smooth (her) feathers   A moribund metaphor (SEE). *allay; appease; assuage; calm; comfort; compose; concil-iate; console; moderate; modulate; mollify; pacify; placate; propitiate; quiet; soften; soothe; still; temper; tranquilize.*

snake in the grass   A moribund metaphor (SEE). *animal; barbarian; beast; brute; degenerate; fiend; knave; lout; monster; rake; rascal; reptile; rogue; ruffian; savage; scamp; scoundrel; villain.*

snatch victory from the jaws of defeat   A moribund metaphor (SEE).

snow job   A moribund metaphor (SEE).

(as) snug as a bug in a rug   An insipid simile (SEE moribund metaphors). *comfortable; cosy; habitable; homey; inhabitable; livable; safe; snug.*

soar to new heights

(as) sober as a judge   An insipid simile (SEE moribund metaphors).
1. *dignified; earnest; formal; grave; pensive; reserved; sedate; self-controlled; self-restrained; serious; severe; sober; solemn; somber; staid; stern; strict; subdued; thoughtful.*
2. *abstemious; sober; teetotal; temperate.*

social butterfly   A moribund metaphor (SEE).

socially redeeming value

so far so good

(as) soft as velvet   An insipid simile (SEE moribund metaphors). *delicate; downy; feathery; fine; fluffy; satiny; silken; silky; smooth; soft; velvety.*

soft landing   A moribund metaphor

(SEE). ■ The airline industry's problem is trying to determine whether this is a *soft landing* for the economy or a recession.

soft spot in (my) heart　A moribund metaphor (SEE).

soft touch　A moribund metaphor (SEE).

solemn vow

(as) solid as a rock　An insipid simile (SEE moribund metaphors).
1. *adamantine; firm; granitelike; hard; petrified; rock-hard; rocklike; rocky; solid; steellike; steely; stonelike; stony.*
2. *athletic; beefy; brawny; burly; firm; fit; hale; hardy; hearty; husky; manly; mighty; muscular; powerful; puissant; robust; rugged; sinewy; solid; stalwart; stout; strapping; strong; sturdy; tough; vigorous; virile; well-built.*
3. *constant; dependable; determined; faithful; fast; firm; fixed; inexorable; inflexible; loyal; obdurate; resolute; resolved; rigid; solid; stable; staunch; steadfast; steady; stern; strong; tenacious; unflinching; unwavering; unyielding.*

somebody's got to do it

some like it hot　An infantile phrase (SEE).

some of my best friends are
A plebeian sentiment (SEE).

(thirty)-something　■ But they're not the typical self-absorbed, *thirty-something* crowd. ■ If you give a speech on social security, your purpose will vary for audiences made up of *twenty-something, forty-something,*

or *seventy-something* individuals.

something has to give

(there's) something in the wind
A moribund metaphor (SEE).

something is rotten in (the state of) Denmark　A moribund metaphor (SEE).

(like) something out of a (Norman Rockwell) painting　An insipid simile (SEE moribund metaphors). ■ Li River cruises can take your clients past dreamlike rock formations; they *look like something out of a Salvador Dali painting.*

(it's) something to do　A plebeian sentiment (SEE). SEE ALSO *(it) gives (me) something to do; (it) keeps (me) busy; (it) keeps (me) out of trouble.*

(it's) something to look forward to　A plebeian sentiment (SEE).

(it's) something to think about
A plebeian sentiment (SEE). This phrase is often a means of dismissing and not dealing with—that is, not thinking about—what a person has said. SEE ALSO *food for thought.*

so near yet so far

song and dance　A moribund metaphor (SEE).

son of a gun　A moribund metaphor (SEE). *brute; degenerate; fiend; knave; lout; rake; rascal; rogue; ruffian; scamp; scoundrel; villain.*

so quiet you could hear a pin drop　A moribund metaphor (SEE).

sordid affair

sorely missed   An inescapable pair (SEE). ■ He is going to be *sorely missed* by his teammates.

sorry about that   An infantile phrase (SEE).

sorry I asked

sorry state of affairs

soul searching

sound advice   An inescapable pair (SEE).

(as) sound as a bell   An insipid simile (SEE moribund metaphors).
1. *cogent; convincing; intelligent; judicious; just; logical; prudent; rational; reasonable; sensible; sound; telling; valid; well-founded; well-grounded; wise.*
2. *athletic; beefy; brawny; energetic; fit; good; hale; hardy; healthful; healthy; hearty; lanky; lean; manly; muscular; powerful; robust; shapely; sinewy; slender; solid; sound; stalwart; strong; sturdy; thin; trim; vigorous; virile; well; well-built.*

(as) sound as a dollar   An insipid simile (SEE moribund metaphors).
1. *cogent; convincing; intelligent; judicious; just; logical; prudent; rational; reasonable; sensible; sound; telling; valid; well-founded; well-grounded; wise.*
2. *athletic; beefy; brawny; energetic; fit; good; hale; hardy; healthful; healthy; hearty; lanky; lean; manly; muscular; powerful; robust; shapely; sinewy; slender; solid; sound; stalwart; strong;*

sturdy; thin; trim; vigorous; virile; well; well-built.

(she) sounds like a broken record   An insipid simile (SEE moribund metaphors).

(as) sour as vinegar   An insipid simile (SEE moribund metaphors).

source of strength

sour grapes   A moribund metaphor (SEE)

sour note   A moribund metaphor (SEE).

so what else is new?   An infantile phrase (SEE).

sow the seeds of   A moribund metaphor (SEE).

sow (his) wild oats   A moribund metaphor (SEE).

spare no expense

spare (me) the details

spare the rod and spoil the child   A popular prescription (SEE).

speak for yourself

speak of the devil

speaks volumes   A moribund metaphor (SEE).

(don't) speak the same language

(she's) special   A suspect superlative (SEE).

(that) special someone   A suspect superlative (SEE). ■ If you're looking for *that special someone*, we're here to help you. ■ I still haven't met *that special someone*, but I am confident it will happen soon.

spending spree

spend money like water   An insipid simile (SEE moribund metaphors).

spick-and-span   An inescapable pair (SEE). *antiseptic; clean; cleansed; disinfected; germ-free; hygienic; immaculate; neat; orderly; sanitary; sanitized; scoured; scrubbed; spotless; spruce; stainless; sterile; tidy; unblemished; unsoiled; unspotted; unsullied; untarnished; washed.*

spilled milk   A moribund metaphor (SEE).

spill (his) guts   A moribund metaphor (SEE). *acknowledge; admit; affirm; allow; avow; concede; confess; disclose; divulge; expose; grant; own; reveal; tell; uncover; unveil.*

spill the beans   A moribund metaphor (SEE). *acknowledge; admit; affirm; allow; avow; concede; confess; disclose; divulge; expose; grant; own; reveal; tell; uncover; unveil.*

spinning (my) wheels   A moribund metaphor (SEE).

spit and image   An inescapable pair (SEE). *clone; copy; counterpart; doppelgänger; double; duplicate; exact likeness; match; twin.*

spit and polish   A moribund metaphor (SEE).

spoiled brat   An inescapable pair (SEE).

spoil rotten   A moribund metaphor (SEE). *coddle; gratify; humor; indulge; mollycoddle; overindulge; overprotect; pamper; spoil.*

spread like wildfire   An insipid simile (SEE moribund metaphors).

spread the word

spread (himself) too thin   A moribund metaphor (SEE).

(I'm no) spring chicken   A moribund metaphor (SEE).

spring has sprung

spring into action

spring to life

sprout up like mushrooms   An insipid simile (SEE moribund metaphors).

(on the) spur of the moment   *abrupt; extemporaneous; extempore; immediate; impromptu; improvised; impulsive; instant; quick; rash; spontaneous; sudden; unexpected; unprepared; unprompted; unrehearsed.*

(caught) squarely in the middle

square meal

square one

square peg in a round hole   A moribund metaphor (SEE).

squeaky clean   A moribund metaphor (SEE).

stab (her) in the back   A moribund metaphor (SEE).

stack the deck   A moribund metaphor (SEE).

(old) stamping ground   A moribund metaphor (SEE).

stamp of approval   *approval; authorization; certification; endorsement; sanction.*

stand a chance

standard operating procedure

stand at the ready

stand idly by

stand (you) in good stead

standing room only   *abounding; brimful; brimming; bursting; chockfull; congested; crammed; crowded; dense; filled; full; gorged; jammed; jampacked; overcrowded; overfilled; overflowing; packed; saturated; stuffed; swarming; teeming.*

stand (it) on (its) head

stand on (his) own two feet   A moribund metaphor (SEE).

stand on the sidelines   A moribund metaphor (SEE). ■ Surgeons who have been *standing on the sidelines* are beginning to take up the procedure themselves.

stand out from (in) the crowd

(pack)   A moribund metaphor (SEE).

stand (stick) out like a sore thumb   An insipid simile (SEE moribund metaphors). *apparent; arresting; blatant; conspicuous; evident; flagrant; glaring; gross; manifest; noticeable; observable; obtrusive; obvious; outstanding; patent; prominent; salient.*

stand up and be counted

(his) star is on the rise   A moribund metaphor (SEE).

stark raving mad   *batty; cracked; crazy; daft; demented; deranged; insane; lunatic; mad; maniacal; neurotic; nuts; nutty; psychotic; raving; squirrelly; touched; unbalanced; unhinged; unsound.*

star-studded (crowd)

(you) started it   An infantile phrase (SEE).

start from scratch

start the ball rolling   A moribund metaphor (SEE).

start with a clean slate   A moribund metaphor (SEE).

state of seige   A moribund metaphor (SEE).

staying power   *determination; durability; endurance; firmness; fortitude; permanence; permanency; perseverance; resolution; resolve; spunk; stability; stamina; steadfastness; tenacity.*

stay on target   A moribund metaphor (SEE).

stay the course

stay tuned   A moribund metaphor (SEE).

(as) steady as a rock   An insipid simile (SEE moribund metaphors).

steady diet of   A moribund metaphor (SEE).

steady stream of   A moribund metaphor (SEE).

steal the show   A moribund metaphor (SEE).

steal (her) thunder   A moribund metaphor (SEE).

steer a (clear) course

steer clear (of)   *avoid; bypass; circumvent; dodge; elude; evade; shun; sidestep; skirt.* ■ It was a signal to the new mayor to *steer cleer of* divisiveness and cliquishness. REPLACE WITH *shun.*

steer wrong   *beguile; betray; deceive; lead astray; misdirect; misguide; mislead.* ■ I trust that you won't *steer* them *wrong.* REPLACE WITH *mislead.*

stellar record

stem the flow   A moribund metaphor (SEE). *arrest; block; check; curb; end; halt; plug; quash; quell; retard; slow; squash; stay; stem; stop; suspend; terminate.*

stem the tide   A moribund metaphor (SEE). *arrest; block; check; curb; end; halt; plug; quash; quell; retard; slow; squash; stay; stem; stop; suspend; terminate.*

step into the breach

step on (his) toes   A moribund metaphor (SEE). *abuse; affront; anger; annoy; bother; displease; harm; hurt; insult; irk; irritate; offend; outrage; provoke; slight; smart; trouble; upset; vex; wound.* ■ During his five months as acting mayor, he *stepped on many people's toes.* REPLACE WITH *offended many people.*

step up to the plate   A moribund metaphor (SEE). ■ Rumors of an imminent buyout circulated, but no one *stepped up to the plate.*

stewed to the gills   A moribund metaphor (SEE). *besotted; crapulous; drunk; inebriated; intoxicated; sodden; stupefied; tipsy.*

stew in (her) own juice   A moribund metaphor (SEE).

stick in (my) craw (throat)   A moribund metaphor (SEE). *acerbate; anger; annoy; bother; bristle; chafe; enrage; envenom; exacerbate; gall; incense; inflame; infuriate; insult; irk; irritate; madden; miff; nettle; offend; rankle; rile; provoke; vex.*

stick (your) neck out   A moribund metaphor (SEE). *chance; dare; endanger; gamble; hazard; imperil; jeopardize; make bold; peril; risk; venture.* ■ They do not *stick their necks out* to initiate change; they are followers. REPLACE WITH *venture.*

sticks and stones will break my bones, but words will never hurt me   An infantile phrase (SEE).

stick together like glue   An insipid

simile (SEE moribund metaphors).

stick to (your) guns   A moribund metaphor (SEE). *hold fast; stand firm.*

stick to (your) ribs   A moribund metaphor (SEE). *fill; sate; satiate; satisfy.*

stick to the knitting   A moribund metaphor (SEE).

sticky wicket   A moribund metaphor (SEE). *affliction; annoyance; bane; bother; burden; curse; difficulty; inconvenience; irritant; irritation; load; nuisance; ordeal; pain; pest; problem; tribulation; trouble; vexation; weight; worry.*

(as) stiff as a board   An insipid simile (SEE moribund metaphors). 1. *firm; inelastic; inflexible; rigid; stiff; unbending; unmalleable; unpliable; unyielding.* 2. *awkward; ceremonious; constrained; formal; precise; priggish; prim; proper; prudish; punctilious; puritanical; reserved; starched; stiff; stilted; straitlaced; stuffy; unrelaxed; uptight.*

still and all   A dimwitted redundancy (SEE). *even so; still; yet.* ■ *Still and all,* I love her. USE *Even so* or *Still.*

(as) still as death   An insipid simile (SEE moribund metaphors).

still kicking   A moribund metaphor (SEE).

still waters run deep   A popular prescription (SEE).

stink like hell   An insipid simile (SEE moribund metaphors). *reek; smell; stink.*

stir up a hornet's nest   A moribund metaphor (SEE).

stitch in time   A moribund metaphor (SEE).

stock in trade

stolen pleasures are sweetest   A popular prescription (SEE).

stone-cold sober

stop and smell the flowers (roses)   A moribund metaphor (SEE). *be idle; be inactive; be lazy; be unoccupied; dally; dawdle; loaf; loiter; loll; lounge; relax; repose; rest; tarry; unwind.*

stop and think about it

stop beating around the bush   A moribund metaphor (SEE).

stop (them) in (their) tracks

(time to) stop talking and start acting

stop the world, I want to get off   An infantile phrase (SEE).

storm brewing   A moribund metaphor (SEE).

(the) story of (my) life   A plebeian sentiment (SEE). ■ I've always felt like an outcast; it's *the story of my life.*

straddle the fence   A moribund metaphor (SEE). *ambivalent; divided; indecisive; in doubt; irresolute; neutral; torn; uncertain; uncommitted; undecided; unsure.*

(as) straight as an arrow   An insipid simile (SEE moribund metaphors).
1. *direct; lineal; linear; straight.*
2. *decent; ethical; exemplary; good; honest; honorable; just; moral; pure; righteous; straight; upright; virtuous; wholesome.*

straight from the horse's mouth
A moribund metaphor (SEE).

straight from the shoulder
A moribund metaphor (SEE). *bluntly; candidly; directly; forthrightly; frankly; openly; outspokenly; plainly; straightforwardly; unambiguously; unequivocally.*

straight shooter   *decent; ethical; forthright; honest; just; moral; righteous; straight; trustworthy; upright; virtuous.*

strange   An overworked word (SEE). *aberrant; abnormal; anomalistic; anomalous; atypical; bizarre; curious; deviant; different; distinct; distinctive; eccentric; exceptional; extraordinary; fantastic; foreign; grotesque; idiosyncratic; independent; individual; individualistic; irregular; novel; odd; offbeat; original; peculiar; puzzling; quaint; queer; rare; remarkable; separate; singular; uncommon; unconventional; unexampled; unique; unnatural; unorthodox; unparalleled; unprecedented; unusual.*

strange bedfellows   A moribund metaphor (SEE).

stranger things have happened

streak of meanness

stressed out   *agitated; anxious; distressed; nervous; pressured; strained; stressed; stressful; tense; uneasy; worried.* ■ I was so *stressed out* that I became physically ill. REPLACE WITH *stressed.*

stretch (my) legs   A moribund metaphor (SEE). *stand; walk.*

stretch the point (truth)   A moribund metaphor (SEE). *elaborate; embellish; embroider; enhance; enlarge; exaggerate; hyperbolize; inflate; magnify; overdo; overstress; overstate; strain; stretch.*

strictly confidential   An inescapable pair (SEE).

strike a (sympathetic) chord
■ These words *struck a familiar chord* with many of the six thousand conference participants.

strike a nerve

strike another blow for

strike fear in the heart of

strike gold   A moribund metaphor (SEE).

strikes again

strike while the iron is hot
A moribund metaphor (SEE). *capitalize on; exploit.*

string of bad luck

(no) strings attached   A moribund metaphor (SEE).

stroke of genius

stroll down memory lane

(as) strong as a horse   An insipid simile (SEE moribund metaphors). *athletic; beefy; brawny; burly; energetic; fit; hale; hardy; healthful; healthy; hearty; husky; manly; mighty; muscular; powerful; puissant; robust; rugged; sinewy; solid; sound; stalwart; stout; strapping; strong; sturdy; vigorous; virile; well-built.*

(as) strong as a lion   An insipid simile (SEE moribund metaphors). *athletic; beefy; brawny; burly; energetic; fit; hale; hardy; healthful; healthy; hearty; husky; manly; mighty; muscular; powerful; puissant; robust; rugged; sinewy; solid; sound; stalwart; stout; strapping; strong; sturdy; vigorous; virile; well-built.*

(as) strong as an ox   An insipid simile (SEE moribund metaphors). *athletic; beefy; brawny; burly; energetic; fit; hale; hardy; healthful; healthy; hearty; husky; manly; mighty; muscular; powerful; puissant; robust; rugged; sinewy; solid; sound; stalwart; stout; strapping; strong; sturdy; vigorous; virile; well-built.*

strong suit   *forte; métier; specialty.*

struggle to make ends meet

(as) stubborn as a mule   An insipid simile (SEE moribund metaphors). *adamant; balky; bullheaded; cantankerous; contrary; contumacious; dogged; headstrong; inflexible; intractable; mulish; obdurate; obstinate; ornery; perverse; refractory; resolute; rigid; stubborn; unyielding; willful.*

stuff and nonsense   *absurdity; fatuousness; folly; foolishness; ludicrousness; nonsense; preposterousness; ridiculousness; rubbish; silliness.*

stuffed shirt   A moribund metaphor (SEE).

stuffed to the gills   A moribund metaphor (SEE). *abounding; brimful; brimming; bursting; chock-full; congested; crammed; crowded; dense; filled; full; gorged; jammed; jam-packed; overcrowded; overfilled; overflowing; packed; replete; saturated; stuffed; swarming; teeming.*

(major) stumbling block   A moribund metaphor (SEE). ■ Modernization of the Chinese HRM system is fraught with significant *stumbling blocks*.

stupid   An overworked word (SEE). This epithet and a few others as common are overused. Let's do our best to convince *stupid* people that they truly are by calling them, instead, *addlebrained; addleheaded; addlepated; Boeotian; bovine; cretinous; doltish; dunderheaded; fatuous; fat-witted; harebrained; hebetudinous; idiotic; imbecilic; incogitant; insensate; ludicrous; mindless; moronic; muddled; nescient; obtuse; oxlike; phlegmatic; sluggish; torpid; vacuous; witless.*

(as) sturdy as an oak   An insipid simile (SEE moribund metaphors). *athletic; beefy; brawny; burly; energetic; fit; hale; hardy; healthful; healthy; hearty; husky; manly; mighty; muscular; powerful; puissant; robust; rugged; sinewy; solid; sound; stalwart; stout; strapping; strong; sturdy; vigorous; virile; well-built.*

subsequent to   A torpid term (SEE). *after; following.* ■ *Subsequent to* the initiation of the Ethics Committee investigation, the senator took back some tapes in my possession that I had not yet transcribed. REPLACE WITH *Following.* SEE ALSO *prior to.*

substantial   An overworked word (SEE).

such is life   A plebeian sentiment (SEE). SEE ALSO *that's how (the way) it goes; that's how (the way) the ball bounces; that's how (the way) the cookie crumbles; that's life; that's life in the big city; that's show biz; what are you going to do; what can you do.*

such stuff as dreams are made of (on)

sudden fury

suddenly and without warning   A dimwitted redundancy (SEE). *suddenly; without warning.*

(don't) suffer fools gladly

suffice (it) to say

sufficient enough   A dimwitted redundancy (SEE). *enough; sufficient.* ■ Just tell them your new number, and that should be *sufficient enough.* USE *sufficient* or *enough.* SEE ALSO *adequate enough.*

sugar and spice   A moribund metaphor (SEE).

sum and substance   An inescapable pair (SEE). *basis; center; core; crux; essence; gist; heart; kernel; pith; substance; sum.*

summer doldrums

(as) sure as death   An insipid simile (SEE moribund metaphors). *assured; certain; destined; established; fated; fixed; foreordained; ineluctable; inescapable; inevitable; inexorable; irresistible; irreversible; irrevocable; ordained; prearranged; predestined; predetermined; sure; unalterable; unavoidable; unchangeable; unpreventable; unstoppable.*

(as) sure as death and taxes   An insipid simile (SEE moribund metaphors). *assured; certain; destined; established; fated; fixed; foreordained; ineluctable; inescapable; inevitable; inexorable; irresistible; irreversible; irrevocable; ordained; prearranged; predestined; predetermined; sure; unalterable; unavoidable; unchangeable; unpreventable; unstoppable.*

survival of the fittest   A popular prescription (SEE).

suspect superlatives   In dimwitted usage, superlatives are suspect. That which seems most laudable is often least, that which seems topmost, bottommost, that which seems best, worst: *a beautiful person; an amazing person; (I'm) a perfectionist; area of expertise; celebrity; class; gentleman; great; personal friend; pursuit of excellence; the best and (the) brightest; the rich and famous.*

swallow (her) pride   A moribund metaphor (SEE). *abase; chasten; debase; degrade; demean; disgrace; dishonor; embarrass; humble; humiliate; lower; mortify; shame.*

swan song   A moribund metaphor (SEE). *farewell; good-bye.*

swear by all that's holy   A moribund metaphor (SEE). *affirm; asseverate; assert; attest; aver; avow; declare; pledge; promise; swear; testify; vow; warrant.*

swear like a trooper   An insipid simile (SEE moribund metaphors). *abusive; blackguardly; coarse; crude; fescennine; foul-mouthed; indecent; lewd; obscene; profane; ribald; scurrilous; thersitical; vulgar.*

swear on a stack of Bibles   A moribund metaphor (SEE). *affirm; asseverate; assert; attest; aver; avow; declare; pledge; promise; swear; testify; vow; warrant.*

sweat bullets   A moribund metaphor (SEE).
1. *excrete; exude; ooze; perspire; sweat; swelter; wilt.*
2. *be afraid; be agitated; be anxious; be apprehensive; be distraught; be distressed; be fearful; be fretful; be impatient; be nervous; be panicky; be tense; be uneasy; be worried.*
3. *drudge; grind; grub; labor; slave; strain; strive; struggle; sweat; toil; travail; work hard.*

sweeping generalization

sweep off (her) feet   A moribund metaphor (SEE). *amaze; astonish; astound; awe; dazzle; dumbfound; flabbergast; overpower; overwhelm; shock; startle; stun; stupefy; surprise.*

sweep (it) under the (carpet) rug   A moribund metaphor (SEE).
1. *avoid; brush aside; discount; disregard; dodge; duck; ignore; neglect; omit; pass over; recoil from; shrink from; shun; shy away from; turn away from;*

withdraw from.
2. *camouflage; cloak; conceal; cover; disguise; enshroud; harbor; hide; keep secret; mask; screen; shroud; suppress; veil; withhold.* ■ The strategy was to *sweep it under the rug.* REPLACE WITH *ignore it.*

sweep (it) under the table   A moribund metaphor (SEE).
1. *avoid; brush aside; discount; disregard; dodge; duck; ignore; neglect; omit; pass over; recoil from; shrink from; shun; shy away from; turn away from; withdraw from.*
2. *camouflage; cloak; conceal; cover; disguise; enshroud; harbor; hide; keep secret; mask; screen; shroud; suppress; veil; withhold.* ■ We see the word *anti-Semitism* every day in our secular newspapers, but the word *anti-Catholic* is *swept under the table.* REPLACE WITH *brushed aside.*

(as) sweet as honey   An insipid simile (SEE moribund metaphors).
1. *honeyed; luscious; saccharine; sugary; sweet; sweetened; syrupy.*
2. *agreeable; ambrosial; beguiling; celestial; charming; delectable; delicious; delightful; divine; enchanting; engaging; enjoyable; fun; heavenly; glorious; gratifying; inviting; joyful; joyous; luscious; pleasant; pleasing; pleasurable.*

(as) sweet as pie   An insipid simile (SEE moribund metaphors).
1. *honeyed; luscious; saccharine; sugary; sweet; sweetened; syrupy.*
2. *agreeable; ambrosial; beguiling; celestial; charming; delectable; delicious; delightful; divine; enchanting; engaging; enjoyable; fun; heavenly; glorious; gratifying; inviting; joyful; joyous; luscious; pleasant; pleasing; pleasurable.*

sweet bird of youth   A moribund metaphor (SEE).

sweeten the pot   A moribund metaphor (SEE).

sweeter than honey   A moribund metaphor (SEE).
1. *honeyed; luscious; saccharine; sugary; sweet; sweetened; syrupy.*
2. *agreeable; ambrosial; beguiling; celestial; charming; delectable; delicious; delightful; divine; enchanting; engaging; enjoyable; fun; heavenly; glorious; gratifying; inviting; joyful; joyous; luscious; pleasant; pleasing; pleasurable.*

(all) sweetness and light

sweet revenge   An inescapable pair (SEE).

sweet smell of success   A moribund metaphor (SEE).

sweet young thing

swift and sure

(as) swift as an arrow   An insipid simile (SEE moribund metaphors).

swim against the tide   A moribund metaphor (SEE).

swim like a fish   An insipid simile (SEE moribund metaphors).

swim upstream   A moribund metaphor (SEE).

swim with the tide   A moribund metaphor (SEE).

swing into action

swing into high gear   A moribund metaphor (SEE).

switch gears   A moribund metaphor (SEE).

symbolic gesture

T

tabula rasa A foreignism (SEE).

tailored to individual (your) needs *customized; custom-made.*

take a back seat to A moribund metaphor (SEE).

take a bath A moribund metaphor (SEE). *lose money.*

take a beating A moribund metaphor (SEE).

take a breather *be idle; be inactive; be lazy; be unemployed; be unoccupied; dally; dawdle; loaf; loiter; loll; lounge; relax; repose; rest; tarry; unwind.*

take (appropriate) action A dim-witted redundancy (SEE). *act.* ■ By the time someone decides to *take action,* the customer may be in too deep. USE *act.*

take a dim view of A moribund metaphor (SEE). *deprecate; disapprove; dislike; frown on; object; protest.*

take a gander (at) *gaze; glance; glimpse; look; observe; stare; watch.*

take a haircut A moribund metaphor (SEE). *lose money.* ■ He sug-gested what has been plain for some time—that holders of $1.7 billion in junk bonds would probably *take a haircut.* REPLACE WITH *lose money.*

take a hit A moribund metaphor (SEE).

take a leaf (page) out of (their) book A moribund metaphor (SEE). *copy; duplicate; emulate; follow; imitate; mimic.*

take a load off (your) mind A moribund metaphor (SEE). *acknowledge; admit; affirm; allow; avow; concede; confess; disclose; divulge; expose; grant; own; reveal; tell; uncover; unveil.*

take a long, hard look (at) *analyze; assay; check out; delve into; examine; investigate; probe; scrutinize; study.* ■ We need leaders with the will and the determination to *take a long, hard look at* the structure of our government. REPLACE WITH *examine.*

take a nose dive A moribund metaphor (SEE). *collapse; crash; dive; drop; fall; nose-dive; plummet; plunge.*

take a powder A moribund metaphor (SEE). *abscond; clear out; decamp; depart; desert; disappear; escape; exit;*

flee; fly; go; go away; leave; move on; part; pull out; quit; retire; retreat; run away; take flight; take off; vacate; vanish; withdraw.

take a shine to   A moribund metaphor (SEE).

take a toll

take a turn for the better   *ameliorate; amend; come round; convalesce; gain strength; get better; heal; improve; look up; meliorate; mend; rally; recover; recuperate; refresh; regain strength; renew; revive; strengthen.*

take a turn for the worse   *decay; decline; degenerate; deteriorate; disintegrate; ebb; erode; fade; fall off; languish; lessen; wane; weaken; wither; worsen.*

take a wait-and-see attitude

take (my) ball (toys) and go home An infantile phrase (SEE).

take (your) breath away   A moribund metaphor (SEE). *amaze; astonish; astound; awe; dazzle; dumbfound; flabbergast; overpower; overwhelm; shock; startle; stun; stupefy; surprise.*

take by storm   A moribund metaphor (SEE). ■ In the two years since it was introduced as the newest drug for depression, Prozac has *taken* the mental health community *by storm*. REPLACE WITH *captivated.*

take each day as it comes   A popular prescription (SEE).

take exception to   A dimwitted redundancy (SEE). *challenge; demur; disagree with; disapprove of; dispute; find* *fault with; object to; oppose; protest; question; resent.* ■ I *take exception to* your analysis of his difficulties. USE *disagree with.* SEE ALSO *take issue with.*

take (him) for a ride   A moribund metaphor (SEE). *bamboozle; befool; beguile; bilk; bluff; cheat; con; deceive; defraud; delude; dupe; feint; fool; gyp; hoodwink; lead astray; misdirect; misguide; misinform; mislead; spoof; swindle; trick; victimize.*

take (my) hat off to   A moribund metaphor (SEE). *admire; applaud; compliment; congratulate; respect.*

take (a lot of) heat   A moribund metaphor (SEE).

take (things) in stride

take into account   A dimwitted redundancy (SEE). *allow for; consider; contemplate; examine; inspect; investigate; look at; ponder; provide for; regard; scrutinize; study; think over; weigh.* ■ The character of the army is also an important factor to *take into account.* USE *consider.* SEE ALSO *take into consideration.*

take (her) into (your) confidence

take into consideration   A dimwitted redundancy (SEE). *allow for; consider; contemplate; examine; inspect; investigate; look at; ponder; provide for; regard; scrutinize; study; think over; weigh.* ■ All this will be *taken into consideration*, and financial analysis will be done. USE *examined.* SEE ALSO *take into account.*

take issue with   A dimwitted redundancy (SEE). *challenge; demur;*

disagree with; disapprove of; dispute; find fault with; object to; oppose; protest; question; resent. ■ Some *take issue with* the state law requiring people to use seat belts. USE *object to.* SEE ALSO *take exception to.*

(I'll) take it any way (I) can get it

take it as it comes   A popular prescription (SEE).

take it a step further

(I) take it (that) back   An infantile phrase (SEE). ■ Joanie is in third place; no, *I take it back* — it's another runner. ■ I always wanted to be with someone more respectable; not respectable, *I take that back*, professional.

(we'll) take it from here (there)

take it one day (step) at a time
A popular prescription (SEE).

take it on the chin   A moribund metaphor (SEE). ■ There's no question that this group of low-waged workers is *taking it on the chin*.

take it or leave it

take it slow (and easy)

take (her) life in (her) hands
A moribund metaphor (SEE). *chance; dare; endanger; gamble; hazard; imperil; jeopardize; make bold; peril; risk; venture.*

take (his) lumps   A moribund metaphor (SEE). ■ We fought our way back to profitability after *taking our lumps*.

take matters (things) into (his) own hands

take (their) medicine   A moribund metaphor (SEE).

take on a life of its own

take the bait   A moribund metaphor (SEE).

take the bit between (in) (her) teeth   A moribund metaphor (SEE). *contumacious; defiant; disobedient; disorderly; obstreperous; rebellious; recalcitrant; refractory; resistant; riotous; unbridled; unconstrained; uncontrollable; uncontrolled; undisciplined; ungovernable; unmanageable; unrestrained; unruly.*

take the bitter with the sweet
A popular prescription (SEE).

take the bull by the horns   A moribund metaphor (SEE).

take the cake   A moribund metaphor (SEE).
1. *be best; be finest; be first; be first-rate; be outstanding; win.*
2. *be disgraceful; be lowest; be outrageous; be poorest; be worst.*

take the good with the bad

take the guesswork out of

take the heat   A moribund metaphor (SEE).

take the high road   A moribund metaphor (SEE).
1. *be beneficent; be benevolent; be broadminded; be charitable; be civil; be courteous; be gracious; be high-minded; be kind; be liberal; be magnanimous; be noble.*
2. *be decent; be ethical; be exemplary; be*

good; be honest; be honorable; be just; be moral; be pure; be respectful; be righteous; be straight; be upright; be virtuous; be wholesome.

take the idea and run with it

take the law into (our) own hands

take the money and run   A moribund metaphor (SEE). *abscond; clear out; decamp; depart; desert; disappear; escape; exit; flee; fly; go; go away; leave; make off; move on; part; pull out; quit; retire; retreat; run away; steal away; take flight; take off; vacate; vanish; withdraw.*

take the plunge   A moribund metaphor (SEE).

take the rough with the smooth
A popular prescription (SEE).

take the wind out of (his) sails
A moribund metaphor (SEE).
1. *abase; chasten; debase; decrease; deflate; degrade; demean; depreciate; depress; disgrace; dishonor; embarrass; humble; humiliate; lower; mortify; puncture; shame.*
2. *arrest; balk; block; bridle; check; curb; derail; detain; end; foil; frustrate; halt; harness; hold up; impede; inhibit; obstruct; restrain; retard; slow; stall; stay; stop; suppress; terminate; thwart.*

(to) take this opportunity (to)   An ineffectual phrase (SEE). ■ I would like *to take this opportunity* to apologize to my family and friends. DELETE *to take this opportunity.* ■ I'd like *to take this opportunity* to renew our commitment to you—to provide you with superior service. DELETE *to take this opportunity.* ■ Let me *take this opportunity to*

thank our most inspirational guest. DELETE *take this opportunity to.*

take (it) to heart

take to (his) heels   A moribund metaphor (SEE). *abscond; clear out; decamp; depart; desert; disappear; escape; exit; flee; fly; go; go away; leave; move on; part; pull out; quit; retire; retreat; run away; take flight; take off; vacate; vanish; withdraw.*

take to (it) like a duck to water
An insipid simile (SEE moribund metaphors).

take (him) to task   *admonish; animadvert; berate; blame; castigate; censure; chasten; chastise; chide; condemn; criticize; denounce; denunciate; discipline; impugn; objurgate; punish; rebuke; remonstrate; reprehend; reprimand; reproach; reprobate; reprove; revile; scold; upbraid; vituperate; warn.*
■ In polite, carefully chosen words, the auditors *take* management *to task* for a multitude of sins. REPLACE WITH *censure.*

take (her) to the cleaners   A moribund metaphor (SEE).

take to the streets

take (them) to the woodshed
A moribund metaphor (SEE). *admonish; animadvert; berate; castigate; censure; chasten; chastise; chide; condemn; criticize; denounce; denunciate; discipline; excoriate; fulminate against; imprecate; impugn; inveigh against; objurgate; punish; rebuke; remonstrate; reprehend; reprimand; reproach; reprobate; reprove; revile; scold; swear at; upbraid; vituperate; warn.*

take umbrage at   A dimwitted redundancy (SEE). *disagree with; dislike; object to; resent.* ■ I *take umbrage at* the comment he made in response to my criticism of the DA's poor performance. USE *resent.*

(I'll) take what (I) can get

(like) taking candy from a baby An insipid simile (SEE moribund metaphors).

(like) taking lambs to the slaughter   An insipid simile (SEE moribund metaphors).

tale of woe

talk a blue streak   A moribund metaphor (SEE). *babbling; blathering; chatty; facile; fluent; garrulous; glib; jabbering; logorrheic; long-winded; loquacious; prolix; talkative; verbose; voluble; windy.*

talk (my) ear (head) off   A moribund metaphor (SEE). *babbling; blathering; chatty; facile; fluent; garrulous; glib; jabbering; logorrheic; long-winded; loquacious; prolix; talkative; verbose; voluble; windy.*

talk is cheap   A quack equation (SEE).

talk on (her) feet

talk (speak) out of both sides of (his) mouth   A moribund metaphor (SEE). *avoid; dodge; doubletalk; equivocate; evade; fence; hedge; palter; prevaricate; quibble; shuffle; sidestep; tergiversate; waffle.*

(he) talks a good game   A moribund metaphor (SEE).

talk through (his) hat   A moribund metaphor (SEE).

talk turkey   A moribund metaphor (SEE).

tall, dark and handsome

tall order

tan (warm) (her) hide   A moribund metaphor (SEE). *spank.*

tar and feather   A moribund metaphor (SEE). *admonish; animadvert; berate; castigate; censure; chasten; chastise; chide; condemn; criticize; denounce; denunciate; discipline; impugn; objurgate; punish; rebuke; remonstrate; reprehend; reprimand; reproach; reprobate; reprove; revile; scold; upbraid; vituperate; warn.*

tar (him) with the same brush A moribund metaphor (SEE).

task force   *board; commission; committee; council; delegation; group; panel.*

teach (me) the ropes   A moribund metaphor (SEE).

team player   This term is much favored by those in the business world for an employee who thinks just as others do and behaves just as he is expected to. A *team player* is a person who has not the spirit to think for or be himself.

Of course, nothing new, nothing innovative is likely to be realized by insisting, as the business world does, on objectivity and consensus.

A team player is often no more than a *bootlicker;* no more than a *fawner,* a *flatterer,* a *follower;* no more than a *lackey,* a *minion,* a *stooge;* no more than a *sycophant,* a *toady,* a *yes-man.* ∎ Mulvey, whose termination is perhaps the most striking—he was one of the bank's stellar performers—was not regarded as a *team player.*

tear (out) (my) hair   A moribund metaphor (SEE).
1. *acerbated; angry; annoyed; bothered; cross; displeased; enraged; furious; grouchy; incensed; inflamed; infuriated; irate; irked; irritated; mad; miffed; peeved; provoked; riled; testy; upset; vexed.*
2. *agitated; anxious; apprehensive; distraught; distressed; fearful; frustrated; nervous; panicky; stressed; stressful; tense; tormented; troubled; uneasy; worried.*

tears (me) apart

teeter on the brink (of)   A moribund metaphor (SEE).

tell it like it is   An infantile phrase (SEE). *be honest; honest; speak the truth; truthful.* ∎ He's not whining; he's just *telling it like it is.* REPLACE WITH *being honest.* ∎ These videos may be informative and *tell it like it is* but are far too explicit and do not belong in a co-ed classroom. REPLACE WITH *truthful.*

tell it to the Marines   A moribund metaphor (SEE).

tell me about it   SEE ALSO *you're telling me.*

telltale signs

tell tales out of school   A moribund metaphor (SEE).

tempest in a teapot   A moribund metaphor (SEE).

term of endearment

terra firma   A foreignism (SEE).

terrific   An overworked word (SEE). *Terrific* means *causing terror* or *terrifying,* but of late, it means only *very bad* or, annoyingly, *very good.* ∎ I have a *terrific* stomachache. REPLACE WITH *very bad.* ∎ We had a *terrific* time at the party. REPLACE WITH *very good.* SEE ALSO *awesome; awful.*

test (their) mettle

test the waters   A moribund metaphor (SEE).

thank goodness it's Friday   An infantile phrase (SEE).

thanks but no thanks   *thanks; thanks all the same; thanks anyway; thanks just the same.*

thank you   A plebeian sentiment (SEE). Even *thank you*—once a sure sign of civility—becomes part of the plebeian patois when it is spoken mechanically.

   Only a dimwitted person is thoughtless enough to thank others for having been abused or berated by them, for having been refused or rejected by them. SEE ALSO *excuse me?; I'm sorry.*

thank(ing) you in advance   A plebeian sentiment (SEE). These phrases are more than plebeian, they are impudent. Only the lowbred or harebrained would presume to thank another for something while requesting it. ∎ We *thank you in advance* for your understanding in this situation. ■ *Thank you in advance* for taking the time to help us.

that fateful day

that makes two of us   *as I do; I do too; neither do I; no more do I; nor do I; so do I.*

that's about the size of it

that's all (I) need

that's all there is to it

that's for me to know and you to find out   An infantile phrase (SEE). SEE ALSO *it's a long story.*

that's how (the way) it goes
A plebeian sentiment (SEE). *That's how (the way) it goes* and other expressions of resignation are often spoken by some people and rarely, if at all, spoken by others.

Plebeian people are too often resigned when they should be complaining, too often resigned when they should be demanding, too often resigned when they should be raging. SEE ALSO *such is life; that's how (the way) the ball bounces; that's how (the way) the cookie crumbles; that's life; that's life in the big city; that's show biz; what are you going to do; what can you do.*

that's how (the way) the ball bounces   A plebeian sentiment (SEE). SEE ALSO *such is life; that's how (the way) it goes; that's how (the way) the cookie crumbles; that's life; that's life in the big city; that's show biz; what are you going to do; what can you do.*

that's how (the way) the cookie crumbles   A plebeian sentiment (SEE). SEE ALSO *such is life; that's how (the way) it goes; that's how (the way) the ball bounces; that's life; that's life in the big city; that's show biz; what are you going to do; what can you do.*

that's interesting   A plebeian sentiment (SEE). *That's interesting,* like *that's nice,* is most often a witless response to what a person has said. It is an acknowledgment of having been bored, a confession of having nothing clever to say. SEE ALSO *every effort is being made; interesting; that's nice.*

that's life   A plebeian sentiment (SEE). SEE ALSO *such is life; that's how (the way) it goes; that's how (the way) the ball bounces; that's how (the way) the cookie crumbles; that's life in the big city; that's show biz; what are you going to do; what can you do.*

that's life in the big city   A plebeian sentiment (SEE). SEE ALSO *such is life; that's how (the way) it goes; that's how (the way) the ball bounces; that's how (the way) the cookie crumbles; that's life; that's show biz; what are you going to do; what can you do.*

that's nice   A plebeian sentiment (SEE). This phrase is used to dismiss what a person has said. *That's nice* is a perfunctory response that, though it suggests interest in a person, actually reveals indifference to the person. SEE ALSO *every effort is being made; that's interesting.*

that's not saying much

that's only natural

that's (your) problem

that's putting it mildly

that's show biz   A plebeian sentiment (SEE). SEE ALSO *such is life; that's how (the way) it goes; that's how (the way) the ball bounces; that's how (the way) the cookie crumbles; that's life; that's life in the big city; what are you going to do; what can you do.*

that's the thing   An ineffectual phrase (SEE). SEE ALSO *here's the thing; the thing about (of) it is; the thing is.*

that's the ticket

that's the trick

that's what it's all about   A popular prescription (SEE). ■ It's the little things — like playing with my son — *that's what it's all about.*

that's where (you) come in

that's where (you) enter the picture   A moribund metaphor (SEE).

that was then and this is now

the Achilles heel of   A moribund metaphor (SEE).

the agony and the ecstasy   A moribund metaphor (SEE).

the agony of defeat

the almighty dollar   A moribund metaphor (SEE).

the alpha and omega of   A moribund metaphor (SEE).

the American dream   A suspect superlative (SEE). ■ *The American dream* has become a nightmare.

the American way

the apple doesn't fall far from the tree   A popular prescription (SEE).

the apple of (my) eye   A moribund metaphor (SEE).

the ax fell   A moribund metaphor (SEE).

the ball's in (your) court   A moribund metaphor (SEE). ■ I think, nationally, *the ball is* definitely *in our court* now.

the bane of (my) existence

the battle of the sexes

(and) the beat goes on

the beginning of the end

the belle of the ball

the best and (the) brightest
A suspect superlative (SEE). *best; brightest; choice; choicest; elite; excellent; finest; first-class; first-rate; foremost; greatest; highest; matchless; outstanding; paramount; peerless; preeminent; premium; prominent; select; superior; superlative; top; unequaled; unexcelled; unmatched; unrivaled; unsurpassed.* ■ He decried the "cult of efficiency" into which have fallen so many of *the best and brightest* of the conservative young. REPLACE WITH *the brightest.*

the best defense is a good offense

A popular prescription (SEE).

the best is still (yet) to come

the best (that) money can buy
A suspect superlative (SEE).

(in) the best of all (possible)
worlds   *ideally*. ■ *In the best of all
possible worlds*, test procedures for
which neither type of error is possible
could be developed. REPLACE WITH *Ideally*.

the best of both worlds

the best show in town

the best thing since sliced bread
A moribund metaphor (SEE).

the best things in life are free
A popular prescription (SEE).

(she's) the best thing that ever
happened to (me)   A plebeian sentiment (SEE).

the big (4)0

the big boys

the bigger the better   A quack
equation (SEE).

the bigger they are, the harder
they fall   A popular prescription
(SEE).

the big picture   A moribund metaphor (SEE). ■ Let's not make decisions
without looking at *the big picture*.

the blind leading the blind   A moribund metaphor (SEE).

the bloom is off the rose   A moribund metaphor (SEE).

the bottom fell out   A moribund
metaphor (SEE). ■ He elected to stop
financing condominium projects nearly two years before *the bottom fell out*
of that business.

the bread always falls on the buttered side   A moribund metaphor
(SEE).

the buck stops here

the calm before the storm   A moribund metaphor (SEE).

the cat's meow   A moribund metaphor (SEE).

the cat's out of the bag   A moribund metaphor (SEE).

(look) (like) the cat that swallowed
the canary   An insipid simile (SEE
moribund metaphors). *complacent;
self-satisfied; smug*.

the chance (opportunity) of a lifetime

the child is father of the man
A popular prescription (SEE).

the clock is ticking   A moribund
metaphor (SEE).

the coast is clear   A moribund metaphor (SEE).

the ... (you've) come (grown) to
love

the common denominator   A moribund metaphor (SEE).

the cook's tour   A moribund metaphor (SEE).

the court of public opinion

the cream of the crop   A moribund metaphor (SEE). *best; brightest; choice; choicest; elite; excellent; finest; first-class; first-rate; foremost; greatest; highest; matchless; outstanding; paramount; peerless; preeminent; premium; prominent; select; superior; superlative; top; unequaled; unexcelled; unmatched; unrivaled; unsurpassed.*

the cruelest of ironies

the customer is always right

the dawn of a new age (era)   A moribund metaphor (SEE).

the dead of night

the dead of winter

the deck stacked against (him)   A moribund metaphor (SEE).

the devil finds work for idle hands to do   A popular prescription (SEE).

the devil take the hindmost   A moribund metaphor (SEE).

(there will be) the devil to pay

the die is cast   A moribund metaphor (SEE).

the difference between night and day

the doctor is in

the dog days of summer   A moribund metaphor (SEE).

(when) the dust settles   A moribund metaphor (SEE).

the early bird catches the worm   A popular prescription (SEE).

(take) the easy way out

the eighth wonder of the world

the element of surprise

the end all and be all

the end justifies the means   A popular prescription (SEE).

the end of an era

the end of civilization as we know it

the end of the line

the enemy within

the envelope, please

the evil empire   A moribund metaphor (SEE).

the exception (and) not the rule   *aberrant; abnormal; anomalistic; anomalous; atypical; bizarre; curious; deviant; different; distinct; distinctive; eccentric; exceptional; extraordinary; fantastic; foreign; grotesque; idiosyncratic; independent; individual; individualistic; irregular; notable; noteworthy; novel; odd; offbeat; original; peculiar; puzzling; quaint; queer; rare; remarkable; separate; singular; uncommon; unconventional; unexampled;*

unique; unnatural; unorthodox; unparalleled; unprecedented; unusual.

Speakers and writers find it easier to mimic a repeatedly used phrase like this — however wordy and inexact, however obtuse and benumbing — than to remember a rarely used word like *aberrant* or *anomalous.* ■ Today, in region after region, single-town school districts are *the exception, not the rule.* REPLACE WITH *exceptional.* ■ Arrest or issuing a citation is *the exception, not the rule.* REPLACE WITH *atypical.*

the exception that proves the rule   An infantile phrase (SEE).

the exception to the rule   *aberrant; abnormal; anomalistic; anomalous; atypical; bizarre; curious; deviant; different; distinct; distinctive; eccentric; exceptional; extraordinary; fantastic; foreign; grotesque; idiosyncratic; independent; individual; individualistic; irregular; notable; noteworthy; novel; odd; offbeat; original; peculiar; puzzling; quaint; queer; rare; remarkable; separate; singular; uncommon; unconventional; unexampled; unique; unnatural; unorthodox; unparalleled; unprecedented; unusual.*

the eyes of the (nation) are upon you

the face that launched a thousand ships   A moribund metaphor (SEE).

the (simple) fact is (that)   An ineffectual phrase (SEE). ■ *The fact is* at least the governor is trying. DELETE *The fact is.* ■ *The simple fact is* we are now spending nearly $1 trillion on health care. DELETE *The simple fact is.* ■ *The simple fact is* American women

are buying guns like they've never bought them before. DELETE *The simple fact is.*

the fact of the matter is   An ineffectual phrase (SEE). ■ *The fact of the matter is* the police took the children from you. DELETE *The fact of the matter is.* ■ Despite her behavior, *the fact of the matter is* I still love her. DELETE *the fact of the matter is.* SEE ALSO *the truth of the matter is.*

the fact remains (that)   An ineffectual phrase (SEE). ■ We call this campaign a "snoozer," but *the fact remains* both candidates did behave responsibly. DELETE *the fact remains.*

the fact that   An ineffectual phrase (SEE). ■ *The fact that* many more computers are in communication with one another increases concern that users' privacy will be violated. USE *That.* ■ *The fact that* she was rather attractive did not escape their notice. USE *That.*

the fair sex   *femaleness; females; femininity; muliebrity; womanhood; womankind; womankind; womanliness; women; womenkind.* SEE ALSO *the weaker sex.*

the family that ... together stays together   A popular prescription (SEE).

the fat's in the fire   A moribund metaphor (SEE).

the feeling's mutual   An infantile phrase (SEE).

the final (last) frontier   A moribund metaphor (SEE).

(that's) the final (last) straw
A moribund metaphor (SEE).

the finer things in life

the first step is always the hardest   A popular prescription (SEE).

the flip side   A moribund metaphor (SEE).

the four corners of the earth (world)   ■ These changes will affect our American patients as well as those who come to the clinic from *the four corners of the world.*

the (date) from hell   A moribund metaphor (SEE).

the fruits of (your) labor

the future is now

the gap between rich and poor

the genie is out of the bottle
A moribund metaphor (SEE).

the genuine article

the gift of time

(get) the go-ahead   *allowance; approval; authority; authorization; blessing; consent; freedom; leave; liberty; license; permission; permit; power; sanction.*

the good die young

the good doctor   An infantile phrase (SEE). ■ I think everything *the good doctor* has said is hogwash.

the good news is (that)   ■ *The*

good news is that most students report that speaking gets easier as the term progresses.

the good news is . . . the bad news is

the good old days   *history; the past; yesterday.*

the good outweighs the bad

the good, the bad and the ugly

(kill) the goose that lays the golden egg   A moribund metaphor (SEE).

the grass is (always) greener (on the other side of)   A popular prescription (SEE).

the great American novel   A suspect superlative (SEE).

the great beyond   *afterlife; eternity; everlastingness.*

the greatest show on earth

the greatest story ever told

(get) the green light   A moribund metaphor (SEE). *allowance; approval; assent; authority; authorization; blessing; consent; freedom; leave; liberty; license; permission; permit; power; sanction.* ■ The Baby Bells — which already have *the green light* to go into just about any other venture — have railed against the remaining restrictions since they were imposed. REPLACE WITH *permission.* ■ The FBI was given *the green light* by the Justice Department to continue its investigation. REPLACE WITH *authorization.* SEE ALSO *(get) the red light.*

the hand that rocks the cradle (rules the world)   A popular prescription (SEE).

the have-nots   *broke; destitute; distressed; impecunious; impoverished; indigent; insolvent; needy; penniless; poor; poverty-stricken; underprivileged.* ■ You, I, and many others can afford to pay a little more for health insurance if it gives some to the *have-nots*. REPLACE WITH *indigent*.

the haves   *affluent; comfortable; moneyed; opulent; privileged; prosperous; rich; wealthy; well-off; well-to-do.*

the heat is on   A moribund metaphor (SEE).

the height of absurdity

the height of hypocrisy

(down) the home stretch   A moribund metaphor (SEE).

the hostess with the mostess   An infantile phrase (SEE).

the human condition

the impossible dream

the ins and outs of

the inside story

the inside track   A moribund metaphor (SEE).

the in thing   ■ Chili peppers and howling wolves are *the in thing* in Sante Fe.

the jewel in the crown

the jig is up

the jury is still out   A moribund metaphor (SEE). ■ *The jury is still out* on how the Medicare cuts will actually be carried out.

the (whole) kit and caboodle   A moribund metaphor (SEE). *aggregate; all; all things; entirety; everything; gross; lot; sum; total; totality; whole.*

the land of milk and honey   A moribund metaphor (SEE).

the land of nod   A moribund metaphor (SEE). *sleep; slumber.*

the land of opportunity

the larger picture

the last thing (I) need (want) is   ■ *The last thing you want* is to discover you are responsible for their mistakes.

(had) the last word

the late, great

the law is the law   A quack equation (SEE).

the law of the land

the lesser of two evils

the less said, the better   A popular prescription (SEE).

the letter of the law

(live) the life of Riley   A moribund metaphor (SEE).
1. *be affluent; be moneyed; be opulent;*

be prosperous; be rich; be wealthy; be well-off; be well-to-do.
2. be extravagant; be lavish; be lush; be luxuriant; be sumptuous; be very well.

the light at the end of the tunnel
A moribund metaphor (SEE). ■ That's when *the light at the end of the tunnel* went out.

the likes of which (we've) never seen before

the lion's share   A moribund metaphor (SEE). *almost all; most; much; nearly all.* ■ The company was late to develop HMOs, and it let competitors grab *the lion's share* of the market. REPLACE WITH *most.*

the little boys' (girls') room   An infantile phrase (SEE).

the little woman   An infantile phrase (SEE). *consort; helpmate; helpmeet; mate; spouse; wife.*

the long and (the) short of (it)
A dimwitted redundancy (SEE). *basis; center; core; crux; essence; gist; heart; kernel; pith; substance.*

the long arm of the law

the look and feel (of)   ■ It's filled with tradition—with campus legends and ritual that go back to 1846—and it has *the look and feel* that evoke nostalgia.

(he's) the love of my life

the luck of the draw

the main event   A moribund metaphor (SEE).

the man in the street   A moribund metaphor (SEE). *citizen; commoner; everyman; pleb; plebeian; vulgarian.*

the manner (means; mechanism; method; procedure; process) by (in) which   A dimwitted redundancy (SEE). These magisterial-sounding phrases should be replaced by one of the least stately of words: *how.* ■ I'm not going to discuss *the methods by which* we achieved that. USE *how.* ■ The philosophical methodology specifies *the procedure by which* concepts will be used to construct a theory. USE *how.* ■ It does less well in explaining *the process by which* a particular firm decides to implement a price change. USE *how.* ■ Virtually all of them have been critical of *the manner in which* the administration dealt with the situation. USE *how.*

the man who came to dinner
An infantile phrase (SEE).

the medium is the message
A quack equation (SEE).

the meek shall inherit the earth
A popular prescription (SEE).

the me generation

the men in white coats   A moribund metaphor (SEE).

the Midas touch   A moribund metaphor (SEE).

the milk of human kindness
A moribund metaphor (SEE). *commiseration; compassion; sympathy; understanding.*

the moment (you've) all been waiting for

the moment of truth

the more the merrier   A quack equation (SEE).

the more things change, the more they stay the same   A popular prescription (SEE).

the morning after

the name of the game

(right) then and there

the nature of the beast

thence   An archaism (SEE).
1. *from that place; from there.*
2. *from that time.*
3. *hence; therefore; thus.*

the object of (my) desire

the only game in town

the only good (cat) is a dead (cat)   A quack equation (SEE).

the opening (latest) salvo   A moribund metaphor (SEE).

the opportunity at hand

the opportunity presented itself

the opposite of love is indifference   A popular prescription (SEE).

the other side of the coin   A moribund metaphor (SEE).

the other woman

the party's over

the path of least resistance

the peace process

the pen is mightier than the sword   A moribund metaphor (SEE).

the picture of health

the pits   A moribund metaphor (SEE).
1. *abhorrent; abominable; appalling; atrocious; awful; beastly; detestable; disagreeable; disgusting; dreadful; frightening; frightful; ghastly; grisly; gruesome; horrendous; horrible; horrid; horrifying; inhuman; loathsome; objectionable; obnoxious; odious; offensive; repellent; repugnant; repulsive; revolting; terrible; terrifying; unspeakable; unutterable.*
2. *calamitous; deplorable; depressing; distressing; disturbing; grievous; lamentable; unfortunate; upsetting; sad; tragic; woeful.*

the plot thickens

the point of no return   A moribund metaphor (SEE).

the possibilities are endless

(like) the pot calling the kettle black   An insipid simile (SEE moribund metaphors).

the power of positive thinking

the power of the purse   A moribund metaphor (SEE).

the powers that be   ■ *The powers that be* have done it again.

the proof of the pudding (is in the

eating) A popular prescription (SEE).

the quick and the dead A moribund metaphor (SEE).

the raw end of the deal

the real McCoy A moribund metaphor (SEE). *actual; authentic; genuine; legitimate; pure; real; sterling; true; unadulterated; unalloyed; veritable.*

the real stuff

the real thing

the real world

there are no easy answers

there are no guarantees

there are no words to describe
There are many more words than people seem to think, and far more is expressible with them than people seem to imagine.

Those who depend on dimwitticisms to convey thought and feeling are more apt to believe *there are no words to describe* . . . , for these people are, necessarily, most frustrated by the limits of language.

Dimwitticisms do permit us to describe our most universal feelings, our most banal thoughts, but they prevent us from describing more individual feelings, more brilliant thoughts. These are reserved for a language largely unknown to everyday speakers and dimwitted writers.

there are only so many hours in a day

there are other fish in the sea
A moribund metaphor (SEE).

there are two sides to every (question) story A popular prescription (SEE).

(so) the reasoning goes

(get) the red light A moribund metaphor (SEE). SEE ALSO *(get) the green light.*

therein lies a tale

there's a first time for everything A popular prescription (SEE).

there's a time and a place for everything A popular prescription (SEE).

there's more than one way to skin a cat A popular prescription (SEE).

there's no accounting for taste
A popular prescription (SEE).

there's no fool like an old fool
A popular prescription (SEE).

there's no (such thing as a) free lunch A popular prescription (SEE).

there's no getting away from (it)

there's no going back A popular prescription (SEE).

there's no harm in trying A popular prescription (SEE).

there's no other word for it

there's no place like home A popular prescription (SEE).

there's no rest for the weary
A popular prescription (SEE).

there's nothing new under the sun   A popular prescription (SEE).

there's no time like the present
A popular prescription (SEE). ■ They say *there's no time like the present* and that's never been truer.

there's no turning back (now)

there's nowhere to go but up
A popular prescription (SEE).

there's only one way to find out

there's plenty more where (that) came from

there's safety (strength) in numbers   A popular prescription (SEE).

there's the rub

(and) the rest is history   An infantile phrase (SEE).

the rich and famous   A suspect superlative (SEE). *The rich and famous* infatuate only dimwitted people, who are as boring to themselves as they are barren of themselves. ■ It has become a summer hideaway for *the rich and famous.* SEE ALSO *celebrity; fame and fortune.*

the rich get richer and the poor get poorer   A popular prescription (SEE).

(a case of) the right hand not knowing what the left hand is doing
A moribund metaphor (SEE).

(all) the right moves

the right stuff   *ability; aptitude; capability; capacity; competence; expertise; intelligence; proficiency; skill; talent.*
■ Why did I hope that Zahn would show us that she has *the right stuff* to outshine her two rivals? REPLACE WITH *the skill.*

the ripe old age of

the rise and fall of

the road to hell is paved with good intentions   A popular prescription (SEE).

the rock of Gibraltar   A moribund metaphor (SEE).
1. *beefy; brawny; burly; energetic; firm; fit; hale; hardy; healthful; healthy; hearty; husky; manly; mighty; muscular; powerful; puissant; robust; rugged; sinewy; solid; sound; stalwart; stout; strapping; strong; sturdy; tough; vigorous; virile; well-built.*
2. *constant; dependable; determined; faithful; fast; firm; fixed; inexorable; inflexible; loyal; obdurate; resolute; resolved; rigid; solid; stable; staunch; steadfast; steady; stern; strong; tenacious; unflinching; unwavering; unyielding.*

the roof fell in   A moribund metaphor (SEE).

(money is) the root of all evil
A popular prescription (SEE).

the rule rather than the exception
basic; common; commonplace; conventional; customary; general; normal; ordinary; quotidian; regular; routine; standard; typical; uneventful; unexcep-

tional; unremarkable; usual. ■ New advertising campaigns costing $5 million or even $10 million are becoming *the rule rather than the exception.* REPLACE WITH *common.*

the rules of the game   A moribund metaphor (SEE).

the rules of the road   A moribund metaphor (SEE).

the salt of the earth   A moribund metaphor (SEE).

the same but different

these are trying times

the second American Revolution A moribund metaphor (SEE).

the second time around

these things happen

(cost) the shirt off (my) back A moribund metaphor (SEE).

the shocking truth

the shoe is on the other foot A moribund metaphor (SEE).

the short end of the stick   A moribund metaphor (SEE).

the short list

the show must go on   A popular prescription (SEE).

the sign of things to come

the silence was deafening

the silent majority   A moribund metaphor (SEE). *all; citizenry; commonage; commonalty; common people; crowd; everybody; everyone; followers; herd; hoi polloi; masses; mob; multitude; plebeians; populace; proletariat; public; rabble.*

the situation is under control

the $64,000 question   An infantile phrase (SEE). ■ That's *the $64,000 question.* REPLACE WITH *the key.*

the sky's the limit   A moribund metaphor (SEE).

the slings and arrows of outrageous fortune   A moribund metaphor (SEE).

the sooner the better   A quack equation (SEE).

the sound and the fury   A moribund metaphor (SEE).

the spirit is willing, but the flesh is weak

the spitting image   *clone; copy; counterpart; doppelgänger; double; duplicate; exact likeness; match; twin.*

the squeaky wheel gets the grease   A popular prescription (SEE).

the staff of life   A moribund metaphor (SEE). *bread.*

the stage has been set   A moribund metaphor (SEE). ■ *The stage has been set* for a contract that will have to contain genuine reforms.

the start of a new day

the straight and narrow (path)
decent; ethical; exemplary; good; honest; honorable; just; moral; pure; righteous; straight; upright; virtuous; wholesome.

the straw that broke the camel's back A moribund metaphor (SEE).

the stuff dreams (legends) are made of A moribund metaphor (SEE).

the summer (winter) of (our) discontent A moribund metaphor (SEE).

the sun, the moon and the stars A moribund metaphor (SEE).

the suspense is killing (me)

(a case of) the tail wagging the dog A moribund metaphor (SEE).

the talk of the town

the temper of our time A moribund metaphor (SEE).

(stand) the test of time

the thing about (of) it is An ineffectual phrase (SEE). ■ *The thing about it is* it's humiliating and destructive to the psyche to be hit. DELETE *The thing about it is.* ■ *The thing about it is,* what they say or do has no influence on what I do. DELETE *The thing about it is.* ■ *The thing about it is,* I could never tell her anything. DELETE *The thing about it is.* SEE ALSO *here's the thing; that's the thing; the thing is.*

the thing is An ineffectual phrase

(SEE). ■ *The thing is,* we know sexual orientation is discovered prior to adolescence. DELETE *The thing is.* ■ *The thing is,* I work two jobs, and when I get home I want to relax. DELETE *The thing is.* ■ But *the thing is,* there's always someone who knows where they are. DELETE *the thing is.* SEE ALSO *here's the thing; that's the thing; the thing about (of) it is.*

the three musketeers A moribund metaphor (SEE).

the thrill of the chase

the thrill of victory

the tide of A moribund metaphor (SEE). SEE ALSO *a barrage of.*

the ties that bind

the time has come ■ *The time has come* to recognize that personal diaries must be accorded greater protection than business records.

the time is now

the time is right

the time is ripe

the time of (your) life

the toast of the town A moribund metaphor (SEE).

the tricks of the trade

the truth of the matter is An ineffectual phrase (SEE). ■ *The truth of the matter is,* half of the people who get married end up divorced. DELETE *The truth of the matter is.* ■ *The truth of the* *matter is,* I don't understand it, but I'm against it. DELETE *The truth of the matter is.* SEE ALSO *the fact of the matter is.*

the truth, the whole truth, and nothing but the truth

the truth will out

the truth will prevail

the truth will set you free   A popular prescription (SEE).

the walking dead   A moribund metaphor (SEE).

the wave of the future   A moribund metaphor (SEE).

the way to a man's heart is through his stomach   A popular prescription (SEE).

the way to go

the weaker sex   *femaleness; females; femininity; muliebrity; womanhood; womankind; womanliness; women; womenkind.* SEE ALSO *the fair sex.*

the weak link (in the chain)   A moribund metaphor (SEE).

the wee small hours (of the morning)

the whole ball of wax   A moribund metaphor (SEE). *aggregate; all; all things; entirety; everything; gross; lot; sum; total; totality; whole.*

the whole is greater than the sum of its parts   A popular prescription (SEE).

the whole nine yards   A moribund metaphor (SEE). *aggregate; all; all things; entirety; everything; gross; lot; sum; total; totality; whole.*

the whole shebang   A moribund metaphor (SEE). *aggregate; all; all things; entirety; everything; gross; lot; sum; total; totality; whole.*

the whole shooting match   A moribund metaphor (SEE). *aggregate; all; all things; entirety; everything; gross; lot; sum; total; totality; whole.*

the who, what and why of

the why and (the) wherefore   A dimwitted redundancy (SEE). *aim; cause; design; end; goal; intent; intention; motive; object; objective; purpose; reason.*

the wisdom of the ages

the wolf at the door   A moribund metaphor (SEE).

the wonderful world of   A moribund metaphor (SEE).

the wonders of modern technology

the (F)-word   An infantile phrase (SEE). ■ Many men have trouble with *the C-word.* REPLACE WITH *commitment.* ■ During the holidays, many people write and ask about *the D-word,* depression. DELETE *the D-word.* ■ Nearly everyone involved with the contract was using *the H-word,* "historic," to describe it. DELETE *the H-word.*

the world is (his) oyster   A moribund metaphor (SEE).

(one of) the world's leading authorities

(and) the world will beat a path to (your) door   A moribund metaphor (SEE).

(looks) the worse for wear   *damaged; decayed; deteriorated; dingy; dirty; filthy; flimsy; foul; frayed; grimy; grubby; grungy; ragged; rickety; seedy; shabby; shaky; soiled; sordid; sullied; squalid; tattered; tottering; unclean; unsound; worn.*

the worst is still (yet) to come

the worst of all (possible) worlds A moribund metaphor (SEE).

the wrong side of the tracks A moribund metaphor (SEE).

they don't make . . . like they used to

the yin and the yang   A moribund metaphor (SEE).

they're made for each other

(as) thick as molasses   An insipid simile (SEE moribund metaphors). *concentrated; congealed; gelatinous; gluey; glutinous; gooey; gummy; inspissated; jellied; jellified; jellylike; mucilaginous; sticky; thick; viscid; viscous.*

(as) thick as thieves   An insipid simile (SEE moribund metaphors). *amiable; amicable; attached; brotherly; chummy; close; confidential; devoted; familiar; friendly; inseparable; intimate; loving; thick.*

(as) thin as a rail   An insipid simile

(SEE moribund metaphors). *attenuated; bony; emaciated; gaunt; lank; lanky; lean; narrow; rail-thin; scraggy; scrawny; skeletal; skinny; slender; slight; slim; spare; spindly; svelte; thin; trim; wispy.*

(as) thin as a reed   An insipid simile (SEE moribund metaphors). *attenuated; bony; emaciated; gaunt; lank; lanky; lean; narrow; rail-thin; scraggy; scrawny; skeletal; skinny; slender; slight; slim; spare; spindly; svelte; thin; trim; wispy.*

(a) thing   An overworked word (SEE). ▪ The mind is *an* amazing *thing.* DELETE *an thing.* ▪ It's *a* very important *thing.* DELETE *a thing.* ▪ We have won the battle, but the war is *an* ongoing *thing.* DELETE *an thing.* ▪ I think that change is *a* good *thing.* DELETE *a thing.*

things are looking up

things are seldom (aren't always) what they seem

things change

things fall apart

think positively

(to) think the unthinkable

thinly veiled

third time's the charm

thirty-something   ▪ But they're not the typical self-absorbed, *thirtysomething* crowd.

this and that   A grammatical gimmick (SEE).

this calls for a celebration

this can't be happening (to me)
A plebeian sentiment (SEE).

this hurts (me) more than it hurts
(you)

this isn't the time or place (to)

this is the first day of the rest of
your life   A popular prescription
(SEE).

this is the happiest day of my life

this is the saddest day of my life

this is to inform you that   An ineffectual phrase (SEE). ■ *This is to inform you that* your credit application
has been approved and your account is
now open. DELETE *This is to inform
you that*. SEE ALSO *(please) be advised
that; (please) be informed that*.

this, too, shall (will) pass

thorn in (my) flesh (side)   A moribund metaphor (SEE). *affliction; annoyance; bane; bother; burden; curse;
difficulty; inconvenience; irritant; irritation; load; nuisance; ordeal; pain;
pest; plague; problem; torment; tribulation; trouble; vexation; weight; worry.*

those who can, do; those who can't,
teach   A popular prescription (SEE).

three sheets to the wind   A moribund metaphor (SEE). *besotted; crapulous; drunk; inebriated; intoxicated;
sodden; stupefied; tipsy.*

three strikes and you're out
A moribund metaphor (SEE).

three-time loser

thrilled to death   *blissful; blithe;
buoyant; cheerful; delighted; ecstatic;
elated; enraptured; euphoric; exalted; excited; exhilarated; exultant; gay; glad;
gleeful; good-humored; happy; intoxicated; jolly; jovial; joyful; joyous; jubilant; merry; mirthful; overjoyed;
pleased; rapturous; thrilled.* SEE ALSO *to
death.*

thrills and chills   An inescapable
pair (SEE).

through and through   *all through;
completely;   entirely;   thoroughly;
throughout; totally; utterly; wholly.*

through thick and thin   A moribund metaphor (SEE).

throw (a dog) a bone   A moribund
metaphor (SEE).

throw (her) a curve   A moribund
metaphor (SEE). *bamboozle; befool; beguile; bilk; bluff; cheat; con; deceive; defraud; delude; dupe; feint; fool; gyp;
hoodwink; lead astray; misdirect; misguide; misinform; mislead; spoof; swindle; trick; victimize.*

throw a monkey wrench into the
works   A moribund metaphor (SEE).
1. *agitate; confuse; disorder; disorganize; disquiet; disrupt; disturb; fluster;
jar; jinx; jolt; jumble; mix up; muddle;
perturb; rattle; ruffle; shake up; stir up;
unnerve; unsettle; upset.*
2. *blight; cripple; damage; disable;
harm; hurt; impair; incapacitate; lame;
mar; mess up; rack; ruin; sabotage;
spoil; subvert; undermine; vitiate;
wrack; wreck.*

throw a wet blanket on   A moribund metaphor (SEE). *bridle; check; constrain; contain; curb; curtail; dampen; discourage; foil; harness; hinder; impede; inhibit; obstruct; quell; repress; restrain; restrict; retard; stifle; subdue; suppress; thwart; weaken.* SEE ALSO *throw cold water on.*

throw caution to the wind   A moribund metaphor (SEE). *chance; dare; endanger; gamble; hazard; imperil; jeopardize; make bold; peril; risk; venture.*

throw cold water on   A moribund metaphor (SEE). *bridle; check; constrain; contain; curb; curtail; dampen; discourage; foil; harness; hinder; impede; inhibit; obstruct; quell; repress; restrain; restrict; retard; stifle; subdue; suppress; thwart; weaken.* SEE ALSO *throw a wet blanket on.*

throw down the gauntlet (glove)   A moribund metaphor (SEE). *affront; brave; call; challenge; confront; dare; defy; encounter; face; meet.*

throw dust in (your) eyes   A moribund metaphor (SEE). *bamboozle; befool; beguile; bilk; bluff; cheat; con; deceive; defraud; delude; dupe; feint; fool; gyp; hoodwink; lead astray; misdirect; misguide; misinform; mislead; spoof; swindle; trick; victimize.*

throw enough dirt, and some will stick   A moribund metaphor (SEE).

throw for a loop   A moribund metaphor (SEE). *amaze; astonish; astound; awe; dazzle; dumbfound; flabbergast; overpower; overwhelm; shock; startle; stun; stupefy; surprise.*

throw good money after bad

throw (toss) (his) hat in the ring   A moribund metaphor (SEE).

throw in the sponge (towel)   A moribund metaphor (SEE). *abdicate; accede; acquiesce; bow; capitulate; cede; concede; give in; give up; quit; relinquish; retreat; submit; succumb; surrender; yield.* ■ The bloated bureaucracy remains unscathed, spending continues uncontrolled, and the House leadership has *thrown in the towel* to the governor. REPLACE WITH *acquiesced.*

throw money at

throw (them) off the scent   A moribund metaphor (SEE). *bamboozle; befool; beguile; bilk; bluff; cheat; conhoodwink; lead astray; deceive; defraud; delude; dupe; feint; fool; gyp; misdirect; misguide; misinform; mislead; spoof; swindle; trick.*

throw out the baby with the bath water   A moribund metaphor (SEE).

throw the book at   A moribund metaphor (SEE). *admonish; animadvert; berate; castigate; censure; chasten; chastise; chide; condemn; criticize; denounce; denunciate; discipline; excoriate; fulminate against; imprecate; impugn; inveigh against; objurgate; penalize; punish; rebuke; remonstrate; reprehend; reprimand; reproach; reprobate; reprove; revile; scold; swear at; upbraid; vituperate; warn.*

throw the bum(s) out

throw (them) to the wolves   A moribund metaphor (SEE).

throw up (my) hands in despair

throw (his) weight around
A moribund metaphor (SEE). *awe;
browbeat; bully; frighten; intimidate;
menace; push around; scare; threaten;
torment.*

thumb (his) nose (at)   A moribund
metaphor (SEE). *contemn; deride; despise; detest; disdain; jeer at; laugh at;
mock; ridicule; scoff at; scorn; shun;
slight; sneer; snub; spurn.* ■ We burden
our own banks with record keeping
and reporting while offshore bankers
thumb their noses at us. REPLACE WITH
mock.

(turn) thumbs down   A moribund
metaphor (SEE). *decline; deny; disallow; disapprove; forbid; nix; prohibit;
proscribe; refuse; reject; rule out; say no;
turn down; veto.*

thunderous applause   An inescapable pair (SEE).

tickled pink   A moribund metaphor
(SEE). *blissful; buoyant; cheerful; delighted; elated; excited; gay; glad; gladdened; gleeful; good-humored; gratified;
happy; jolly; jovial; joyful; joyous; jubilant; merry; mirthful; pleased; tickled.*

tickled to death   *blissful; buoyant;
cheerful; delighted; elated; excited; gay;
glad; gladdened; gleeful; good-humored;
gratified; happy; jolly; jovial; joyful; joyous; jubilant; merry; mirthful; pleased;
tickled.* SEE ALSO *to death.*

tied to (her) apron strings   A moribund metaphor (SEE). *clinging; dependent; subject; subordinate; subservient.*

tie the knot   A moribund metaphor
(SEE). *marry; wed.*

tie up loose ends   A moribund metaphor (SEE).

(as) tight as a drum   An insipid
simile (SEE moribund metaphors).
*firm; snug; strained; stretched; taut;
tense; tight.*

tighten the screws   A moribund
metaphor (SEE).

tight rein on   A moribund metaphor
(SEE).

(talk) till (I'm) blue in the face
A moribund metaphor (SEE). *always;
ceaselessly; constantly; continually; continuously; endlessly; eternally; everlastingly; evermore; forever; forevermore;
immortally; indefinitely; interminably;
permanently; perpetually; persistently;
unceasingly; unremittingly.*

till (her) dying days   *always; ceaselessly; constantly; continually; continuously; endlessly; eternally; everlastingly;
evermore; forever; forevermore; immortally; indefinitely; interminably; permanently; perpetually; persistently; unceasingly; unremittingly.*

till (until) hell freezes over
A moribund metaphor (SEE). *always;
ceaselessly; constantly; continually; continuously; endlessly; eternally; everlastingly; evermore; forever; forevermore;
immortally; indefinitely; interminably;
permanently; perpetually; persistently;
unceasingly; unremittingly.*

till it's coming out (of) (my) ears
A moribund metaphor (SEE).

(not) till the cows come home
A moribund metaphor (SEE). *always;
ceaselessly; constantly; continually; con-*

tinuously; endlessly; eternally; everlastingly; evermore; forever; forevermore; immortally; indefinitely; interminably; permanently; perpetually; persistently; unceasingly; unremittingly.

tilt at windmills   A moribund metaphor (SEE).

time and (time) again   A dimwitted redundancy (SEE). *frequently; habitually; often; recurrently; regularly; repeatedly.* ■ *Time and time again* people are fooled into thinking their survival depends on pleasing everyone. USE *Repeatedly.* SEE ALSO *again and again; over and over (again).*

time and effort   An inescapable pair (SEE). ■ He still puts a lot of *time and effort* into his commercials.

time and energy   An inescapable pair (SEE). ■ Boiling water also is cheaper than buying bottled water, but it takes more *time and energy.*

time and tide wait for no man
A popular prescription (SEE).

time bomb (just) waiting to go off

time flies

time flies when you're having fun   A popular prescription (SEE).

time hangs heavy

(our) time has come

time heals all wounds   A popular prescription (SEE).

time-honored (American) tradition

time is a great healer   A popular prescription (SEE).

time is money   A quack equation (SEE).

time is of the essence

time is on (our) side

time is running out

time marches on

time period   A dimwitted redundancy (SEE). *period; time.* ■ Would you go along with this for a *time period*? USE *period* or *time.*

times are tough

times (have) change(d)

(have) time to kill

time was when   *before; earlier; formerly; long ago; once; previously.*

time will tell   ■ We have made many changes in attitude and practice, and only *time will tell* whether these are for the ultimate good or merely more mischief.

timing is everything

tip (my) hat to   A moribund metaphor (SEE). *flag; greet; hail; salute; wave to; welcome.*

tip of the iceberg   A moribund metaphor (SEE). ■ We have just seen the *tip of the iceberg* of corporations that have loaded up with too much debt and gone broke because of the merger and takeover wars. REPLACE WITH *beginning*.

And here is an example no less than wonderful: ■ It's difficult to tell whether my study is the iceberg and the tip is yet to be found, or whether my study was the *tip of the iceberg*.

tip the scales   A moribund metaphor (SEE).

(as) tired as a dog   An insipid simile (SEE moribund metaphors). *beat; bushed; debilitated; depleted; drained; enervated; exhausted; fatigued; sapped; spent; tired; weary; worn out*.

tit for tat

to all intents and purposes
A dimwitted redundancy (SEE). *effectively; essentially; in effect; in essence; practically; virtually*. ■ *To all intents and purposes*, you were dating two women at a time. USE *In effect*. SEE ALSO *for all intents and purposes; for all practical purposes; to all practical purposes*.

to all practical purposes   A dimwitted redundancy (SEE). *effectively; essentially; in effect; in essence; practically; virtually*. ■ The ruling Unionist party is, *to all practical purposes*, a Protestant party. USE *in essence*. SEE ALSO *for all intents and purposes; for all practical purposes; to all intents and purposes*.

to beat the band   A moribund metaphor (SEE). *aggressively; dynamically; emphatically; energetically; ferociously; fervently; fiercely; forcefully; frantically; frenziedly; furiously; hard; intensely; intently; mightily; passionately; powerfully; robustly; savagely; spiritedly;* *strenuously; strongly; vehemently; viciously; vigorously; violently; wildly; with vigor*. ■ When you wake up, it should be snowing *to beat the band*. REPLACE WITH *mightily*.

to be honest (with you)   An ineffectual phrase (SEE).

today is the first day of the rest of (your) life   A popular prescription (SEE).

today . . . , tomorrow the world

to die for

to death   *consumedly; enormously; exceedingly; excessively; exorbitantly; extraordinarily; extremely; greatly; hugely; immensely; immoderately; inordinately; intemperately; intensely; mightily; prodigiously; unreasonably; unrestrainedly; very much*.

to each (his) own   A popular prescription (SEE).

to err is human   A popular prescription (SEE).

to err is human, to forgive divine
A popular prescription (SEE).

toe the line (mark)   A moribund metaphor (SEE). *abide by; accede; accommodate; accord; acquiesce; adapt; adhere to; agree; behave; comply; concur; conform; correspond; follow; harmonize; heed; mind; obey; observe; submit; yield*.

(leveraged) to (their) eyebrows
A moribund metaphor (SEE).

together, we can make a difference

to (his) heart's content

token gesture

token of appreciation (esteem)

to know (him) is to love (him)

to make a long story short   *briefly; concisely; in brief; in short; in sum; succinctly; tersely.*

tomorrow is another day

(with) tongue in cheek   A moribund metaphor (SEE). *facetiously; humorously; in fun; in jest; in play; jocosely; jokingly; kiddingly; playfully; teasingly.*

too big for (his) breeches   A moribund metaphor (SEE). *arrogant; cavalier; condescending; contemptuous; despotic; dictatorial; disdainful; dogmatic; domineering; haughty; imperious; insolent; lofty; overbearing; overweening; patronizing; pompous; pretentious; scornful; self-important; supercilious; superior; vainglorious.*

too close for comfort

too close to call

(I'm) too close to it

too (funny) for words

(sounds) too good to be true

too good to pass up

too hot to handle   A moribund metaphor (SEE).

(you) took the words (right) out of

(my) mouth   A moribund metaphor (SEE).

too little too late

too many chiefs (and not enough Indians)   A moribund metaphor (SEE).

too many cooks spoil the broth (brew)   A popular prescription (SEE).

too much of a good thing

too much too soon

to . . . or not to . . . (that is the question)

too smart for (his) own good   A plebeian sentiment (SEE).

(fight) tooth and nail   A moribund metaphor (SEE). *aggressively; dynamically; emphatically; energetically; ferociously; fervently; fiercely; forcefully; frantically; frenziedly; furiously; hard; intensely; intently; mightily; passionately; powerfully; robustly; savagely; spiritedly; strenuously; strongly; vehemently; viciously; vigorously; violently; wildly; with vigor.* ■ Bank of Boston, the state's largest bank, lobbied *tooth and nail* against the interstate law. RE-PLACE WITH *intensely.*

too (numerous) to mention

toot (your) own horn   A moribund metaphor (SEE). *acclaim; applaud; bluster; boast; brag; celebrate; cheer; commend; compliment; congratulate; crow; extol; flatter; gloat; hail; honor; laud; praise; puff; salute; self-congratulate; strut; swagger.* ■ Engineers are the world's worst at *tooting their own horn*. REPLACE WITH *applauding themselves*.

top brass   A moribund metaphor (SEE). *administrator; boss; brass; chief; commander; director; executive; foreman; head; headman; leader; manager; master; (high) muckamuck; officer; official; overseer; president; principal; superintendent; supervisor.*

top of the heap   A moribund metaphor (SEE).

top priority   A torpid term (SEE). ■ *The top priority in my life is my kids.* REPLACE WITH *Most important.* SEE ALSO *first priority; number-one priority.*

torpid terms   Torpid terms are vapid words and phrases that we use in place of vital ones: *a majority of; a number of; a step in the right direction; cautiously optimistic; degree; effectuate; extent; (a) factor; incumbent upon; indicate; input; move forward; negative feelings; operative; prioritize; pursuant to; remedy the situation; represent(s); send a message; significant other; subsequent to; utilize; weight proportionate to height.*

Formulas as flat as these keep us dumb and dispassionate. They elicit the least from us.

With these unsound formulas, little can be communicated and still less can be accomplished. Torpid terms interfere with our understanding and even with our taking action. SEE ALSO *overworked words.*

toss a bone

toss and turn   An inescapable pair (SEE).

toss in the towel   A moribund metaphor (SEE). *abdicate; accede; acquiesce; bow; capitulate; cede; concede; give in; give up; quit; relinquish; retreat; submit; succumb; surrender; yield.*

to tell you the truth   An ineffectual phrase (SEE).

(march) to the beat of a different drummer   A moribund metaphor (SEE). *aberrant; abnormal; anomalistic; anomalous; atypical; bizarre; curious; deviant; different; distinct; distinctive; eccentric; exceptional; extraordinary; fantastic; foreign; grotesque; idiosyncratic; independent; individual; individualistic; irregular; novel; odd; offbeat; original; peculiar; puzzling; quaint; queer; rare; remarkable; separate; singular; strange; uncommon; unconventional; unexampled; unique; unnatural; unorthodox; unparalleled; unprecedented; unusual; weird.*

to the best of (our) ability

to the breaking point

to the brink of extinction

to the ends (far reaches) of the earth   A moribund metaphor (SEE). 1. *always; ceaselessly; constantly; continually; continuously; endlessly; eternally; everlastingly; evermore; forever; forevermore; frequently; interminably; nonstop; permanently; perpetually; persistently; recurrently; regularly; repeatedly; unceasingly; unremittingly.* 2. *all during; all over; all through; everyplace; everywhere; throughout.*

(up) to the hilt   A moribund metaphor (SEE). *altogether; completely; entirely; fully; perfectly; quite; thoroughly;*

totally; unreservedly; utterly; wholly.

(follow instructions) to the letter
carefully; conscientiously; deliberately; faithfully; exactly; meticulously; painstakingly; precisely; religiously; rigorously; scrupulously; strictly; with care. ■ We followed all of her advice *to the letter* with no results. REPLACE WITH *scrupulously.*

to the manner (manor) born

to the point of (that; where)
A dimwitted redundancy (SEE). *so; so far (that); so much (that); so that; to; to when; to where.* ■ It's gotten *to the point that* I even flirt with operators. REPLACE WITH *so that.* ■ But it has now evolved *to the point where* they do it all the time. REPLACE WITH *to where.*

to the teeth   *altogether; completely; entirely; fully; perfectly; quite; thoroughly; totally; unreservedly; utterly; wholly.*

to the tune of   A dimwitted redundancy (SEE). It cost him *to the tune of* $4,500 to buy his new computer system. DELETE *to the tune of.*

to the victor belong the spoils
A popular prescription (SEE).

to thine own self be true   A popular prescription (SEE).

touch and go   *dangerous; precarious; risky; uncertain.*

touch a raw nerve   A moribund metaphor (SEE).

touch base with   A moribund metaphor (SEE).

touch of class

(as) tough as leather   An insipid simile (SEE moribund metaphors).
1. *athletic; beefy; brawny; burly; energetic; firm; fit; hale; hardy; hearty; healthful; healthy; husky; leathery; manly; mighty; muscular; powerful; puissant; robust; rugged; sinewy; solid; sound; stalwart; stout; strapping; strong; sturdy; tough; vigorous; virile; well-built.*
2. *constant; dependable; determined; faithful; fast; firm; fixed; inexorable; inflexible; loyal; obdurate; resolute; resolved; rigid; solid; stable; staunch; steadfast; steady; stern; strong; tenacious; unflinching; unwavering; unyielding.*

(as) tough as nails   An insipid simile (SEE moribund metaphors).
1. *athletic; beefy; brawny; burly; energetic; firm; fit; hale; hardy; healthful; healthy; hearty; leathery; manly; mighty; muscular; powerful; puissant; robust; rugged; sinewy; solid; sound; stalwart; stout; strapping; strong; sturdy; tough; vigorous; virile; well-built.*
2. *constant; dependable; determined; faithful; fast; firm; fixed; inexorable; inflexible; loyal; obdurate; resolute; resolved; rigid; solid; stable; staunch; steadfast; steady; stern; strong; tenacious; unflinching; unwavering; unyielding.*

tough choices

tough sell

tough sledding   A moribund metaphor (SEE). *arduous; backbreaking; burdensome; difficult; exhausting; fatiguing; hard; herculean; laborious; not easy; onerous; severe; strenuous; toilful;*

toilsome; tough; trying; wearisome.

tough (economic) times

tough to swallow   A moribund metaphor (SEE).

(it's) tough to teach an old dog new tricks   A moribund metaphor (SEE).

to wit   An archaism (SEE). *namely; that is; that is to say.* ■ The ones who hold the key to the problem are the problem themselves, *to wit*, drug abusers. USE *namely.*

track record   A moribund metaphor (SEE).

trample on the rights of individuals

travel broadens the mind   A popular prescription (SEE).

travel the same road   A moribund metaphor (SEE).

travesty of justice

treacherous waters   A moribund metaphor (SEE).

tread water   A moribund metaphor (SEE). ■ He is now *treading water*, deciding what to do next.

treasure house of   A moribund metaphor (SEE).

treat (us) like royalty   An insipid simile (SEE moribund metaphors).

très   A foreignism (SEE). *very.* ■ She is *très* happy now that she is working. REPLACE WITH *very.*

trial and error

trials and tribulations   *adversity; affliction; calamity; catastrophe; difficulty; distress; hardship; misadventure; misfortune; ordeal; trial; tribulation; trouble; woe.* ■ It also presents a firsthand account of the *trials and tribulations* of living in a lesbian family. REPLACE WITH *ordeal.*

tried and true   An inescapable pair (SEE). *constant; dependable; faithful; firm; loyal; reliable; solid; staunch; steadfast; strong; true; trustworthy; trusty.*

trim (his) sails   A moribund metaphor (SEE).

trip the light fantastic   A moribund metaphor (SEE). *dance.*

triumphant return   An inescapable pair (SEE).

triumph of good over evil

trivial pursuit   An infantile phrase (SEE).

trouble in paradise   A moribund metaphor (SEE).

true believer   *addict; devotee; extremist; fanatic; partisan; radical; sectarian; votary; zealot.*

true blue   A moribund metaphor (SEE). *constant; dependable; faithful; firm; loyal; reliable; solid; staunch; steadfast; strong; true; trustworthy; trusty.*

true facts   A dimwitted redundancy (SEE). *facts; truth.* ■ Sometimes I wish the papers would print the *true facts*. USE *facts* or *truth*.

true love A suspect superlative (SEE).

(the course of) true love never runs smooth A popular prescription (SEE).

true to form

trust your feelings A popular prescription (SEE).

truthfully honest A dimwitted redundancy (SEE). *honest; truthful.* ■ To be *truthfully honest*, I do want to be her friend. USE *truthful.*

truth is stranger than fiction
A popular prescription (SEE).

truth, justice and the American way An infantile phrase (SEE).

try it, you'll like it An infantile phrase (SEE).

try (my) level best

try, try again A popular prescription (SEE).

turn a blind eye to A moribund metaphor (SEE). *avoid; brush aside; discount; disregard; dodge; duck; ignore; neglect; omit; pass over; recoil from; shrink from; shun; shy away from; turn away from; withdraw from.*

turnabout is fair play A popular prescription (SEE).

turn a deaf ear to A moribund metaphor (SEE). *avoid; brush aside; dis-*

count; disregard; dodge; duck; ignore; neglect; omit; pass over; recoil from; shrink from; shun; shy away from; turn away from; withdraw from.

turn a negative into a positive
■ The revolution in traditional family ties has *turned a negative into a positive* for most singles today. SEE ALSO *negative; positive.*

turn (things) around

turn (their) back on A moribund metaphor (SEE). *abandon; abdicate; avoid; brush aside; deny; desert; disavow; discount; disinherit; disown; disregard; dodge; drop; duck; forgo; forsake; give up; ignore; leave; neglect; omit; pass over; quit; recoil from; reject; relinquish; renounce; shrink from; shun; shy away from; snub; surrender; turn away from; withdraw from; yield.* ■ It will be unfortunate, indeed, if the countries of Western Europe *turn their backs on* their Eastern European neighbors. REPLACE WITH *disregard.*

turn back the clock (of time)
A moribund metaphor (SEE).

turn (your) dreams into reality
A popular prescription (SEE).

turning point (in history)

turn inside out A moribund metaphor (SEE). *agitate; confuse; disorder; disorganize; disquiet; disrupt; disturb; fluster; jar; jolt; jumble; mess up; mix up; muddle; perturb; rattle; ruffle; shake up; stir up; unnerve; unsettle; upset.*

turn like the weather An insipid simile (SEE moribund metaphors). *capricious; changeable; erratic; fickle; fit-*

ful; flighty; fluctuating; haphazard; inconsistent; inconstant; intermittent; irregular; mercurial; occasional; random; sometime; spasmodic; sporadic; unpredictable; unsettled; unstable; unsteady; vacillating; volatile; wavering; wayward.

(unexpected) turn of events

(another) turn of the screw
A moribund metaphor (SEE).

turn over a new leaf   A moribund metaphor (SEE). *alter; begin again; change; convert; improve; metamorphose; modify; reform; remake; transform.*

turn over in (his) grave   A moribund metaphor (SEE).

turn sour   A moribund metaphor (SEE). ■ Banks caught in the euphoria of a construction boom have watched the economy *turn sour.*

turn (my) stomach   A moribund metaphor (SEE). *appall; disgust; horrify; nauseate; offend; outrage; repel; repulse; revolt; shock; sicken.*

turn tail   *abscond; clear out; decamp; depart; desert; disappear; escape; exit; flee; fly; go; go away; leave; move on; part; pull out; quit; retire; retreat; run away; take flight; take off; vacate; vanish; withdraw*

turn the corner   A moribund metaphor (SEE). *advance; awaken; better; expand; flourish; gain; gain strength; grow; heal; improve; increase; pick up; progress; prosper; rally; recover; recuperate; refresh; renew; revive; rouse; strengthen; thrive.* ■ Our number one

goal is to reestablish reliability and customer satisfaction, and we think we have started to *turn the corner.* REPLACE WITH *improve.*

turn the other cheek   A moribund metaphor (SEE).

turn the tables (on)   A moribund metaphor (SEE).

turn the tide   A moribund metaphor (SEE).

turn up (her) nose   A moribund metaphor (SEE). *contemn; deride; despise; detest; disdain; jeer at; laugh at; mock; ridicule; scoff at; scorn; shun; slight; sneer; snub; spurn.*

turn up the heat   A moribund metaphor (SEE). *coerce; command; compel; constrain; demand; enforce; force; goad; impel; importune; incite; induce; insist; instigate; make; oblige; press; pressure; prod; push; spur; urge.*

(sit and) twiddle (our) thumbs
A moribund metaphor (SEE). *be idle; be inactive; be lazy; be unemployed; be unoccupied; dally; dawdle; loaf; loiter; loll; lounge; relax; repose; rest; tarry; unwind.*

twilight zone   A moribund metaphor (SEE).

twist and turn in the wind   A moribund metaphor (SEE).

twist (his) arm   A moribund metaphor (SEE). *bulldoze; bully; coerce; compel; constrain; demand; drive; enforce; enjoin; goad; force; impel; incite; intimidate; make; necessitate; obligate; oblige;*

order; press; pressure; prod; require; threaten; tyrannize; urge.

twist (wrap) around (her) little finger   A moribund metaphor (SEE). *administer; boss; command; control; dictate; direct; dominate; domineer; govern; in charge; in control; in command; manage; manipulate; master; misuse; order; overpower; oversee; predominate; prevail; reign over; rule; superintend; tyrannize; use.*

twist of fate   A moribund metaphor (SEE).

twists and turns (of fate)   A moribund metaphor (SEE).

two for the price of one

two heads are better than one

A popular prescription (SEE).

(like) two peas in a pod   An insipid simile (SEE). *akin; alike; correspondent; corresponding; equal; equivalent; identical; indistinguishable; kindred; like; matching; one; same; selfsame; similar.*

two's company, three's a crowd   A popular prescription (SEE).

(take) two steps backward for every step forward

two strikes against (him)

two-way street   A moribund metaphor (SEE).

two wrongs don't make a right   A popular prescription (SEE).

U

(as) ugly as a toad   An insipid simile (SEE moribund metaphors). *deformed; disfigured; disgusting; displeasing; distorted; freakish; frightful; ghastly; gorgonian; grisly; grotesque; gruesome; hideous; homely; horrendous; horrible; horrid; monstrous; offensive; plain; repellent; repulsive; revolting; ugly; unsightly.*

(as) ugly as sin   An insipid simile (SEE moribund metaphors). *deformed; disfigured; disgusting; displeasing; distorted; freakish; frightful; ghastly; gorgonian; grisly; grotesque; gruesome; hideous; homely; horrendous; horrible; horrid; monstrous; offensive; plain; repellent; repulsive; revolting; ugly; unsightly.*

ugly duckling   A moribund metaphor (SEE). *deformed; disfigured; disgusting; displeasing; distorted; freakish; frightful; ghastly; gorgonian; grisly; grotesque; gruesome; hideous; homely; horrendous; horrible; horrid; monstrous; offensive; plain; repellent; repulsive; revolting; ugly; unsightly.*

unassailable logic

unbeknownst   An archaism (SEE). *unbeknown; unknown.* ■ *Unbeknownst*

to his girlfriend, he made a videotape of them. USE *Unknown*.

unbelievable   An overworked word (SEE).
1. *beyond belief; beyond comprehension; doubtful; dubious; implausible; improbable; incomprehensible; inconceivable; inexplicable; questionable; unfathomable; unimaginable; unthinkable.*
2. *astonishing; astounding; breathtaking; extraordinary; fabulous; fantastic; marvelous; miraculous; overwhelming; prodigious; sensational; spectacular; wonderful.* One of the hallmarks of dimwitted language is the unimaginativeness of those who use it. ■ It's just *unbelievable* that something like this could happen to us. REPLACE WITH *inexplicable*. ■ It's an almost *unbelievable* challenge to the country to change this. REPLACE WITH *overwhelming*. SEE ALSO *incredible*.

unbridled enthusiasm

uncharted waters   A moribund metaphor (SEE).

under a cloud   A moribund metaphor (SEE). *discredited; disfavored; disgraced; dishonored; distrusted; in disfavor; in disgrace; in disrepute; in ignominy; in shame; suspect; under suspi-*

cion. ∎ He became the only vice president to leave *under a cloud*. REPLACE WITH *in disgrace*. ∎ He left the police department *under a cloud of suspicion*. REPLACE WITH *under suspicion*.

under (my) belt   A moribund metaphor (SEE). *background; education; experience; grooming; grounding; instruction; learning; knowledge; maturity; practice; preparation; qualifications; schooling; seasoning; skill; teaching; training.*

(come) under fire   A moribund metaphor (SEE). *be admonished; be assailed; be attacked; be castigated; be censured; be chastised; be chided; be condemned; be criticized; be denounced; be rebuked; be reprimanded; be reproached; be reproved; be scolded; be set on; be upbraided.*

(keep) under lock and key
A moribund metaphor (SEE).
1. *confined; imprisoned; in jail; locked up.*
2. *guarded; protected; safe; secure; sheltered; shielded.*

under (his) own steam   A moribund metaphor (SEE).

understaffed and overworked   An inescapable pair (SEE).

under the gun   A moribund metaphor (SEE).

under the influence   *besotted; crapulous; drunk; inebriated; intoxicated; sodden; stupefied; tipsy.*

under the same roof   A moribund metaphor (SEE).

under the table   A moribund metaphor (SEE). *clandestinely; confidentially; covertly; furtively; mysteriously; in private; in secret; privately; secludedly; secretly; slyly; stealthily; surreptitiously; undercover.*

under the weather   A moribund metaphor (SEE).
1. *afflicted; ailing; diseased; ill; indisposed; infirm; not (feeling) well; sick; sickly; suffering; unhealthy; unsound; unwell; valetudinarian.*
2. *besotted; crapulous; drunk; inebriated; intoxicated; sodden; stupefied; tipsy.*

under the wire   A moribund metaphor (SEE).

under (his) thumb   A moribund metaphor (SEE). *dependent; subject; subordinate; subservient; under.*

under (his) wing   A moribund metaphor (SEE).

undivided attention

uneasy lies the head that wears a crown   A popular prescription (SEE).

uneasy truce

uneducated English
Whereas people who aspire to elegant English still maintain standards of speech and observe distinctions between words, the uneducated, like some juggernaut, massacre and obliterate.

They slay nearly all that they say: ∎ He knew they *was* out there for ten to fifteen minutes before he *done* anything. ∎ I *seen* things out there in the world that I never thought I would see. ■ My mom is the one that *brung* me up. ■ We were a close family; we *done* things together. ■ Don't you have family members that you could *of went* to? ■ Men have treated me *terrible*. ■ I took everything *literate*. ■ She wasn't being abused about *nothing*. ■ We don't go to parties *no* more; we don't go *no* where. ■ That *don't* matter, I'm still there with you, *ain't* I? ■ I shot *me* a burglar. ■ Let's start over here with the two of *yous*.

Uneducated English offends people less than does elegant English. People neither fume nor flinch when they hear sentences like these. But let them listen to someone speaking elegantly, and they are instantly repelled.

Doubtless, well-turned phrases and orotund tones suggest to them a soul unslain.

afeared (ascared). ■ He says he's *afeared* of being alone in the dark. USE *afraid* or *scared*.

ain't. ■ It *ain't* right to take the law into your own hands, but he got what he had coming. USE *isn't*. ■ I *ain't* interested. USE *am not*.

allow as (to) how. ■ He *allowed as to how* it would be a good way to learn about presenting cooking on television. USE *allowed that*. ■ I quit singing after I asked my voice trainer what I should do the third semester and she *allowed as how* I needed to repeat 101. USE *allowed that*.

alls. ■ *Alls* I can say is he was a good cop. USE *All*. ■ *Alls* you hear them talk about is their baby. USE *All*.

anyways. ■ *Anyways*, I have to go now. USE *Anyway* or DELETE. ■ You shouldn't be sleeping around when you're married *anyways*. USE *anyway* or DELETE.

anywheres. ■ He hasn't got *any-*

wheres to go. USE *anywhere*.

a (long) ways. ■ I think magazines can go *a long ways* to effecting that. USE *a long way*. ■ Is it *a long ways*? USE *a long way*.

being as. ■ *Being as* he's such a great dad, I thought he wouldn't mind. USE *because, considering, in that* or *since*.

being as how. ■ That's not so bad, *being as how* we didn't even know we would be on the ballot. USE *because, considering, in that*, or *since*.

being that. ■ *Being that* we seem to be getting along so well, I thought we might go to dinner. USE *because, considering, in that* or *since*.

better had. ■ You *better had* do as your father says. USE *had better, ought to* or *should*.

complected. ■ I'm 5'2", 110 lbs., and very light-*complected*. USE *complexioned*.

could of. ■ I *could of* if I wanted to. USE *could have*.

drownded. ■ Two men *drownded* when their boat capsized. USE *drowned*.

drug. ■ He *drug* up the past and complained about the argument we had that time. USE *dragged*.

had(n't) ought. ■ I *had ought* to go. USE *ought* or *should*. ■ You *hadn't ought* tell him what she said. USE *ought not to* or *should not*.

heighth. ■ She's over six feet in *heighth*. USE *height*.

hisself. ■ I heard it from Walter *hisself*. USE *himself*. ■ I was afraid he was going to hurt *hisself*. USE *himself*.

in regards to. ■ The system has failed me *in regards to* disciplining my kids. USE *in regard to*. ■ *In regards to* your question, the most important thing is that we don't have a father figure in our lives. USE *Concerning*.

irregardless (of). ■ Remember to treat all patients with respect and compassion *irregardless of* their health status. USE *despite, irrespective of, no matter what, regardless of* or *whatever.* ■ This would have happened *irregardless of* the Chapter 11 decision. USE *despite, irrespective of, no matter what, regardless of* or *whatever.*

irregardless of the fact that. ■ *Irregardless of the fact that* she was raised by someone else, she is still our daughter. USE *Although, Even though* or *Though.*

leastways. ■ There's no sense of accomplishment, *leastways* not for me. USE *at least.*

leave us. ■ *Leave us* go now before it starts to pour. USE *Let us.*

may of. ■ I *may of* met him once before. USE *may have.*

might of. ■ It *might of* been me; I *might of* been sitting in the back seat. USE *might have.*

more -(i)er. ■ You're probably *more busier* than I am. USE *busier* or *more busy.* ■ I've gotten a lot *more braver.* USE *braver* or *more brave.*

most -(i)est. ■ We want to express our *most sincerest* appreciation for the many expressions of sympathy you have shown us. USE *most sincere* or *sincerest.* ■ The panel consisted of some of the town's *most lustiest* women. USE *most lusty* or *lustiest.*

muchly. ■ Thank you *muchly.* USE *very much.*

not hardly. ■ Is she plump? *Not hardly.* USE *Hardly.* ■ I *couldn't hardly* breathe because he had broken my ribs. USE *could hardly.*

not scarcely. ■ I *can't scarcely* hear you. USE *can scarcely.*

nowheres. ■ He was *nowheres* near their house. USE *nowhere.*

seeing as. ■ *Seeing as* you're a woman, does the audience respond to you differently? USE *Because, Considering, In that* or *Since.*

seeing as how. ■ Quite possibly it is my fault *seeing as how* I did not respond the way I thought I would. USE *because, considering, in that* or *since.*

seeing that. ■ *Seeing that* this isn't a programming book, you should have little trouble. USE *Because, Considering, In that* or *Since.*

should of. ■ I *should of* known. USE *should have.*

somewheres. ■ I left it *somewheres.* USE *somewhere.*

that (those) there. ■ *That there* man was the one who hit her. DELETE *there.* ■ *That* way *there,* I can get my degree a few months sooner. DELETE *there.*

theirself (theirselves). ■ Irish people I know don't think of *theirselves* as Irish. USE *themselves.*

this (these) here. ■ *This* is my little brother *here.* DELETE *here.* ■ *These* shirts *here* are lighter than those. DELETE *here.*

thusly. ■ *Thusly,* I feel he was irresponsible and I feel I should tell him. USE *Thus.*

went and. ■ We *went and* called 911. DELETE *went and.* ■ He *went and* left me. DELETE *went and.*

what all. ■ She can't seem to find anyone who understands *what all* she has been through. DELETE *all.* ■ I don't know *what all* the deal was with her, but she rejected me. DELETE *all.*

where at. ■ Nobody knows *where* the $100 is *at.* DELETE *at.* ■ I know *where* she is *at.* I know *where* she works *at.* DELETE *at.*

who all. ■ I don't know *who all* you mean. DELETE *all.*

with regards to. ■ Customers are looking for standard-based applications *with regards to* networking. USE *with regard to.* ■ *With regards to* the paper you gave out recently, I don't want to read about what you have against your opponent but what you are going to do for the city. USE *With regard to.*

　would of. ■ I asked myself what I *would of, could of* and *should of* done. USE *would have, could have* and *should have.* SEE ALSO *elegant English; everyday English.*

unfinished business

unholy alliance

unified front

united we stand (divided we fall) A popular prescription (SEE).

unite in holy wedlock (marriage) A dimwitted redundancy (SEE). *marry; wed.*

unless and until A dimwitted redundancy (SEE). *unless; until.* ■ I am opposed to the imposition of any new taxes *unless and until* major cuts in spending have been implemented. USE *unless* or *until.*

unmitigated gall An inescapable pair (SEE).

unprecedented move (step)

unsung hero

unswerving devotion

untenable position An inescapable pair (SEE).

until and unless A dimwitted redundancy (SEE). *unless; until.* ■ *Until*

and unless these two conditions are met, the second rule does not fire. USE *Unless* or *Until.*

until death do us part

until such time as A dimwitted redundancy (SEE). *until.* ■ Lessee shall not be liable for any rent *until such time as* Lessor can deliver possession. USE *until.*

untimely end

up a blind alley A moribund metaphor (SEE).
1. *at risk; endangered; hard-pressed; imperiled; in a bind; in a dilemma; in a fix; in a jam; in a predicament; in a quandary; in danger; in difficulty; in jeopardy; in peril; in trouble; jeopardized.*
2. *caught; cornered; enmeshed; ensnared; entangled; entrapped; netted; snared; trapped.*

up a creek A moribund metaphor (SEE). *at risk; endangered; hard-pressed; imperiled; in a bind; in a dilemma; in a fix; in a jam; in a predicament; in a quandary; in danger; in difficulty; in jeopardy; in peril; in trouble; jeopardized.*

up against (it)

up against the wall A moribund metaphor (SEE).
1. *at risk; endangered; hard-pressed; imperiled; in a bind; in a dilemma; in a fix; in a jam; in a predicament; in a quandary; in danger; in difficulty; in jeopardy; in peril; in trouble; jeopardized.*
2. *caught; cornered; enmeshed; en-*

snared; entangled; entrapped; netted; snared; trapped.

(right) up (her) alley   A moribund metaphor (SEE).

up and about   *healthy.*

up and running   A moribund metaphor (SEE). *at work; functioning; going; in action; in operation; operational; operating; performing; producing; running; working.* ▪ We intend to have a smoothly functioning, well-integrated unit *up and running* when we start in February. REPLACE WITH *in operation.*

up a tree   A moribund metaphor (SEE).
1. *at risk; endangered; hard-pressed; imperiled; in a bind; in a fix; in a jam; in a predicament; in danger; in difficulty; in jeopardy; in peril; in trouble; jeopardized.*
2. *caught; cornered; enmeshed; ensnared; entangled; entrapped; netted; snared; trapped.*

up close and personal   An infantile phrase (SEE).

update   (*v*) A torpid term (SEE). *adjust; alter; bring up to date; change; modernize; modify; recreate; redo; reform; refresh.* ▪ We will *update you* on this story at eleven o'clock. REPLACE WITH *bring you up to date.* ▪ Copy the sheet so that as conditions change you can *update* the directions. REPLACE WITH *modify.*

up for grabs

up in arms   A moribund metaphor (SEE).
1. *agitated; alarmed; angry; annoyed; aroused; choleric; enraged; fierce; fuming; furious; incensed; indignant; inflamed; infuriated; irate; irked; irritable; mad; maddened; raging; resentful; splenetic; vexatious.*
2. *factious; insubordinate; insurgent; mutinous; rebellious; seditious.* ▪ These investors are *up in arms* about seeing their investment damaged by amalgamation with a less profitable bank. REPLACE WITH *incensed.*

up in the air   A moribund metaphor (SEE). *confused; dubious; indecisive; in doubt; irresolute; open; questionable; tentative; uncertain; unconcluded; undecided; undetermined; unresolved; unsettled.* ▪ The issue is still very much *up in the air* despite a series of rulings in the 1980s. REPLACE WITH *unsettled.*

ups and downs   *complications; fluctuations; troubles; uncertainties; vicissitudes.*

upset the apple cart   A moribund metaphor (SEE). *confuse; damage; disorder; disrupt; disturb; jumble; mess up; mix up; muddle; ruin; scramble; spoil; upset.*

up the ante   A moribund metaphor (SEE).

up the creek (without a paddle)   A moribund metaphor (SEE).
1. *at risk; endangered; hard-pressed; imperiled; in a bind; in a dilemma; in a fix; in a jam; in a predicament; in a quandary; in danger; in difficulty; in jeopardy; in peril; in trouble; jeopardized.*
2. *caught; cornered; enmeshed; ensnared; entangled; entrapped; netted; snared; trapped.*

up till (until)   A dimwitted redundancy (SEE). *till (until)*. ■ *Up until* the day he left, they hoped he would play a major role in the new company as a key senior executive. USE *Until*.

up till (until) this point (time)
A dimwitted redundancy (SEE). *until now*. ■ *Up until this point* we have been working in the dark. USE *Until now*.

up to (my) eyeballs (eyebrows)
A moribund metaphor (SEE). *bury; immerse; inundate; infest; overrun; overwhelm*. ■ The campaigns' organizations are all *up to their eyeballs* with delegate-counting. REPLACE WITH *overrun*.

up to (his) old tricks

up to par   A moribund metaphor (SEE).
1. *average; common; commonplace; customary; everyday; mediocre; middling; normal; ordinary; quotidian; regular; routine; standard; typical; uneventful; unexceptional; unremarkable; usual*.
2. *acceptable; adequate; fine; good; good enough; healthy; passable; satisfactory; sufficient; suitable; tolerable; well*.

up to scratch   A moribund metaphor (SEE). *acceptable; adequate; fine; good; good enough; healthy; passable; satisfactory; sufficient; suitable; tolerable; well*.

up to snuff   A moribund metaphor (SEE). *acceptable; adequate; fine; good; good enough; healthy; passable; satisfactory; sufficient; suitable; tolerable; well*.

up to speed   A moribund metaphor (SEE). *acceptable; adequate; fine; good; good enough; healthy; passable; satisfactory; sufficient; suitable; tolerable; well*.

up-to-the-minute

upwardly mobile

use and abuse   An inescapable pair (SEE).

utilize   A torpid term (SEE). *apply; employ; make use of; use*. ■ I *utilize* my bike for nearly everything. REPLACE WITH *use*. SEE ALSO *finalize*.

V

valuable asset   An inescapable pair (SEE). This phrase is, like many inescapable pairs, also redundant, for an *asset* is *valuable*.

valued customer

variation on a theme

variety is the spice of life   A popular prescription (SEE).

various and sundry   An inescapable pair (SEE). *assorted; diverse; sundry; varied; various; varying.* ■ I tried *various and sundry* ways to get her to see me. REPLACE WITH *various*. SEE ALSO *all and sundry*.

vast wasteland   A moribund metaphor (SEE).

vehemently oppose   An inescapable pair (SEE). ■ MCA *vehemently opposed* Sony's Betamax and the VCR invasion.

verboten   A foreignism (SEE). *banned; disallowed; enjoined; forbidden; prohibited; proscribed.*

verily   An archaism (SEE). *actually; indeed; in fact; in faith; in reality; in truth; truly.*

very   An overworked word (SEE). The word *very* is often a needless intensive, but preceding words like *excellent, major* and *delightful*, it is ridiculous. ■ I think that's a *very* excellent thought. DELETE *very*. ■ It's a *very* major plus for our state and our region. DELETE *very*. ■ You seem *very* delightful. DELETE *very*. ■ She's a biochemist and *very* brilliant. DELETE *very*. ■ If the test cells were to be shut down, it would be *very* detrimental to the operation. DELETE *very*. SEE ALSO *really*.

vested interest   An inescapable pair (SEE).

viable alternative   An inescapable pair (SEE).

vicious circle   An inescapable pair (SEE).

vicious rumor   An inescapable pair (SEE).

victim of circumstances

victim of (his) own good fortune

(snatch) victory from the jaws of defeat

view with alarm

vim and vigor   An inescapable pair (SEE). *animation; ardor; dash; dynamism; élan; energy; fervor; force; intensity; liveliness; passion; potency; power; spirit; stamina; strength; verve; vigor; vitality; vivacity; zeal.*

virtue is its own reward   A popular prescription (SEE).

vis-à-vis   A foreignism (SEE).

viselike grip   An insipid simile (SEE moribund metaphors).

visible (invisible) to the eye
A dimwitted redundancy (SEE). *visible (invisible)*. SEE ALSO *audible (inaudible) to the ear*.

vive la différence   A foreignism (SEE).

vivid reminder

voice (concern)   A torpid term (SEE). ■ He *voiced scorn at* their claim that the government had undercounted. REPLACE WITH *scorned.* ■ They also *voiced concern* that many people may be expecting too much from biotech research regarding job creation. REPLACE WITH *worried*. SEE ALSO *express (concern)*.

voice (crying) in the wilderness
A moribund metaphor (SEE).

vote of confidence

vote with (their) feet   ■ People are *voting with their feet*, and politicians know this.

W

wages of sin　A moribund metaphor (SEE).

wait and see (what happens)

wait for the ax to fall　A moribund metaphor (SEE).

wait for the other shoe to drop　A moribund metaphor (SEE).

waiting for Godot　An infantile phrase (SEE).

waiting in the wings　A moribund metaphor (SEE).

wait on hand and foot

wait (it) out

wait with bated breath　A moribund metaphor (SEE).

wake the dead　A moribund metaphor (SEE). *blaring; boisterous; booming; deafening; earsplitting; fulminating; loud; noisy; obstreperous; piercing; plangent; resounding; roaring; shrill; stentorian; strident; thundering; thunderous; tumultuous; vociferous.*

wake up and smell the coffee　A moribund metaphor (SEE).

wake-up call　A moribund metaphor (SEE).

walk a fine line　A moribund metaphor (SEE).

walk a tightrope　A moribund metaphor (SEE). *chance; dare; endanger; gamble; hazard; imperil; jeopardize; make bold; peril; risk; venture.*

walk away from　A moribund metaphor (SEE). *abandon; abdicate; avoid; brush aside; deny; desert; disavow; discount; disinherit; disown; disregard; dodge; drop; duck; forgo; forsake; give up; ignore; leave; neglect; omit; pass over; quit; recoil from; reject; relinquish; renounce; shrink from; shun; shy away from; snub; spurn; surrender; turn away from; withdraw from; yield.* ■ The state cannot *walk away from* that obligation. REPLACE WITH *disregard.*

walk on air　A moribund metaphor (SEE). *blissful; blithe; buoyant; cheerful; delighted; ecstatic; elated; enraptured; euphoric; exalted; excited; exhilarated; exultant; gay; glad; gleeful; good-humored; happy; intoxicated; jolly; jovial; joyful; joyous; jubilant; merry; mirthful; overjoyed; pleased; rapturous; thrilled.*

walk on eggs (eggshells)　A moribund metaphor (SEE). ■ For years, Robinson *walked on eggshells* as the first black baseball player in the major leagues.

(all) walks of life   A moribund metaphor (SEE).

wall of silence   A moribund metaphor (SEE).

wallow in self-pity

(the) walls have ears   A moribund metaphor (SEE).

want(s) and need(s)   An inescapable pair (SEE). ■ It contains many important nutrients your body *wants and needs*. SEE ALSO *need(s) and want(s)*.

want to bet?   An infantile phrase (SEE).

war clouds   A moribund metaphor (SEE).

(as) warm as toast   An insipid simile (SEE moribund metaphors). *heated; lukewarm; mild; temperate; tepid; toasty; warm; warmish.*

warm spot in my heart

warm the cockles of (my) heart   A moribund metaphor (SEE).

warn in advance   A dimwitted redundancy (SEE). *warn*. ■ Management should be *warned in advance* that fines are no longer the way to satisfy the system for a careless disaster. DELETE *in advance*. SEE ALSO *advance warning; forewarn*.

war of words   A moribund meta-

phor (SEE). *altercation; argument; bickering; conflict; contention; controversy; disagreement; disputation; dispute; feud; polemics; quarrel; row; spat; squabble; strife; wrangle.* ■ Yesterday's *war of words* seemed like a replay of the bitter 1988 campaign. REPLACE WITH *squabble*.

war on crime

war on drugs

warring camps   A moribund metaphor (SEE).

wash (their) dirty linen in public A moribund metaphor (SEE).

(all) washed up   *beaten; condemned; conquered; cowed; cursed; damned; defunct; doomed; fated; finished; gone; lost; ruined; vanquished.*

wash (her) hands of (it)   A moribund metaphor (SEE). *abandon; abdicate; avoid; brush aside; deny; desert; disavow; discount; disinherit; disown; disregard; dodge; drop; duck; forgo; forsake; give up; ignore; leave; neglect; omit; pass over; quit; recoil from; reject; relinquish; renounce; shrink from; shun; shy away from; snub; surrender; turn away from; withdraw from; yield.*

(I) wasn't born yesterday

(don't) waste (your) breath

waste not, want not   A popular prescription (SEE).

watch and wait

watch (him) like a hawk   An insipid simile (SEE moribund metaphors).

watch your manners

water over the dam   A moribund metaphor (SEE).
1. *completed; concluded; done; ended; finished; over; past; through.*
2. *history; the past; yesterday.*

water under the bridge   A moribund metaphor (SEE).
1. *completed; concluded; done; ended; finished; over; past; through.*
2. *history; the past; yesterday.*

water, water everywhere (and not a drop to drink)

(like) waving a red flag (rag) in front of a bull   An insipid simile (SEE moribund metaphors).

wax   An archaism (SEE).
1. *become; grow.*
2. *express oneself; speak.* ■ He *waxes* eloquent about his love for her. RE-PLACE WITH *becomes.*

wax and wane   An inescapable pair (SEE).

way back when

ways and means   An inescapable pair (SEE). *approaches; means; mechanisms; methods; techniques; ways.*

way to go

(as) weak as a baby   An insipid simile (SEE moribund metaphors). *dainty; debilitated; delicate; enervated; feeble; fragile; frail; infirm; nonmuscu-lar; puny; sickly; unhealthy; unwell; valetudinarian; weak; weakly.*

(as) weak as a kitten   An insipid simile (SEE moribund metaphors). *dainty; debilitated; delicate; enervated; feeble; fragile; frail; infirm; nonmuscu-lar; puny; sickly; unhealthy; unwell; valetudinarian; weak; weakly.*

weak in the knees   A moribund metaphor (SEE).

we all have to die (go) sometime

wealth of information

wears (her) heart on (her) sleeve   A moribund metaphor (SEE).

wear the pants   A moribund metaphor (SEE). *administer; boss; command; control; dictate; direct; dominate; govern; in charge; in command; in control; manage; manipulate; master; order; overpower; oversee; predominate; prevail; reign over; rule; superintend.*

wear (your) true colors

weather permitting

weather the storm   A moribund metaphor (SEE). ■ A tremendous thank-you goes out to each of you who has helped our family *weather this storm.*

web of lies   A moribund metaphor (SEE).

we have to talk

weighed down by facts and figures

weigh heavily on

weight proportionate to height
A torpid term (SEE).

weird   An overworked word (SEE). *aberrant; abnormal; anomalistic; anomalous; atypical; bizarre; curious; deviant; different; distinct; distinctive; eccentric; exceptional; extraordinary; fantastic; foreign; grotesque; idiosyncratic; independent; individual; individualistic; irregular; novel; odd; offbeat; original; peculiar; puzzling; quaint; queer; rare; remarkable; separate; singular; uncommon; unconventional; unexampled; unique; unnatural; unorthodox; unparalleled; unprecedented; unusual.* SEE ALSO *strange.*

welcome addition

welcome change

welcome news

welcome to the club

welcome (them) with open arms
■ We have *welcomed them with open arms.*

(all) well and good   An inescapable pair (SEE). *adequate; all right; excellent; fine; good; O.K.; satisfactory; well.* ■ That's *all well and good,* but what about my son? REPLACE WITH *fine.* SEE ALSO *fine and dandy.*

well-kept secret

well-known fact

well-nigh   An archaism (SEE). *almost; nearly.*

well on (our) way (to)

we'll see what happens

wend (its) way

we're (a thousand) miles apart

wet behind the ears   A moribund metaphor (SEE). *artless; awkward; callow; green; guileless; immature; inexperienced; inexpert; ingenuous; innocent; naive; raw; simple; undeveloped; unfledged; unskilled; unskillful; unsophisticated; untaught; untrained; unworldly.*

wet (my) whistle   A moribund metaphor (SEE). *drink; guzzle; imbibe; quaff.*

we've all got to go sometime
A popular prescription (SEE).

we've got to stop meeting like this
An infantile phrase (SEE).

what a difference a day makes

what are (we) waiting for?

what are you going to do   A plebeian sentiment (SEE). This is still another expression of resignation. Though phrased as a question, it is rarely spoken interrogatively, so resigned, so hopeless are those who use it. SEE ALSO *such is life; that's how (the way) it goes; that's how (the way) the ball bounces; that's how (the way) the cookie crumbles; that's life; that's life in the big city; that's show biz; what can you do.*

what can I say?   An infantile phrase (SEE).

what can I tell you?   An infantile phrase (SEE).

what can you do A plebeian sentiment (SEE). SEE ALSO *such is life; that's how (the way) it goes; that's how (the way) the ball bounces; that's how (the way) the cookie crumbles; that's life; that's life in the big city; that's show biz; what are you going to do.*

what (he) doesn't know won't hurt (him) A popular prescription (SEE).

whatever happens happens An infantile phrase (SEE). SEE ALSO *it just happened; what(ever) must (will) be, must (will) be.*

what goes around, comes around A popular prescription (SEE). This is the secular equivalent of *as you sow, so shall you reap.* As such, it is nonetheless a moralistic prescription — intoned by those who think in circles — that too easily explains the way of the world.

what goes up must come down A popular prescription (SEE).

what happened (is) An ineffectual phrase (SEE). ■ *What happened was* I woke up one morning and just decided to leave. DELETE *What happened was.* ■ *What happened was* we applied for welfare. DELETE *What happened was.* ■ *What happened was* when I said that to him he got upset and left in a huff. DELETE *What happened was.* SEE ALSO *what is.*

what have (I) got to lose?

what is An ineffectual phrase (SEE). ■ *What* you want *is* someone who will stand by his work once it is completed. DELETE *What is.* ■ *What* we are finding *is* that they want to measure up to our

standards of integrity. DELETE *What is.* ■ *What* this course is about *is* empowerment. DELETE *What is.* SEE ALSO *what happened (is).*

(it's) what makes America great

what makes (her) run?

what makes (him) tick?

what might have been

what more do you want?

what(ever) must (will) be, must (will) be SEE ALSO *whatever happens happens.*

what's done is done A quack equation (SEE).

what's good for (the goose) is good for (the gander) A popular prescription (SEE).

what's in a name?

what's the story?

what's wrong with this picture?

what's yours is mine, and what's mine is mine

what's yours is mine, and what's mine is yours

what we have (here) is a failure to communicate

what will they think of next? A plebeian sentiment (SEE).

what you don't know can't (won't)

hurt you   A popular prescription (SEE).

what you see is not always what you get   A popular prescription (SEE).

what you see is what you get
A popular prescription (SEE).

wheel and deal   An inescapable pair (SEE). *bargain; contrive; deal; do business; negotiate; plan; plot; scheme.*

when all is said and done   A dimwitted redundancy (SEE). *all in all; all told; altogether; eventually; finally; in all; in the end; on the whole; overall; ultimately.* ■ *When all is said and done,* we humans are a curious species. USE *All told.* SEE ALSO *after all is said and done.*

when and if   A dimwitted redundancy (SEE). *if; when.* ■ People are asking *when and if* there will be a democratic government. USE *if* or *when.* SEE ALSO *if and when; if, as and when; when and whether; when, as and if; whether and when.*

when and whether   A dimwitted redundancy (SEE). *when; whether.* ■ She will decide *when and whether* and under what circumstances she'll become a mother. USE *when* or *whether.* SEE ALSO *if and when; if, as and when; when and if; when, as and if; whether and when.*

when, as and if   A dimwitted redundancy (SEE). *if; when.* SEE ALSO *if and when; if, as and when; when and if; when and whether; whether and when.*

whence   An archaism (SEE).
1. *from where.*

2. *from what source.*
3. *from which.*

when hell freezes over   A moribund metaphor (SEE). *never; no; not at all; not ever; not in any way; not in the least.*

when in Rome (do as the Romans do)   A popular prescription (SEE). *abide by; accede; accommodate; accord; acquiesce; adapt; adhere to; agree; behave; comply; concur; conform; correspond; follow; harmonize; heed; mind; obey; observe; submit; yield.*

when it comes to   A dimwitted redundancy (SEE). *about; as for; as to; concerning; for; in; of; on; over; regarding; respecting; to; toward; when; with.* ■ I feel I'm more experienced *when it comes to* looking for a job. USE *in.* ■ I'm an expert *when it comes to* marriage. USE *about.* ■ *When it comes to* middle-age dating, there are four stages. USE *As for.* ■ She is not reasonable *when it comes to* me. USE *with.*

when it rains, it pours   A moribund metaphor (SEE).

when I was your age

when push comes to shove
A moribund metaphor (SEE). ■ *When push comes to shove,* liberalism collapses, society polarizes itself, and the gloves are removed.

when (heroes) still walked the earth

when the cat's away, the mice will play   A moribund metaphor (SEE).

when the chips are down

when the going gets tough, the tough get going A popular prescription (SEE).

when you come right down to it

where angels fear to tread A moribund metaphor (SEE).

whereat An archaism (SEE). *at which point.*

where did (I) go wrong?

where do (we) go from here?

wherefore An archaism (SEE).
1. *why.*
2. *for which.*
3. *therefore.*

where (I) hang (my) hat

where I come from

wherein An archaism (SEE). *how; in what way.*

where . . . is concerned A dimwitted redundancy (SEE). *about; as for; as to; concerning; for; in; of; on; over; regarding; respecting; to; toward; with.* ■ Our gangs are just getting off the ground *where* violence *is concerned.* USE *concerning.* ■ Obviously, time doesn't heal all wounds, especially *where* the Red Sox *are concerned.* USE *regarding.* SEE ALSO *as far as . . . (goes; is concerned).*

whereon An archaism (SEE). *on what; on which.*

where's the beef? An infantile phrase (SEE).

(it's) where the action is

where there's a will there's a way A popular prescription (SEE).

where there's smoke there's fire A popular prescription (SEE).

wherethrough An archaism (SEE). *through which.*

whereto An archaism (SEE). *to what; to which.*

whereunto An archaism (SEE). *to what; to which.*

where will it (all) end?

wherewith An archaism (SEE). *with what; with which.*

whet (my) appetite A moribund metaphor (SEE).

whether and when A dimwitted redundancy (SEE). *when; whether.* ■ Lee will be the one to determine *whether and when* he isn't up to the job. USE *when* or *whether.* SEE ALSO *if and when; if, as and when; when and if; when and whether; when, as and if.*

which way the wind blows A moribund metaphor (SEE).

while at the same time A dimwitted redundancy (SEE). *at the same time; while.* ■ It provides us with an opportunity to honor his memory *while at the same time* assisting future students. USE *at the same time* or *while.* SEE ALSO *simultaneously at the same time.*

while away the time *be idle; be inactive; be lazy; be unemployed; be unoc-*

cupied; dally; dawdle; loaf; loiter; loll; lounge; relax; repose; rest; tarry; unwind.

whilst An archaism (SEE). *while.*

whip into a frenzy A moribund metaphor (SEE). *acerbate; anger; annoy; bother; bristle; chafe; enrage; incense; inflame; infuriate; irk; irritate; madden; miff; provoke; rile; vex.*

whip into shape A moribund metaphor (SEE).

whirlwind of activity

whirlwind tour

whistle in the dark A moribund metaphor (SEE).

whistling Dixie A moribund metaphor (SEE).

(as) white as a sheet An insipid simile (SEE moribund metaphors).
1. *anemic; ashen; blanched; bloodless; cadaverous; colorless; deathlike; doughy; haggard; pale; pallid; pasty; peaked; sallow; sickly; wan; whitish.*
2. *achromatic; alabaster-white; albescent; bleached; chalky; colorless; ivory; milk-white; milky; niveous; pearly; pearly-white; snow-white; snowy; uncolored; whitish.*

(as) white as snow An insipid simile (SEE moribund metaphors).
1. *achromatic; alabaster-white; albescent; bleached; chalky; colorless; ivory; milk-white; milky; niveous; pearly; pearly-white; snow-white; snowy; uncolored; whitish.*
2. *anemic; ashen; blanched; bloodless; cadaverous; colorless; deathlike; doughy;*

haggard; pale; pallid; pasty; peaked; sallow; sickly; wan; whitish.

whither An archaism (SEE).
1. *where.*
2. *wherever.*

(my) whole, entire (life) An infantile phrase (SEE). ■ People like you laughed at me *my whole, entire life.* ■ With this on, you will attract more women than you have in *your whole, entire lives.*

who let the cat out of the bag? A moribund metaphor (SEE).

who needs it?

whoop it up A moribund metaphor (SEE).
1. *be merry; carouse; carry on; celebrate; frolic; party; play; revel; riot; roister; rollick; romp; skylark.*
2. *bay; bawl; bellow; blare; caterwaul; cheer; clamor; cry; holler; hoot; howl; roar; screak; scream; screech; shout; shriek; shrill; squawk; squeal; vociferate; wail; whoop; yell; yelp; yowl.*

whose side are you on (anyway)?

who's minding the store? A moribund metaphor (SEE).

who would have (ever) thought A plebeian sentiment (SEE).

(the) why and (the) wherefore A dimwitted redundancy (SEE). *aim; cause; goal; motive; purpose; reason.*

why didn't I think of that?

why me? A plebeian sentiment (SEE).

wide open spaces

wild and crazy   An inescapable pair
(SEE).

wild and woolly   An inescapable
pair (SEE).

wild blue yonder   A moribund metaphor (SEE). *air; atmosphere; biosphere;
empyrean; ether; firmament; heaven;
heavens; outer space; sky; space; strato-
sphere.*

wild goose chase   A moribund metaphor (SEE).

**wild horses couldn't (keep me
away)**   A moribund metaphor (SEE).

**wild horses couldn't drag it from
(me)**   A moribund metaphor (SEE).

(she) will get (hers)

win a few, lose a few

window dressing   A moribund metaphor (SEE).

window of opportunity   A moribund metaphor (SEE). *chance; occasion; opening; opportunity; possibility;
prospect.* ■ I think we have a terrific
window of opportunity to make progress this year. REPLACE WITH *chance.*

window on the (world)   A moribund metaphor (SEE).

winds of change   A moribund metaphor (SEE).

wine and dine   An inescapable pair
(SEE).

wine, women and song

win hands down   A moribund metaphor (SEE). *beat; conquer; crush; defeat; outdo; overcome; overpower; overwhelm; prevail; quell; rout; succeed;
triumph; trounce; vanquish; win.*

win, lose or draw   *regardless.*

(their) winning ways

win (his) spurs   A moribund metaphor (SEE).

winter blahs

winter wonderland

wipe the slate clean   A moribund
metaphor (SEE).

(as) wise as Solomon   An insipid
simile (SEE moribund metaphors). *astute; bright; brilliant; clever; discerning;
enlightened; insightful; intelligent; judicious; keen; knowledgeable; learned;
logical; luminous; penetrating; perceptive; perspicacious; rational; reasonable;
sagacious; sage; sapient; sensible;
sharp; shrewd; smart; sound; understanding; wise.*

wishful thinking

wish list

wit and wisdom   An inescapable
pair (SEE).

with a capital (A)   An infantile
phrase (SEE). ■ It's crisp, *with a capital
C.* DELETE *with a capital C.*

(take) with a grain of salt   A moribund metaphor (SEE). *doubtingly;*

dubiously; skeptically; suspiciously.

with a heavy hand   A moribund metaphor (SEE). *coercively; harshly; oppressively; severely.*

with a heavy heart

with a little luck

with all due respect   Far from conveying respect, this phrase suggests disrespect.
Implicit in its utterance is the meaning that though you with whom I speak are venerable or experienced or thoughtful, you are less so than I.
With all due respect, at other times, conveys nothing more than the abject obsequiousness of those who use it.
In all instances, this is a wearing, not a caring, sentiment. ■ *With all due respect* to all parties involved, the Merrimack Valley economy relies on these industries that in turn rely on prompt access to their elected officials.

with all (my) heart   A moribund metaphor (SEE). *earnestly; fervently; genuinely; heartily; honestly; sincerely; unreservedly; wholeheartedly.*

with an open hand   A moribund metaphor (SEE). *altruistically; beneficently; bountifully; charitably; generously; liberally; munificently; unselfishly; unstintingly.*

with a vengeance   *aggressively; dynamically; emphatically; energetically; ferociously; fervently; fiercely; forcefully; frantically; frenziedly; furiously; hard; intensely; intently; mightily; passionately; powerfully; robustly; savagely; spiritedly; strenuously; strongly; vehe-*

mently; viciously; vigorously; violently; wildly; with vigor.

with bated breath   *agitatedly; anxiously; apprehensively; excitedly; fearfully; timidly; timorously; tremulously.*

with bells on   A moribund metaphor (SEE). *animatedly; eagerly; ebulliently; effervescently; effusively; enthusiastically; excitedly; lively; spiritedly; sprightly; vivaciously.*

with flying colors   A moribund metaphor (SEE). *beautifully; brilliantly; dazzlingly; excellently; grandly; impressively; magnificently; marvelously; outstandingly; splendidly; sublimely; successfully; superbly; triumphally; triumphantly; victoriously; wonderfully.*

with friends like (her) who needs enemies

with (her) heart in (her) mouth   A moribund metaphor (SEE). *anxiously; apprehensively; fearfully; timidly; timorously; tremblingly; tremulously.*

within a hair's breadth of   A moribund metaphor (SEE). ■ Some visionaries are *within a hair's breadth of* achieving unattended computer center operation.

(beaten) within an inch of (his) life   A moribund metaphor (SEE).

within a whisker of   A moribund metaphor (SEE).

(handle) with kid gloves   A moribund metaphor (SEE). *carefully; cautiously; delicately; gently; gingerly; mildly; sensitively; with care.*

with machinelike precision An insipid simile (SEE moribund metaphors). *accurately; exactly; excellently; faultlessly; flawlessly; methodically; perfectly; precisely; regularly; systematically; well.*

with might and main *aggressively; dynamically; emphatically; energetically; ferociously; fervently; fiercely; forcefully; frantically; frenziedly; furiously; hard; intensely; intently; mightily; passionately; powerfully; robustly; savagely; spiritedly; strenuously; strongly; vehemently; viciously; vigorously; violently; wildly; with vigor.*

with (her) nose in the air A moribund metaphor (SEE). *arrogant; cavalier; condescending; contemptuous; despotic; dictatorial; disdainful; dogmatic; domineering; haughty; imperious; insolent; lofty; overbearing; overweening; patronizing; pompous; pretentious; scornful; self-important; supercilious; superior; vainglorious.*

with open arms A moribund metaphor (SEE). *affectionately; eagerly; gladly; happily; joyously; warmly.*

without cost or obligation A dimwitted redundancy (SEE). *free.*

without further ado *at once; directly; forthwith; immediately; instantly; now; promptly; right away; straightaway; summarily; without delay.*

without missing a beat A moribund metaphor (SEE).

without rhyme or reason A moribund metaphor (SEE). *foolish; idiotic; illogical; incomprehensible; meaning-less; nonsensical; senseless; stupid; unintelligent; unintelligible.*

with (my) tail between (my) legs A moribund metaphor (SEE). *abjectly; ashamedly; humbly; ignobly; ignominiously; ingloriously; in humility; in shame; meekly; shamefully; submissively.* ■ But she was not happy at the school and left before graduation *with her tail between her legs.* REPLACE WITH *ingloriously.*

with the exception of A dimwitted redundancy (SEE). *apart from; aside from; barring; besides; but for; except; except for; excepting; excluding; other than; outside of.* ■ We found that our first fifty patients were wide awake and alert the next day *with the exception of* one patient. USE *except for.*

woefully inadequate An inescapable pair (SEE).

woe is me An infantile phrase (SEE).

wolf in sheep's clothing A moribund metaphor (SEE). *apostate; charlatan; deceiver; dissembler; fake; fraud; hypocrite; impostor; knave; mountebank; pharisee; phony; pretender; quack; rascal; recreant; renegade; scoundrel; swindler; tergiversator; traitor.*

(will) wonders never cease

(he) won't bite A moribund metaphor (SEE).

won't budge (an inch)

won the battle but lost the war A moribund metaphor (SEE).

won't take no for an answer
insist.

word gets around

words can't describe (express)
■ *Words cannot express* the terrible emptiness we feel or how much we miss her.

words escape me   Most often, words escape those who have managed to flee from themselves.

words get in the way

words of encouragement

words of wisdom

word to the wise

work (my) butt (tail) off   A moribund metaphor (SEE). *drudge; grind; grub; labor; slave; strain; strive; struggle; sweat; toil; travail; work hard.*

work day and night   *drudge; grind; grub; labor; slave; strive; struggle; sweat; toil; travail; work hard.*

work (his) fingers to the bone   A moribund metaphor (SEE). *drudge; grind; grub; labor; slave; strain; strive; struggle; sweat; toil; travail; work hard.*

working stiff   A moribund metaphor (SEE). *aide; apparatchik; assistant; cog; dependent; drudge; flunky; helper; hireling; inferior; junior; minion; secondary; servant; slave; subaltern; subordinate; underling; vassal.*

work like a dog   An insipid simile (SEE moribund metaphors). *drudge; grind; grub; labor; slave; strain; strive;*

struggle; sweat; toil; travail; work hard.

work long and hard   *drudge; grind; grub; labor; slave; strain; strive; struggle; sweat; toil; travail; work hard.*

works like magic   An insipid simile (SEE moribund metaphors).

work wonders

worlds apart   A moribund metaphor (SEE).

worn threadbare   A moribund metaphor (SEE).
1. *banal; bromidic; common; commonplace; hackneyed; overused; overworked; pedestrian; platitudinous; prosaic; stale; trite.*
2. *damaged; decayed; decrepit; deteriorated; dilapidated; ragged; shabby; shopworn; tattered; worn.*

worried to death   A moribund metaphor (SEE). *agitated; anxious; apprehensive; distraught; distressed; fearful; nervous; panicky; stressed; stressful; tense; tormented; troubled; uneasy; worried.* SEE ALSO *to death.*

(he) worships the ground (I) walk on   A moribund metaphor (SEE). *adore; cherish; esteem; eulogize; exalt; extol; glorify; honor; idealize; idolize; laud; love; panegyrize; prize; revere; treasure; venerate; worship.*

(every parent's) worst nightmare   A moribund metaphor (SEE). ■ It's every mother's *worst nightmare.* ■ This defendant is every person's *worst nightmare.* ■ Being a stepparent is my *worst nightmare.* ■ Perhaps the cliché is true about its being a woman's greatest fantasy and a man's *worst nightmare.* SEE ALSO *it was a nightmare.*

worth (her) salt A moribund metaphor (SEE).

(well) worth the wait

worth (its) weight in gold A moribund metaphor (SEE).
1. *costly; dear; expensive; inestimable; invaluable; precious; priceless; prized; valuable.*
2. *advantageous; beneficial; effective; effectual; efficacious; essential; helpful; indispensable; profitable; serviceable; useful; valuable; vital; worthwhile.*

worthy opponent

would appear (hope; imagine; seem; submit; suggest; suspect; think) A dimwitted redundancy (SEE). *appear (hope; imagine; seem; submit; suggest; suspect; think)* ■ I *would think* so. DELETE *would.* ■ I *would hope* a decision would be reached before the term of office expires. DELETE *would.* ■ It *would appear* that the state wants to jeopardize the project. USE *appears.*

would I lie to you?

(I) wouldn't be caught dead

(he) wouldn't give (me) the time of day

(I) wouldn't have it any other way

(he) wouldn't hurt a flea (fly)

(I) wouldn't touch it with a ten-foot pole A moribund metaphor (SEE).

wouldn't you know it

wrapped up in (herself) A moribund metaphor (SEE). *egocentric; egoistic; egotistic; egotistical; narcissistic; self-absorbed; selfish; solipsistic.*

wreak havoc An inescapable pair (SEE). *demolish; destroy; devastate; obliterate; rack; ravage; ruin; shatter; smash; undo; wrack; wreck.* ■ A handful of companies is *wreaking havoc* on the rest of the industry. REPLACE WITH *ravaging.*

wreathed in smiles A moribund metaphor (SEE).

writhe in pain

(it's) written all over (you) A moribund metaphor (SEE).

wrong end of the stick A moribund metaphor (SEE).

(what's) wrong is wrong A quack equation (SEE).

(he) wrote the book (on) A moribund metaphor (SEE).

X Y Z

x marks the spot

year in (and) year out   *always; ceaselessly; constantly; continually; continuously; endlessly; eternally; everlastingly; evermore; forever; forevermore; immortally; indefinitely; interminably; permanently; perpetually; persistently; unceasingly; unremittingly.*

(eight) years in the making

(sixty-two) years young   An infantile phrase (SEE). ■ I'm forty-three *years young.* DELETE *years young.*

yell and scream   An inescapable pair (SEE). *bay; bawl; bellow; blare; caterwaul; clamor; cry; holler; hoot; howl; roar; screak; scream; screech; shout; shriek; shrill; squawk; squeal; vociferate; wail; whoop; yell; yelp; yowl.* ■ Two months later, he'd lost all his hair, and his wife started *yelling and screaming* about my not making him continue. REPLACE WITH *scream* or *yell.* SEE ALSO *yell and scream.*

yell at the top of (my) lungs   *bay; bawl; bellow; blare; caterwaul; clamor; cry; holler; hoot; howl; roar; screak; scream; screech; shout; shriek; shrill; squawk; squeal; vociferate; wail; whoop; yell; yelp; yowl.*

yell (her) head off   A moribund metaphor (SEE). *bay; bawl; bellow; blare; caterwaul; clamor; cry; holler; hoot; howl; roar; screak; scream; screech; shout; shriek; shrill; squawk; squeal; vociferate; wail; whoop; yell; yelp; yowl.*

ye of little faith

yes and no

yes, Virginia, (there is)   An infantile phrase (SEE).

you ain't seen nothing yet

you and you alone

you are what you eat   A popular prescription (SEE).

you better believe it

you can ask anyone

you can catch more flies with honey than with vinegar   A popular prescription (SEE).

you can fool some of the people some of the time, but you can't fool all of the people all of the time   A popular prescription (SEE).

you can lead a horse to water, but you can't make (him) drink A popular prescription (SEE).

you can make a difference A popular prescription (SEE).

you can say that again An infantile phrase (SEE).

you can't be all things to all people A popular prescription (SEE).

you can't buy love A popular prescription (SEE).

you can't change the world in a day A popular prescription (SEE).

you can't fight city hall A popular prescription (SEE).

you can't fit a square peg in a round hole A popular prescription (SEE).

you can't get blood from (out of) a stone A popular prescription (SEE).

you can't get there from here An infantile phrase (SEE).

you can't go home again A popular prescription (SEE).

you can't have everything A popular prescription (SEE).

you can't have it both ways A popular prescription (SEE).

you can't have something for nothing A popular prescription (SEE).

you can't have your cake and eat it too A popular prescription (SEE).

you can't judge a book by its cover A popular prescription (SEE).

you can't live on love alone A popular prescription (SEE).

you can't live with (them) and you can't live without (them) A popular prescription (SEE).

you can't lose what you never had A popular prescription (SEE).

you can't make a silk purse out of a sow's ear A popular prescription (SEE).

you can't please everyone A popular prescription (SEE).

you can't put new wine in old bottles A popular prescription (SEE).

you can't serve God and mammon A popular prescription (SEE).

you can't take it with you A popular prescription (SEE).

you can't teach an old dog new tricks A popular prescription (SEE).

you can't win them all A popular prescription (SEE).

(so quiet) you could hear a pin drop A moribund metaphor (SEE). *dumb; hushed; motionless; mum; mute; noiseless; quiet; reticent; silent; speechless; stationary; still; subdued; taciturn; unmoving; voiceless; wordless.*

you couldn't be more wrong

you don't have to be a rocket scientist to An infantile phrase (SEE).

you don't know the half of it

you don't miss what you never had   A popular prescription (SEE).

you (have to) do what you have to (do)   A popular prescription (SEE).

you get used to it

you get what you pay for   A popular prescription (SEE).

you had to be there   A grammatical gimmick (SEE). This is merely an admission of having badly told a tale.

(well) you have a funny way of showing it

you have everything to gain and nothing to lose   A popular prescription (SEE).

you have nothing to lose   A popular prescription (SEE).

you haven't seen anything yet

you have to get out more

you have to give to get   A popular prescription (SEE).

you have to see (it) to believe (it)

you have (got) to start somewhere   A popular prescription (SEE).

you have to understand (that)   An ineffectual phrase (SEE). ■ First of all, *you have to understand that* many young men are in prison. DELETE *you have to understand that.* SEE ALSO *it is important to understand (that).*

you heard it (here) first

(do) you know?   An ineffectual phrase (SEE). ■ I felt like I was enlightened, *you know?* DELETE *you know?* ■ You never know what's going to happen, *you know?* DELETE *you know?* ■ The translation sounded too straightforward, *you know?* DELETE *you know?* ■ To an extent, I think everybody is racist. *You know?* DELETE *You know?* SEE ALSO *(you) hear what I'm saying?; (you) know what I mean?; (you) know what I'm saying?; (you) know what I'm telling you?.*

you know how it goes (is)

you learn something new every day   A plebeian sentiment (SEE). This phrase is typically spoken by those who learn nothing day after day.
It's the event of having learned something — something taught or told to them, nothing thought or found by them — that gives rise to the remark.

you'll be sorry

you'll be the first to know

you made your bed, now lay in it   A popular prescription (SEE).

you name it   A grammatical gimmick (SEE). ■ Today, in our state, those who do the public's work — teachers, cops, public-health nurses, social workers, highway builders, prison guards, *you name it* — are held up to ridicule.

you never know   A plebeian sentiment (SEE).

you never know till you try   A popular prescription (SEE).

young and foolish   An inescapable pair (SEE).

young at heart

you owe it to yourself   ■ Believe me, *you owe it to yourself* to take advantage of this exciting opportunity.

you're (only) as old as you feel   A popular prescription (SEE).

you're either part of the solution or part of the problem   A popular prescription (SEE).

you're either with (me) or against (me)   A popular prescription (SEE).

you're kidding   An infantile phrase (SEE). This expression is among the most banal we utter. We say it uncontrollably — less in stupefaction than in stupidity — and without a moment's reflection.
   The more commonplace the words you use, the more commonplace the person you are. SEE ALSO *really?; you've got to be kidding*.

you're not alone   A plebeian sentiment (SEE). ■ Feeling depressed, lonely, restless, bored, upset? *You're not alone*.

you're not the only one   *as I do; I do too; neither do I; no more do I; nor do I; so do I*.

you're only young once   A popular prescription (SEE).

you're telling me   SEE ALSO *tell me about it*.

your guess is as good as mine   An infantile phrase (SEE). *I don't know; (it's) not (yet) known; (that's) uncertain; (that's) unclear; (it's) unknown*. SEE ALSO *(it) remains to be seen*.

yours truly   *I; me*.

your wish is my command

you scratch my back, I'll scratch yours   A popular prescription (SEE).

you think too much   A plebeian sentiment (SEE). *You think too much* is, of course, commentary that only those who think not at all or hardly at all could ever offer.

you think you know someone

you've come a long way (baby)   An infantile phrase (SEE).

you've got to be kidding   An infantile phrase (SEE). SEE ALSO *really?; you've got to be kidding*.

you win a few (some), you lose a few (some)   A popular prescription (SEE).

zigs and zags   An inescapable pair (SEE).

(a) zillion(s) (of)   An infantile phrase (SEE). Doubly infantile are the *bazillion* and *gazillion*. ■ I'll bet their mothers spent *a zillion* hours trying to get their sons to clean up after themselves.

More Great Books for Writers!

Writing the Short Story — With Bickham's unique "workshop on paper" you'll plan, organize, write, revise, and polish a short story. Clear instruction, helpful charts and practical exercises will lead you every step of the way! *#10421/$16.99/224 pages*

The Complete Guide to Self-Publishing — By Tom and Marilyn Ross! Discover how to make the publishing industry work for you! You'll get step-by-step guidance on every aspect of publishing from cover design and production tips to sales letters and publicity strategies. *#10411/$18.99/432 pages/paperback*

Writer's Digest Guide to Good Writing — Put the best advice and inspiration from the past 75 years of Writer's Digest magazine to work for you! You'll be inspired by authors like Vonnegut, Sinclair, Michener, Steinbeck, and over a dozen others! *#10391/$18.95/352 pages*

Beginner's Guide to Getting Published — This comprehensive collection of articles will calm your worries, energize your work, and help you get published! You'll find in-depth, expertly written articles on idea generation, breaking into the business, moving up the ladder and much more! *#10418/$16.99/208 pages*

The Art & Craft of Novel Writing — With help from John Steinbeck, Joyce Carol Oates, Anton Chekhov, and many others, Hall shows you what works in novel writing and why. You'll gain inspiration along with instruction from this enlightening discussion of the elements of fiction. *#48002/$14.99/240 pages/paperback*

The Best Writing on Writing — This is the first in a series that will bring you the most provocative new articles, essays and lectures on fiction, nonfiction, poetry, playwriting, and the writing life. You'll enjoy this lively feast on the well-written word and how it is crafted. *#48001/$16.99/208 pages/paperback*

The Writer's Digest Guide to Manuscript Formats — Don't take chances with your hard work! Learn how to prepare and submit books, poems, scripts, stories and more with the professional look editors expect from a good writer. *#10025/$18.95/200 pages*

Beginning Writer's Answer Book — Discover everything you need to know to get published — from how to generate great ideas, to the most up-to-date business advice and tax tips. *#10394/$16.95/336 pages*

Writing the Blockbuster Novel — Discover how to make your novel a sure-fire success with memorable characters, exotic settings, clashing conflicts and universal plots. *#10393/$17.95/224 pages*

Magazine Writing That Sells — Discover the secrets to sensational queries, in-depth interviewing, reader-grabbing leads, solidly-written pieces and can't miss marketing strategies. *#10409/$16.95/240 pages*

Creating Characters — Learn how to build characters that jump off the page. In-depth instruction shows you how to infuse characters with emotion so powerful they will touch every reader. *#10417/$14.99/192 pages/paperback*

20 Master Plots — Write great contemporary fiction from timeless plots. This guide outlines 20 plots from various genres and illustrates how to adapt them into your own fiction. *#10366/$16.95/240 pages*

The Writer's Digest Character Naming Sourcebook — Finally, you'll discover how to choose the perfect name to reflect your character's personality, ethnicity, and place in history. Here you'll find 20,000 first and last names (and their meanings) from around the world! *#10390/$18.95/352 pages*

The Complete Guide to Magazine Article Writing — You'll write articles that are clear, focused, effective, and best of all salable with the practical explanations and easy-to-follow instructions in this comprehensive guide. *#10369/$17.95/304 pages*

How To Write and Sell Children's Picture Books — If you yearn to put smiles on little faces, you need this charming guide. You'll discover how to put your picture book on paper and get it published — whether you're retelling a wonderful old tale, or spinning a splendid new yarn. *#10410/$16.95/192 pages*

Children's Writer's Word Book — Even the most original children's story won't get published if its language usage or sentence structure doesn't speak to young readers. You'll avoid these pitfalls with this fast-reference guide full of word lists, reading levels for synonyms, and more! *#10316/$19.95/352 pages*

The Craft of Writing Science Fiction That Sells — Discover how to fascinate audiences (and a editors) with imaginative, well-told science fiction. *#10395/$16.95/224 pages*

The Writer's Complete Crime Reference Book — Now completely revised and updated! Incre encyclopedia of hard-to-find facts about the ways of criminals and cops, prosecutors and defen victims and juries — everything the crime and mystery writer needs is at your fingertips. *#1 $19.95/304 pages*

Police Procedural: A Writer's Guide to the Police and How They Work — Learn how police off work, when they work, what they wear, who they report to, and how they go about controllin investigating crime. *#10374/$16.95/272 pages/paperback*

Private Eyes: A Writer's Guide to Private Investigators — How do people become investiga What procedures do they use? What tricks/tactics do they use? This guide gives you the "i scoop" on the world of private eyes! *#10373/$15.95/208 pages/paperback*

Setting — Expert instruction on using sensual detail, vivid language and keen observation will you create settings that provide the perfect backdrop to every story. *#10397/$14.95/176 pages*

Conflict, Action & Suspense — Discover how to grab your reader with an action-packed begin build the suspense throughout your story, and bring it all to a fever pitch through powerful, grip conflict. *#10396/$14.95/176 pages*

The Writer's Guide to Everyday Life in the 1800s — From clothes to food, social customs to fur ings, you'll find everything you need to write an accurate story about this century. Plus, the e are dated so you don't invent something before its creation. *#10353/$18.95/320 pages*
